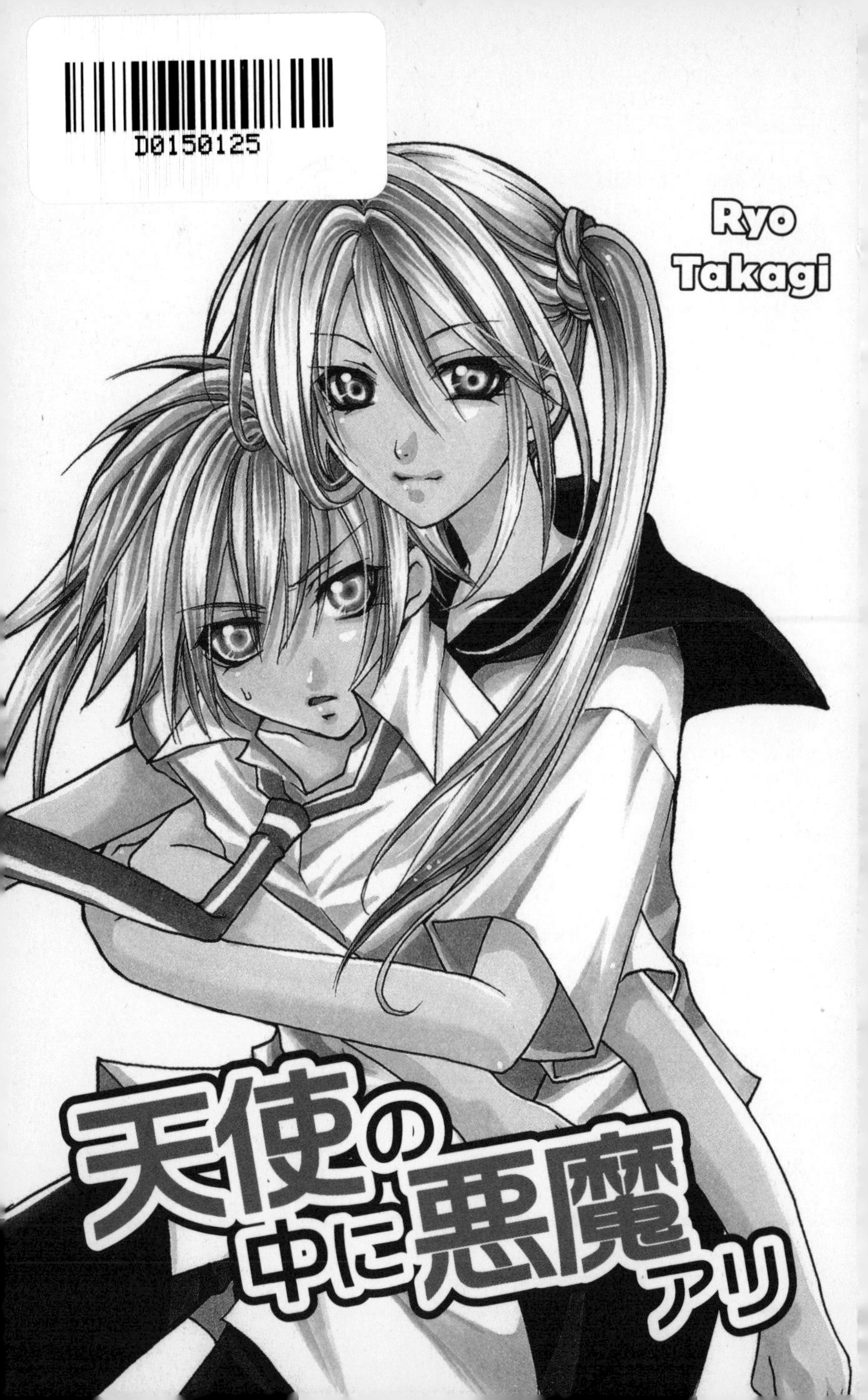
Ryo
Takagi
天使の
中に悪魔アリ

Translation – Christine Schilling
Adaptation – Brynne Chandler
Editorial Assistant –Mallory Reaves
Lettering & Retouch –Jennifer Skarupa
Production Manager – James Dashiell
Editor – Brynne Chandler

A Go! Comi manga

Published by Go! Media Entertainment, LLC

Tenshi no Naka ni Akuma Ari Volume 1
© 2003 RYO TAKAGI
All rights reserved.
First published in Japan in 2003 by SHINSHOKAN Co., Ltd. Tokyo
English Version published by Go! Media Entertainment, LLC under license
from SHINSHOKAN Co., Ltd.

Visit us online at www.gocomi.com
e-mail: info@gocomi.com

ISBN 978-1-933617-44-2

First printed in August 2007

1 2 3 4 5 6 7 8 9

Manufactured in the United States of America.

The Devil Within?

STORY AND ART BY

Ryo Takagi

VOLUME 1

go!comi

The Devil Within!

VOLUME 1

CONTENTS

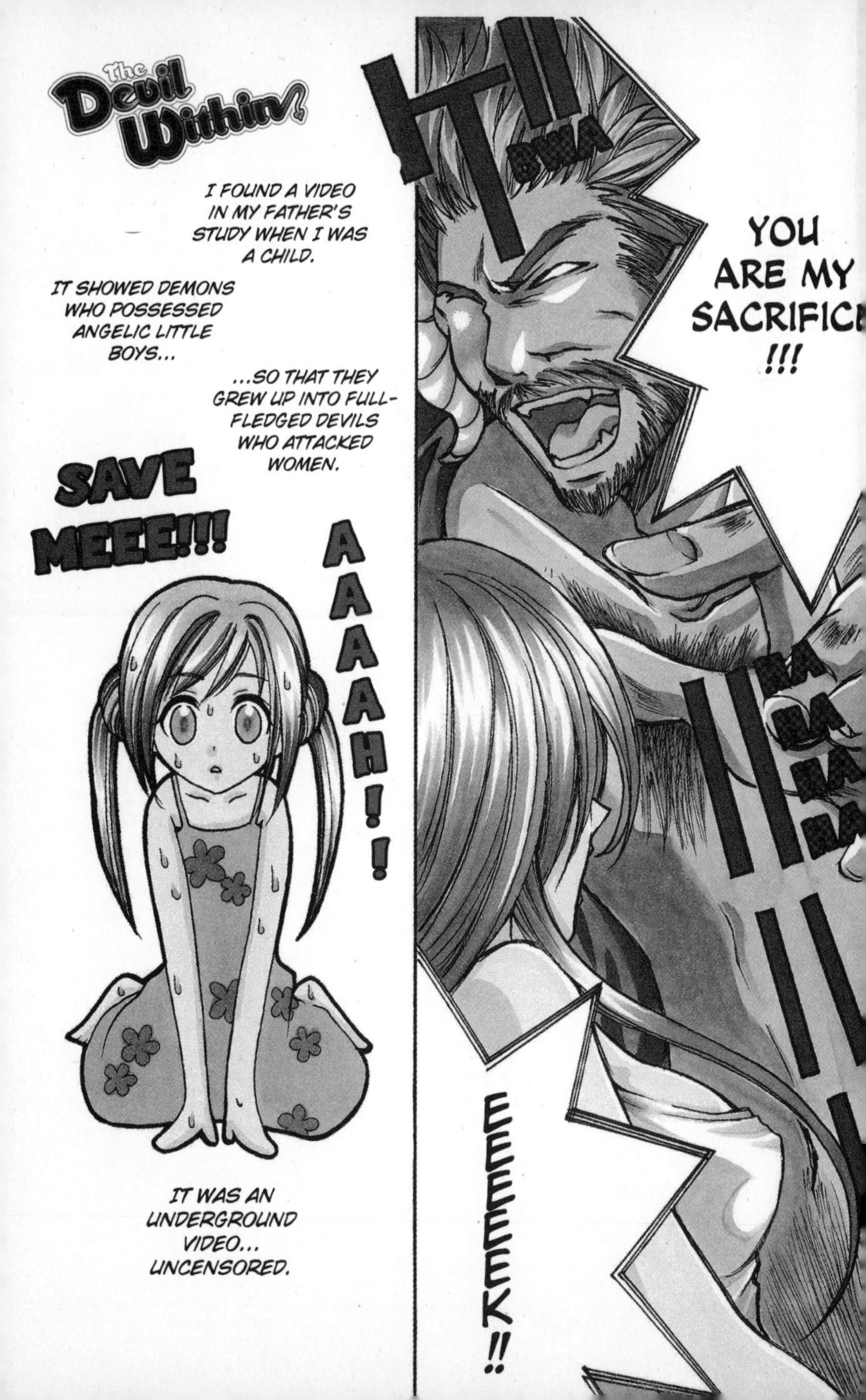

BWA
HA HA HA
YOU ARE MY SACRIFIC !!!
EEEEEEK!!
The Devil Within
I FOUND A VIDEO IN MY FATHER'S STUDY WHEN I WAS A CHILD.
IT SHOWED DEMONS WHO POSSESSED ANGELIC LITTLE BOYS...
...SO THAT THEY GREW UP INTO FULL-FLEDGED DEVILS WHO ATTACKED WOMEN.
SAVE MEEE!!!
AAAAAH!!
IT WAS AN UNDERGROUND VIDEO... UNCENSORED.

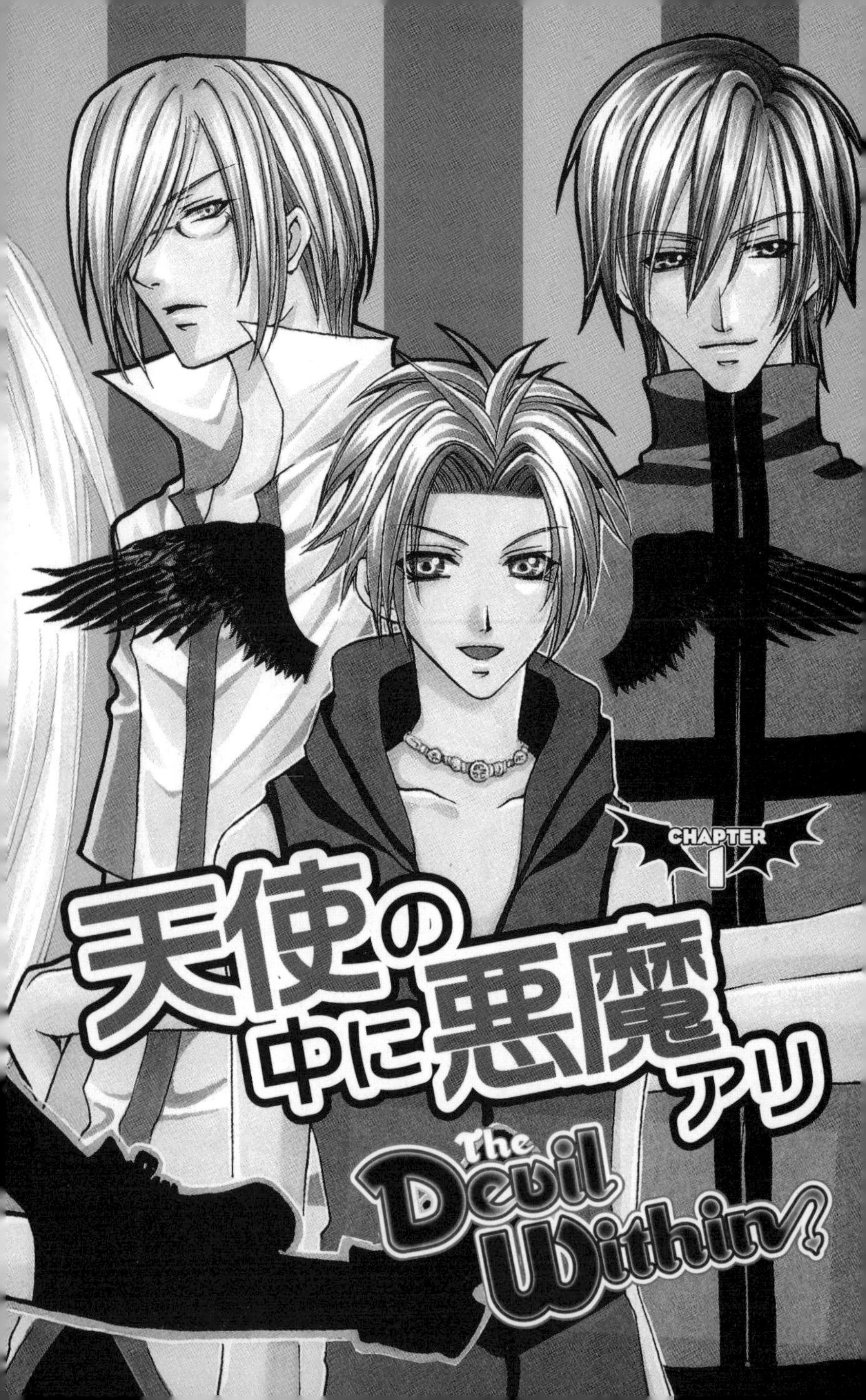
CHAPTER 1
天使の中に悪魔アリ
The Devil Within!

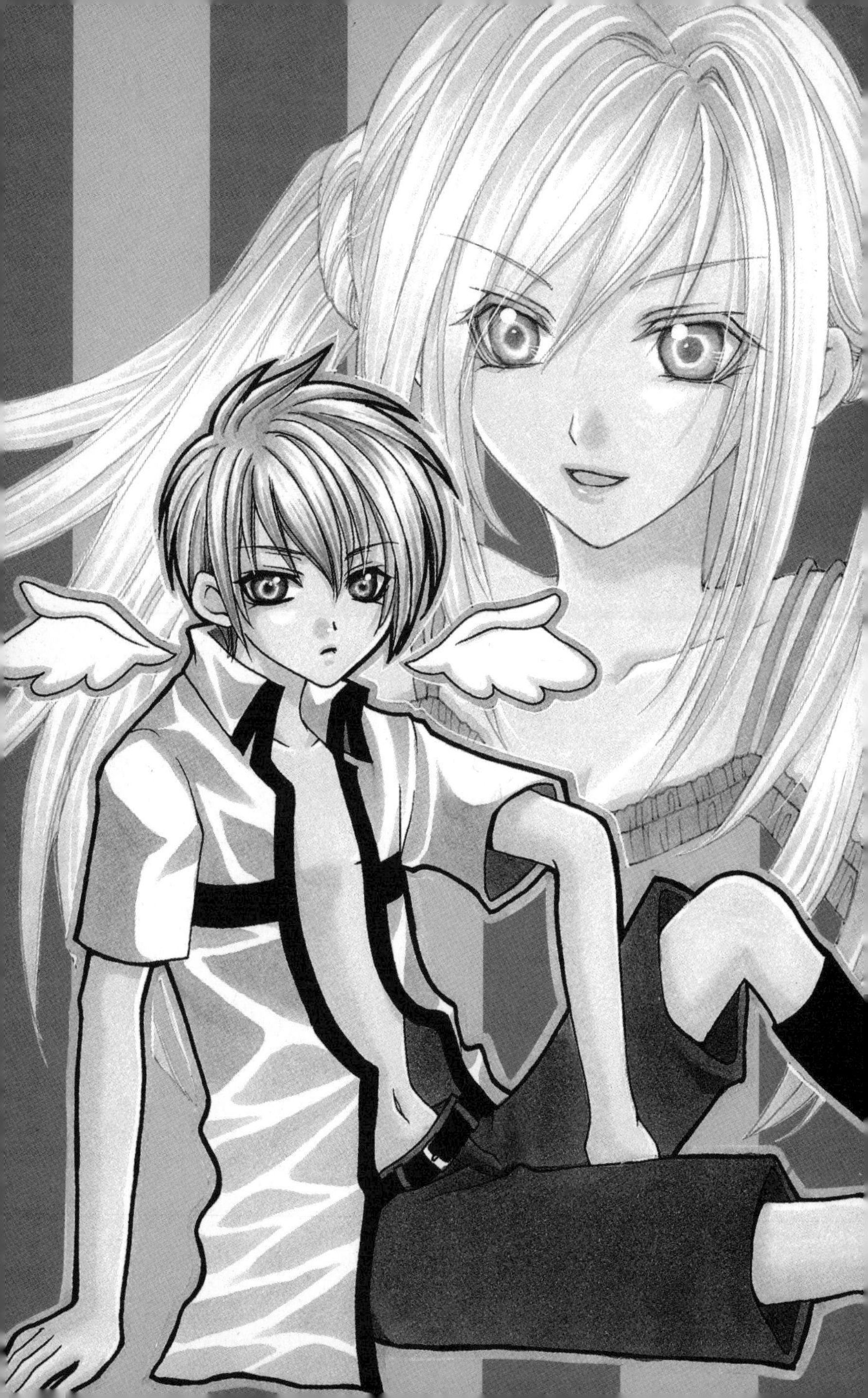

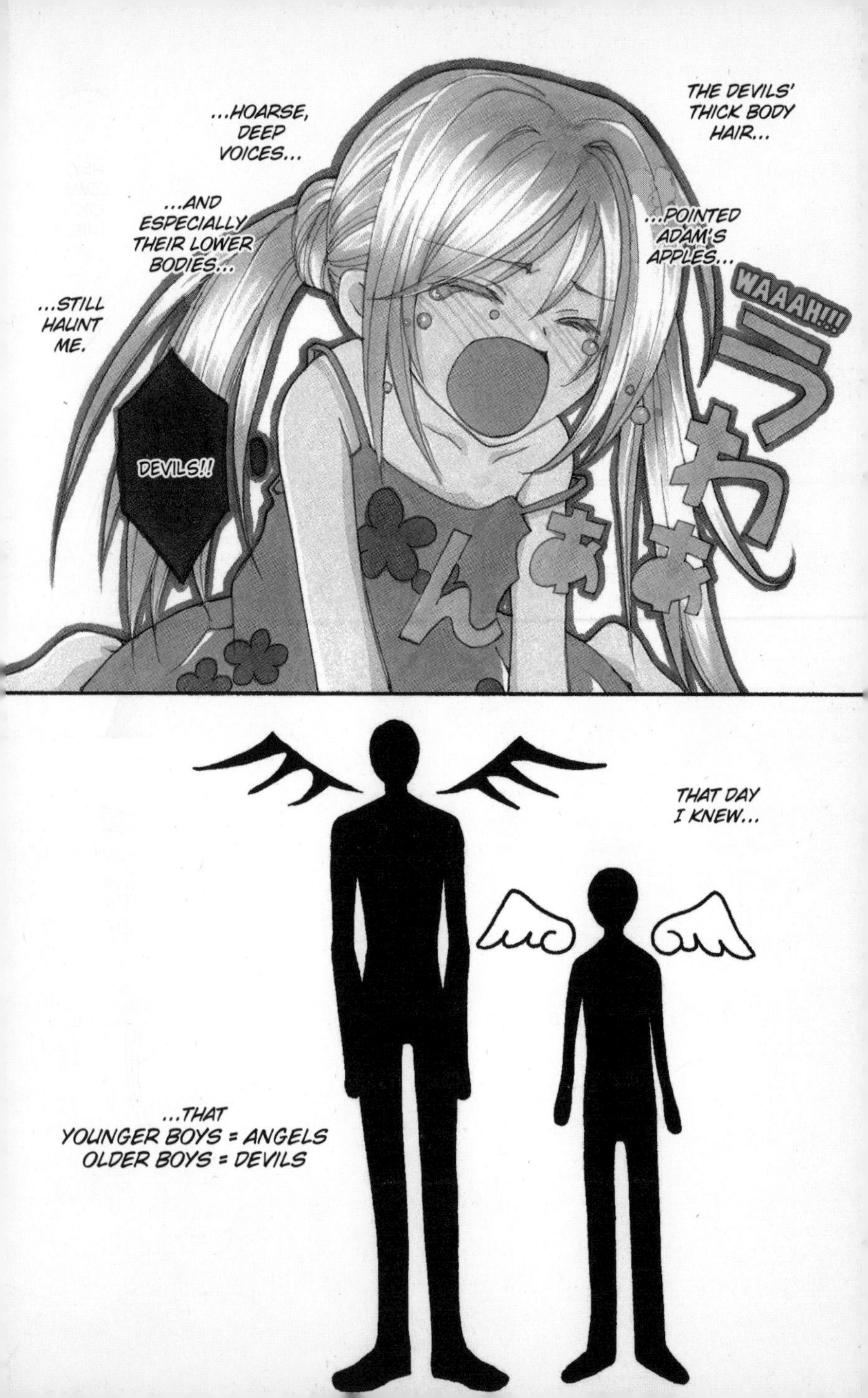
THE DEVILS' THICK BODY HAIR...
...HOARSE, DEEP VOICES...
...POINTED ADAM'S APPLES...
...AND ESPECIALLY THEIR LOWER BODIES...
...STILL HAUNT ME.
WAAAH!!!
うわぁぁん
DEVILS!!
THAT DAY I KNEW...
...THAT
YOUNGER BOYS = ANGELS
OLDER BOYS = DEVILS

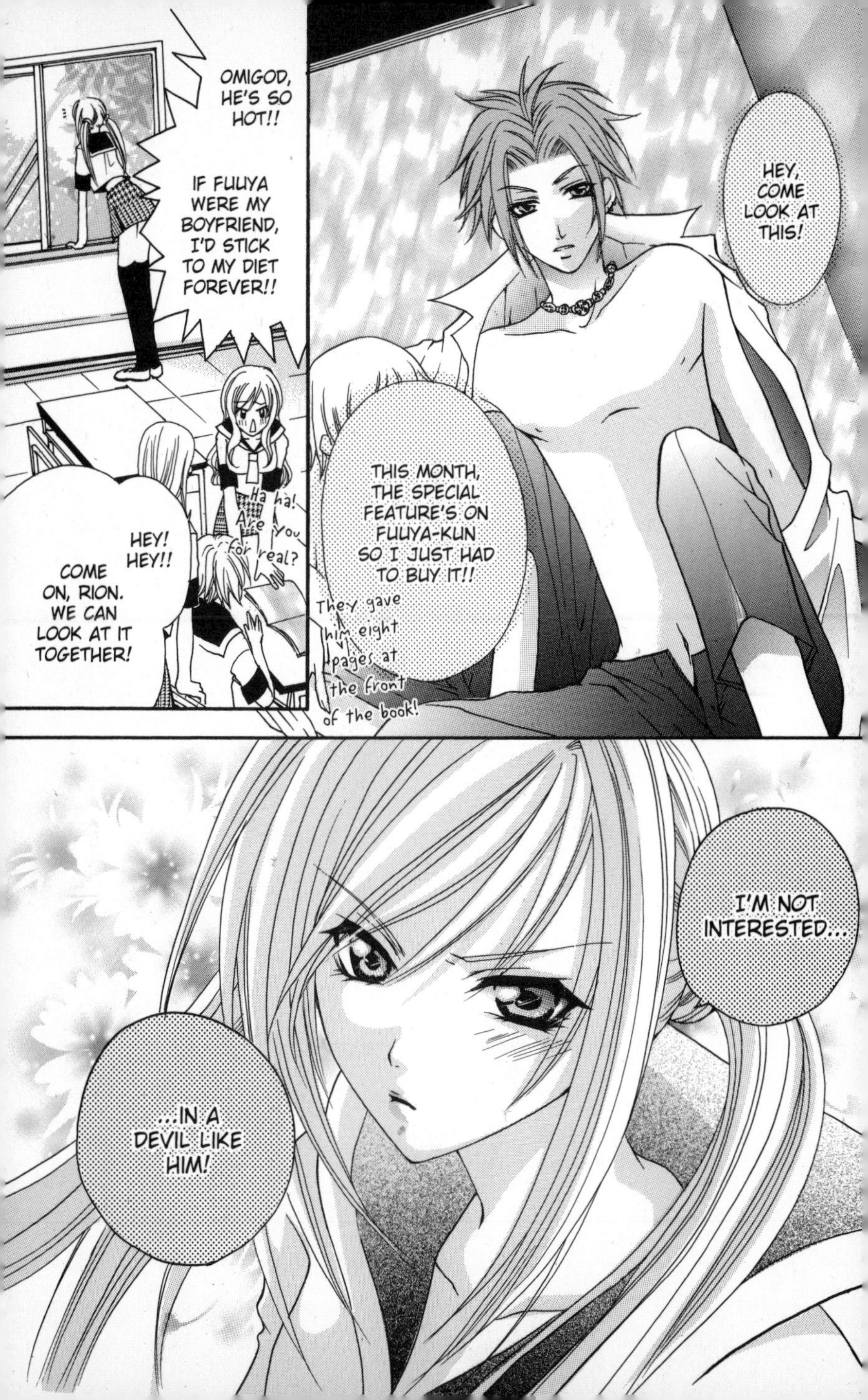
HEY, COME LOOK AT THIS!
THIS MONTH, THE SPECIAL FEATURE'S ON FUUYA-KUN SO I JUST HAD TO BUY IT!!
They gave him eight pages at the front of the book!
OMIGOD, HE'S SO HOT!!
IF FUUYA WERE MY BOYFRIEND, I'D STICK TO MY DIET FOREVER!!
Ha ha! Are you for real?
HEY! HEY!!
COME ON, RION. WE CAN LOOK AT IT TOGETHER!
I'M NOT INTERESTED...
...IN A DEVIL LIKE HIM!

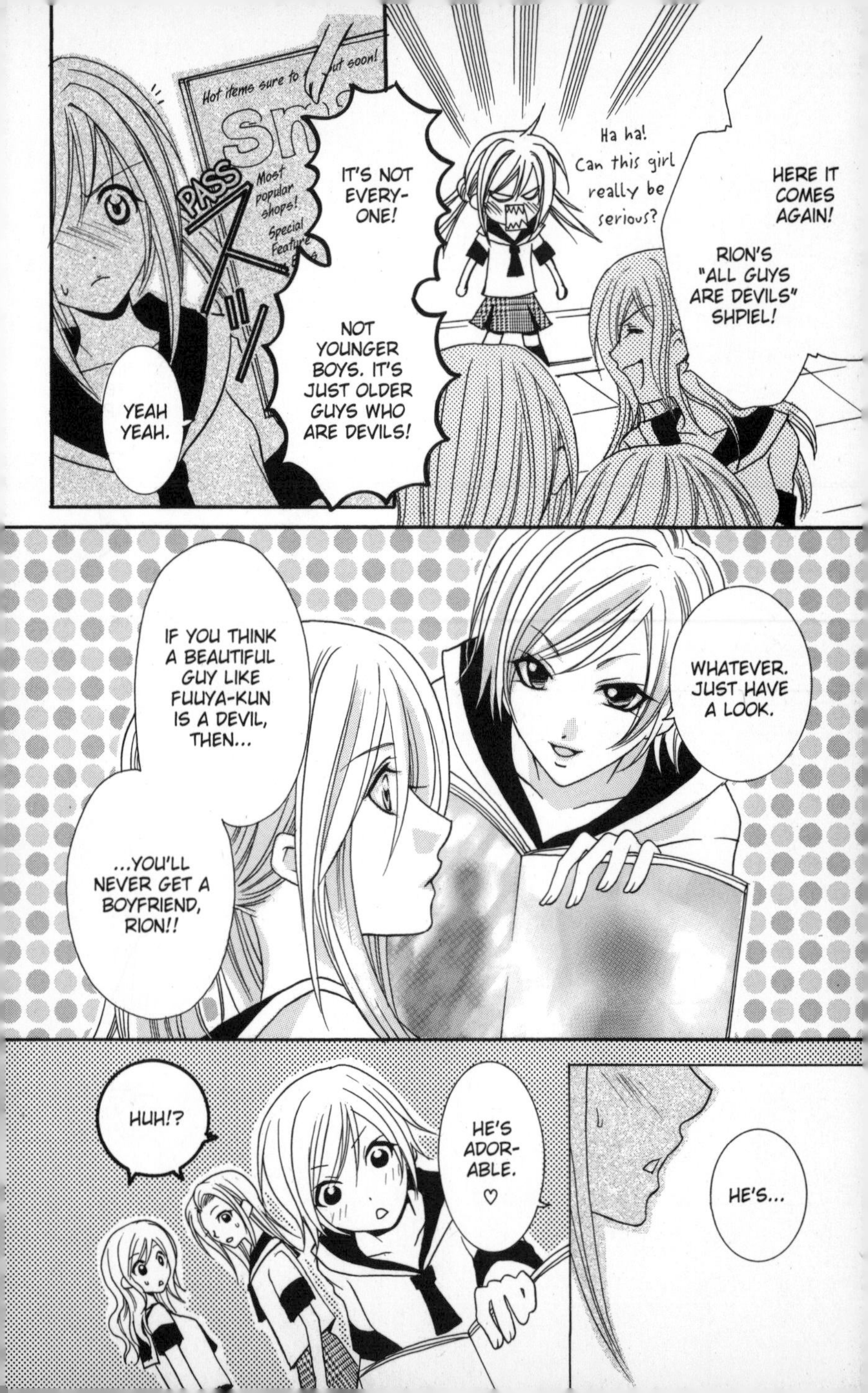
HERE IT COMES AGAIN!
RION'S "ALL GUYS ARE DEVILS" SHPIEL!
Ha ha! Can this girl really be serious?
IT'S NOT EVERY-ONE!
NOT YOUNGER BOYS. IT'S JUST OLDER GUYS WHO ARE DEVILS!
PASS
Most popular shops!
YEAH YEAH.
WHATEVER. JUST HAVE A LOOK.
IF YOU THINK A BEAUTIFUL GUY LIKE FUUYA-KUN IS A DEVIL, THEN...
...YOU'LL NEVER GET A BOYFRIEND, RION!!
HE'S...
HE'S ADOR-ABLE. ♡
HUH!?

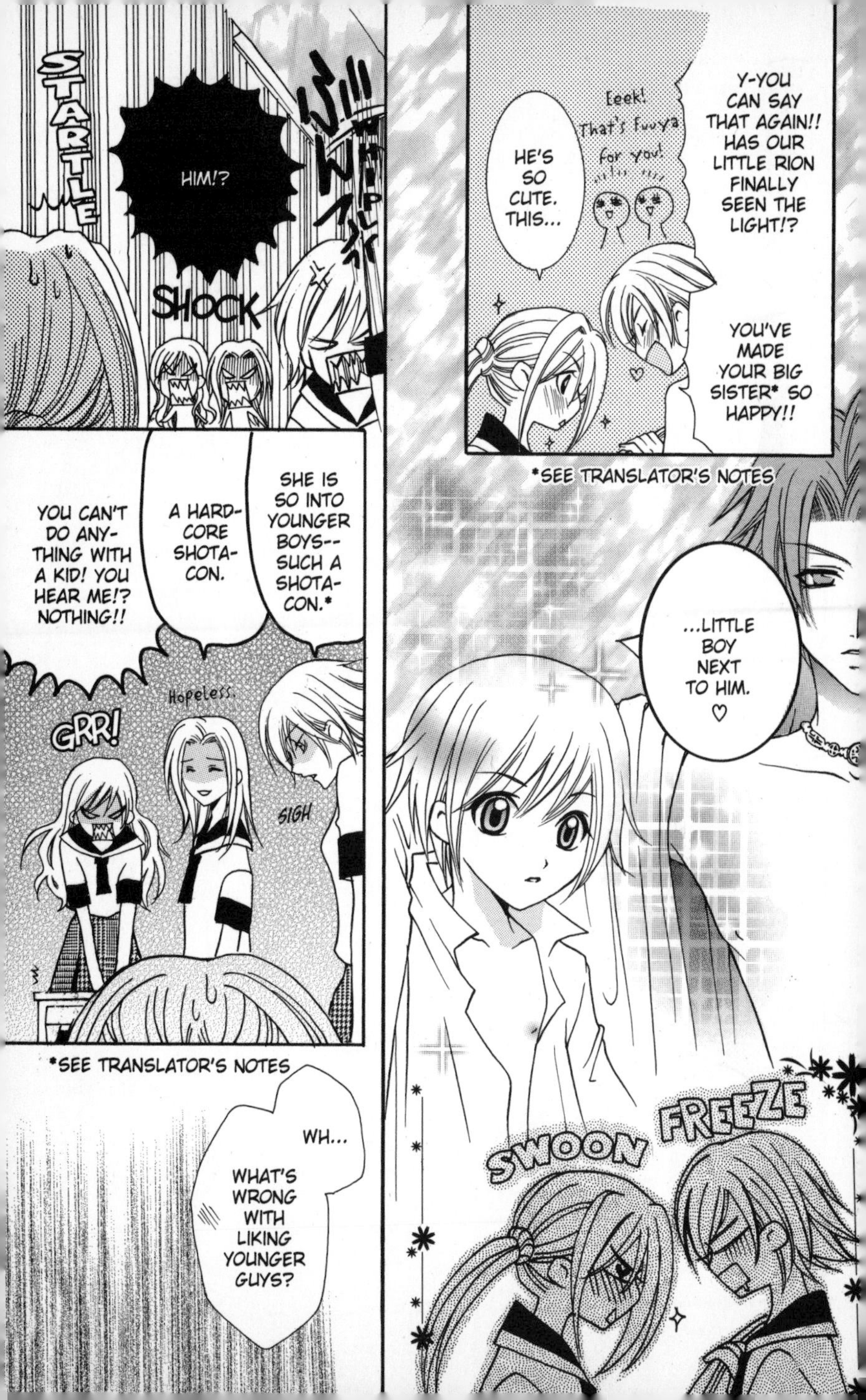

Y-YOU CAN SAY THAT AGAIN!! HAS OUR LITTLE RION FINALLY SEEN THE LIGHT!?
Eeek! That's Fuuya for you!
HE'S SO CUTE. THIS...
YOU'VE MADE YOUR BIG SISTER* SO HAPPY!!
*SEE TRANSLATOR'S NOTES
...LITTLE BOY NEXT TO HIM. ♡
SWOON
FREEZE
STARTLE
HIM!?
SHOCK
SHE IS SO INTO YOUNGER BOYS--SUCH A SHOTA-CON.*
A HARD-CORE SHOTA-CON.
YOU CAN'T DO ANY-THING WITH A KID! YOU HEAR ME!? NOTHING!!
Hopeless.
GRR!
SIGH
*SEE TRANSLATOR'S NOTES
WH...
WHAT'S WRONG WITH LIKING YOUNGER GUYS?

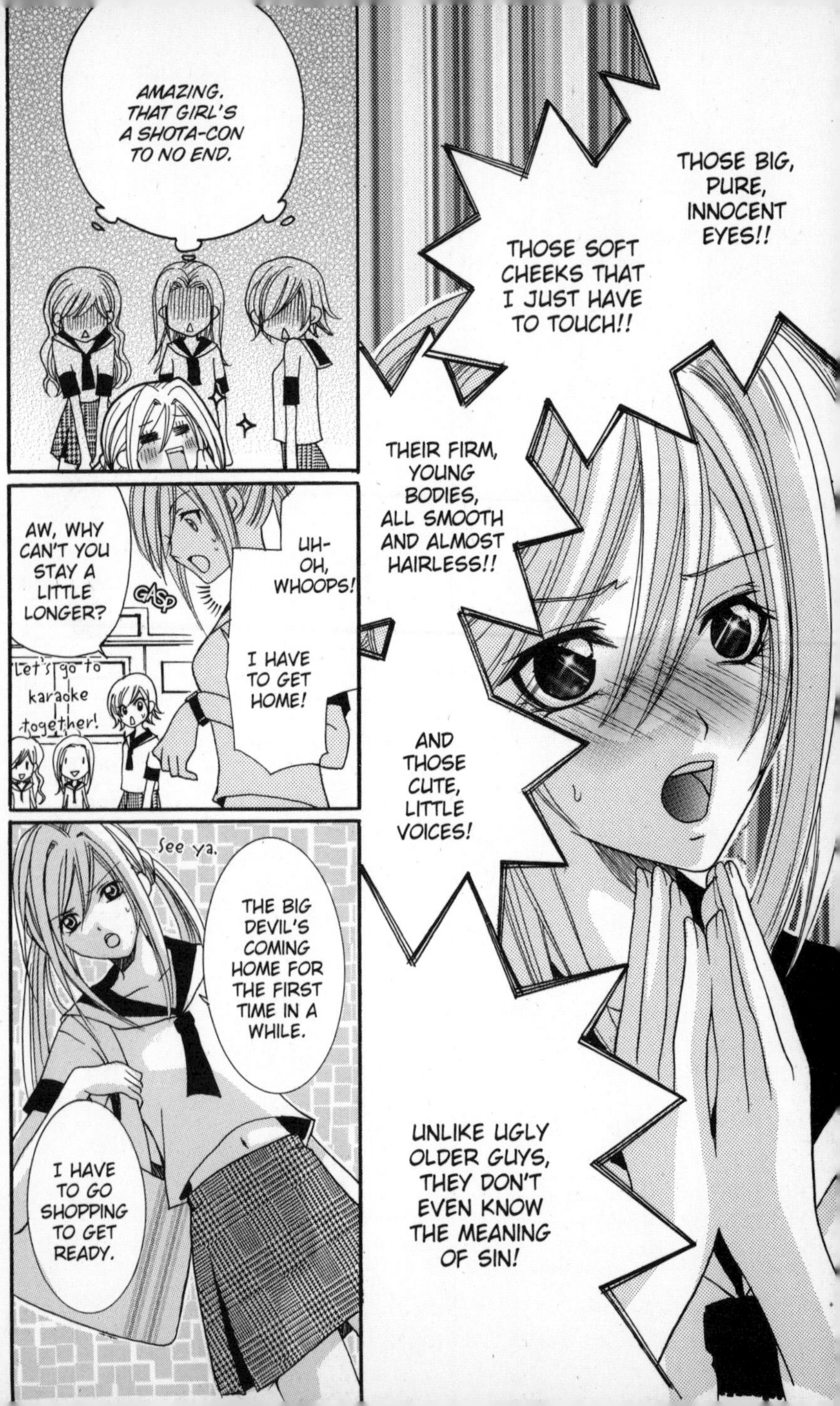
THOSE BIG, PURE, INNOCENT EYES!!
THOSE SOFT CHEEKS THAT I JUST HAVE TO TOUCH!!
THEIR FIRM, YOUNG BODIES, ALL SMOOTH AND ALMOST HAIRLESS!!
AND THOSE CUTE, LITTLE VOICES!
UNLIKE UGLY OLDER GUYS, THEY DON'T EVEN KNOW THE MEANING OF SIN!
AMAZING. THAT GIRL'S A SHOTA-CON TO NO END.
UH-OH, WHOOPS!
I HAVE TO GET HOME!
GASP
AW, WHY CAN'T YOU STAY A LITTLE LONGER?
Let's go to karaoke together!
See ya.
THE BIG DEVIL'S COMING HOME FOR THE FIRST TIME IN A WHILE.
I HAVE TO GO SHOPPING TO GET READY.

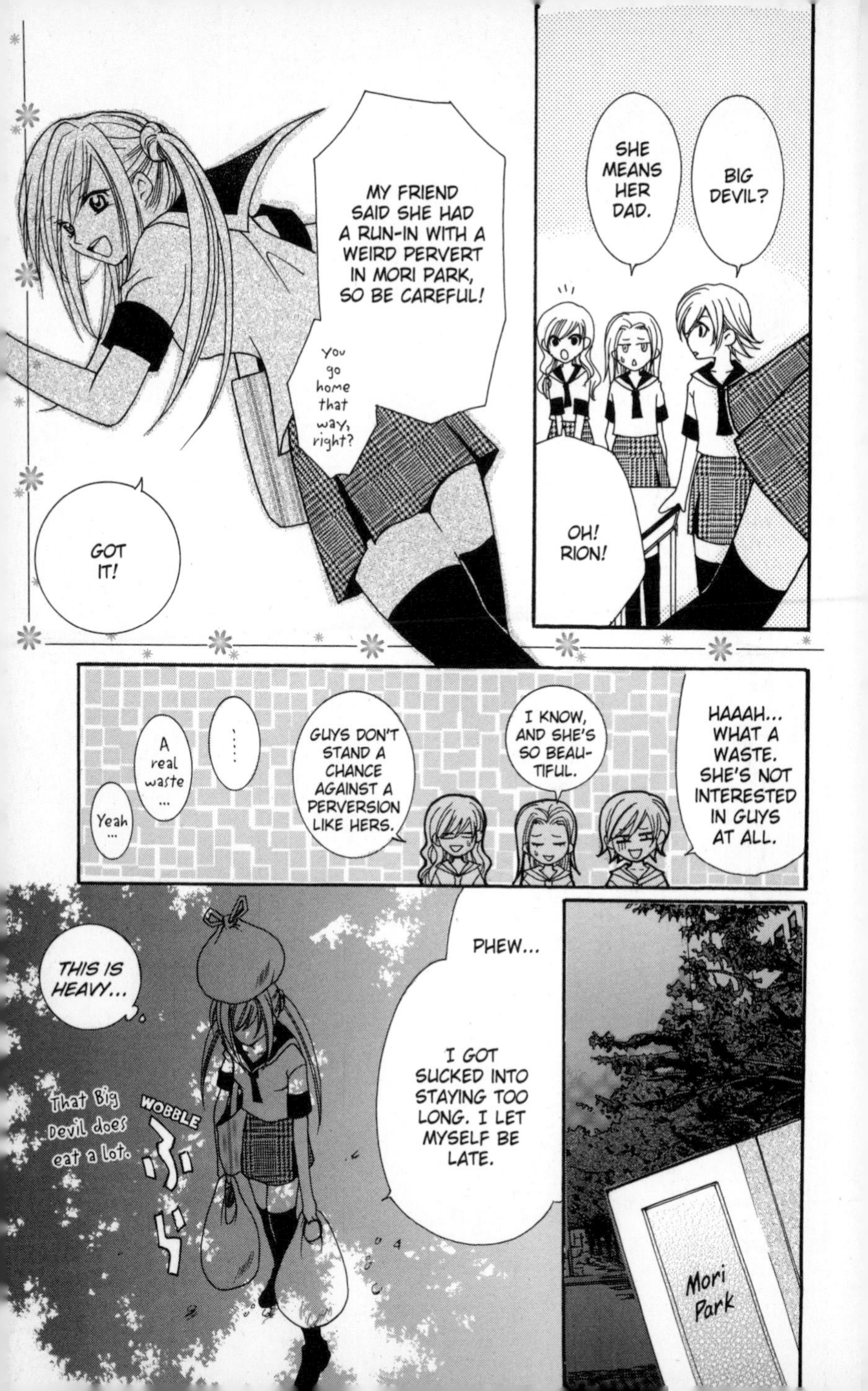
BIG DEVIL?
SHE MEANS HER DAD.
OH! RION!
MY FRIEND SAID SHE HAD A RUN-IN WITH A WEIRD PERVERT IN MORI PARK, SO BE CAREFUL!
You go home that way, right?
GOT IT!
HAAAH... WHAT A WASTE. SHE'S NOT INTERESTED IN GUYS AT ALL.
I KNOW, AND SHE'S SO BEAU-TIFUL.
GUYS DON'T STAND A CHANCE AGAINST A PERVERSION LIKE HERS.
.....
A real waste...
Yeah...
Mori Park
PHEW...
I GOT SUCKED INTO STAYING TOO LONG. I LET MYSELF BE LATE.
THIS IS HEAVY...
WOBBLE
That Big Devil does eat a lot.

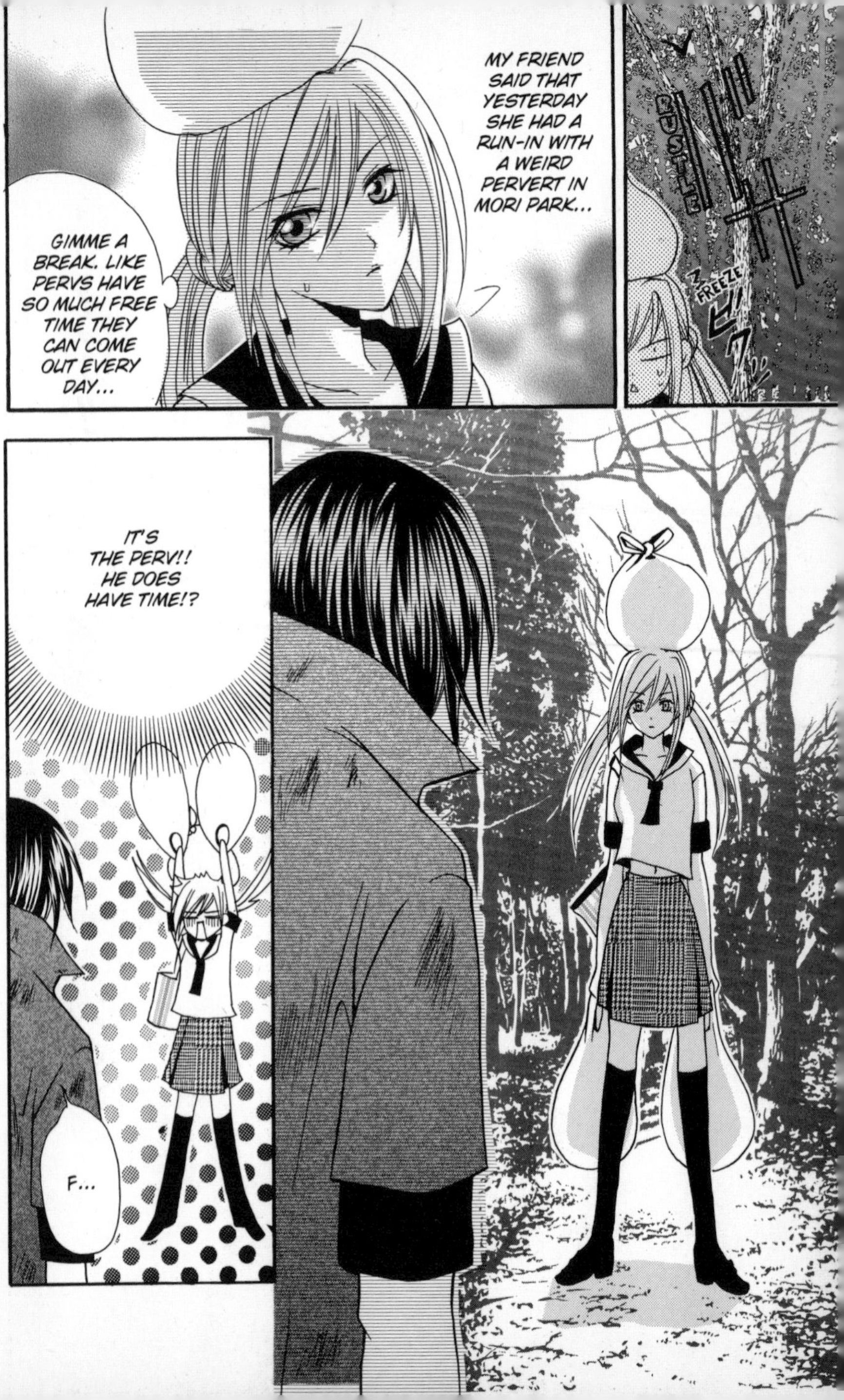
MY FRIEND SAID THAT YESTERDAY SHE HAD A RUN-IN WITH A WEIRD PERVERT IN MORI PARK...
GIMME A BREAK. LIKE PERVS HAVE SO MUCH FREE TIME THEY CAN COME OUT EVERY DAY...
RUSTLE
FREEZE
IT'S THE PERV!! HE DOES HAVE TIME!?
F...

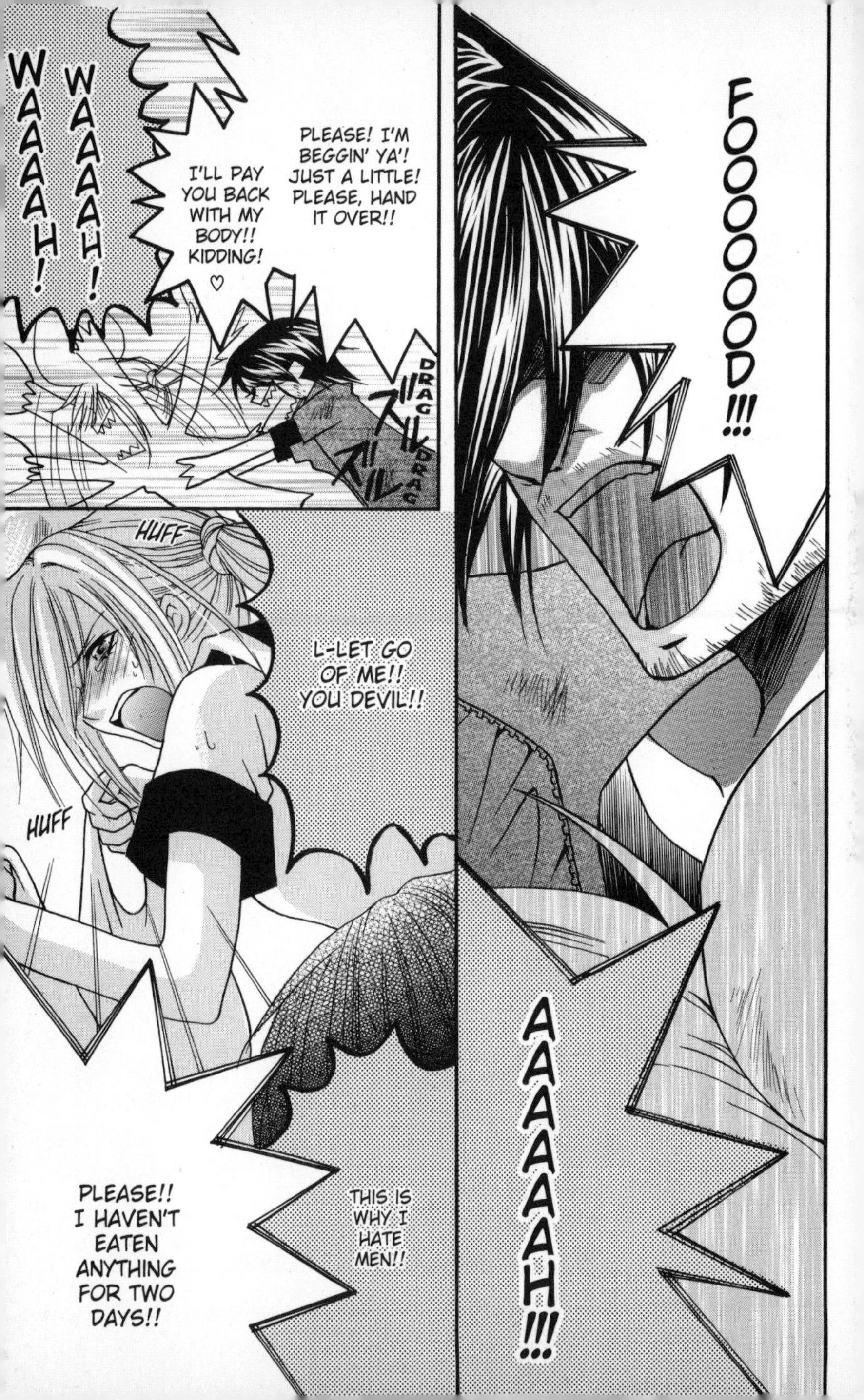

FOOOOOOD!!!
AAAAAAAH!!!
PLEASE! I'M BEGGIN' YA'! JUST A LITTLE! PLEASE, HAND IT OVER!!
I'LL PAY YOU BACK WITH MY BODY!! KIDDING! ♡
WAAAAAH!
WAAAAAH!
DRAG DRAG
HUFF
L-LET GO OF ME!! YOU DEVIL!!
HUFF
THIS IS WHY I HATE MEN!!
PLEASE!! I HAVEN'T EATEN ANYTHING FOR TWO DAYS!!

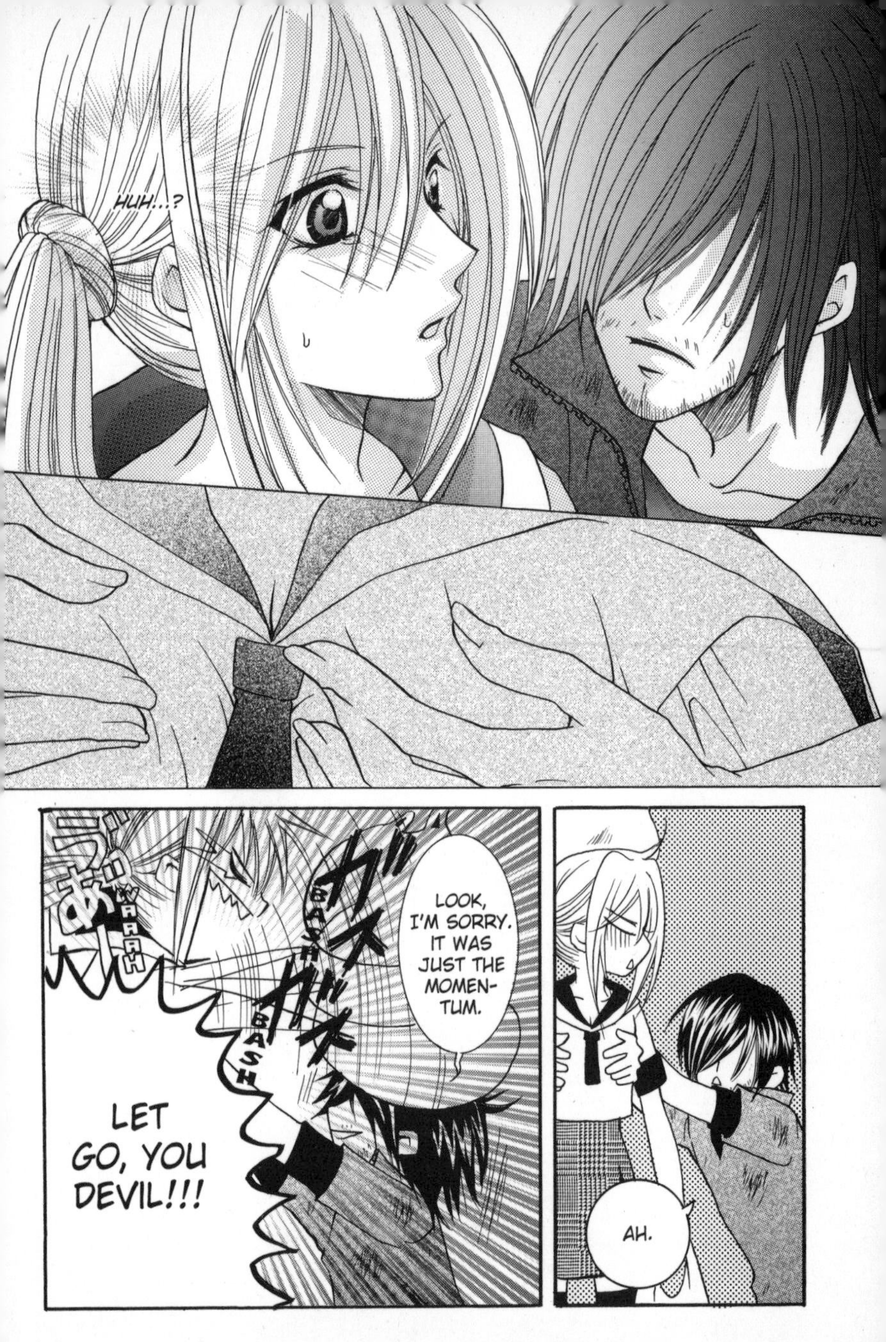
HUH...?
AH.
LOOK, I'M SORRY. IT WAS JUST THE MOMEN-TUM.
BASH
BASH
LET GO, YOU DEVIL!!!

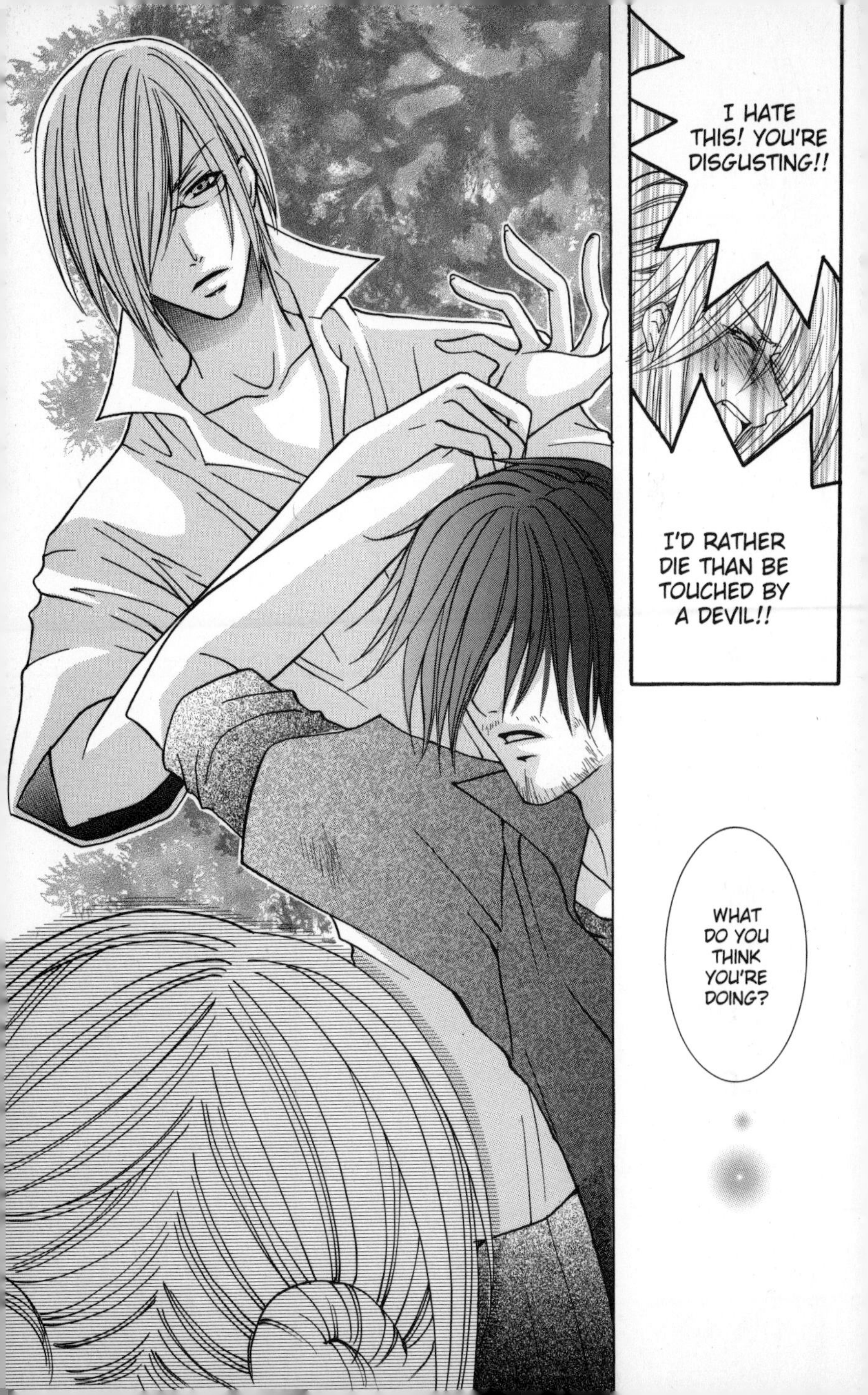
I HATE THIS! YOU'RE DISGUSTING!!
I'D RATHER DIE THAN BE TOUCHED BY A DEVIL!!
WHAT DO YOU THINK YOU'RE DOING?

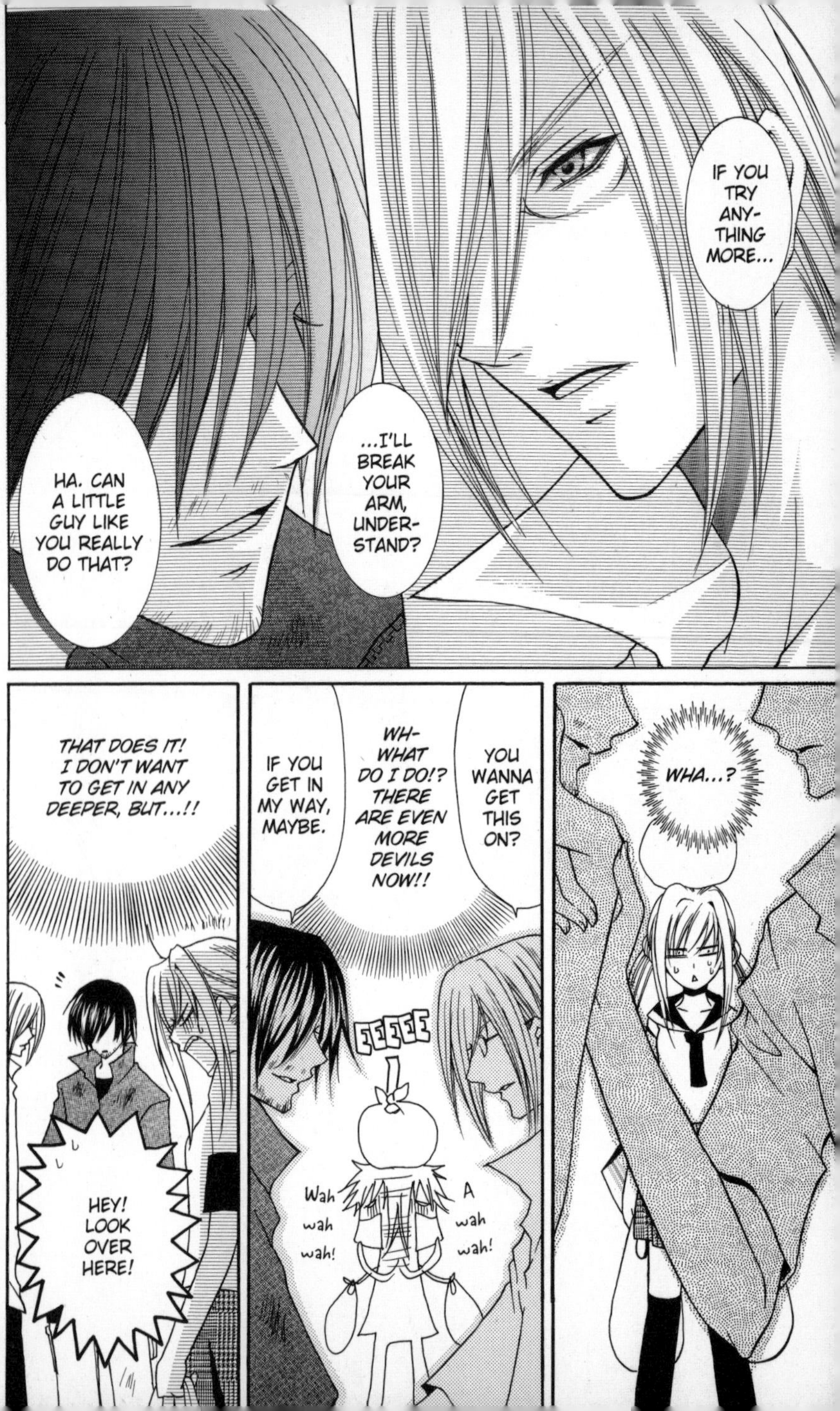
IF YOU TRY ANYTHING MORE...
...I'LL BREAK YOUR ARM, UNDERSTAND?
HA. CAN A LITTLE GUY LIKE YOU REALLY DO THAT?
WHA...?
YOU WANNA GET THIS ON?
WH-WHAT DO I DO!? THERE ARE EVEN MORE DEVILS NOW!!
IF YOU GET IN MY WAY, MAYBE.
EEEEE
A wah wah!
Wah wah wah!
THAT DOES IT! I DON'T WANT TO GET IN ANY DEEPER, BUT...!!
HEY! LOOK OVER HERE!

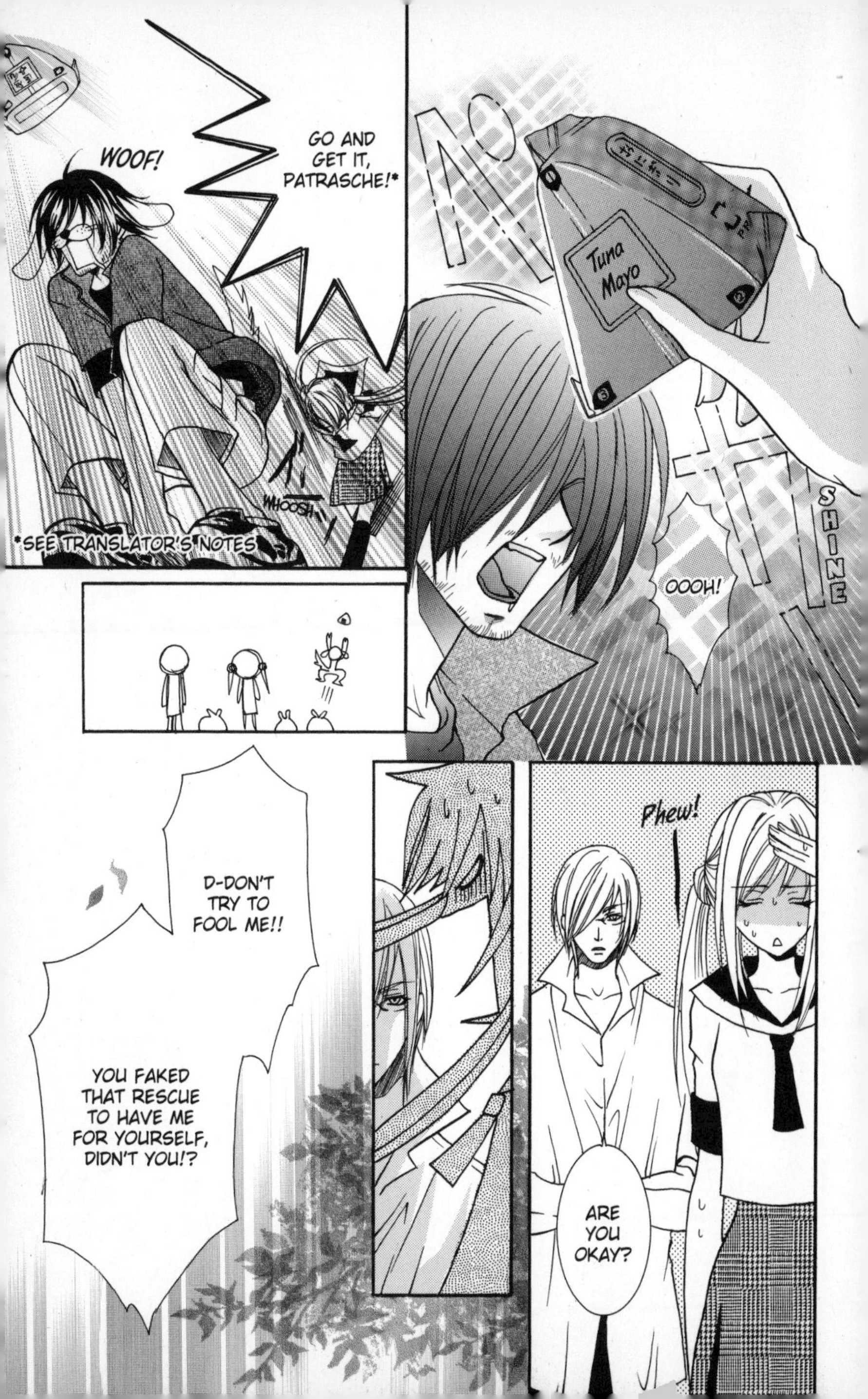
GO AND GET IT, PATRASCHE!*
WOOF!
WHOOSH
*SEE TRANSLATOR'S NOTES
Tuna Mayo
OOOH!
SHINE
Phew!
ARE YOU OKAY?
D-DON'T TRY TO FOOL ME!!
YOU FAKED THAT RESCUE TO HAVE ME FOR YOURSELF, DIDN'T YOU!?

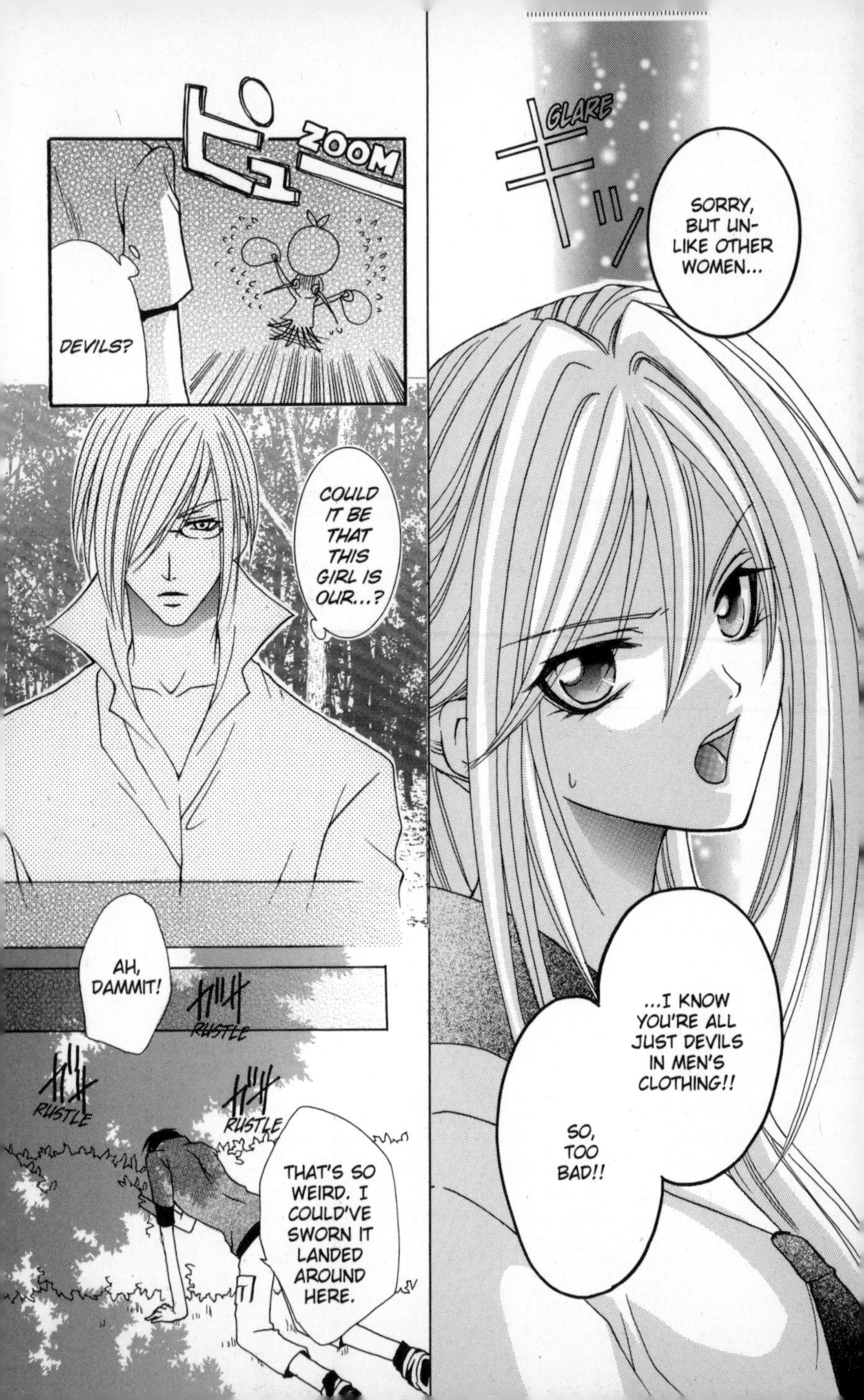
GLARE
SORRY, BUT UN-LIKE OTHER WOMEN...
...I KNOW YOU'RE ALL JUST DEVILS IN MEN'S CLOTHING!!
SO, TOO BAD!!
ZOOM
DEVILS?
COULD IT BE THAT THIS GIRL IS OUR...?
AH, DAMMIT!
RUSTLE
RUSTLE
RUSTLE
THAT'S SO WEIRD. I COULD'VE SWORN IT LANDED AROUND HERE.

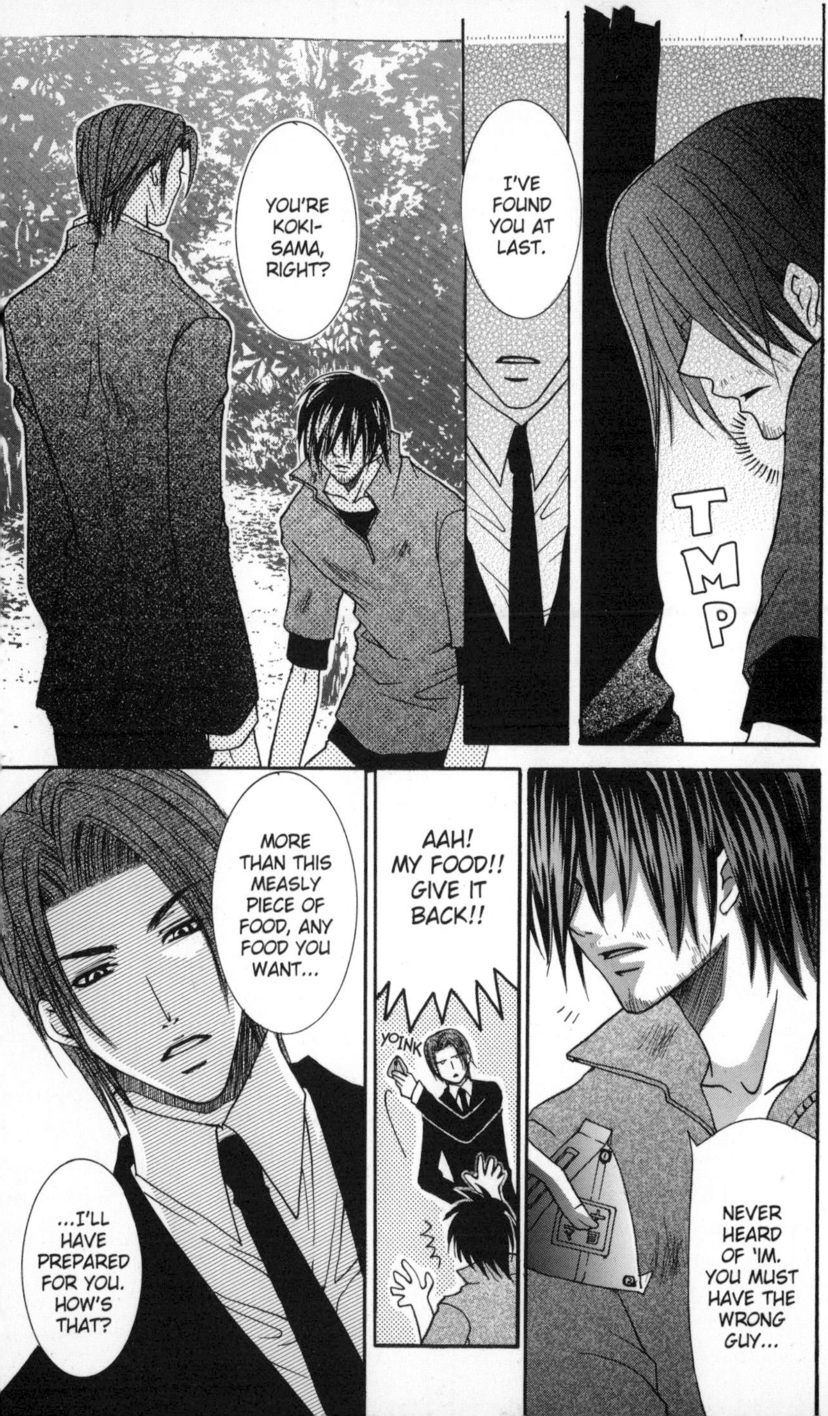
TMP
I'VE FOUND YOU AT LAST.
YOU'RE KOKI-SAMA, RIGHT?
NEVER HEARD OF 'IM. YOU MUST HAVE THE WRONG GUY...
YOINK
AAH! MY FOOD!! GIVE IT BACK!!
MORE THAN THIS MEASLY PIECE OF FOOD, ANY FOOD YOU WANT...
...I'LL HAVE PREPARED FOR YOU. HOW'S THAT?

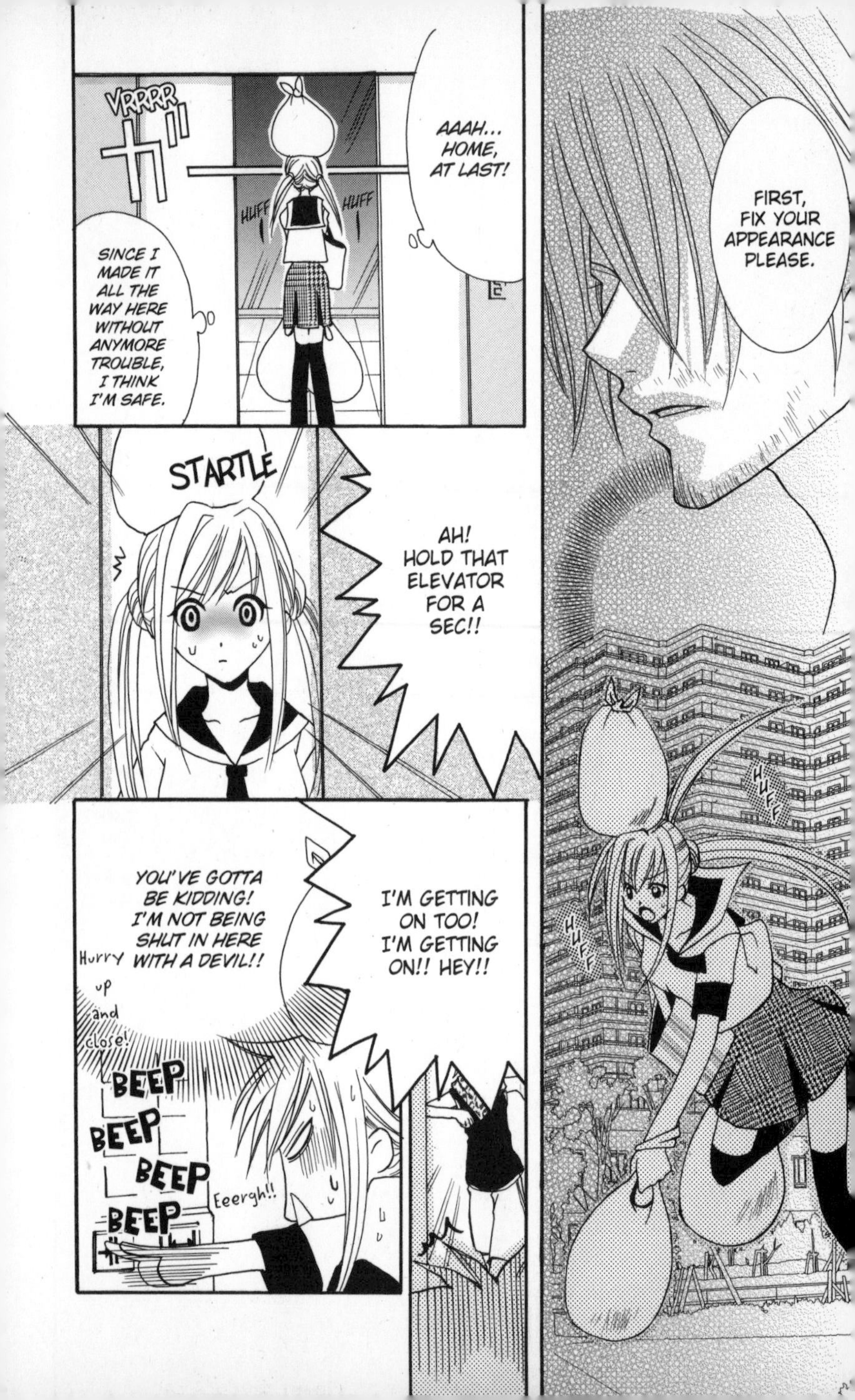
FIRST, FIX YOUR APPEARANCE PLEASE.
HUFF
HUFF
AAAH... HOME, AT LAST!
VRRRR
HUFF
HUFF
SINCE I MADE IT ALL THE WAY HERE WITHOUT ANYMORE TROUBLE, I THINK I'M SAFE.
AH! HOLD THAT ELEVATOR FOR A SEC!!
STARTLE
I'M GETTING ON TOO! I'M GETTING ON!! HEY!!
YOU'VE GOTTA BE KIDDING! I'M NOT BEING SHUT IN HERE WITH A DEVIL!!
Hurry up and close!
BEEP
BEEP
BEEP
BEEP
Eeergh!!

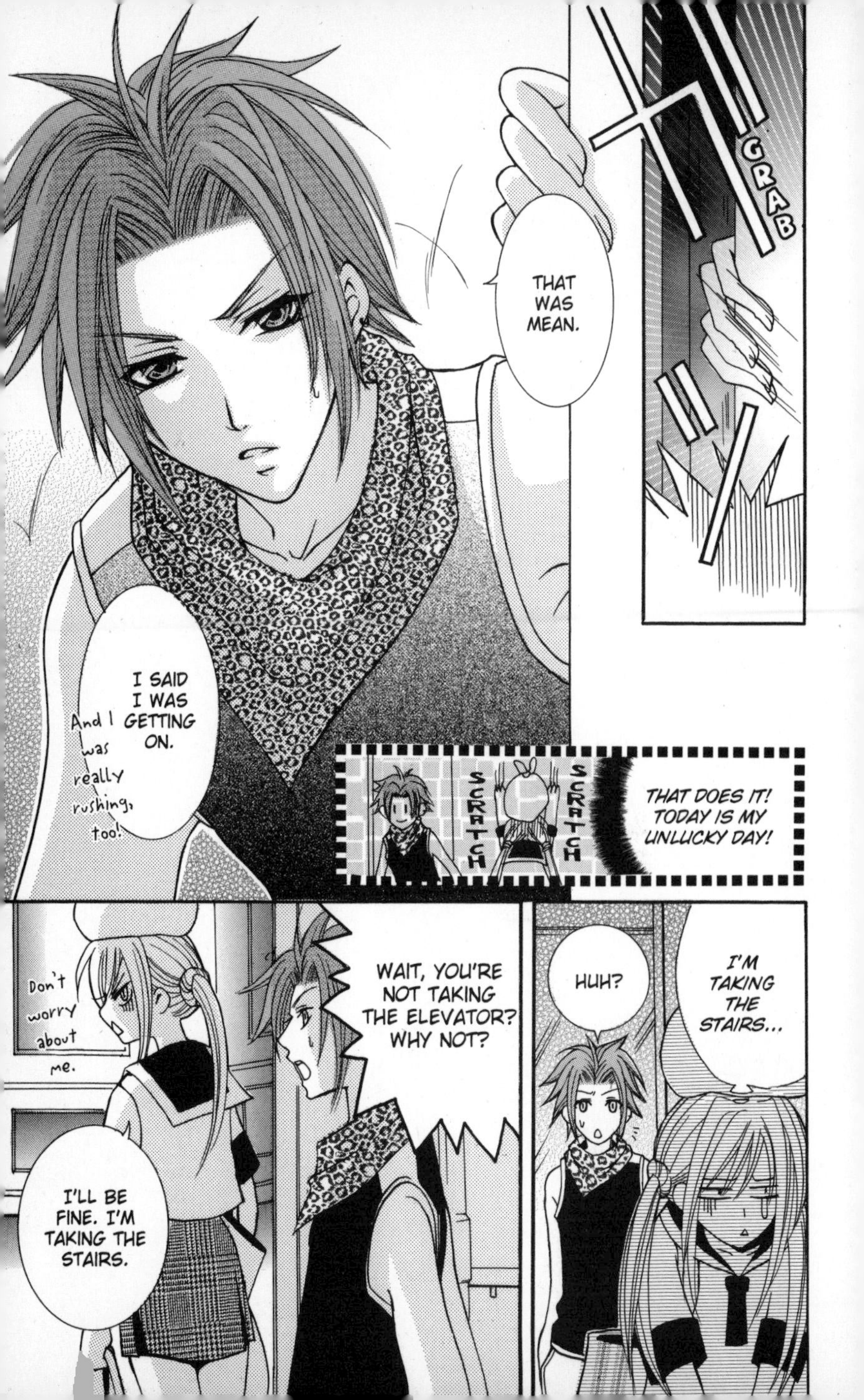
GRAB
THAT WAS MEAN.
I SAID I WAS GETTING ON.
And I was really rushing, too!
SCRATCH
SCRATCH
THAT DOES IT! TODAY IS MY UNLUCKY DAY!
I'M TAKING THE STAIRS...
HUH?
WAIT, YOU'RE NOT TAKING THE ELEVATOR? WHY NOT?
Don't worry about me.
I'LL BE FINE. I'M TAKING THE STAIRS.

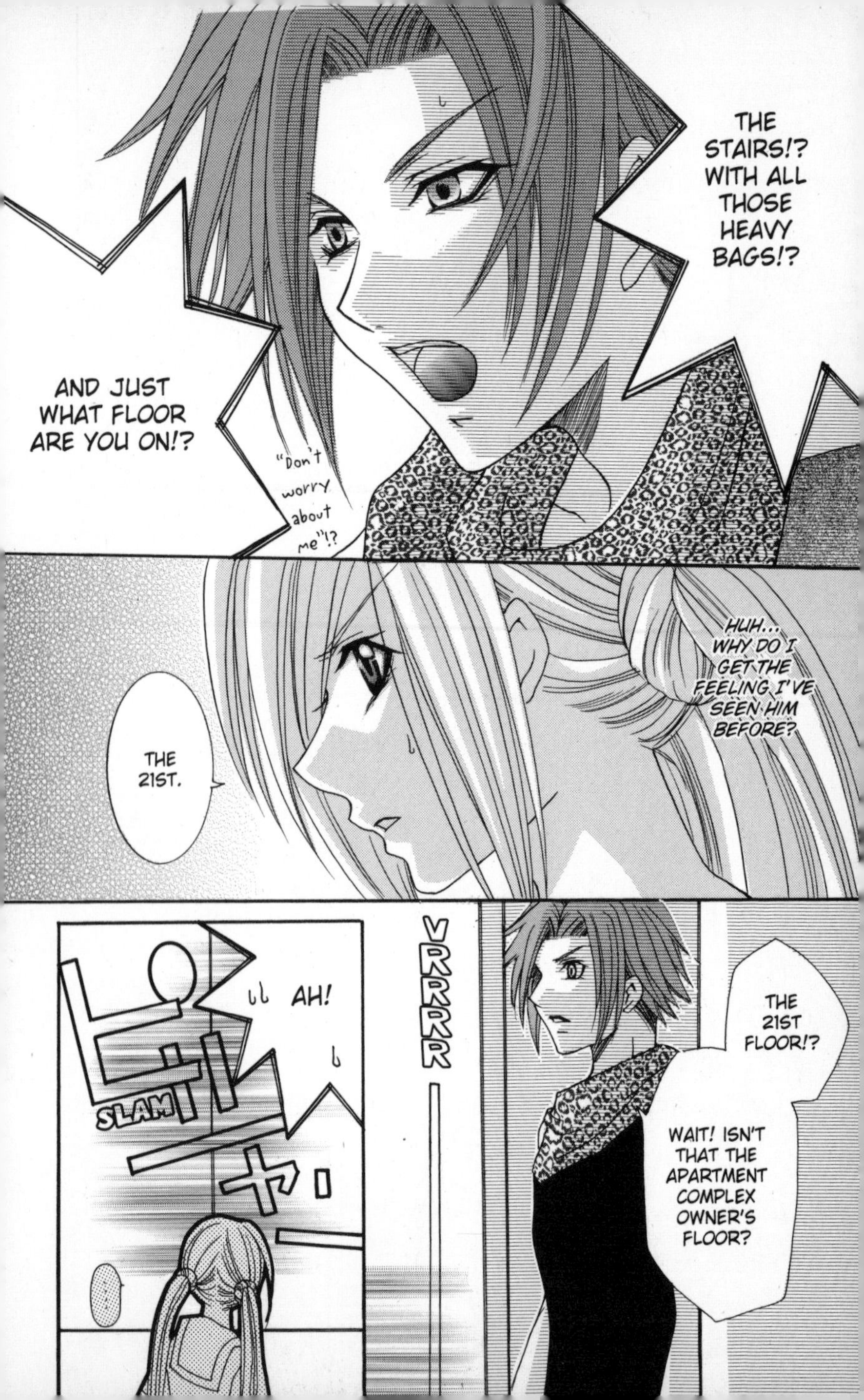
THE STAIRS!? WITH ALL THOSE HEAVY BAGS!?
AND JUST WHAT FLOOR ARE YOU ON!?
"Don't worry about me"!?
HUH... WHY DO I GET THE FEELING I'VE SEEN HIM BEFORE?
THE 21ST.
THE 21ST FLOOR!?
WAIT! ISN'T THAT THE APARTMENT COMPLEX OWNER'S FLOOR?
VRRRR
AH!
SLAM

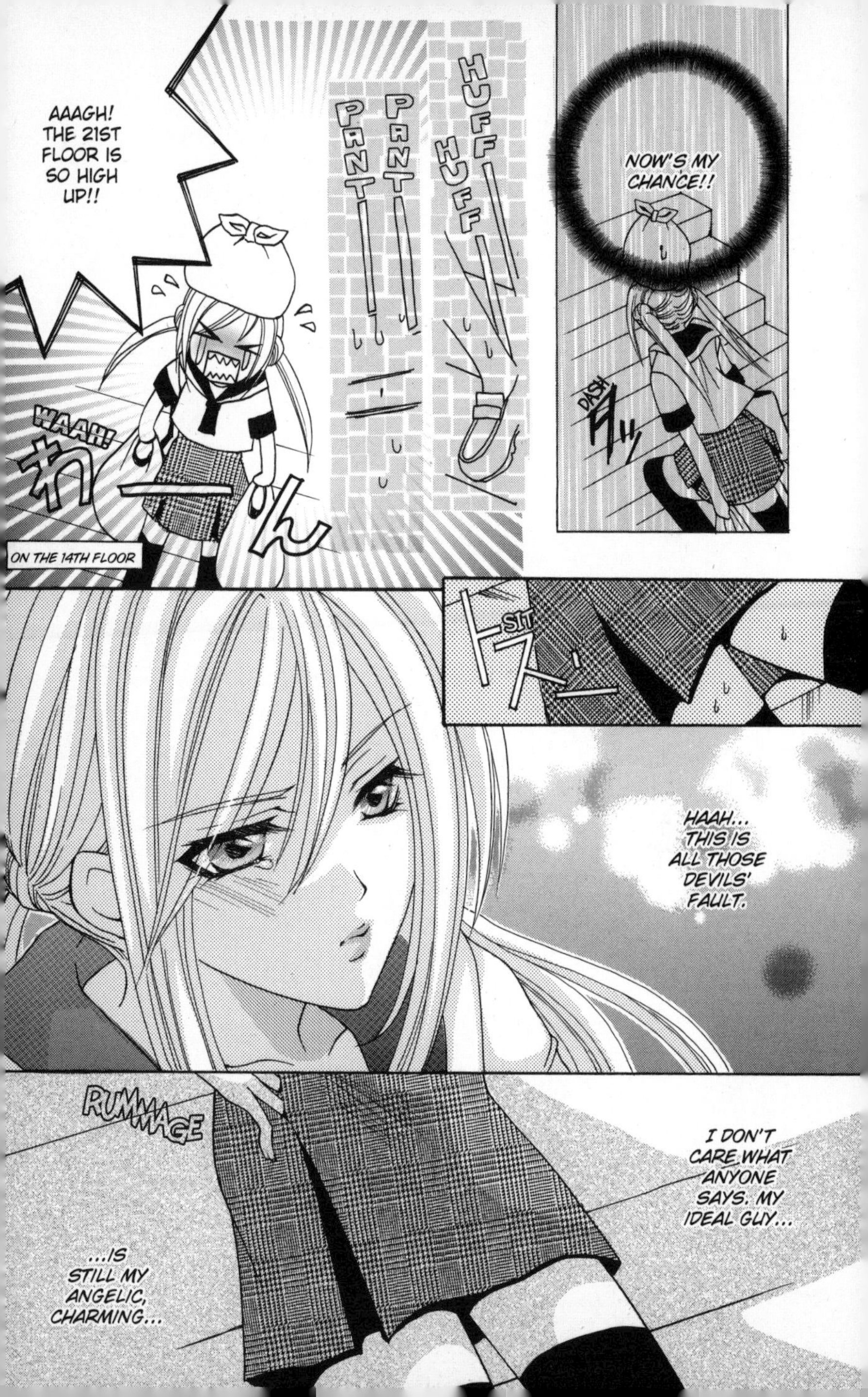
NOW'S MY CHANCE!!
DASH
HUFF HUFF
PANT PANT
AAAGH! THE 21ST FLOOR IS SO HIGH UP!!
WAAAH!
ON THE 14TH FLOOR
SIT
HAAH... THIS IS ALL THOSE DEVILS' FAULT.
RUMMAGE
I DON'T CARE WHAT ANYONE SAYS. MY IDEAL GUY...
...IS STILL MY ANGELIC, CHARMING...

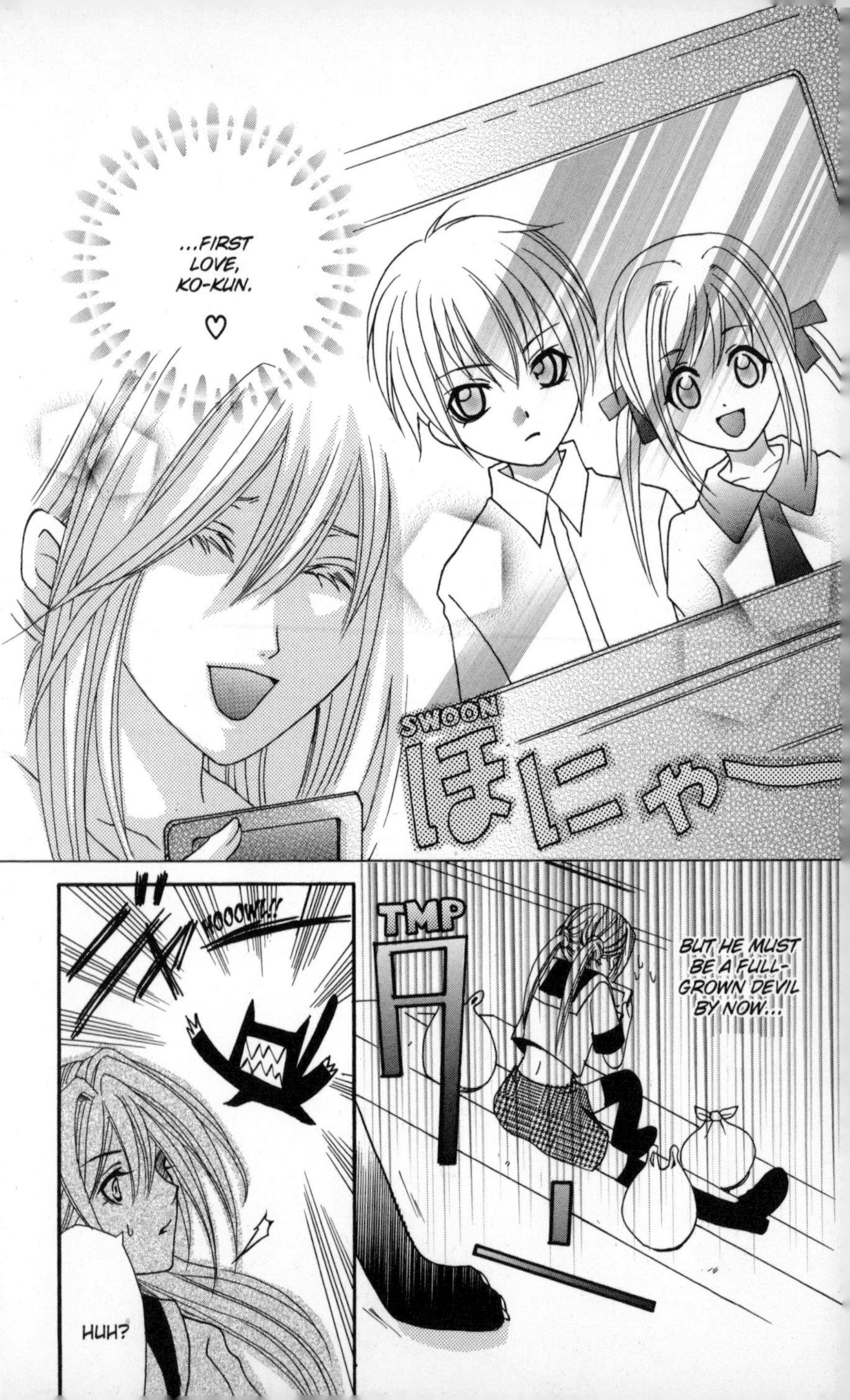
...FIRST LOVE, KO-KUN.
♡
SWOON
ほにゃー
TMP
BUT HE MUST BE A FULL-GROWN DEVIL BY NOW...
HOOOWL!!
HUH?

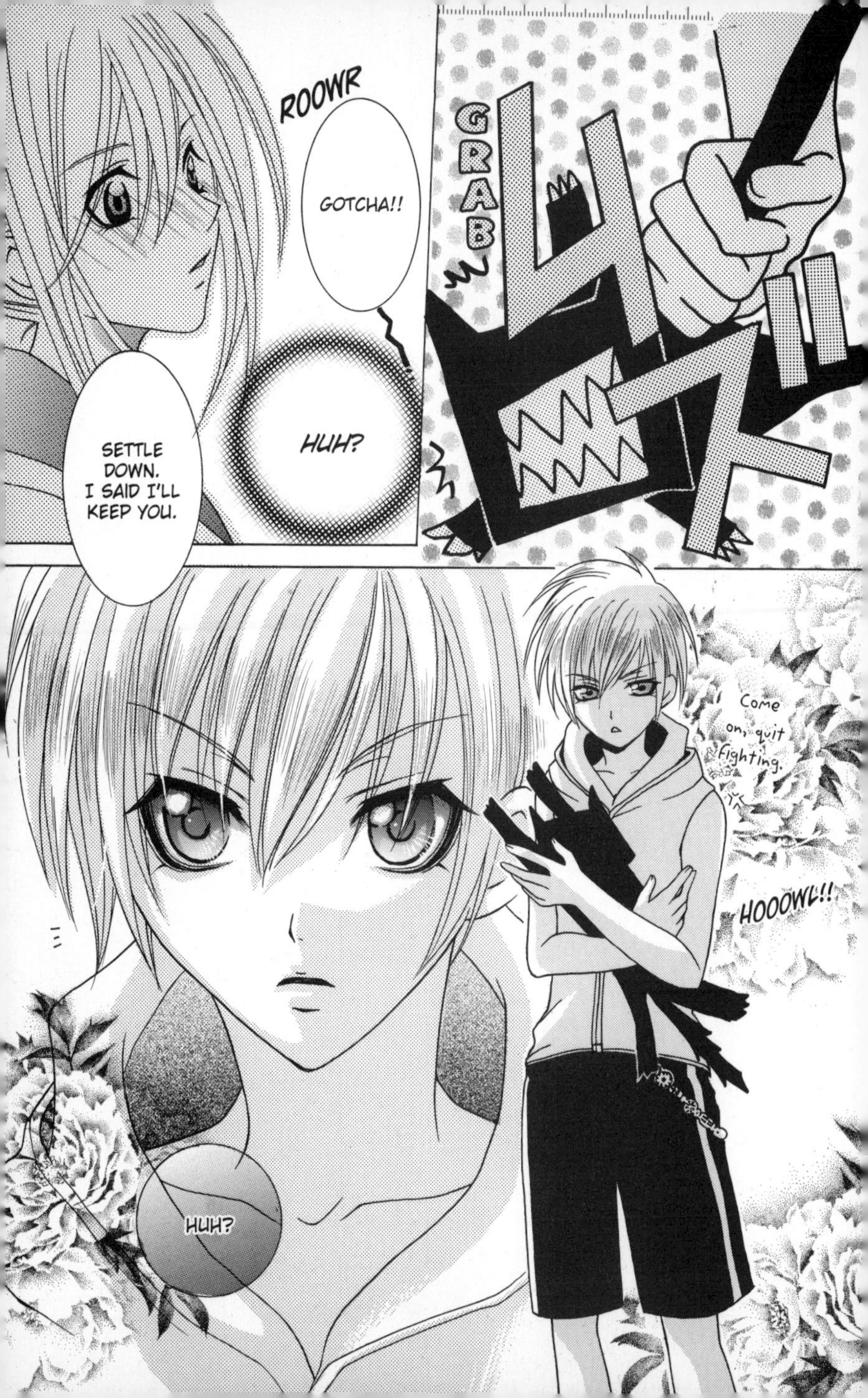
GRAB
ROOWR
GOTCHA!!
HUH?
SETTLE DOWN. I SAID I'LL KEEP YOU.
Come on, quit fighting.
HOOOWL!!
HUH?

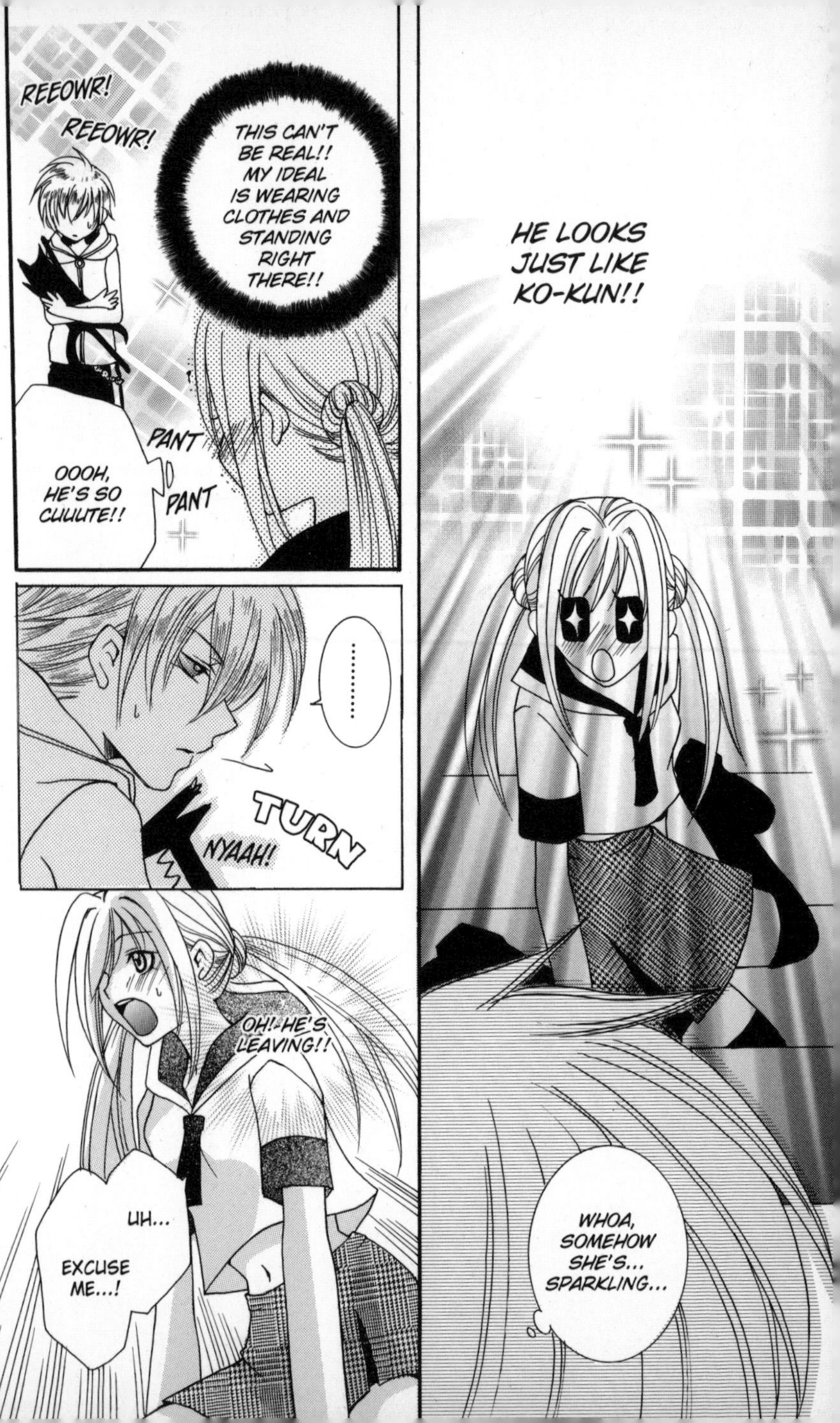
HE LOOKS JUST LIKE KO-KUN!!
WHOA, SOMEHOW SHE'S... SPARKLING...
REEOWR!
REEOWR!
THIS CAN'T BE REAL!! MY IDEAL IS WEARING CLOTHES AND STANDING RIGHT THERE!!
PANT
PANT
OOOH, HE'S SO CUUUTE!!
....
TURN
NYAAH!
OH! HE'S LEAVING!!
UH...
EXCUSE ME...!

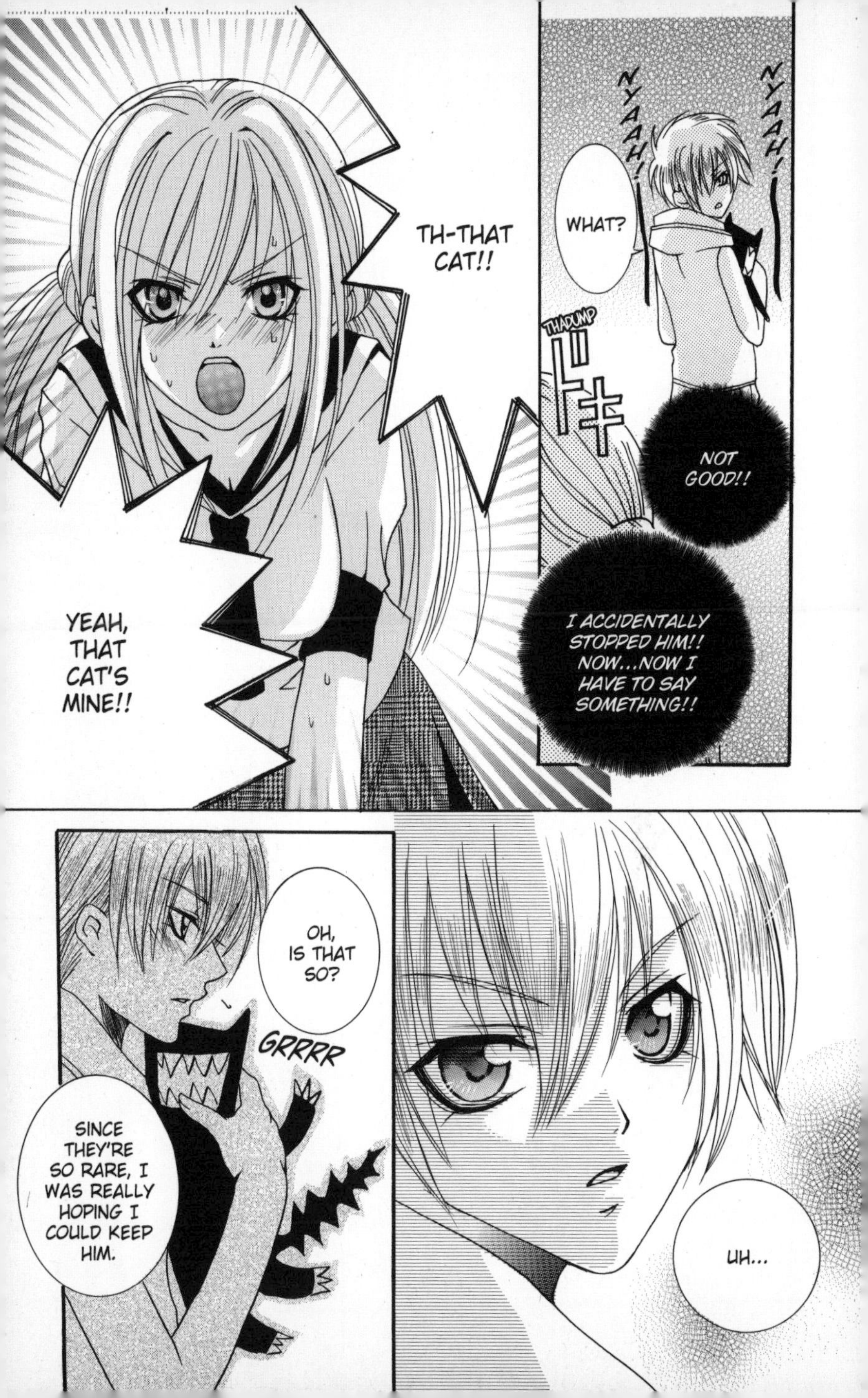
NYAAH!
NYAAH!
WHAT?
THADUMP
ドキ
NOT GOOD!!
I ACCIDENTALLY STOPPED HIM!! NOW...NOW I HAVE TO SAY SOMETHING!!
TH-THAT CAT!!
YEAH, THAT CAT'S MINE!!
UH...
OH, IS THAT SO?
GRRRR
SINCE THEY'RE SO RARE, I WAS REALLY HOPING I COULD KEEP HIM.

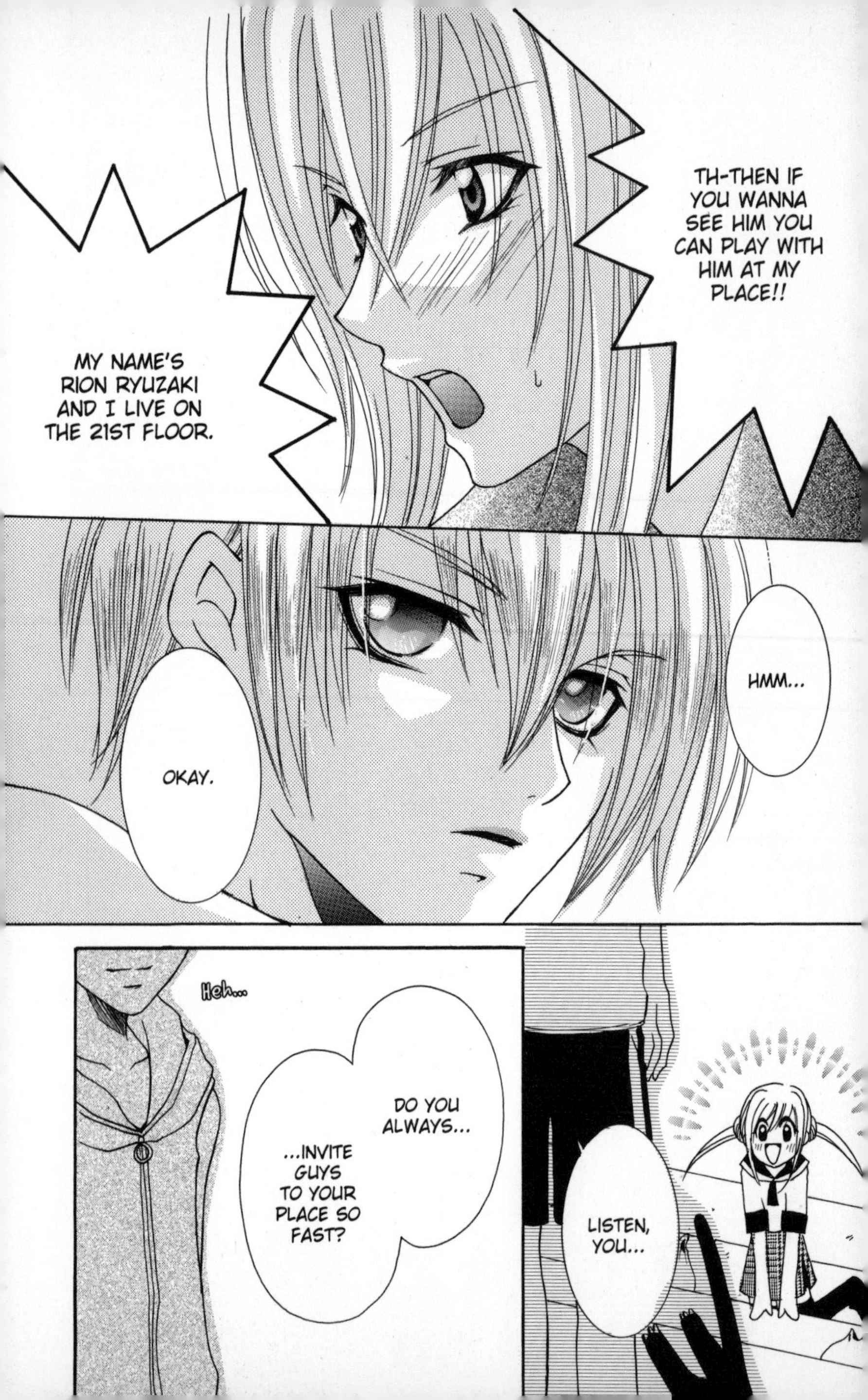
TH-THEN IF YOU WANNA SEE HIM YOU CAN PLAY WITH HIM AT MY PLACE!!
MY NAME'S RION RYUZAKI AND I LIVE ON THE 21ST FLOOR.
HMM...
OKAY.
LISTEN, YOU...
Heh...
DO YOU ALWAYS...
...INVITE GUYS TO YOUR PLACE SO FAST?

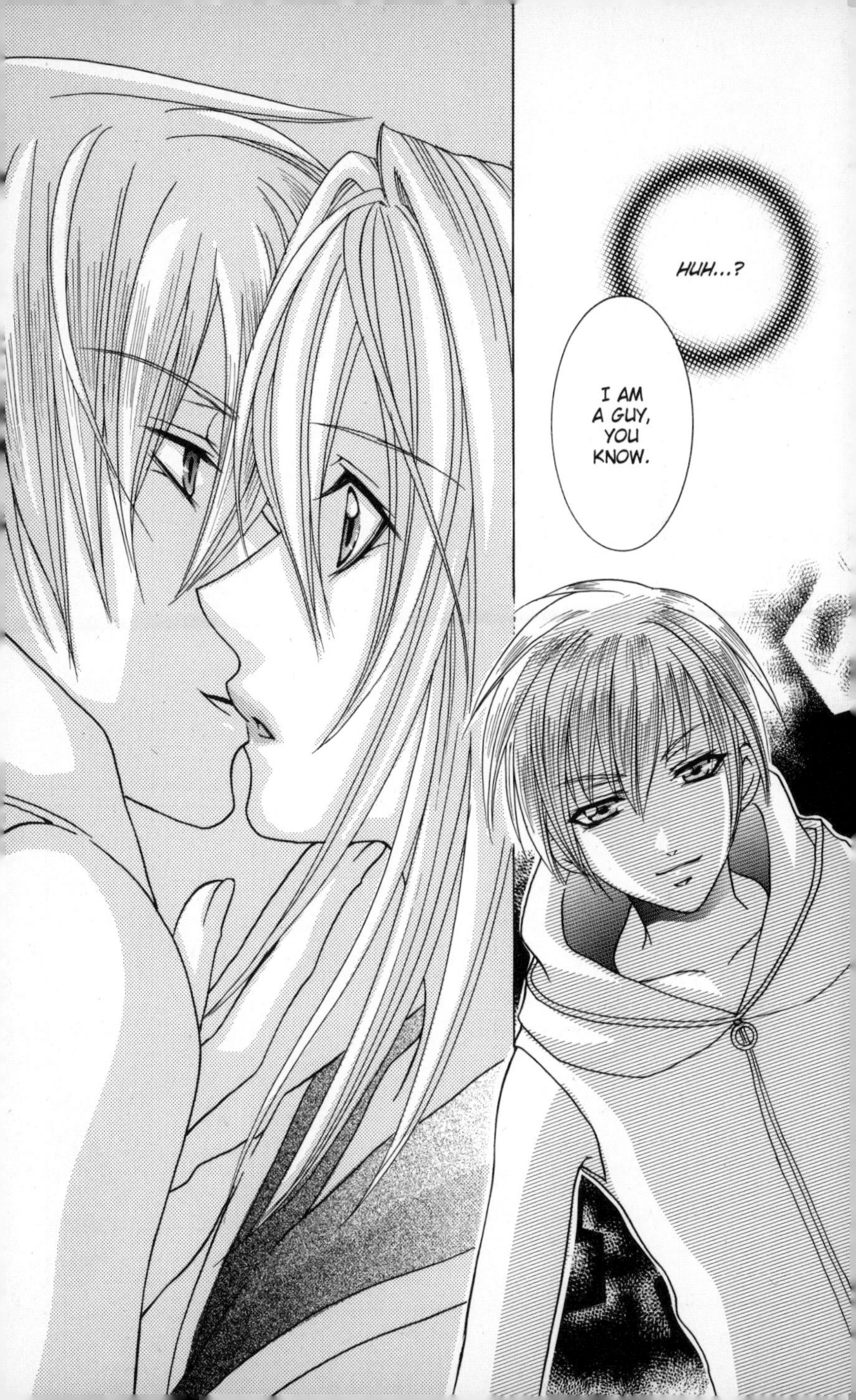
HUH...?
I AM A GUY, YOU KNOW.

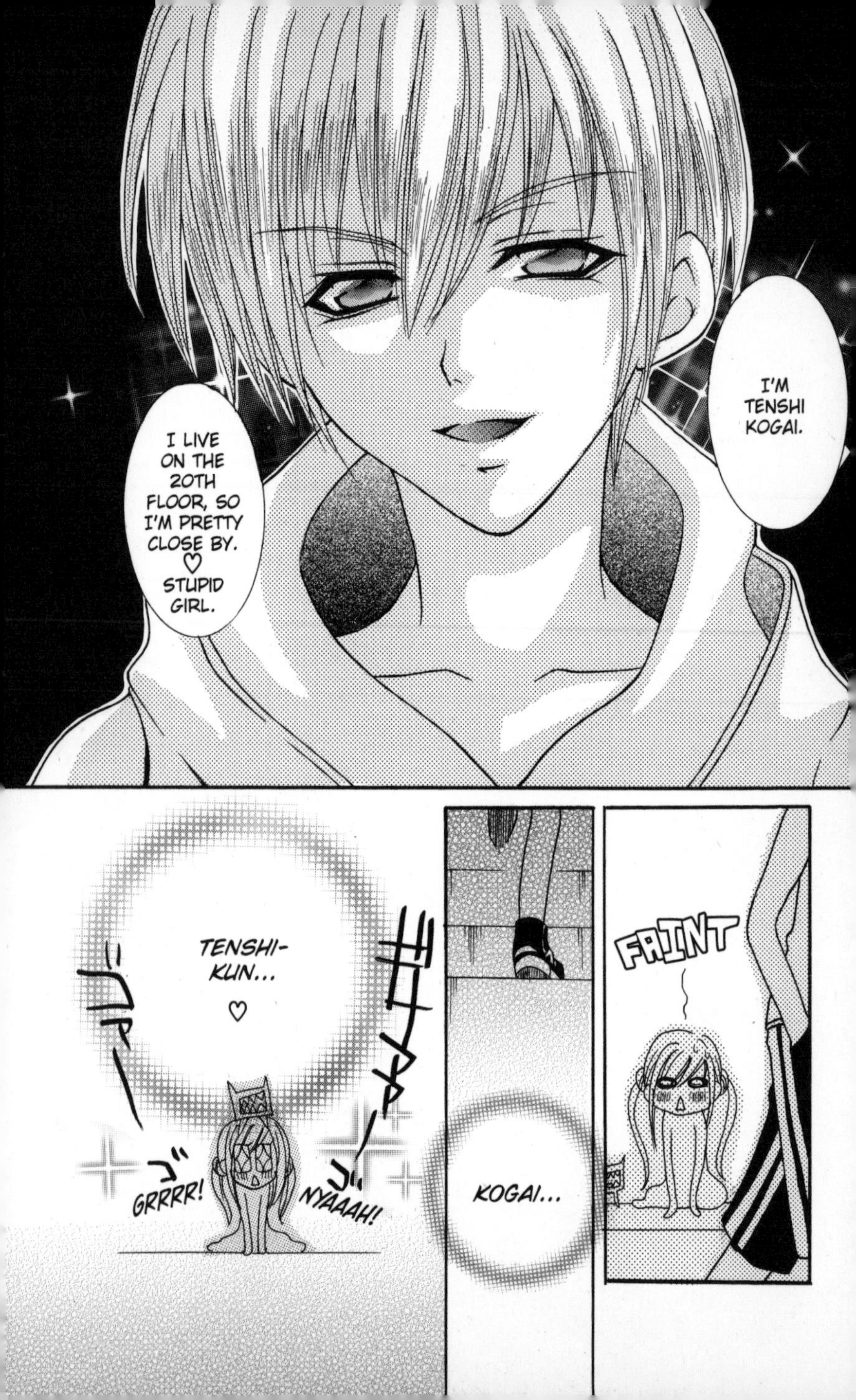
I'M TENSHI KOGAI.
I LIVE ON THE 20TH FLOOR, SO I'M PRETTY CLOSE BY. ♡ STUPID GIRL.
FAINT
KOGAI...
TENSHI-KUN... ♡
NYAAAH!
GRRRR!

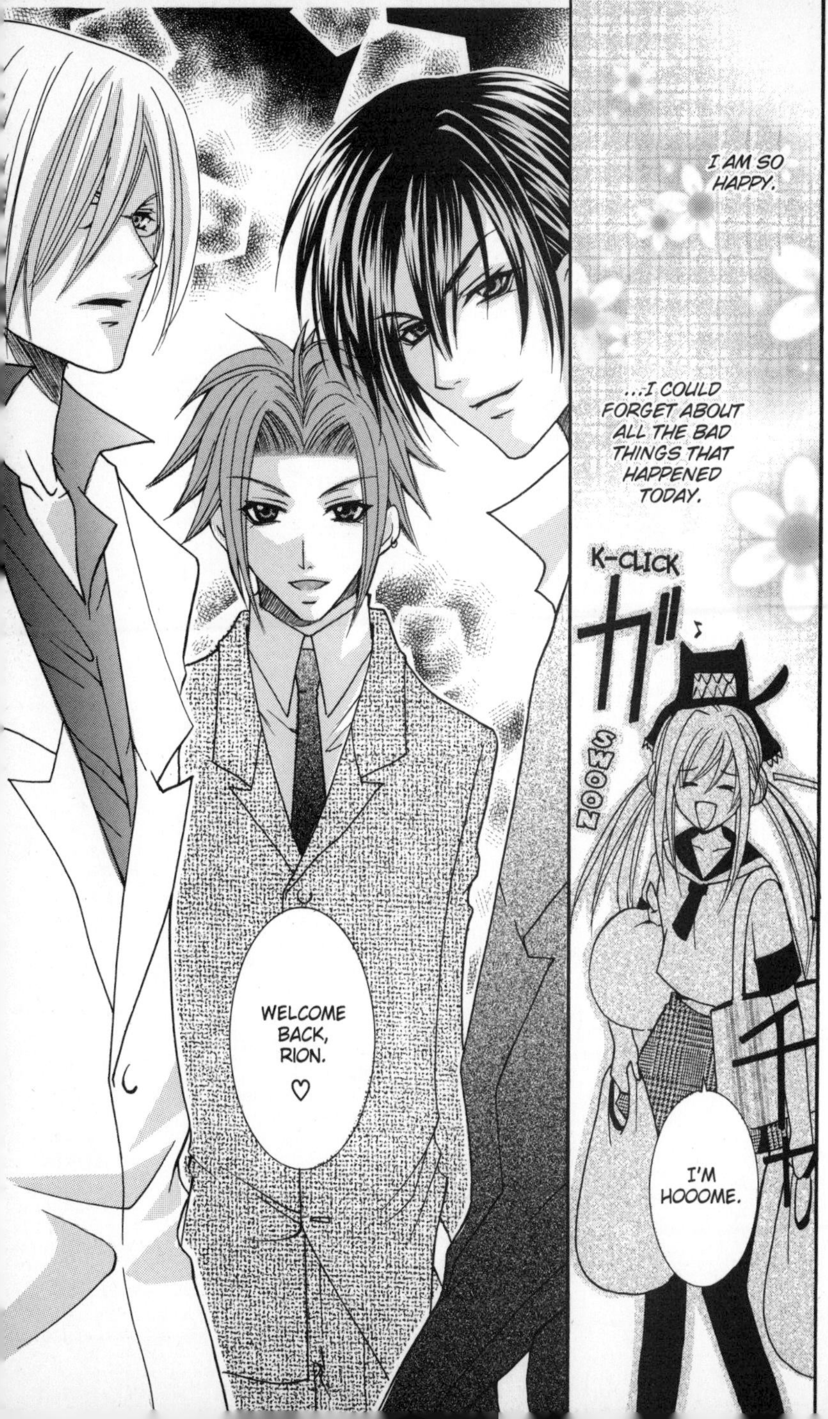
I AM SO HAPPY.
...I COULD FORGET ABOUT ALL THE BAD THINGS THAT HAPPENED TODAY.
K-CLICK
SWOON
I'M HOOOME.
WELCOME BACK, RION. ♡

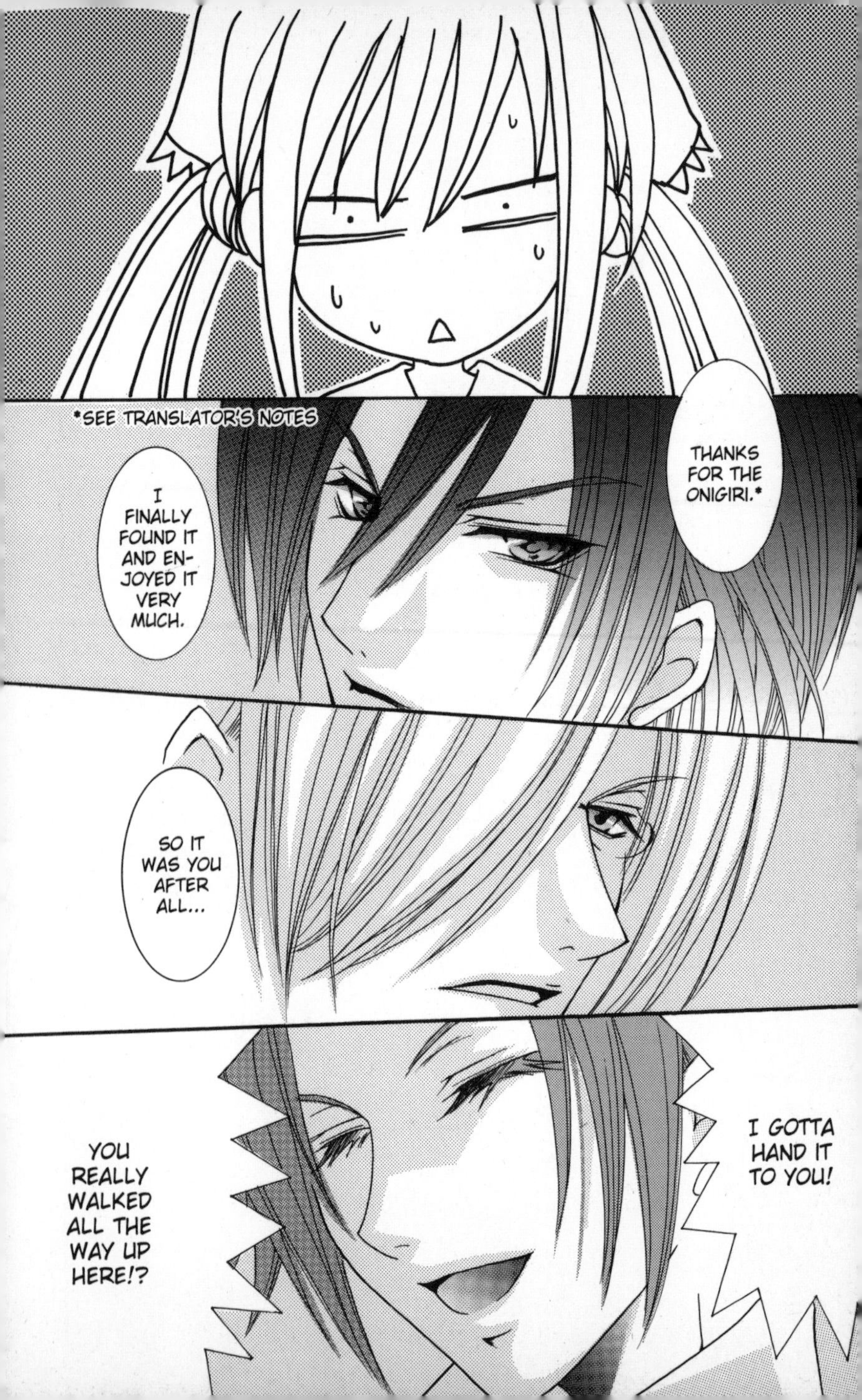
THANKS FOR THE ONIGIRI.*
I FINALLY FOUND IT AND EN-JOYED IT VERY MUCH.
*SEE TRANSLATOR'S NOTES
SO IT WAS YOU AFTER ALL...
I GOTTA HAND IT TO YOU!
YOU REALLY WALKED ALL THE WAY UP HERE!?

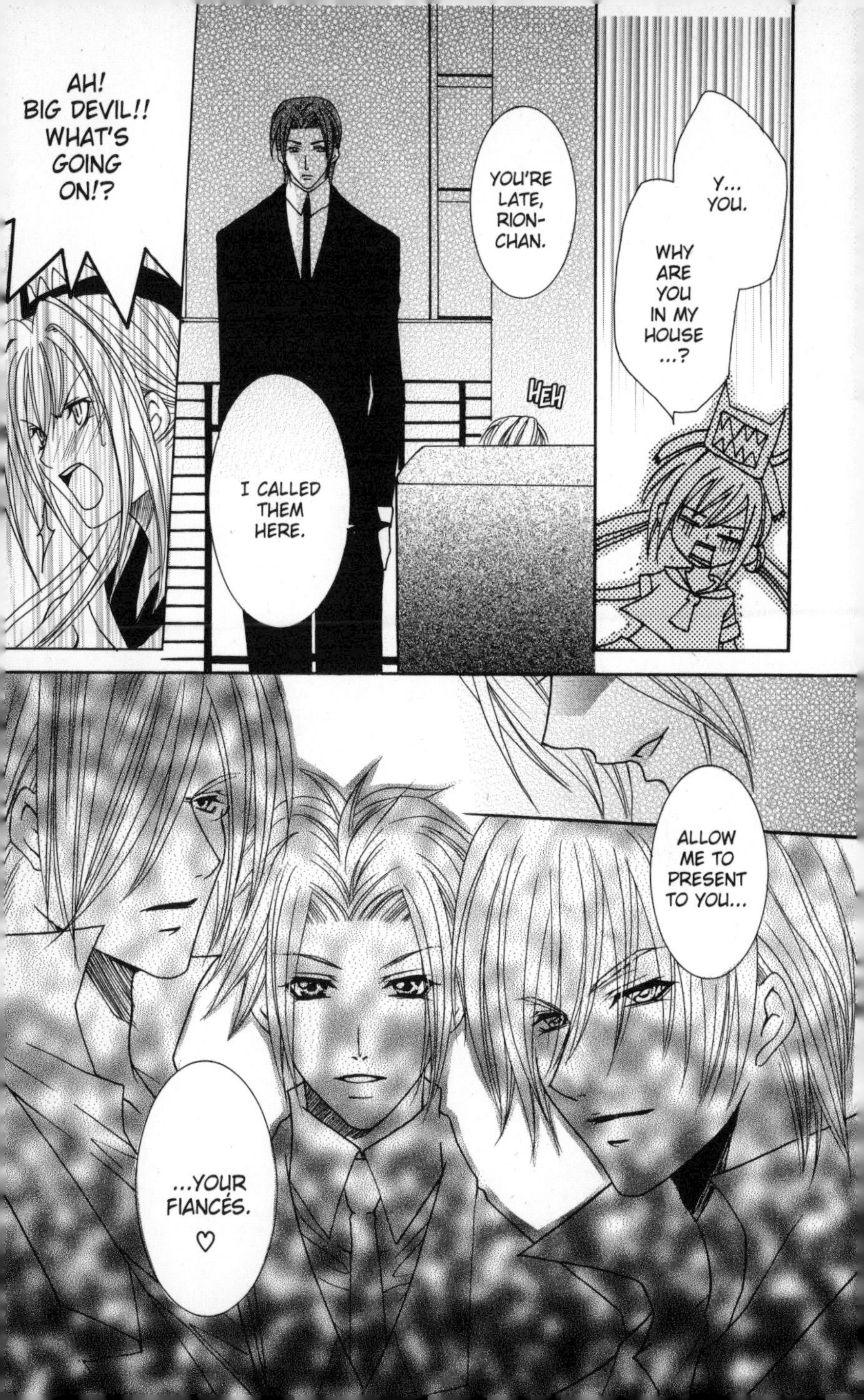
Y... YOU.
WHY ARE YOU IN MY HOUSE ...?
HEH
YOU'RE LATE, RION-CHAN.
AH! BIG DEVIL!! WHAT'S GOING ON!?
I CALLED THEM HERE.
ALLOW ME TO PRESENT TO YOU...
...YOUR FIANCÉS. ♡

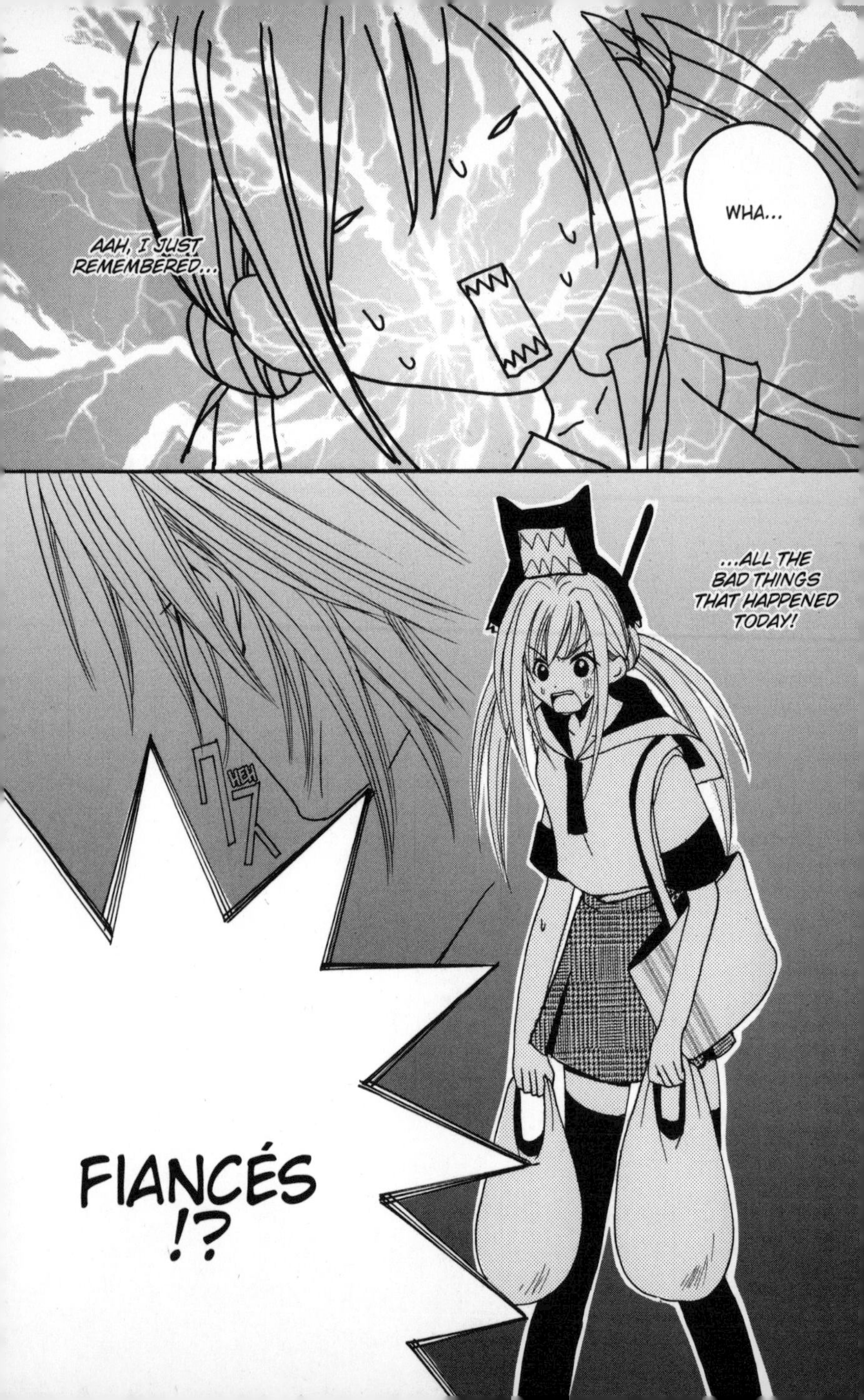
WHA...
AAH, I JUST REMEMBERED...
...ALL THE BAD THINGS THAT HAPPENED TODAY!
HEH
FIANCÉS !?

Chibi Angel Chibi Devil (1)

◀Chibi Light Version▶

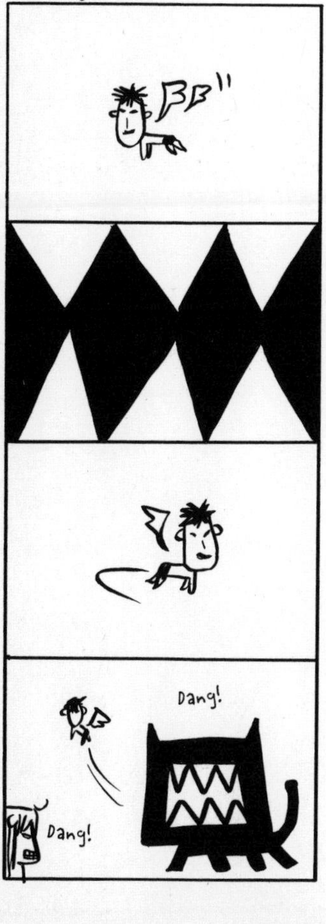
Dang!
Dang!

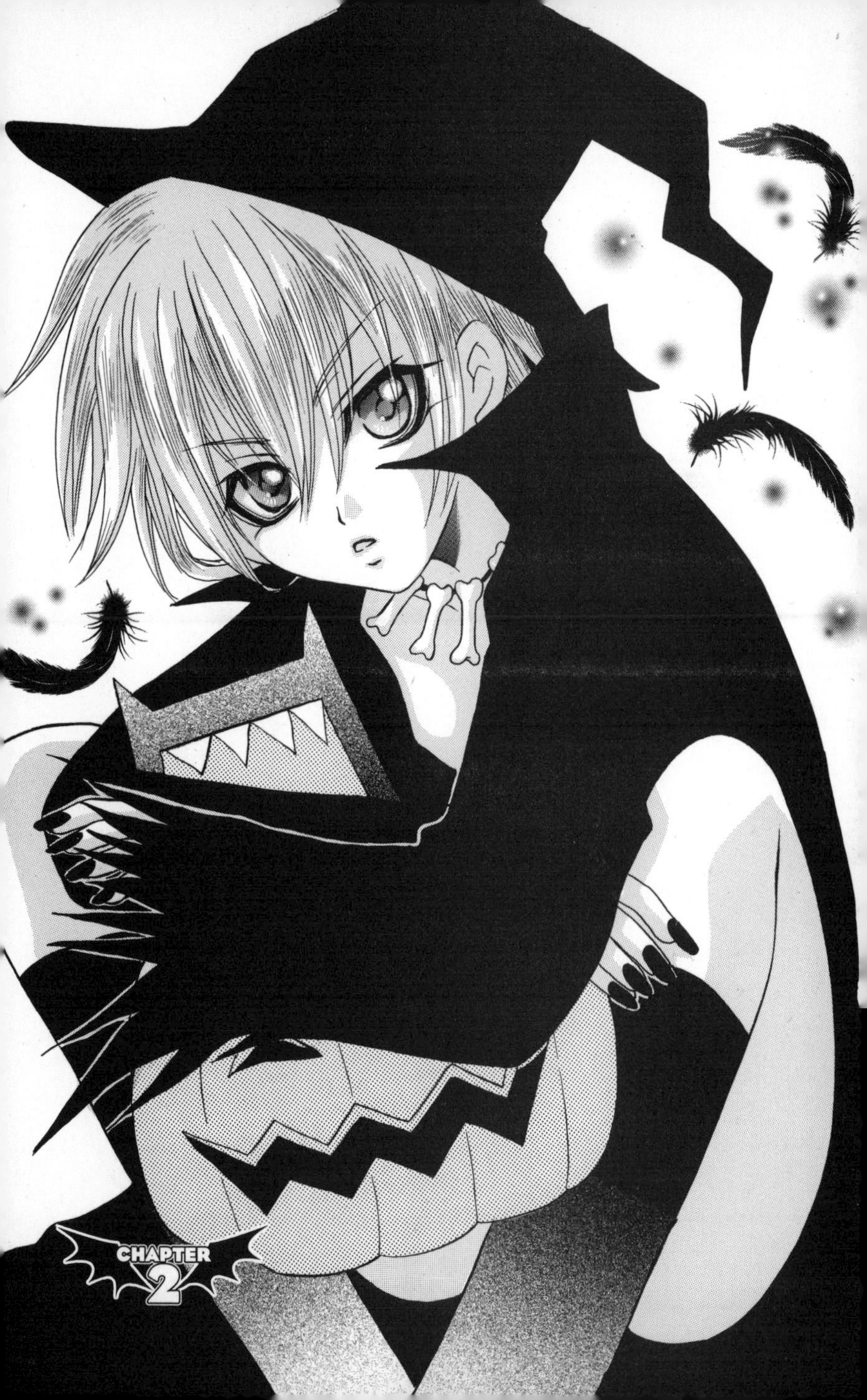
CHAPTER
2

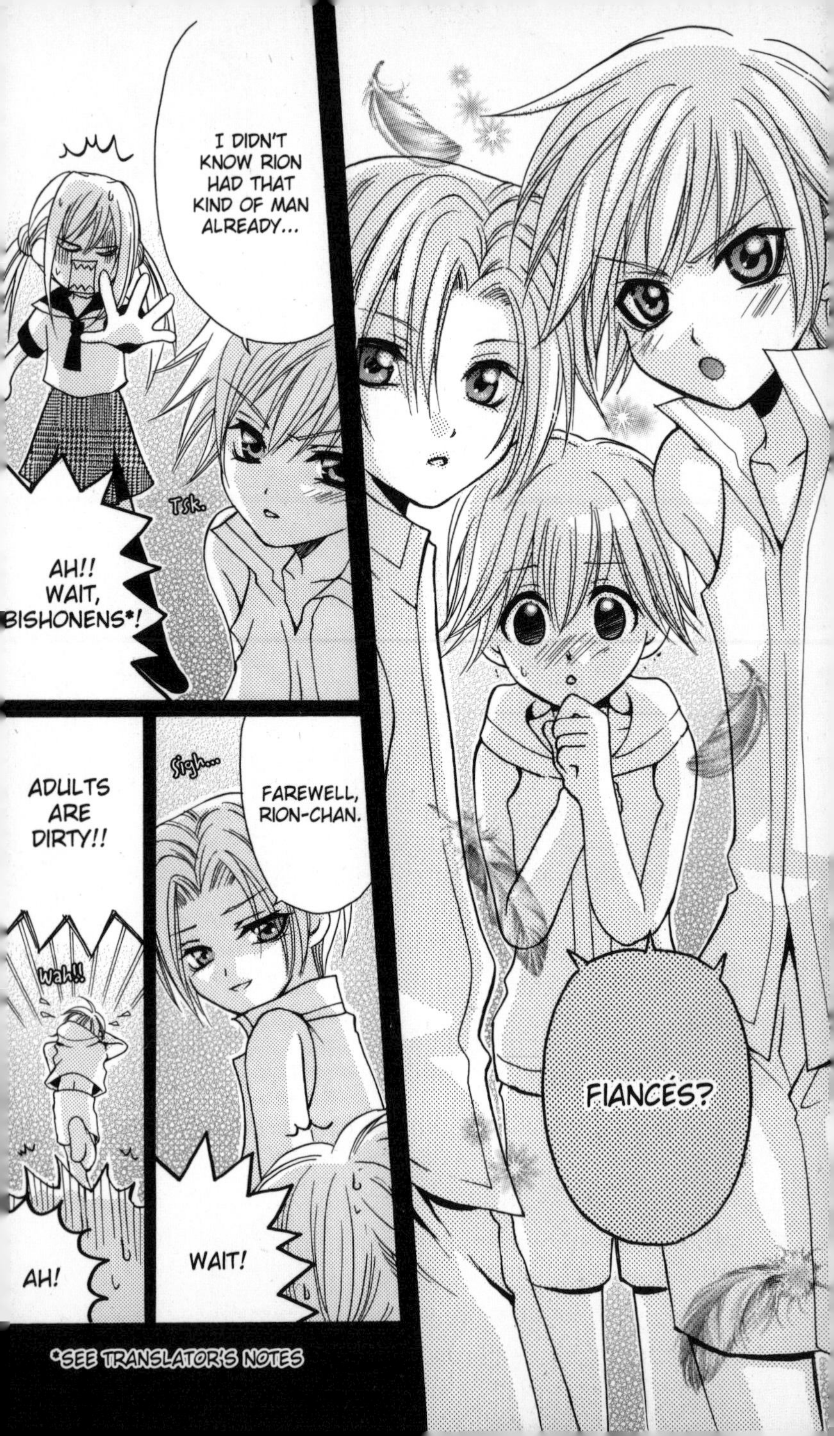
FIANCÉS?
I DIDN'T KNOW RION HAD THAT KIND OF MAN ALREADY...
Tsk.
AH!! WAIT, BISHONENS*!
Sigh...
FAREWELL, RION-CHAN.
WAIT!
ADULTS ARE DIRTY!!
Wah!!
AH!

*SEE TRANSLATOR'S NOTES

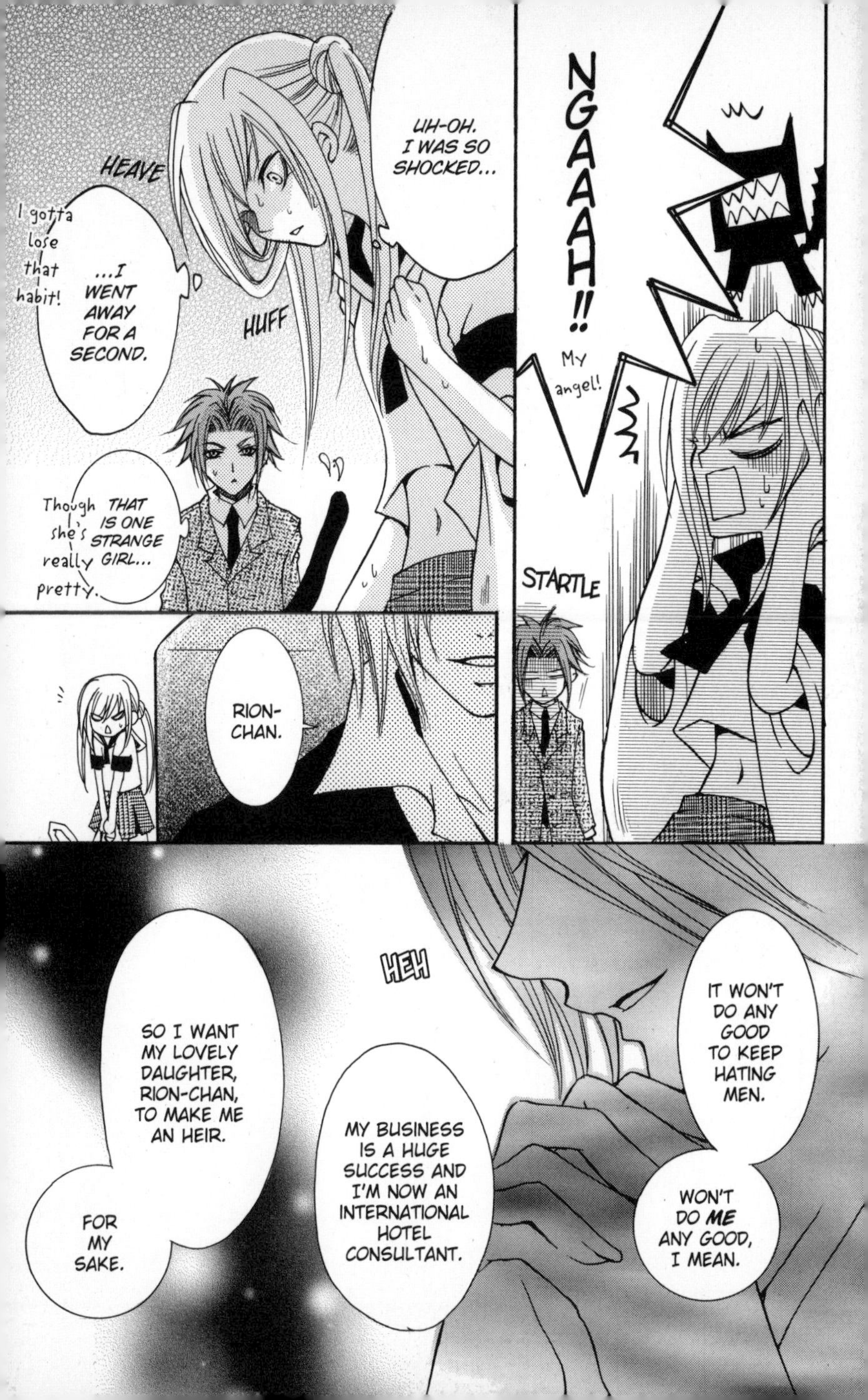
NGAAAAH!!
My angel!
STARTLE
UH-OH. I WAS SO SHOCKED...
HEAVE
...I WENT AWAY FOR A SECOND.
I gotta lose that habit!
HUFF
THAT IS ONE STRANGE GIRL...
Though she's really pretty.
RION-CHAN.
IT WON'T DO ANY GOOD TO KEEP HATING MEN.
WON'T DO *ME* ANY GOOD, I MEAN.
HEH
MY BUSINESS IS A HUGE SUCCESS AND I'M NOW AN INTERNATIONAL HOTEL CONSULTANT.
SO I WANT MY LOVELY DAUGHTER, RION-CHAN, TO MAKE ME AN HEIR.
FOR MY SAKE.

SO, I BROUGHT YOU THESE MEN.

AND SOMI-KUN.

FUUYA-KUN.

KOKI-KUN.

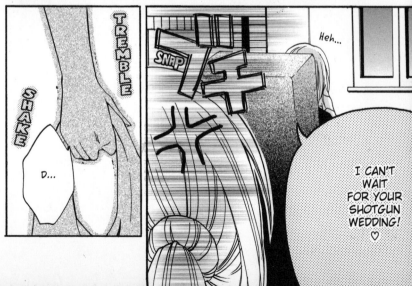

TREMBLE

SHAKE

D...

SNAP

Heh...

I CAN'T WAIT FOR YOUR SHOTGUN WEDDING! ♡

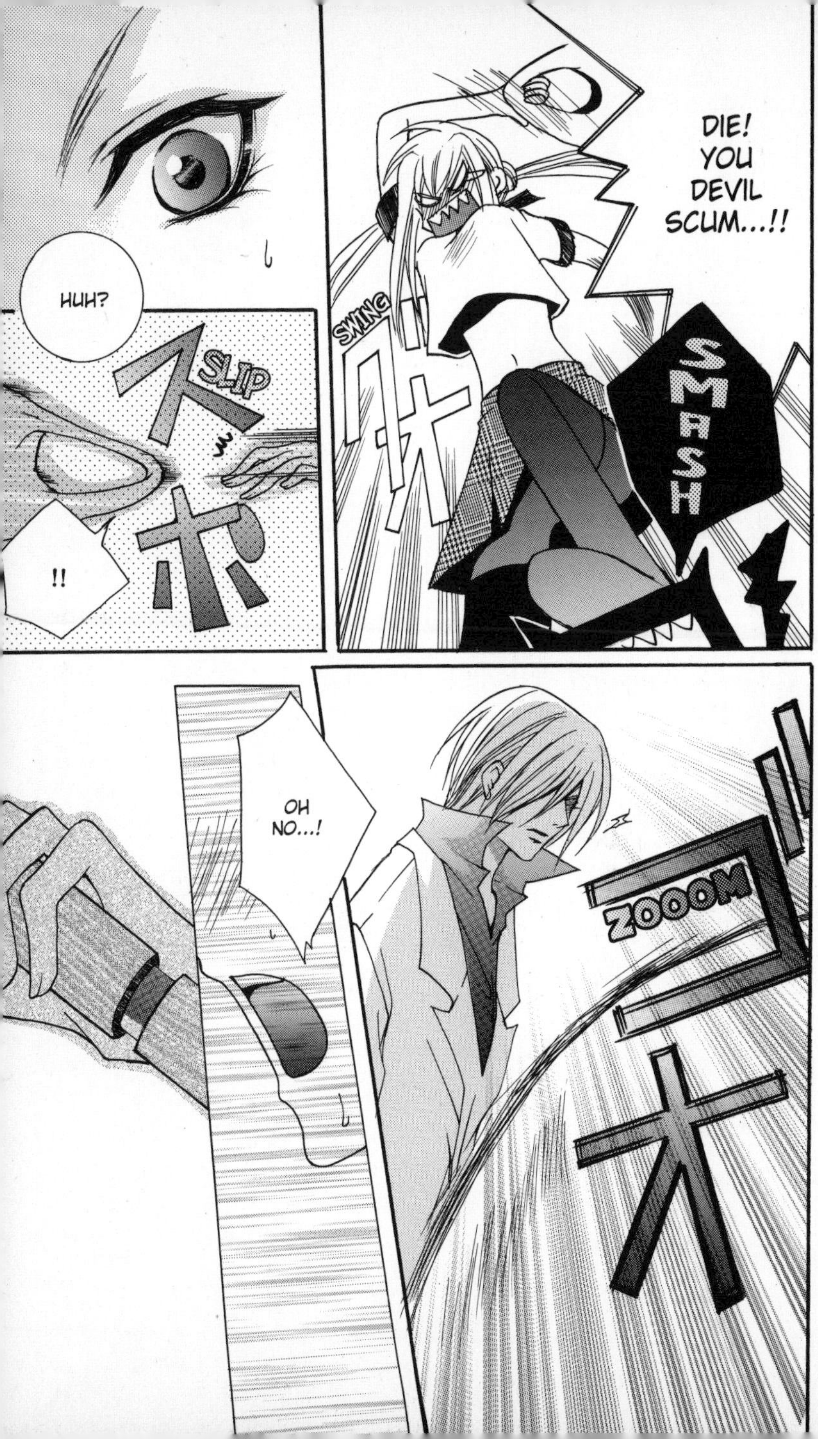
DIE! YOU DEVIL SCUM...!!
SWING
SMASH
HUH?
SLIP
!!
ZOOOM
OH NO...!

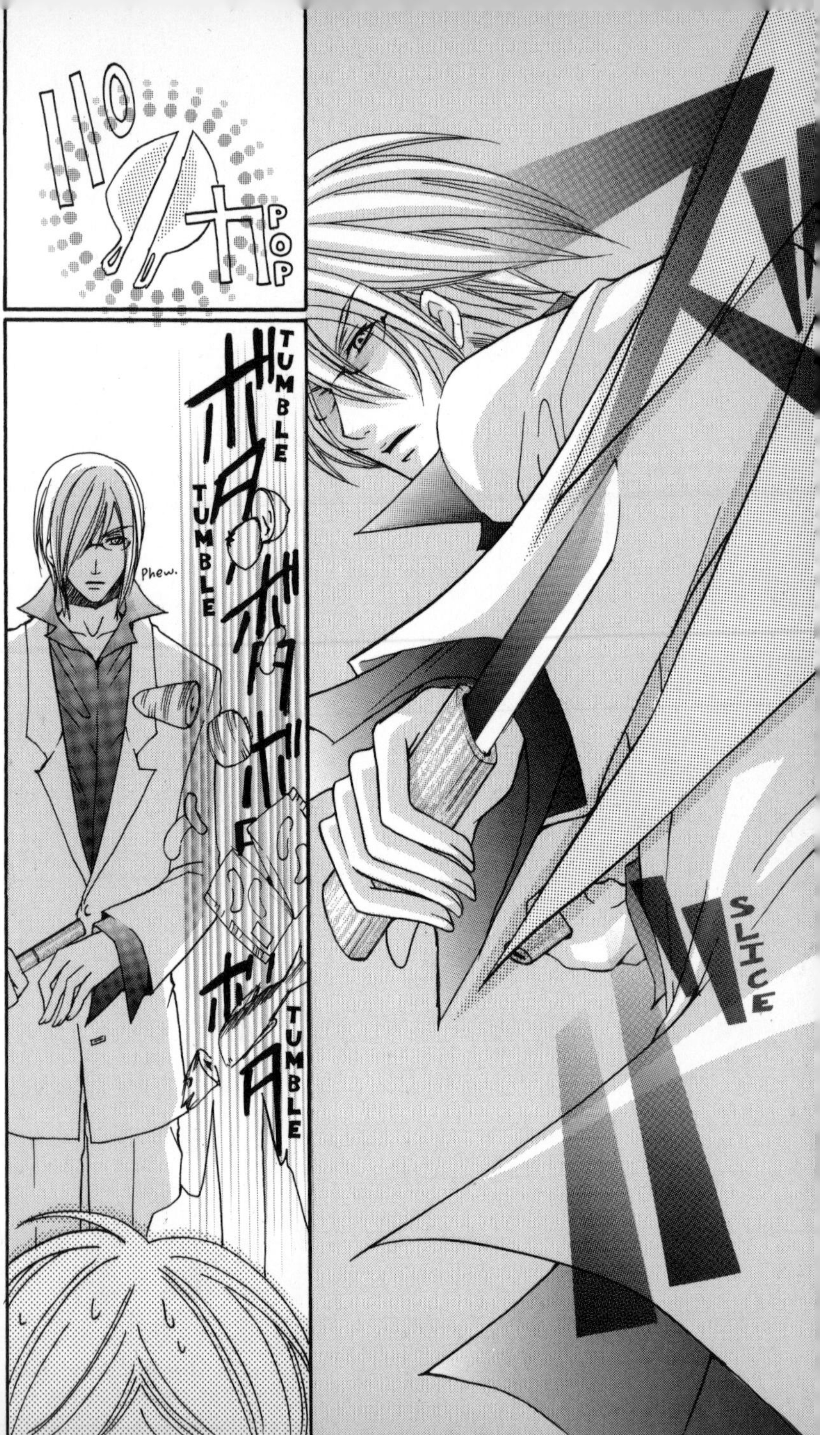
SLICE
POP
TUMBLE
TUMBLE
Phew.
TUMBLE

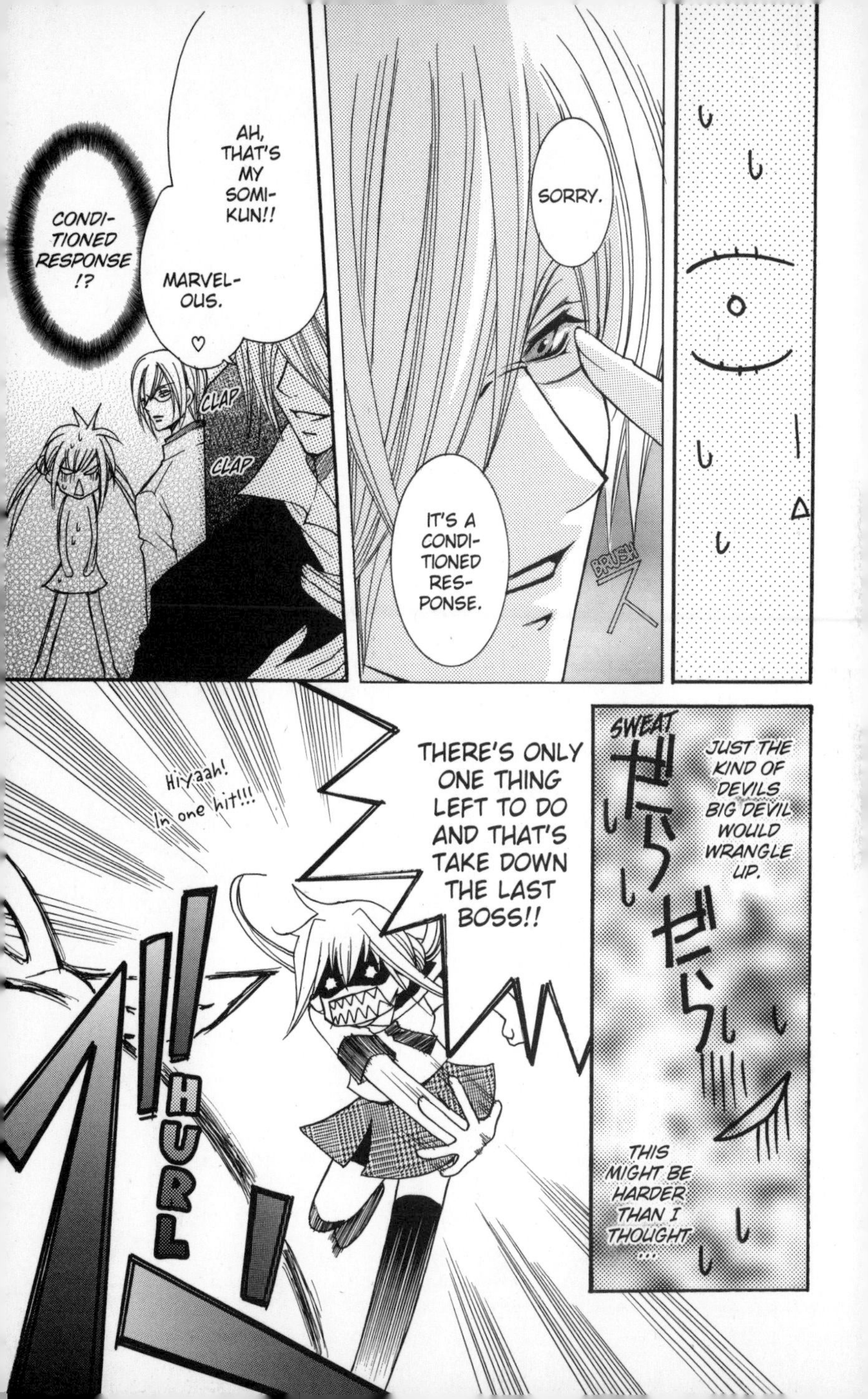
SORRY.
IT'S A CONDITIONED RESPONSE.
BRUSH
AH, THAT'S MY SOMI-KUN!!
MARVELOUS. ♡
CLAP
CLAP
CONDITIONED RESPONSE!?
SWEAT
JUST THE KIND OF DEVILS BIG DEVIL WOULD WRANGLE UP.
THIS MIGHT BE HARDER THAN I THOUGHT...
THERE'S ONLY ONE THING LEFT TO DO AND THAT'S TAKE DOWN THE LAST BOSS!!
Hiyaah! In one hit!!!
HURL

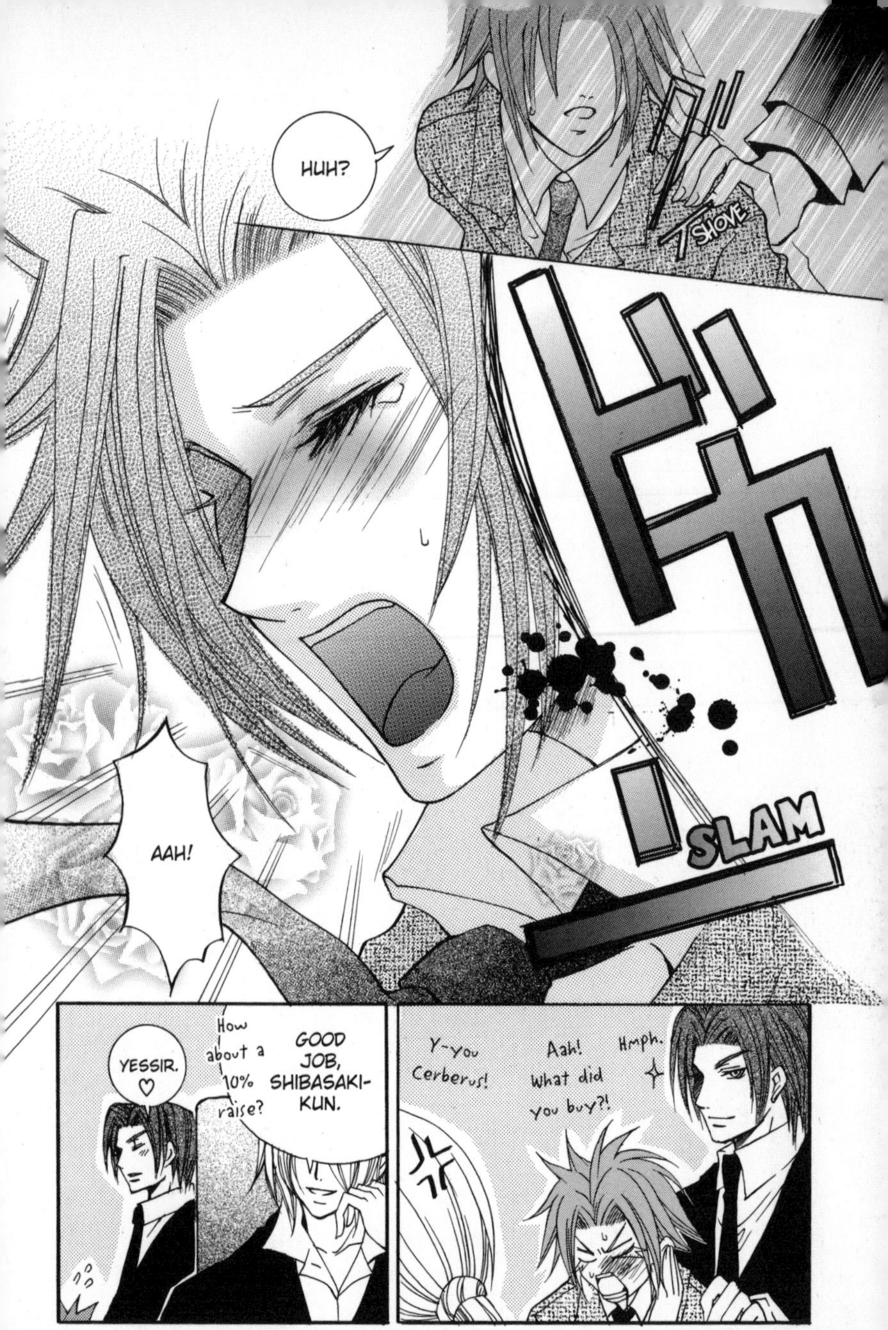
HUH?
SHOVE
SLAM
AAH!
Hmph.
Aah! What did you buy?!
Y-you Cerberus!
GOOD JOB, SHIBASAKI-KUN.
How about a 10% raise?
YESSIR. ♡

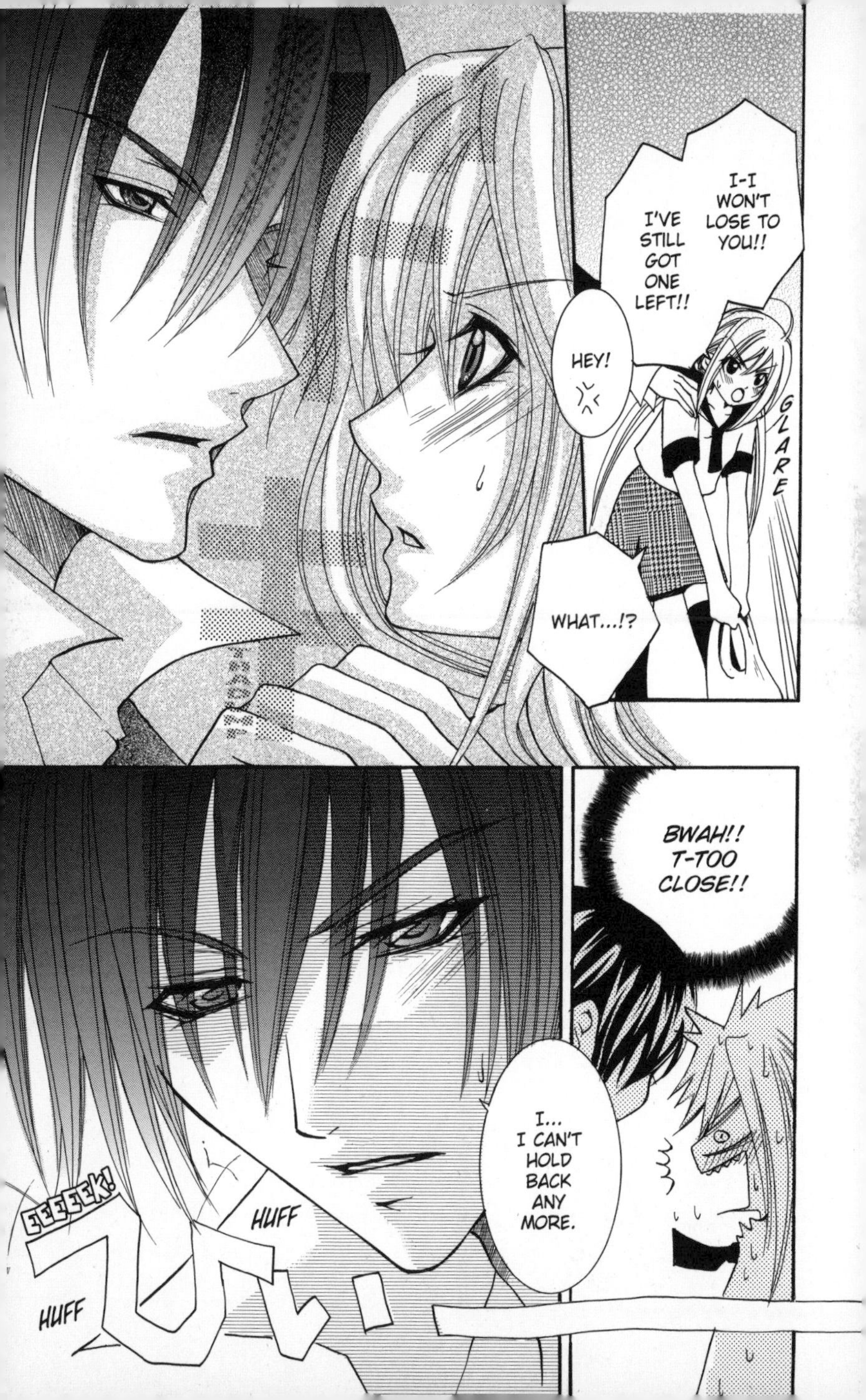
I-I WON'T LOSE TO YOU!!
I'VE STILL GOT ONE LEFT!!
HEY!
GLARE
WHAT...!?
BWAH!! T-TOO CLOSE!!
I... I CAN'T HOLD BACK ANY MORE.
HUFF
EEEEEK!
HUFF

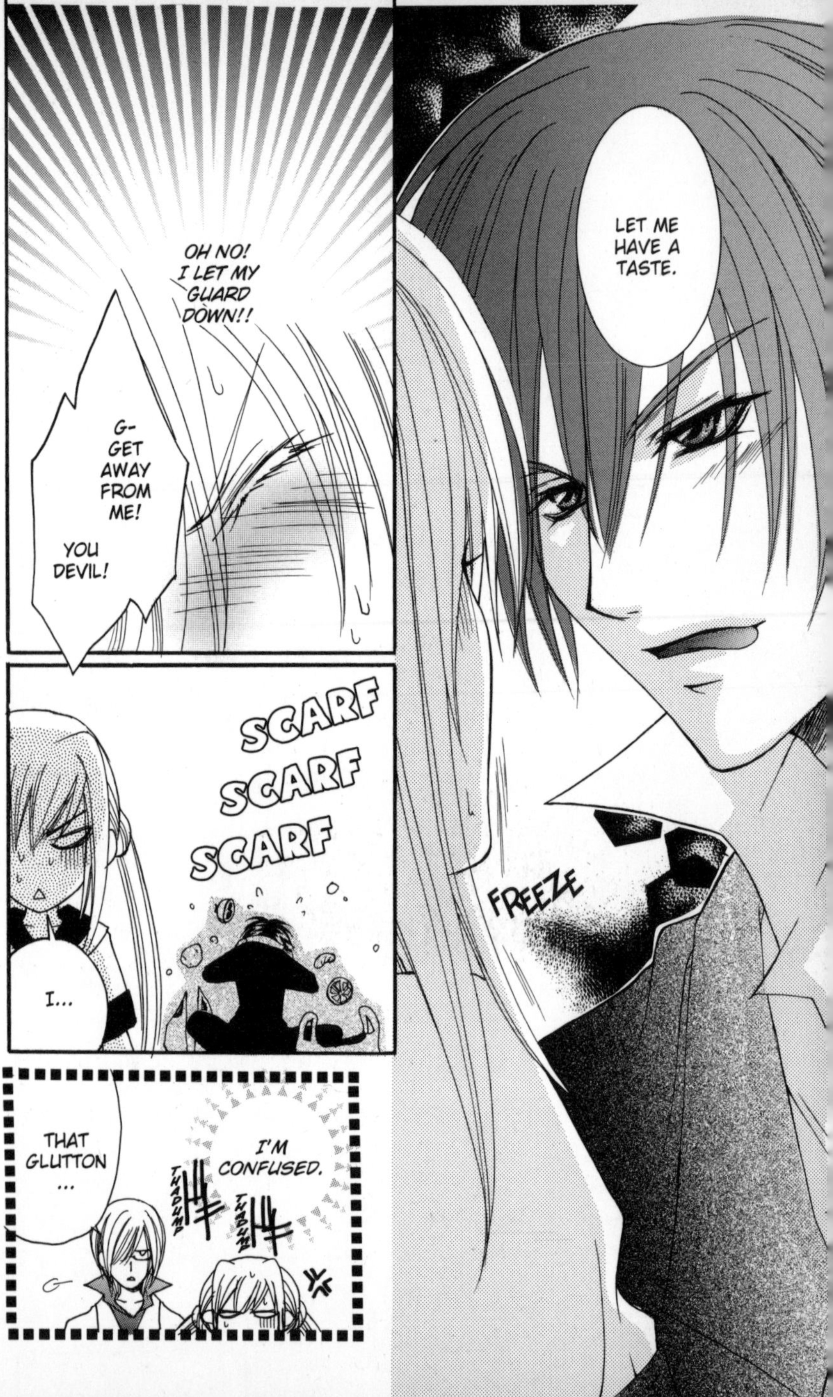
LET ME HAVE A TASTE.
FREEZE
OH NO! I LET MY GUARD DOWN!!
G- GET AWAY FROM ME!
YOU DEVIL!
SCARF
SCARF
SCARF
I...
I'M CONFUSED.
THADUMP
THADUMP
THAT GLUTTON ...

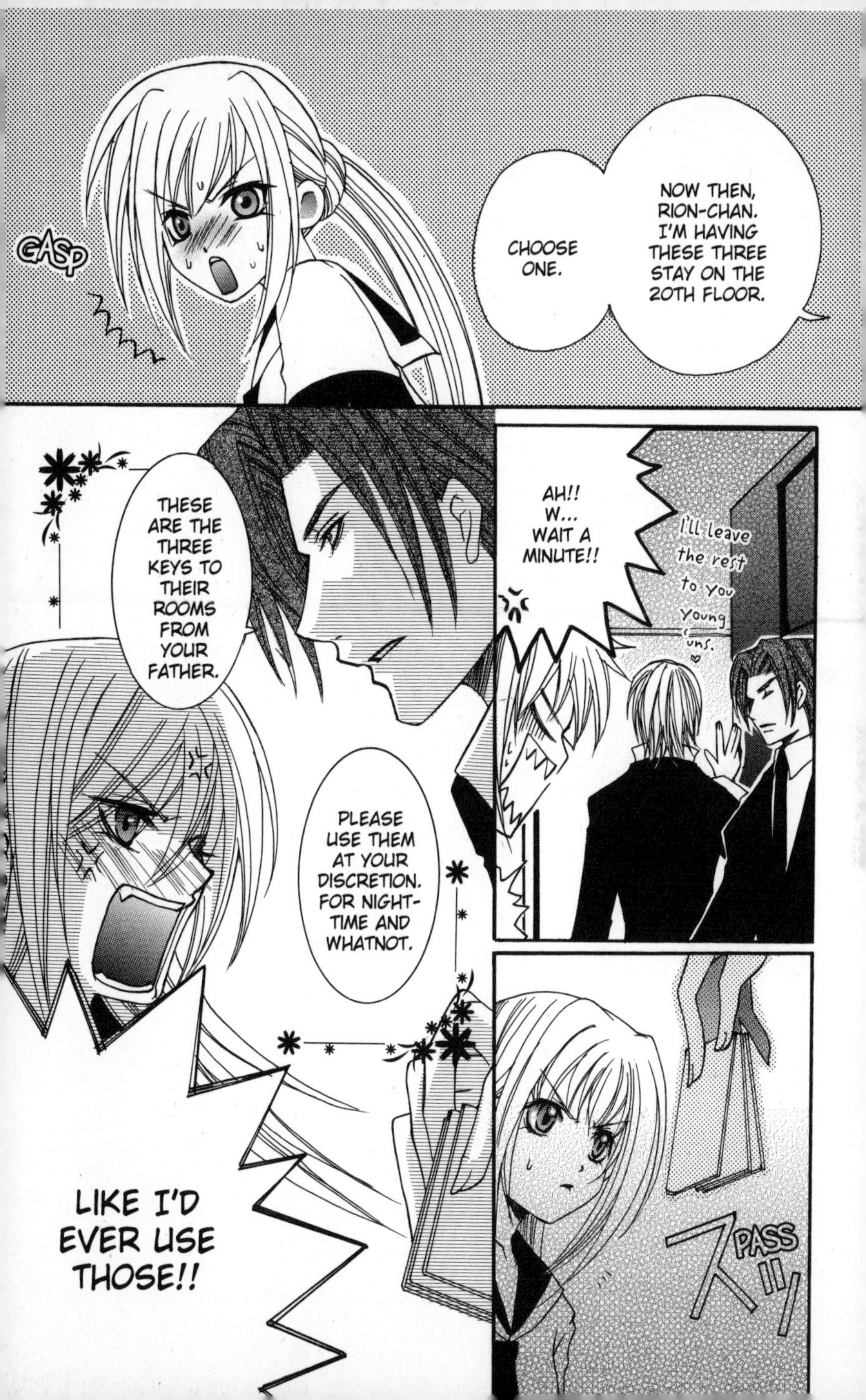
NOW THEN, RION-CHAN. I'M HAVING THESE THREE STAY ON THE 20TH FLOOR.
CHOOSE ONE.
GASP
I'll leave the rest to you young 'uns.
AH!! W... WAIT A MINUTE!!
THESE ARE THE THREE KEYS TO THEIR ROOMS FROM YOUR FATHER.
PLEASE USE THEM AT YOUR DISCRETION. FOR NIGHT-TIME AND WHATNOT.
PASS
LIKE I'D EVER USE THOSE!!

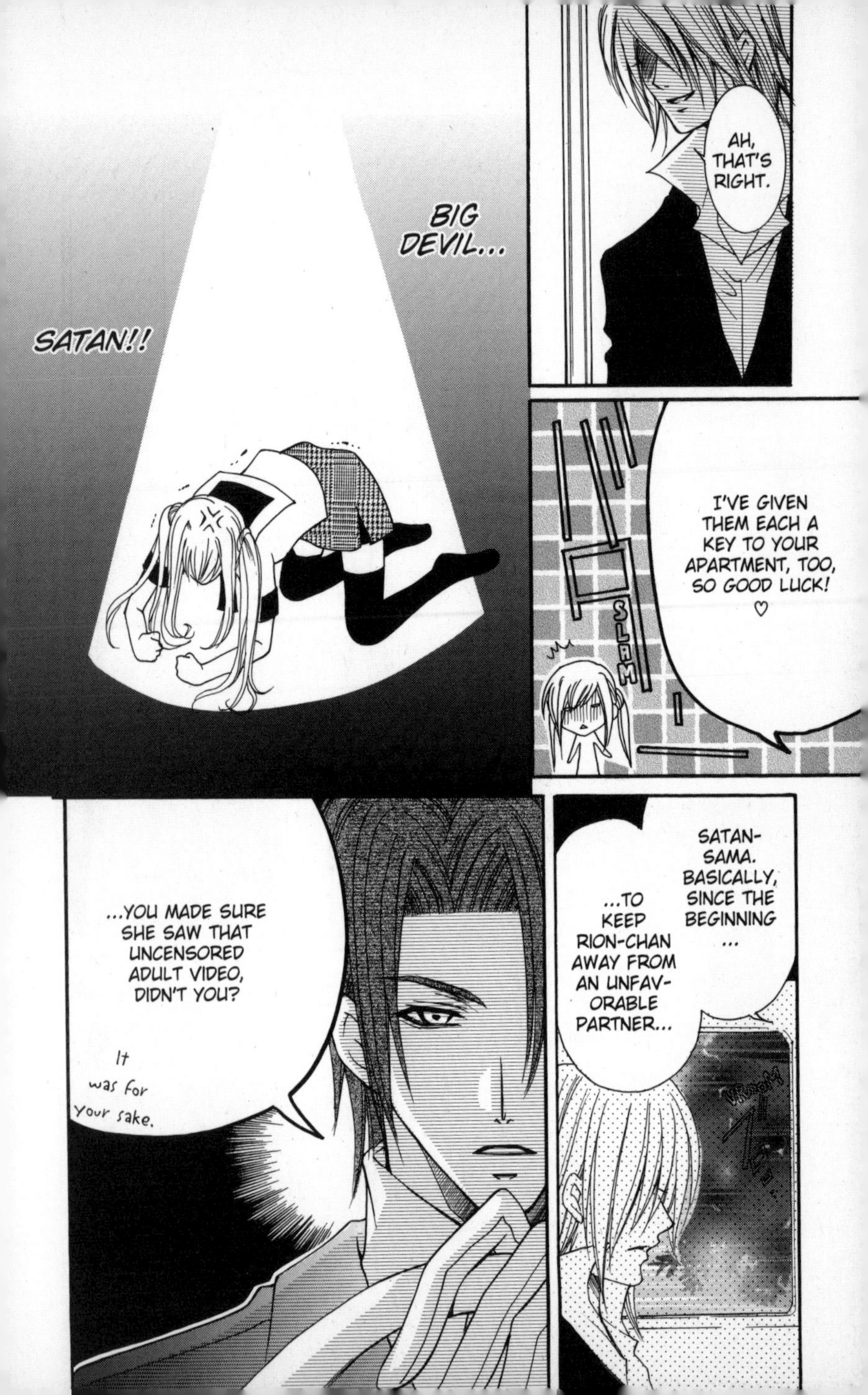
AH, THAT'S RIGHT.
I'VE GIVEN THEM EACH A KEY TO YOUR APARTMENT, TOO, SO GOOD LUCK! ♡
SLAM
BIG DEVIL...
SATAN!!
SATAN-SAMA. BASICALLY, SINCE THE BEGINNING ...
...TO KEEP RION-CHAN AWAY FROM AN UNFAVORABLE PARTNER...
...YOU MADE SURE SHE SAW THAT UNCENSORED ADULT VIDEO, DIDN'T YOU?
It was for your sake.

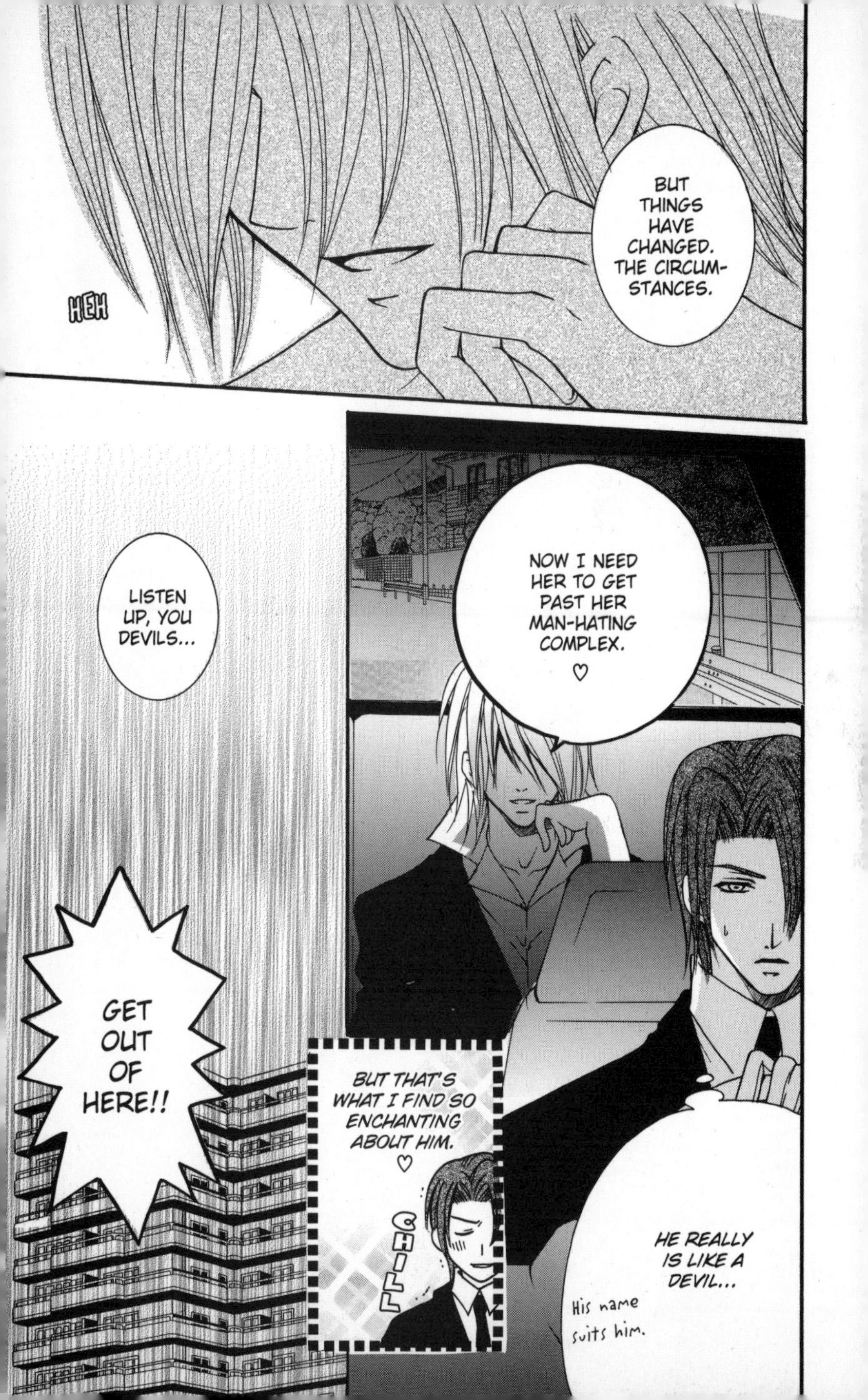
BUT THINGS HAVE CHANGED. THE CIRCUM-STANCES.
HEH
NOW I NEED HER TO GET PAST HER MAN-HATING COMPLEX. ♡
LISTEN UP, YOU DEVILS...
HE REALLY IS LIKE A DEVIL...
His name suits him.
BUT THAT'S WHAT I FIND SO ENCHANTING ABOUT HIM. ♡
CHILL
GET OUT OF HERE!!

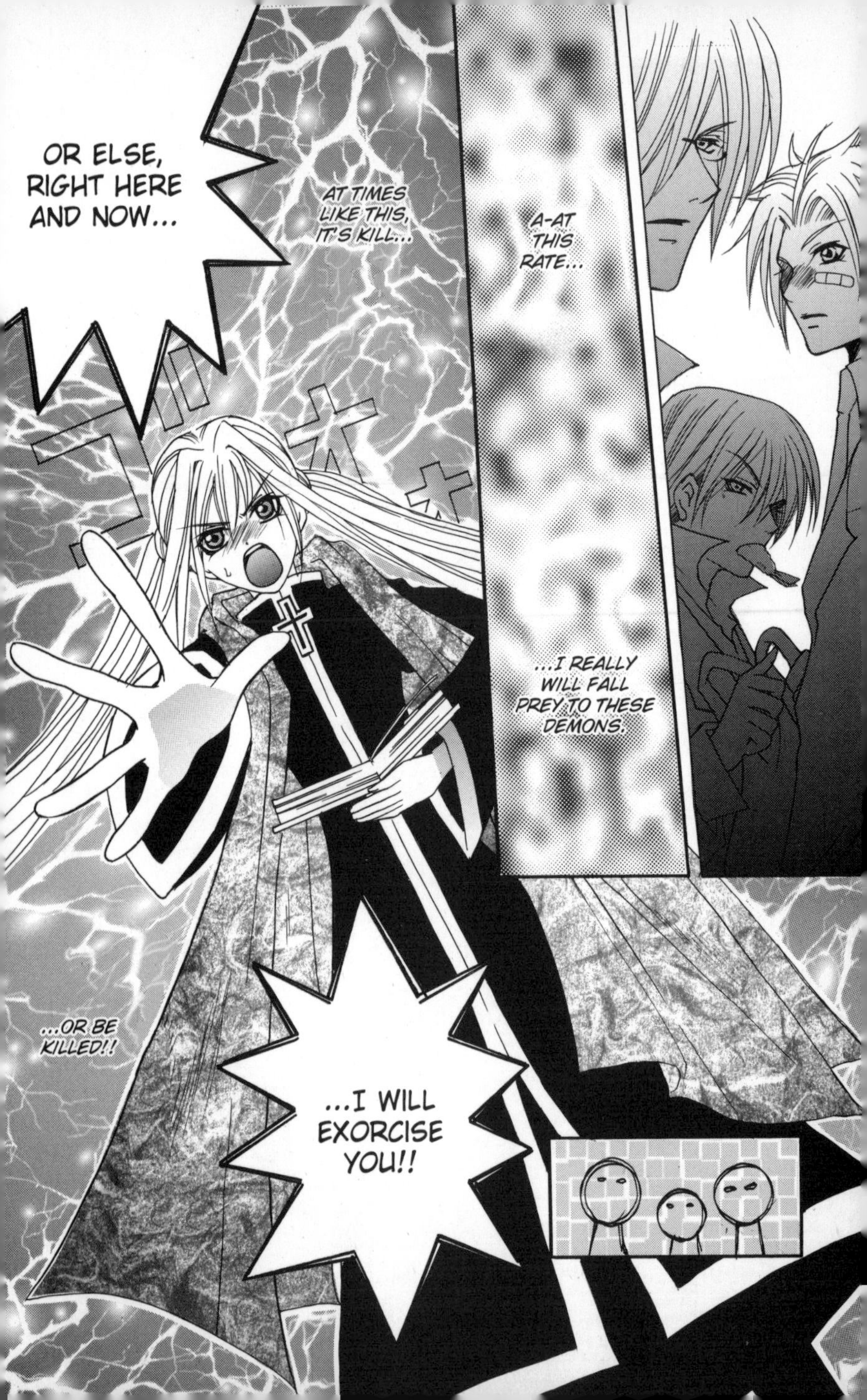
A-AT THIS RATE...
...I REALLY WILL FALL PREY TO THESE DEMONS.
OR ELSE, RIGHT HERE AND NOW...
AT TIMES LIKE THIS, IT'S KILL...
...OR BE KILLED!!
...I WILL EXORCISE YOU!!

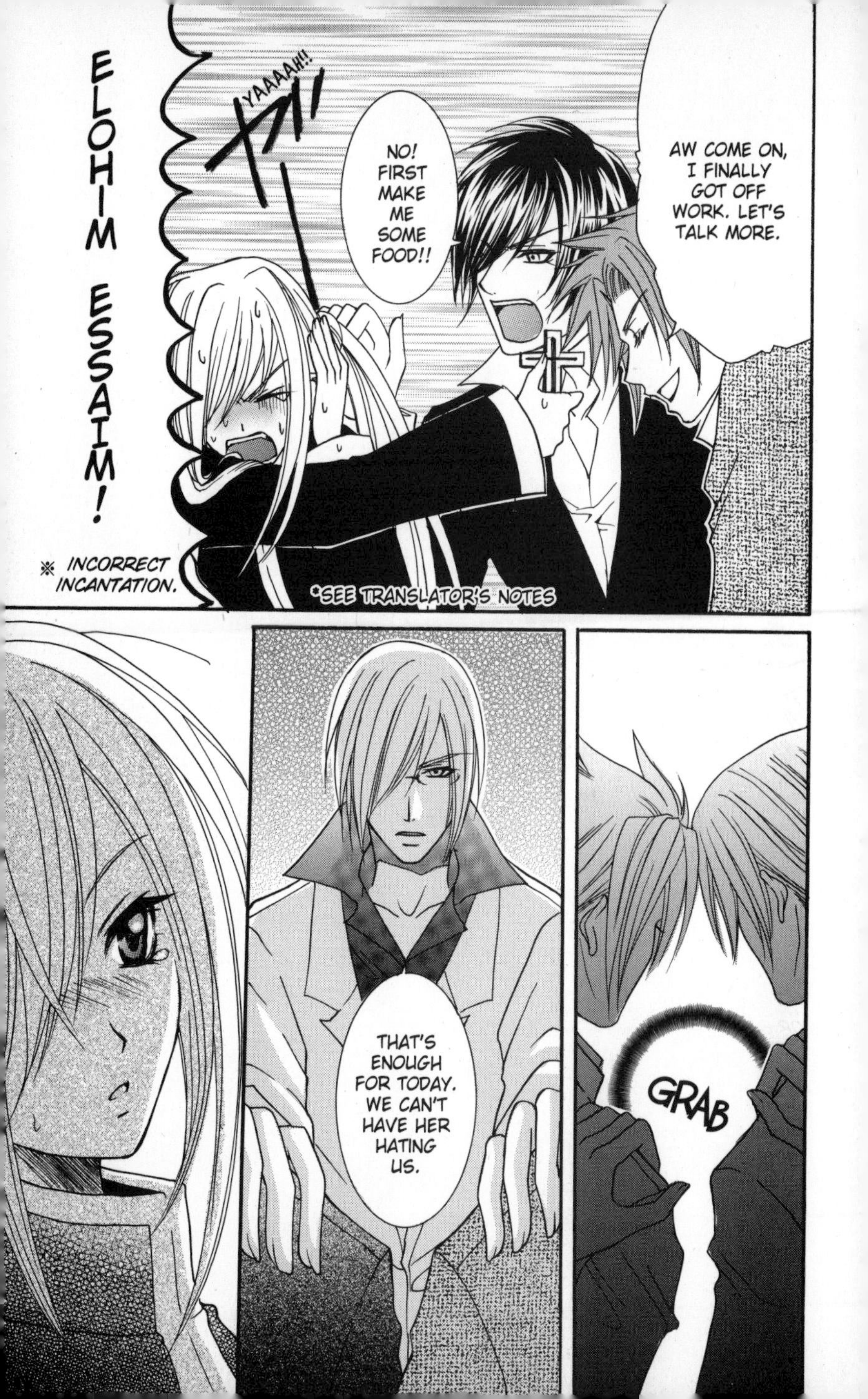
AW COME ON, I FINALLY GOT OFF WORK. LET'S TALK MORE.
NO! FIRST MAKE ME SOME FOOD!!
YAAAAH!!
ELOHIM ESSAIM!
※ INCORRECT INCANTATION.
*SEE TRANSLATOR'S NOTES
GRAB
THAT'S ENOUGH FOR TODAY. WE CAN'T HAVE HER HATING US.

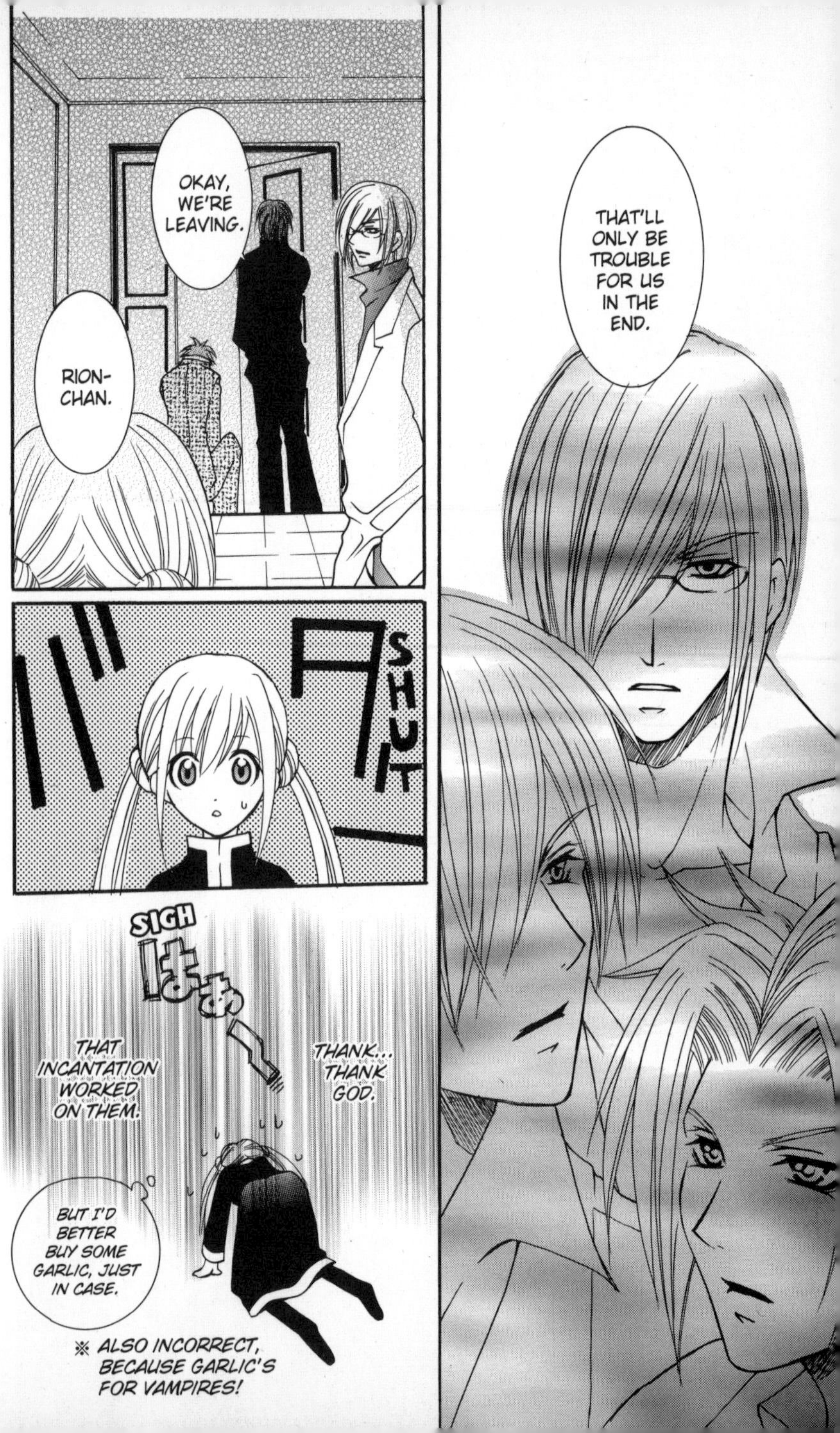
THAT'LL ONLY BE TROUBLE FOR US IN THE END.
OKAY, WE'RE LEAVING.
RION-CHAN.
SHUT
SIGH
はぁ
THANK... THANK GOD.
THAT INCANTATION WORKED ON THEM.
BUT I'D BETTER BUY SOME GARLIC, JUST IN CASE.
※ ALSO INCORRECT, BECAUSE GARLIC'S FOR VAMPIRES!

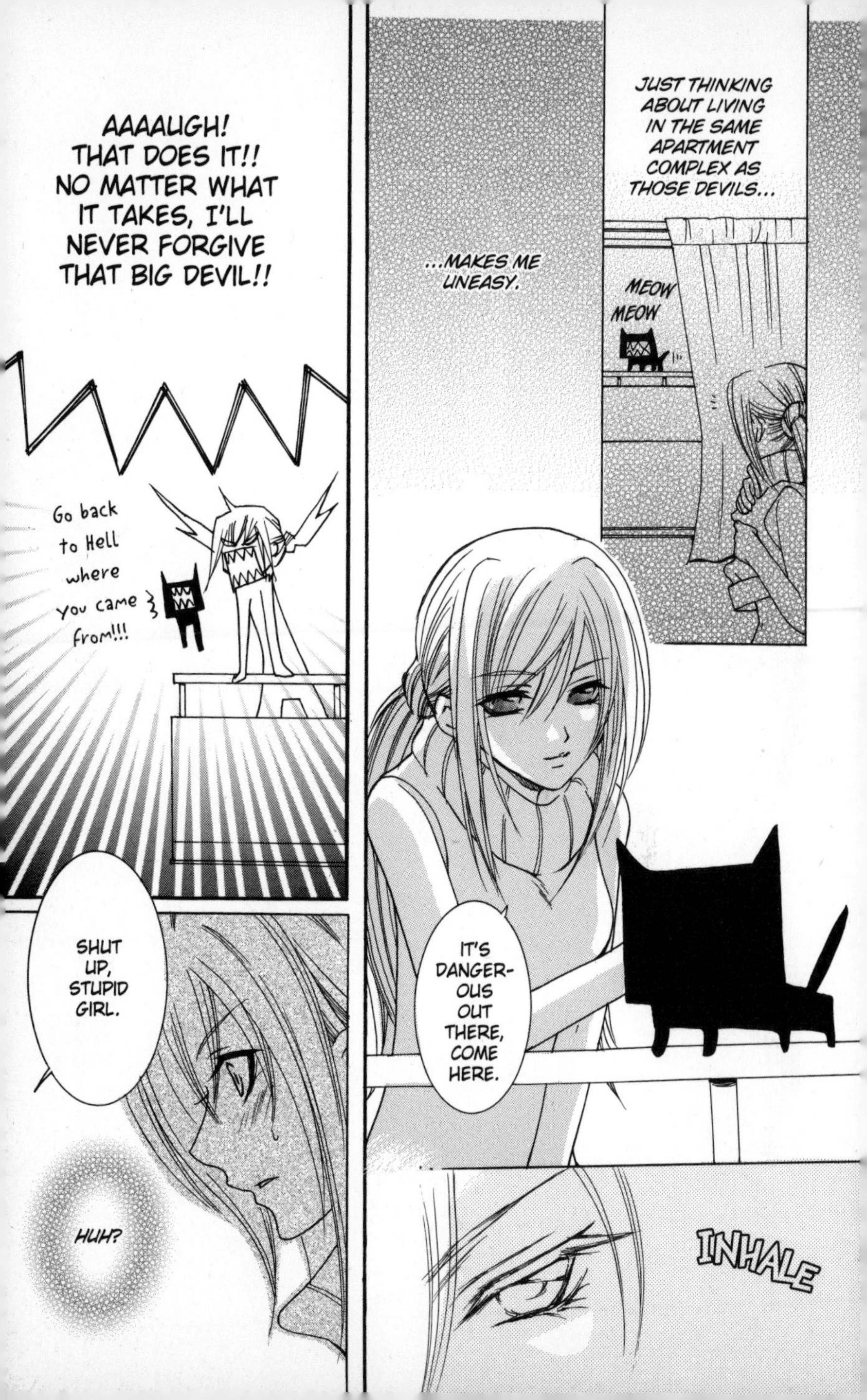
JUST THINKING ABOUT LIVING IN THE SAME APARTMENT COMPLEX AS THOSE DEVILS...
...MAKES ME UNEASY.
MEOW MEOW
IT'S DANGER-OUS OUT THERE, COME HERE.
INHALE
AAAAUGH! THAT DOES IT!! NO MATTER WHAT IT TAKES, I'LL NEVER FORGIVE THAT BIG DEVIL!!
Go back to Hell where you came from!!!
SHUT UP, STUPID GIRL.
HUH?

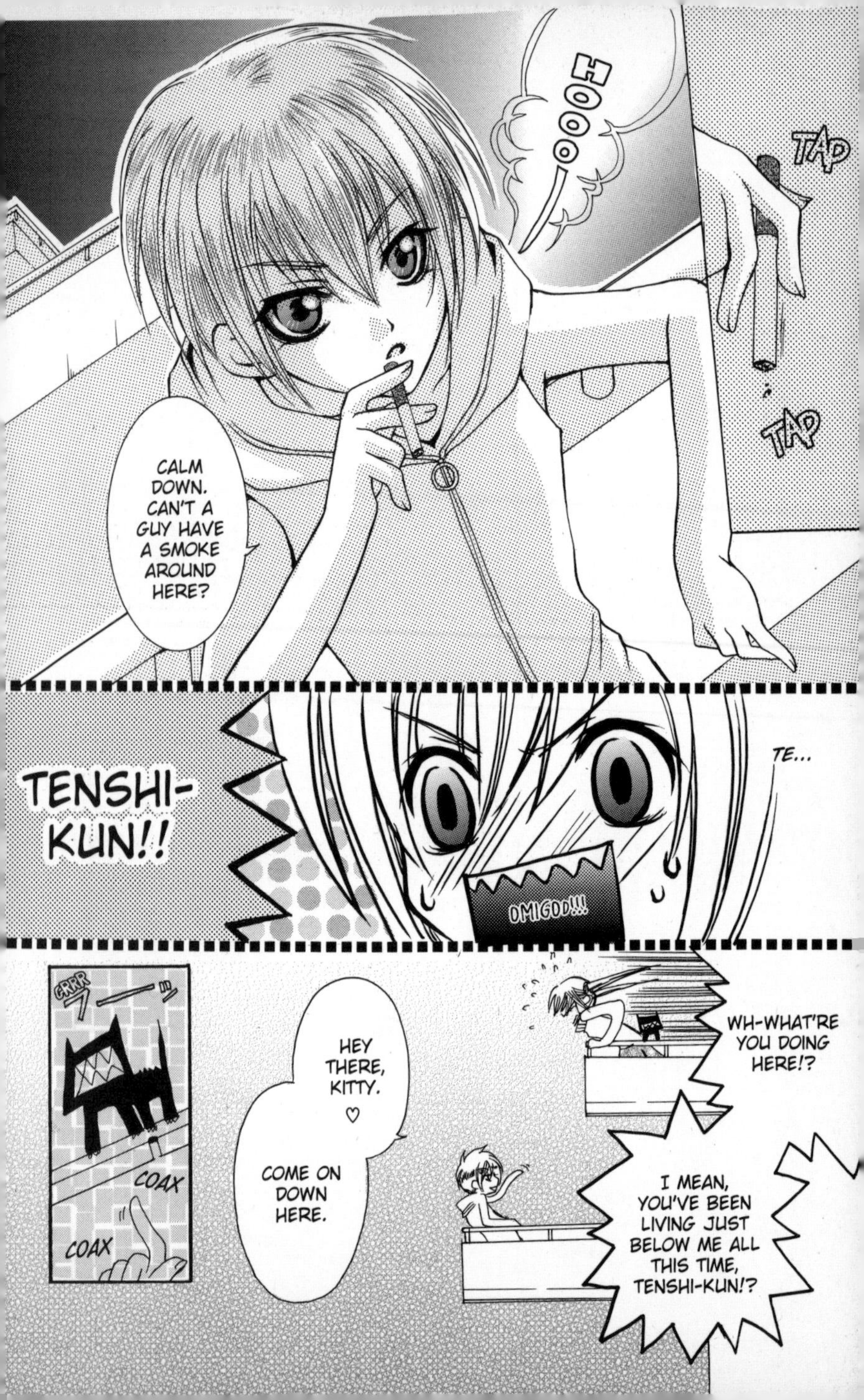
HOOO
TAP
TAP
CALM DOWN. CAN'T A GUY HAVE A SMOKE AROUND HERE?
TE...
OMIGOD!!!
TENSHI-KUN!!
WH-WHAT'RE YOU DOING HERE!?
I MEAN, YOU'VE BEEN LIVING JUST BELOW ME ALL THIS TIME, TENSHI-KUN!?
HEY THERE, KITTY. ♡
COME ON DOWN HERE.
GRRR
COAX
COAX

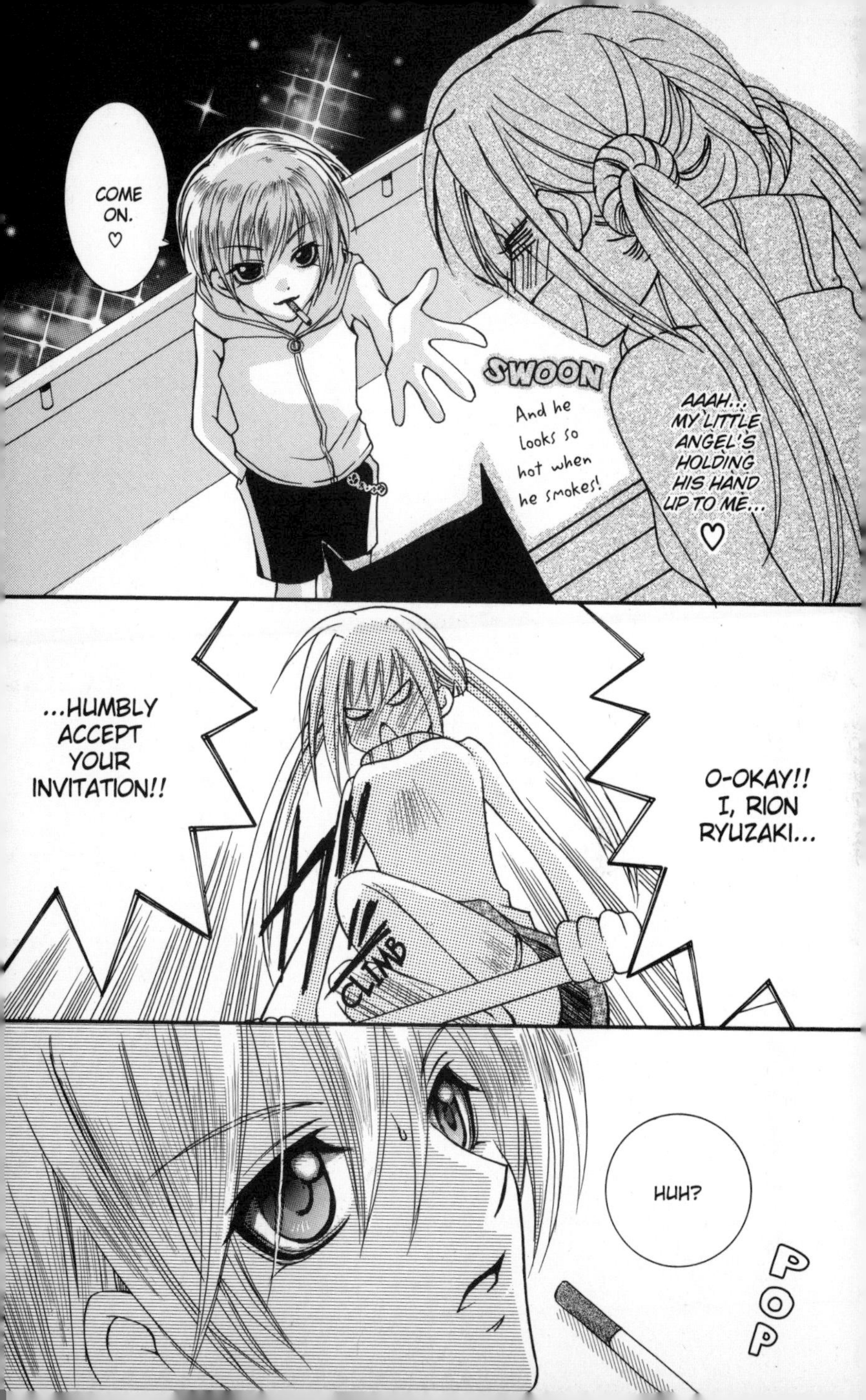

COME ON. ♡
AAAH... MY LITTLE ANGEL'S HOLDING HIS HAND UP TO ME... ♡
SWOON
And he looks so hot when he smokes!
O-OKAY!! I, RION RYUZAKI...
...HUMBLY ACCEPT YOUR INVITATION!!
CLIMB
HUH?
POP

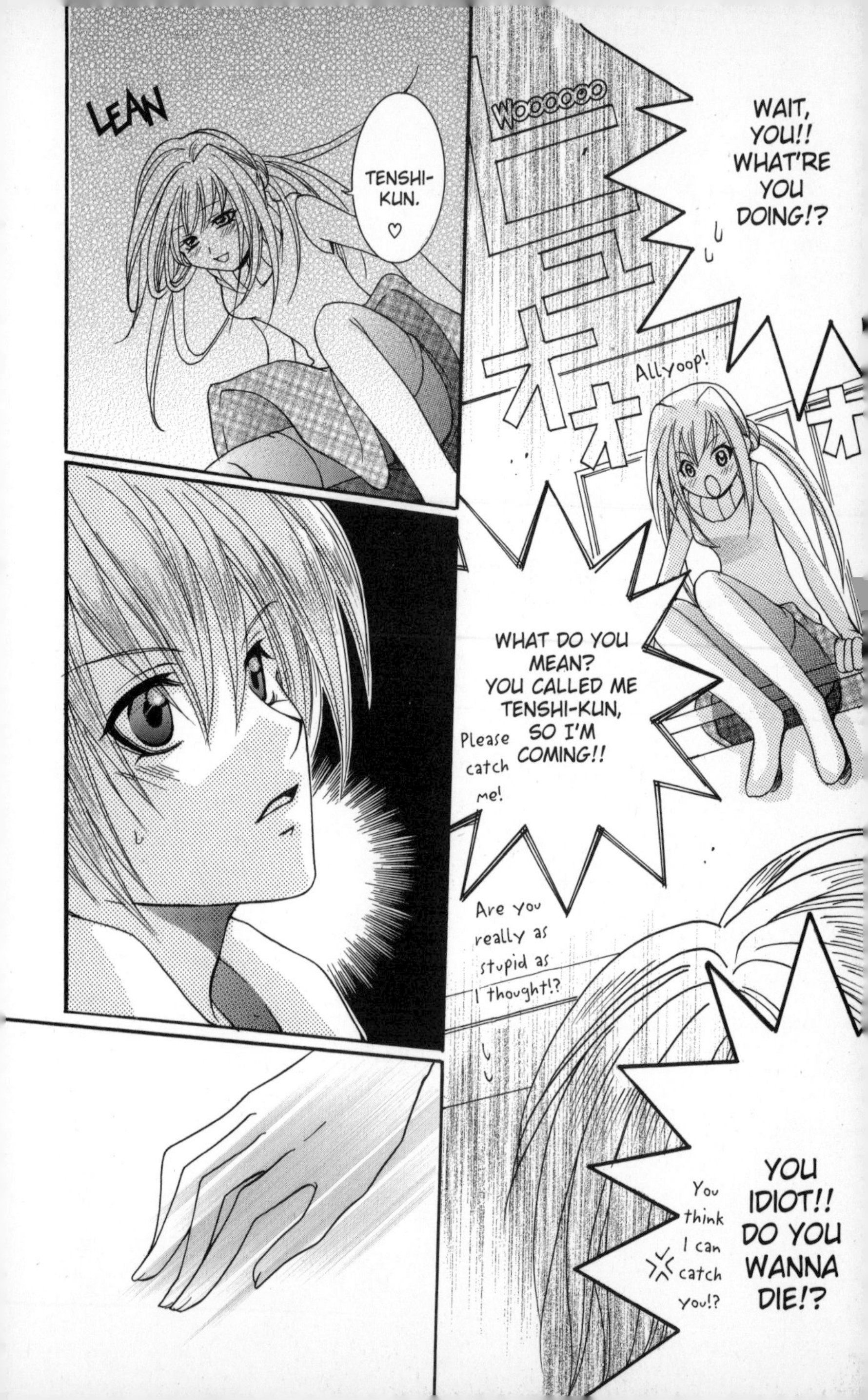
LEAN
TENSHI-KUN. ♡
WOOOOOO
WAIT, YOU!! WHAT'RE YOU DOING!?
Allyoop!
WHAT DO YOU MEAN? YOU CALLED ME TENSHI-KUN, SO I'M COMING!!
Please catch me!
Are you really as stupid as I thought!?
YOU IDIOT!! DO YOU WANNA DIE!?
You think I can catch you!?

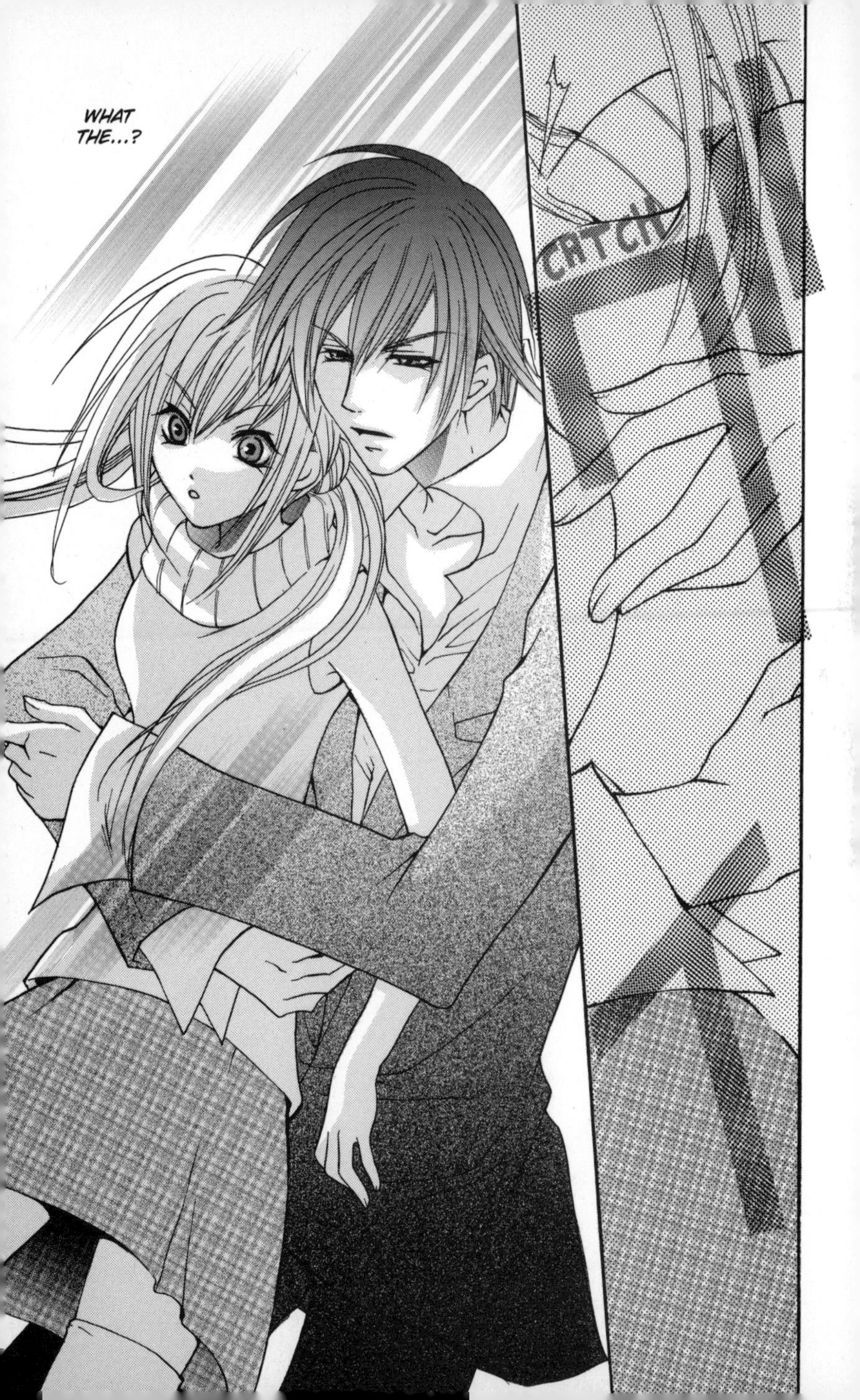
WHAT THE...?
CATCH

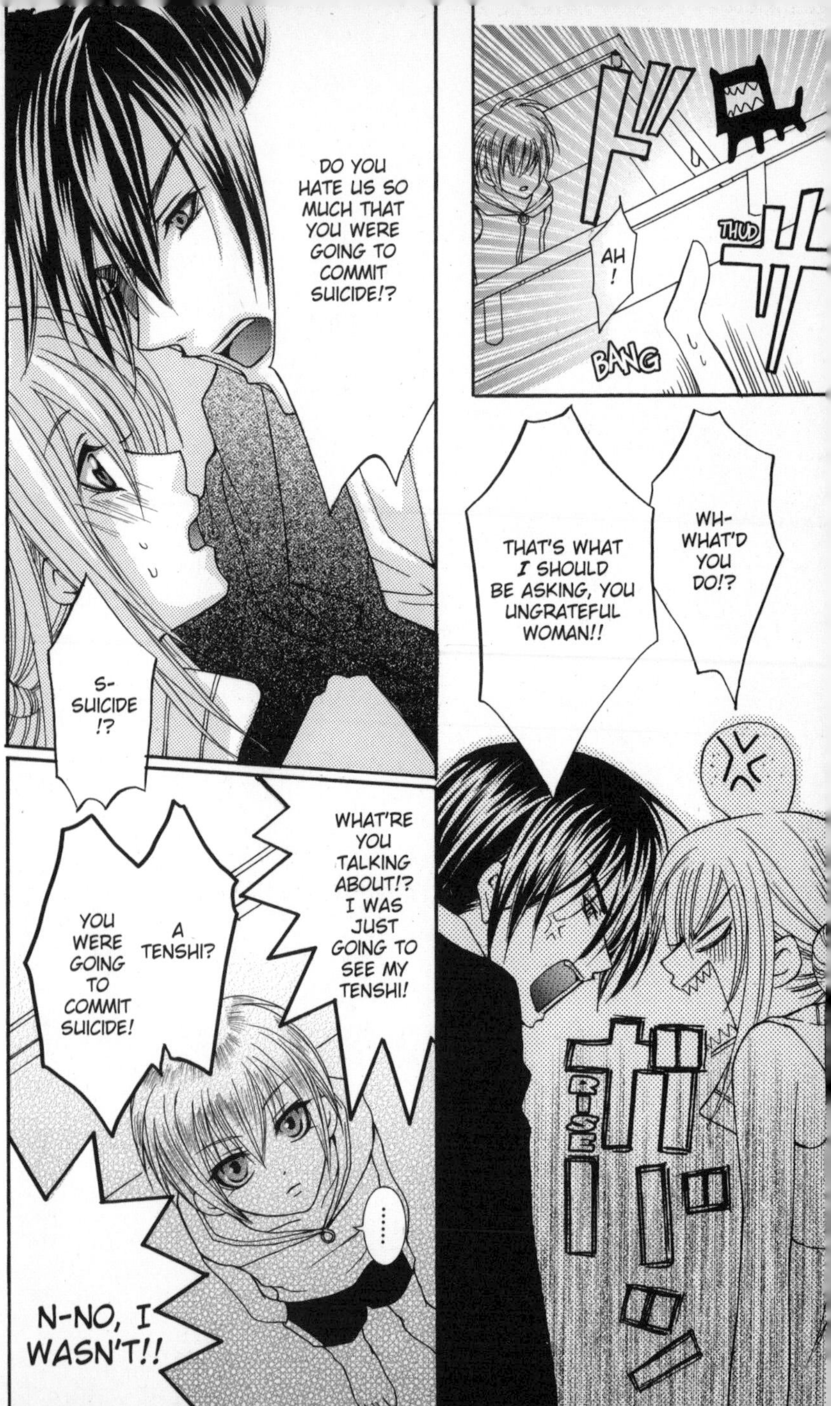
THUD
AH!
BANG
WH-WHAT'D YOU DO!?
THAT'S WHAT *I* SHOULD BE ASKING, YOU UNGRATEFUL WOMAN!!
RISE
DO YOU HATE US SO MUCH THAT YOU WERE GOING TO COMMIT SUICIDE!?
S-SUICIDE!?
WHAT'RE YOU TALKING ABOUT!? I WAS JUST GOING TO SEE MY TENSHI!
A TENSHI?
YOU WERE GOING TO COMMIT SUICIDE!
......
N-NO, I WASN'T!!

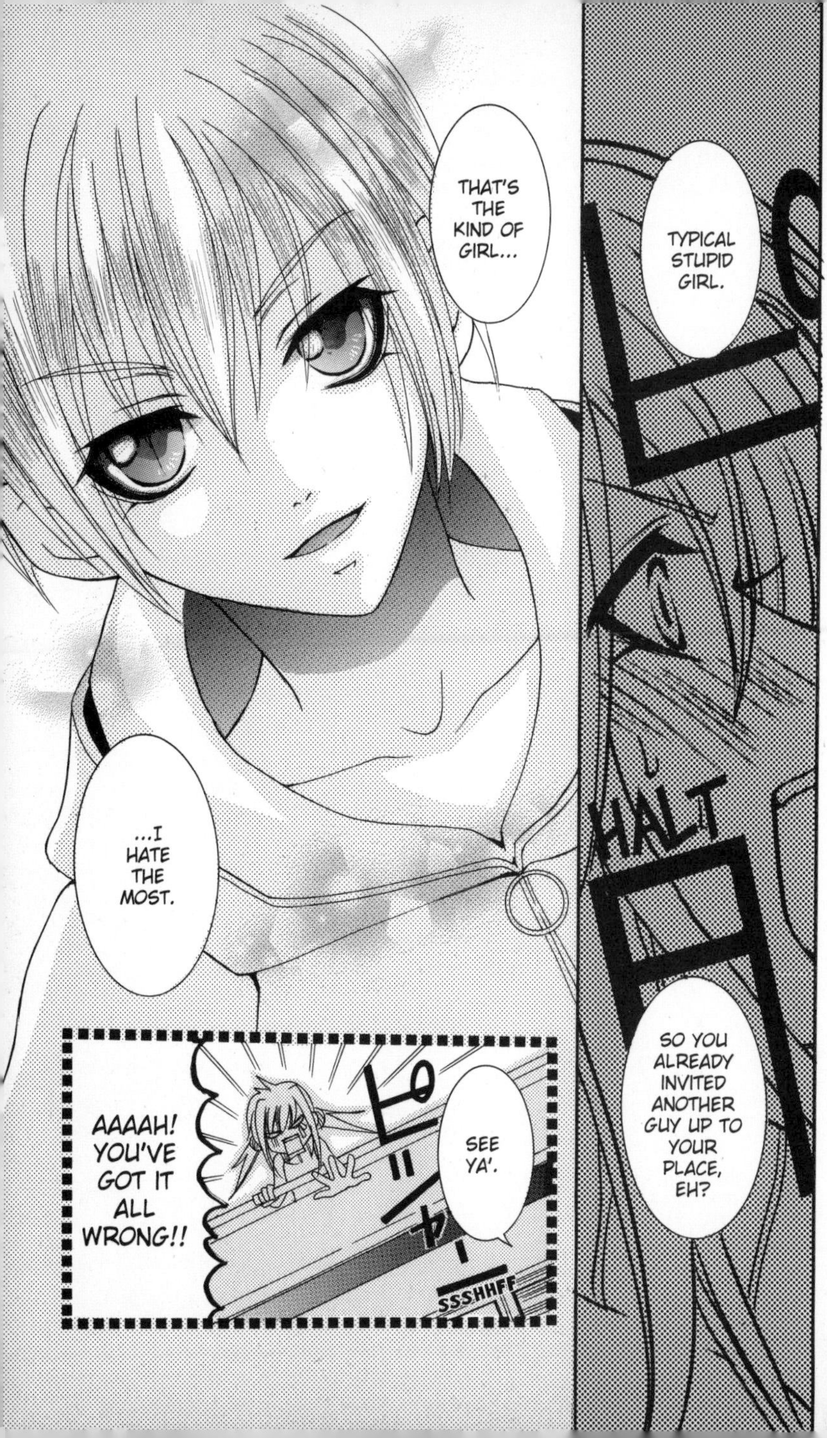
TYPICAL STUPID GIRL.
HALT
SO YOU ALREADY INVITED ANOTHER GUY UP TO YOUR PLACE, EH?
THAT'S THE KIND OF GIRL...
...I HATE THE MOST.
SEE YA'.
SSSHHFF
AAAAH! YOU'VE GOT IT ALL WRONG!!

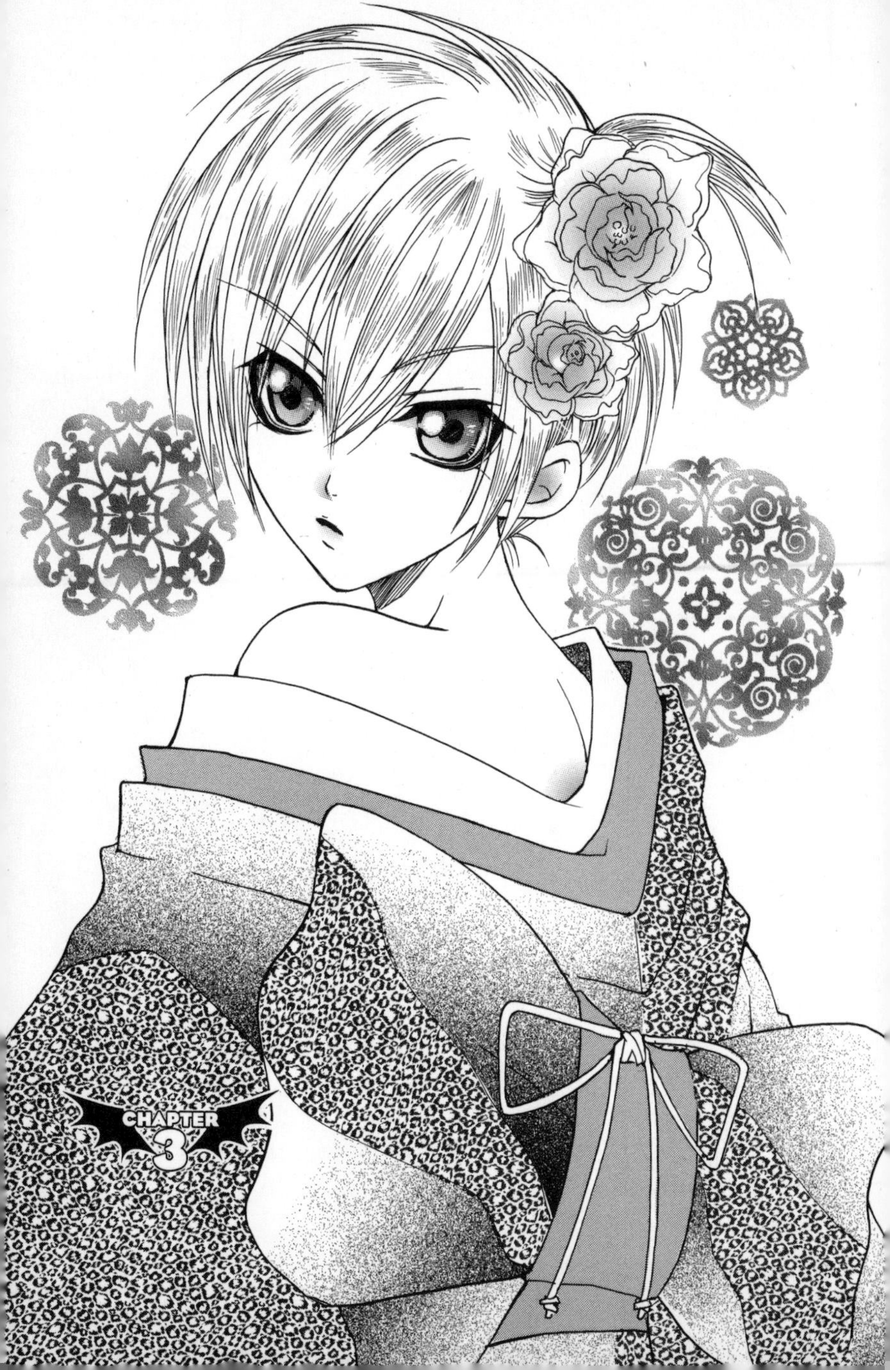
CHAPTER
3

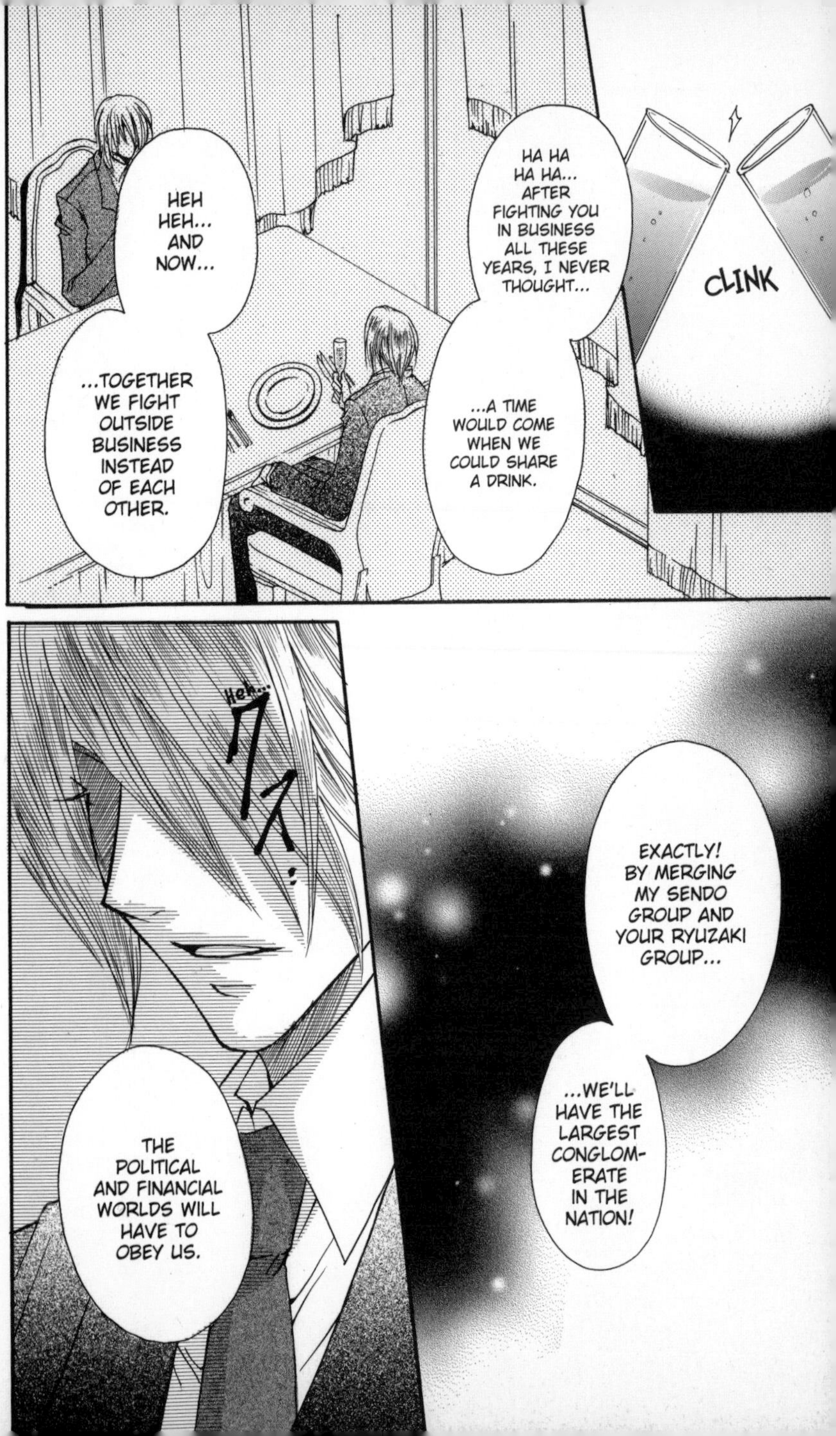
CLINK
HA HA HA HA... AFTER FIGHTING YOU IN BUSINESS ALL THESE YEARS, I NEVER THOUGHT...
...A TIME WOULD COME WHEN WE COULD SHARE A DRINK.
HEH HEH... AND NOW...
...TOGETHER WE FIGHT OUTSIDE BUSINESS INSTEAD OF EACH OTHER.
EXACTLY! BY MERGING MY SENDO GROUP AND YOUR RYUZAKI GROUP...
...WE'LL HAVE THE LARGEST CONGLOM-ERATE IN THE NATION!
Heh...
THE POLITICAL AND FINANCIAL WORLDS WILL HAVE TO OBEY US.

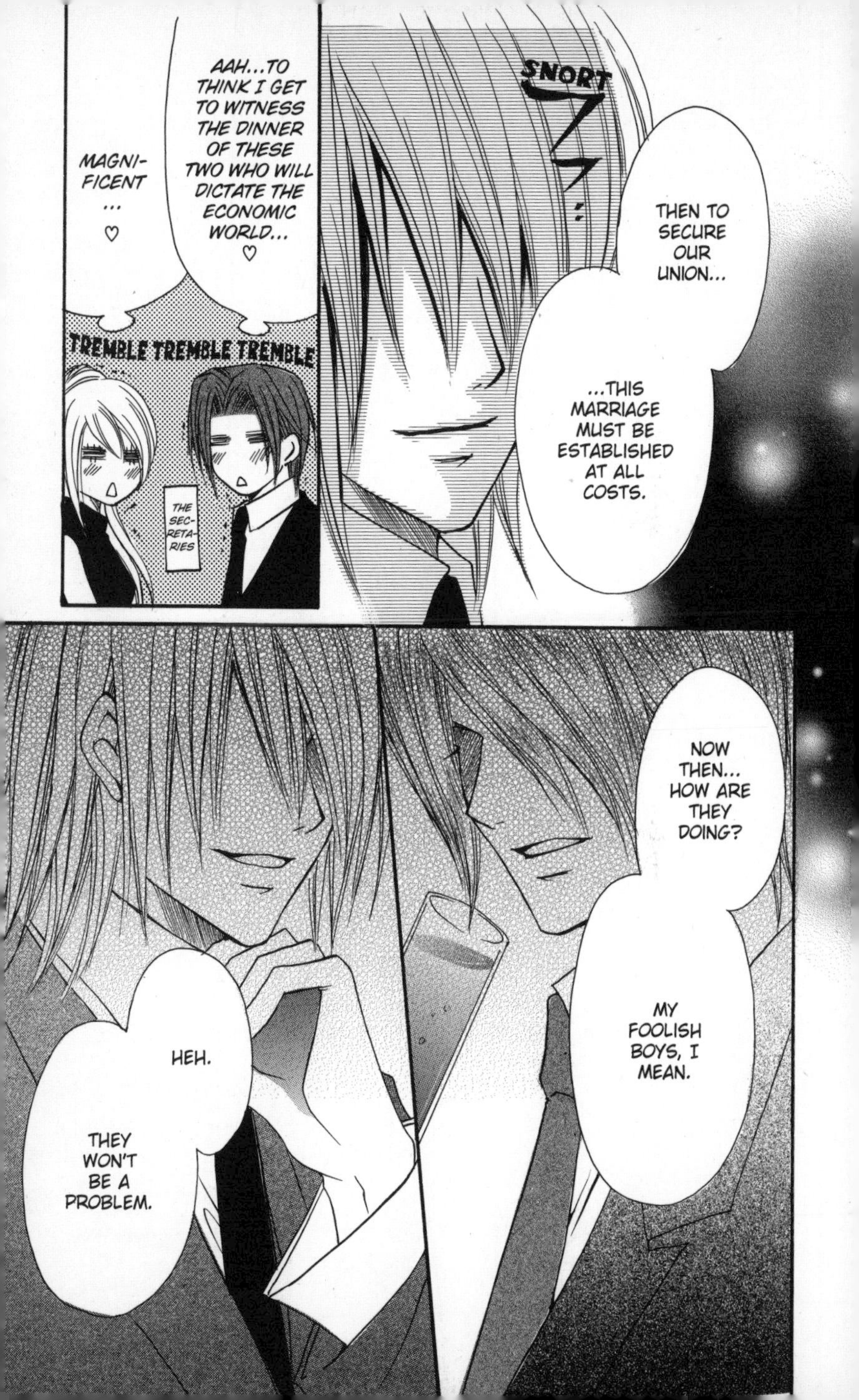
SNORT
THEN TO SECURE OUR UNION...
...THIS MARRIAGE MUST BE ESTABLISHED AT ALL COSTS.
AAH...TO THINK I GET TO WITNESS THE DINNER OF THESE TWO WHO WILL DICTATE THE ECONOMIC WORLD... ♡
MAGNIFICENT... ♡
TREMBLE TREMBLE TREMBLE
THE SECRETARIES
NOW THEN... HOW ARE THEY DOING?
MY FOOLISH BOYS, I MEAN.
HEH.
THEY WON'T BE A PROBLEM.

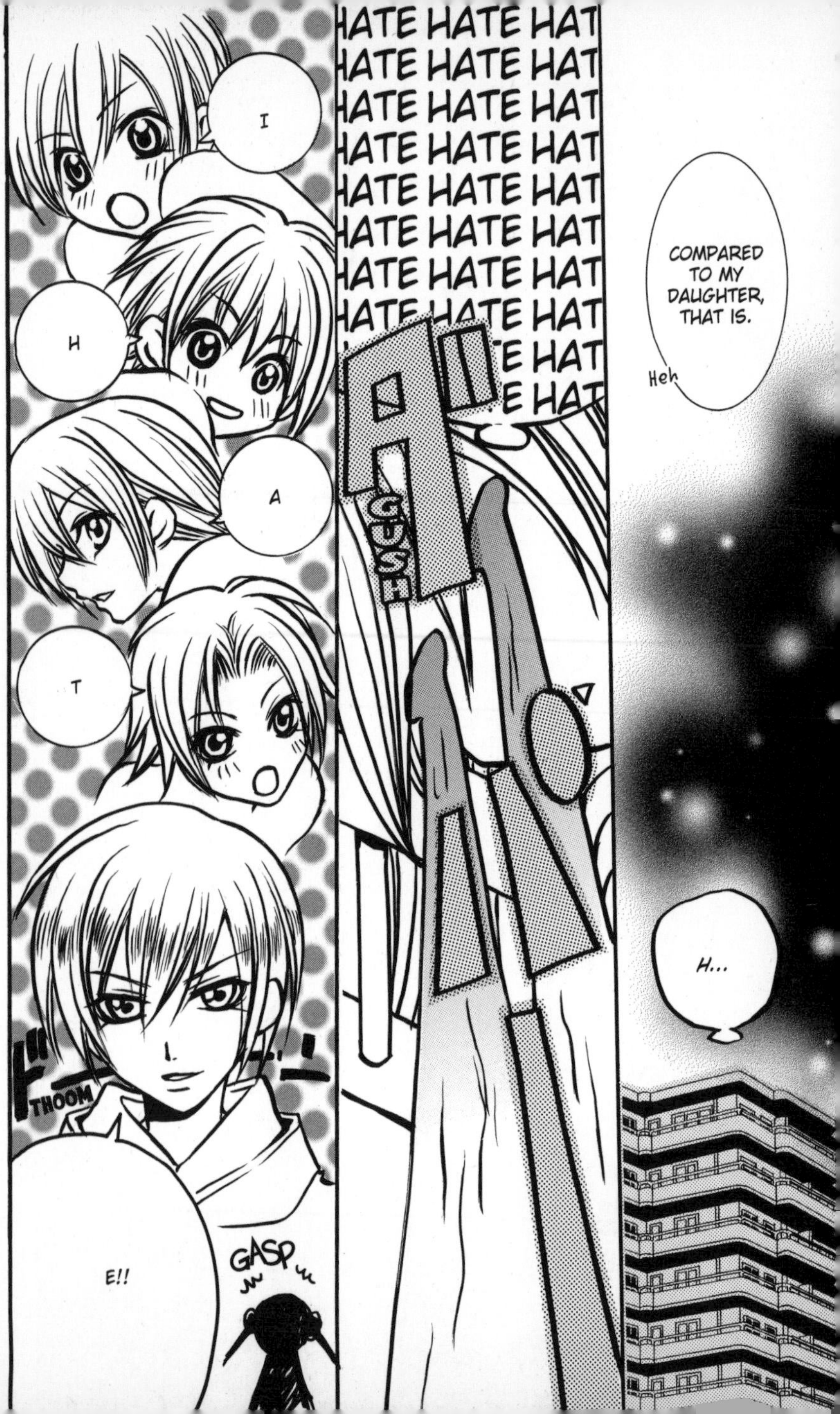
COMPARED TO MY DAUGHTER, THAT IS.
Heh
H...
HATE HATE HAT
HATE HATE HAT
HATE HATE HAT
HATE HATE HAT
HATE HATE HAT
HATE HATE HAT
HATE HATE HAT
HATE HATE HAT
E HAT
E HAT
GUSH
I
H
A
T
E!!
THOOM
GASP

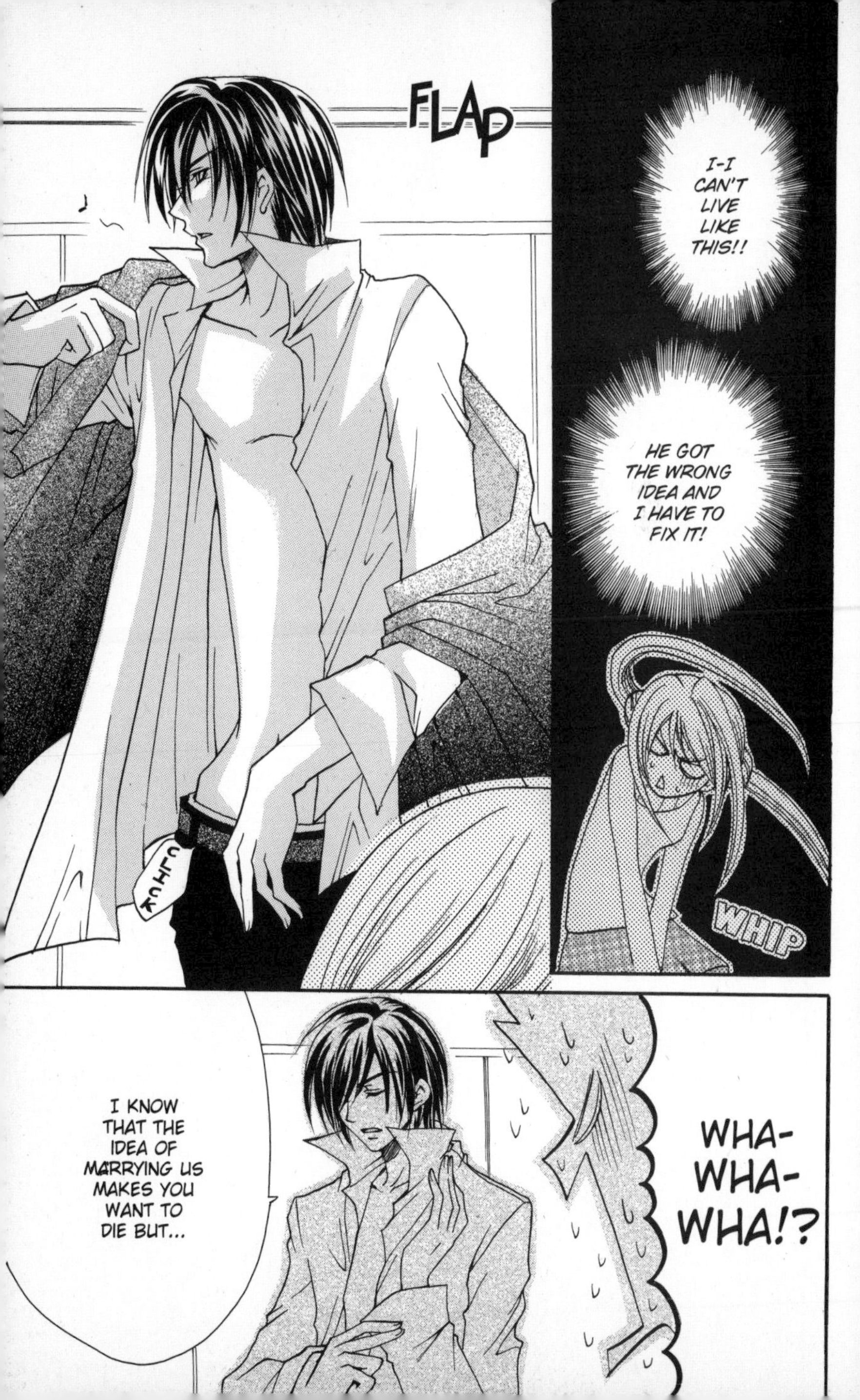
I-I CAN'T LIVE LIKE THIS!!
HE GOT THE WRONG IDEA AND I HAVE TO FIX IT!
WHIP
FLAP
CLICK
WHA-WHA-WHA!?
I KNOW THAT THE IDEA OF MARRYING US MAKES YOU WANT TO DIE BUT...

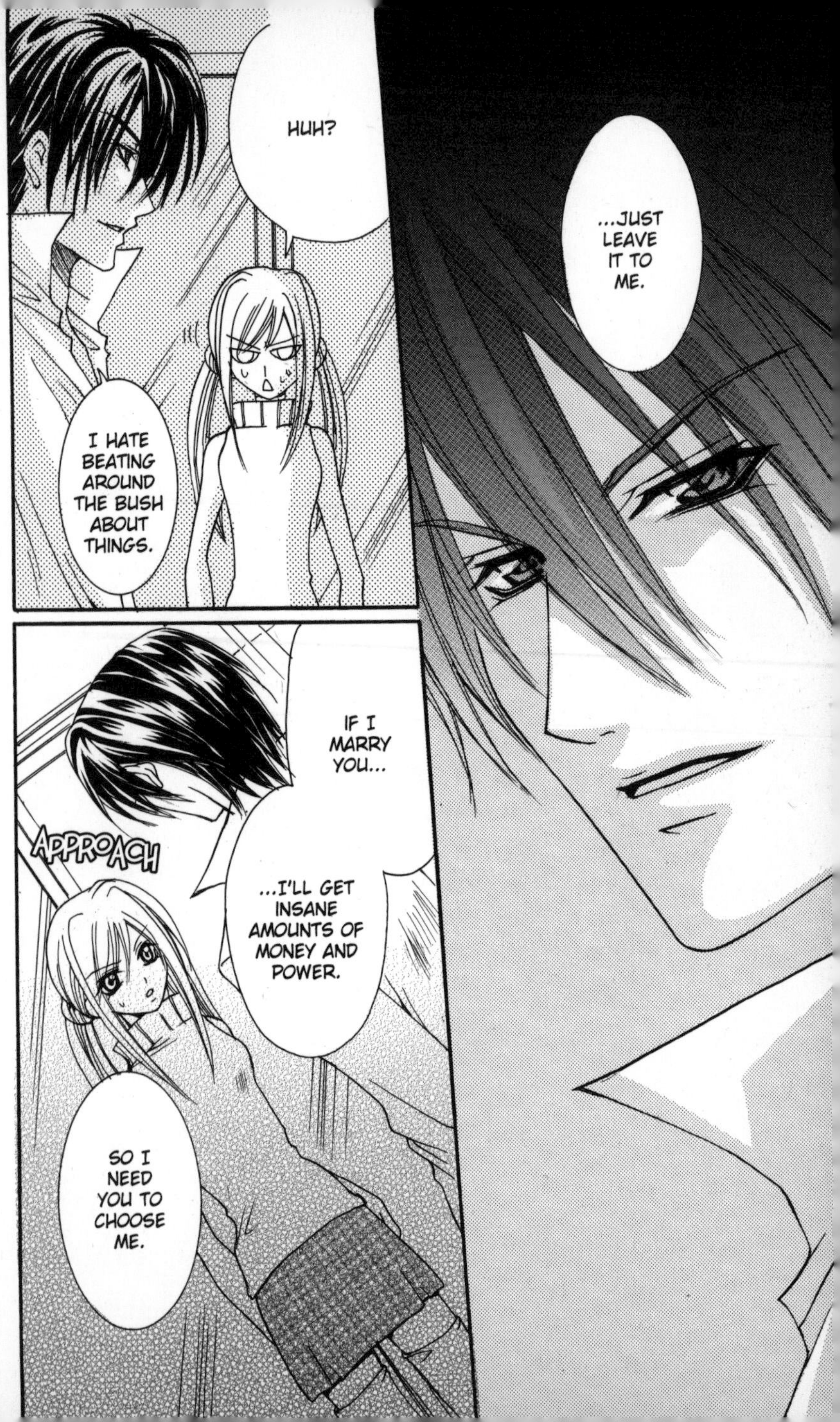
...JUST LEAVE IT TO ME.
HUH?
I HATE BEATING AROUND THE BUSH ABOUT THINGS.
IF I MARRY YOU...
APPROACH
...I'LL GET INSANE AMOUNTS OF MONEY AND POWER.
SO I NEED YOU TO CHOOSE ME.

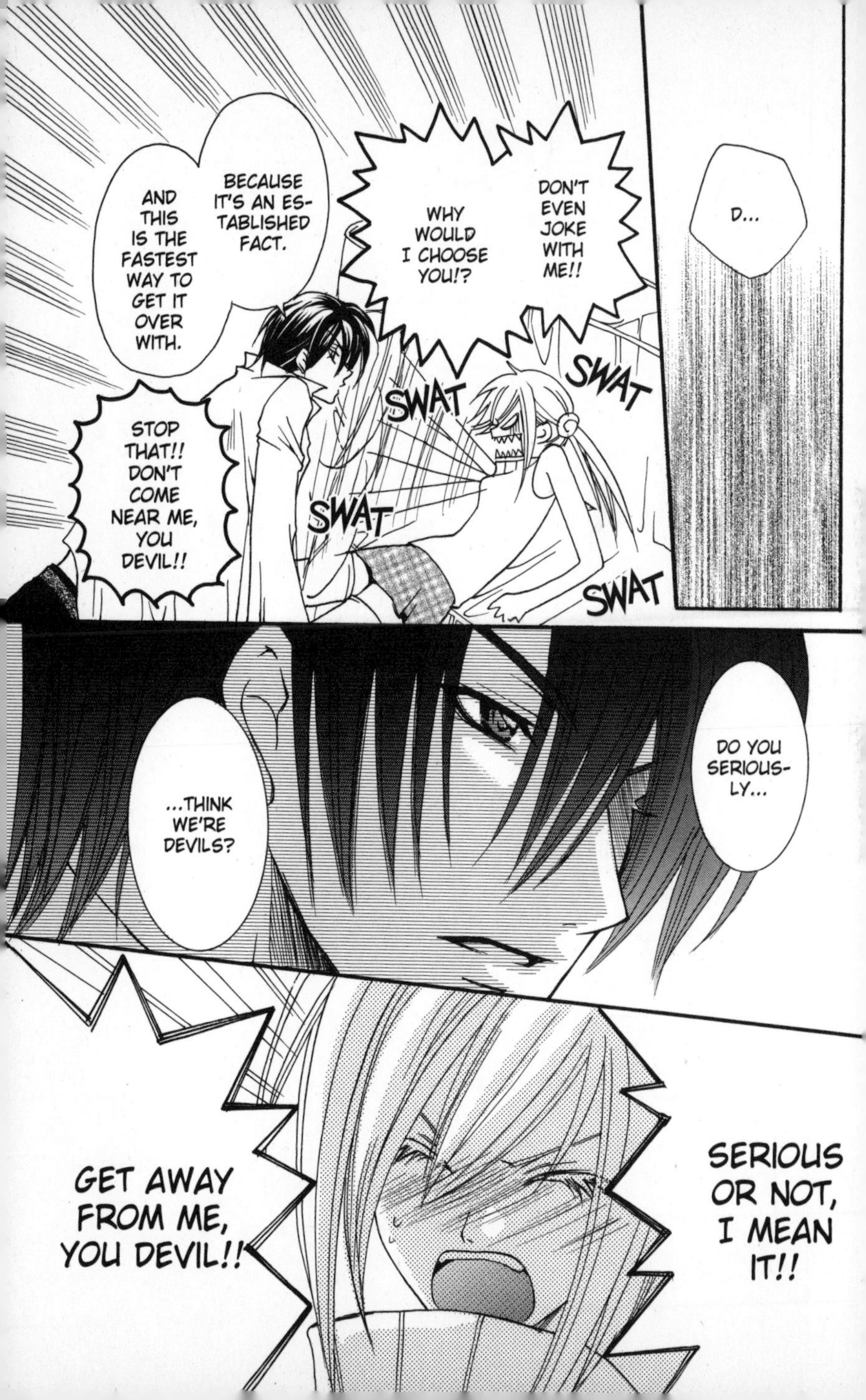
D...
DON'T EVEN JOKE WITH ME!!
WHY WOULD I CHOOSE YOU!?
SWAT
SWAT
BECAUSE IT'S AN ESTABLISHED FACT.
AND THIS IS THE FASTEST WAY TO GET IT OVER WITH.
SWAT
SWAT
STOP THAT!! DON'T COME NEAR ME, YOU DEVIL!!
DO YOU SERIOUSLY...
...THINK WE'RE DEVILS?
SERIOUS OR NOT, I MEAN IT!!
GET AWAY FROM ME, YOU DEVIL!!

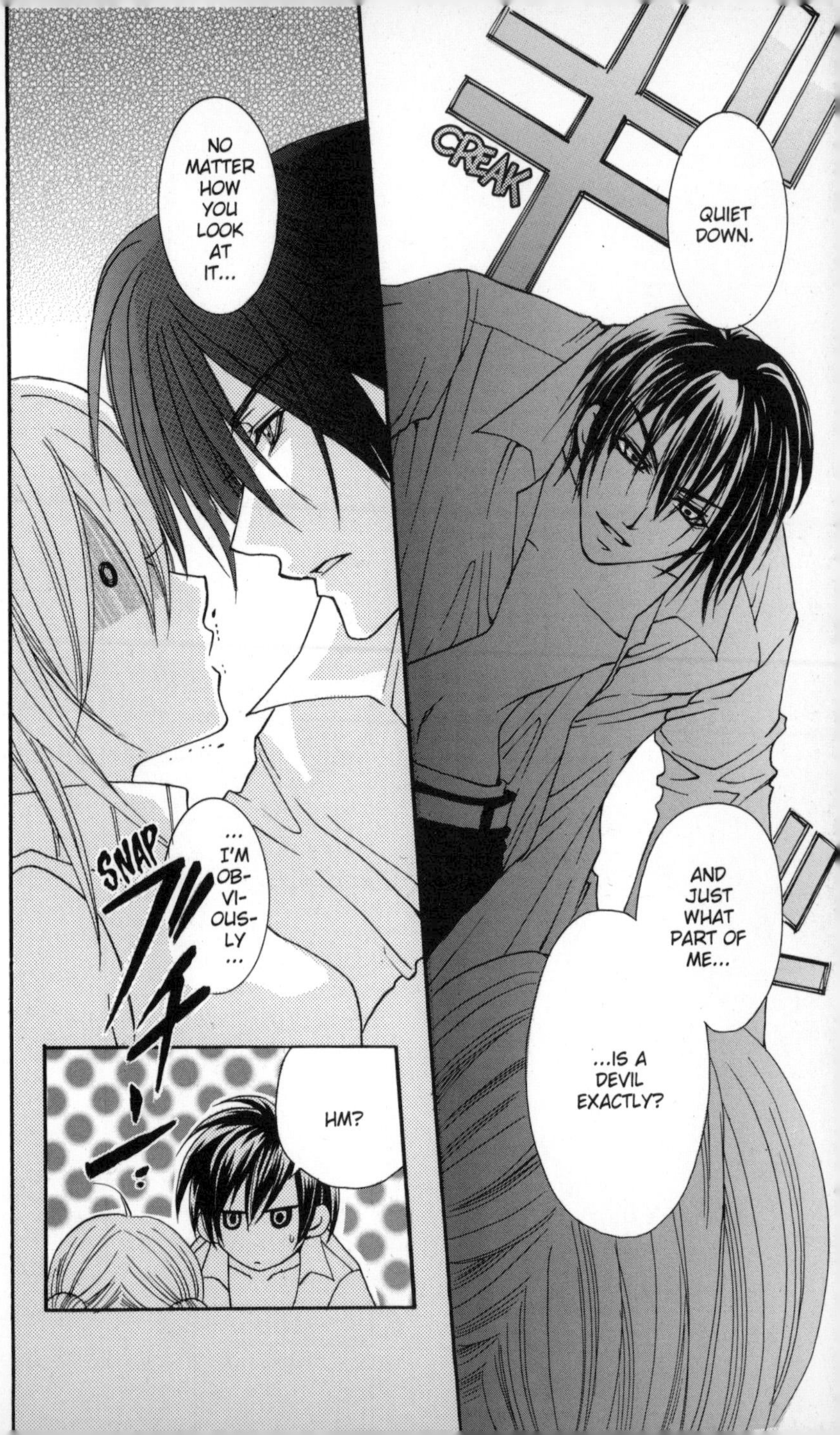
CREAK
QUIET DOWN.
NO MATTER HOW YOU LOOK AT IT...
...I'M OBVIOUSLY...
SNAP
AND JUST WHAT PART OF ME...
...IS A DEVIL EXACTLY?
HM?

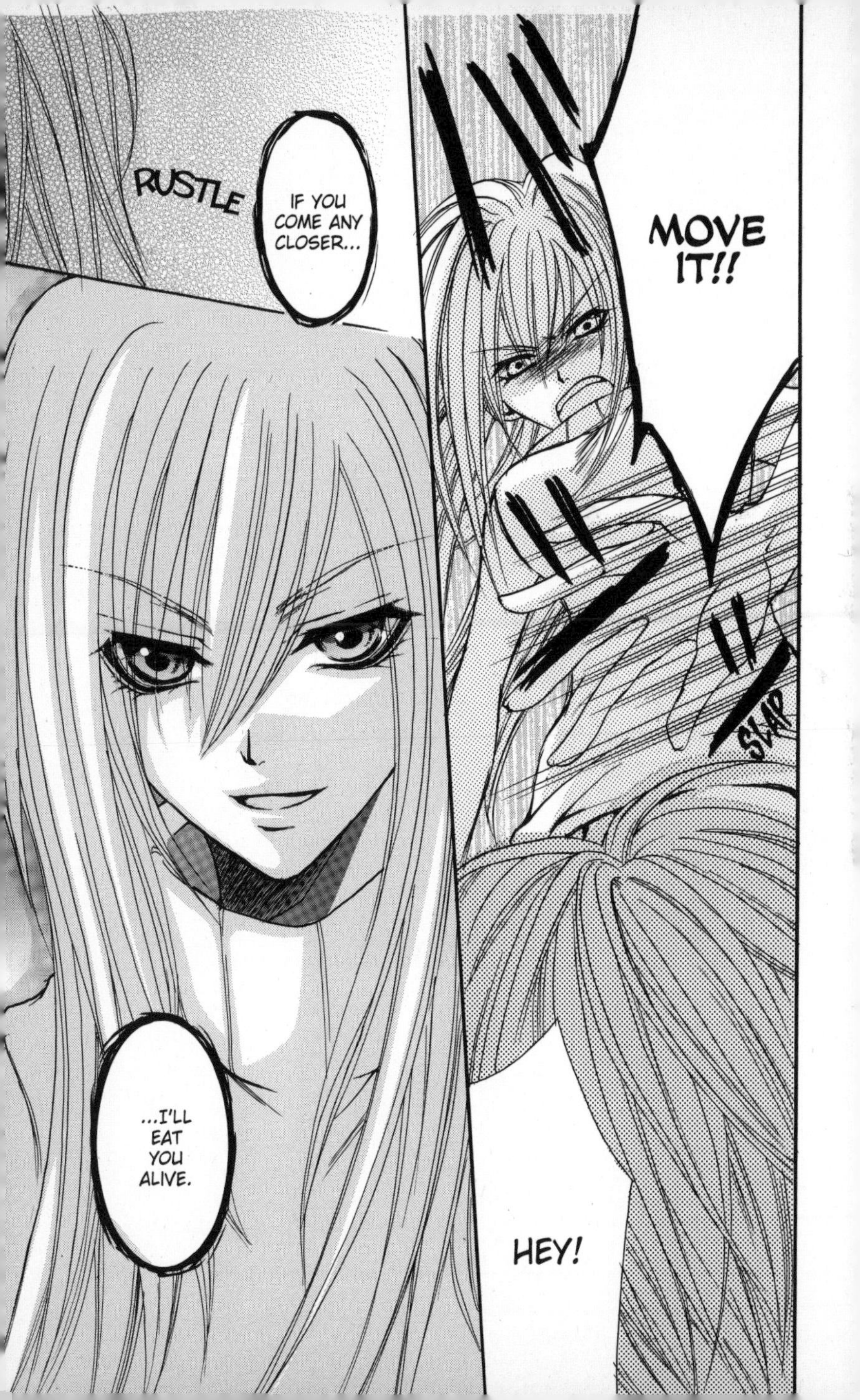
MOVE IT!!
SLAP
HEY!
RUSTLE
IF YOU COME ANY CLOSER...
...I'LL EAT YOU ALIVE.

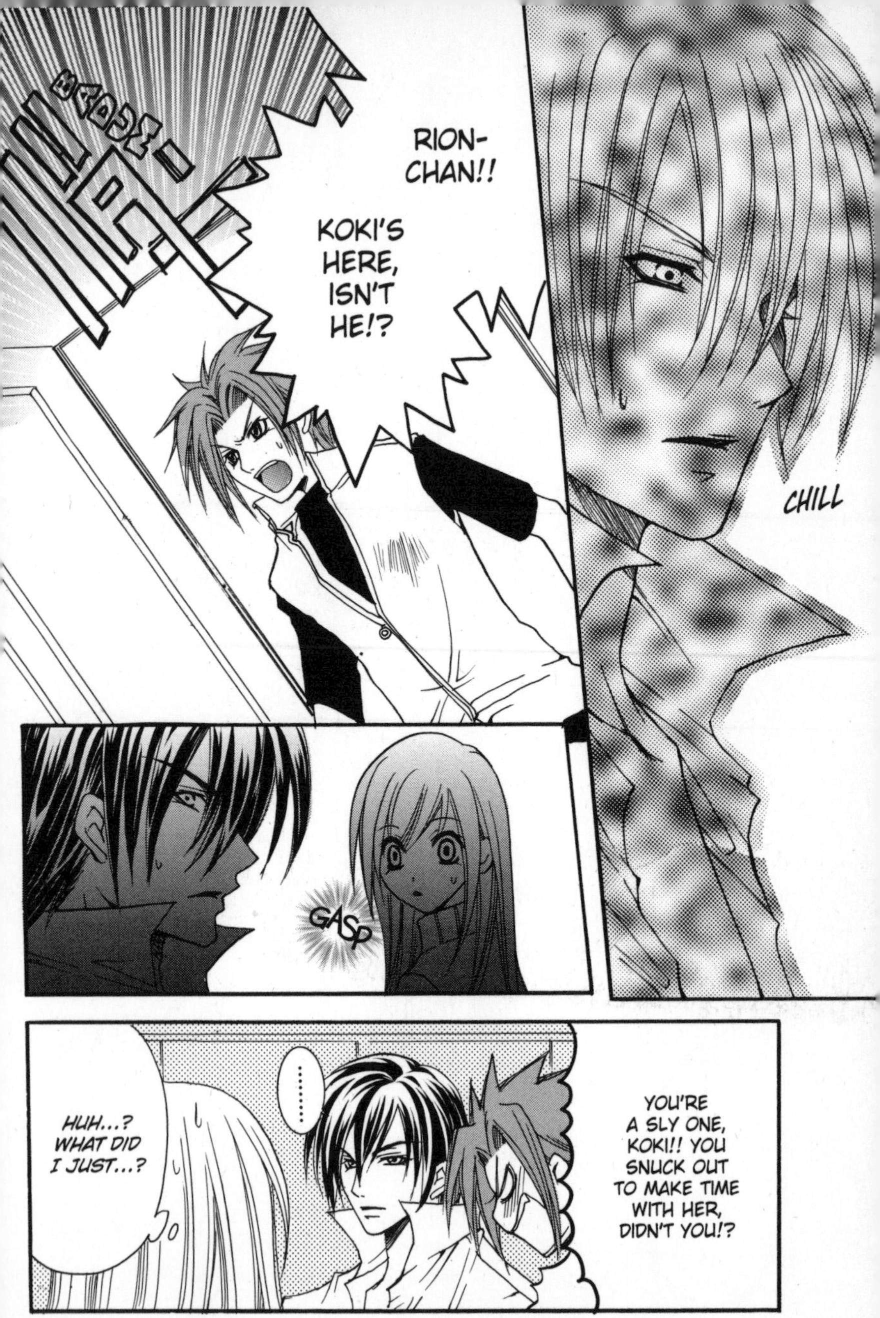
RION-CHAN!!
KOKI'S HERE, ISN'T HE!?
CHILL
GASP
YOU'RE A SLY ONE, KOKI!! YOU SNUCK OUT TO MAKE TIME WITH HER, DIDN'T YOU!?
......
HUH...? WHAT DID I JUST...?

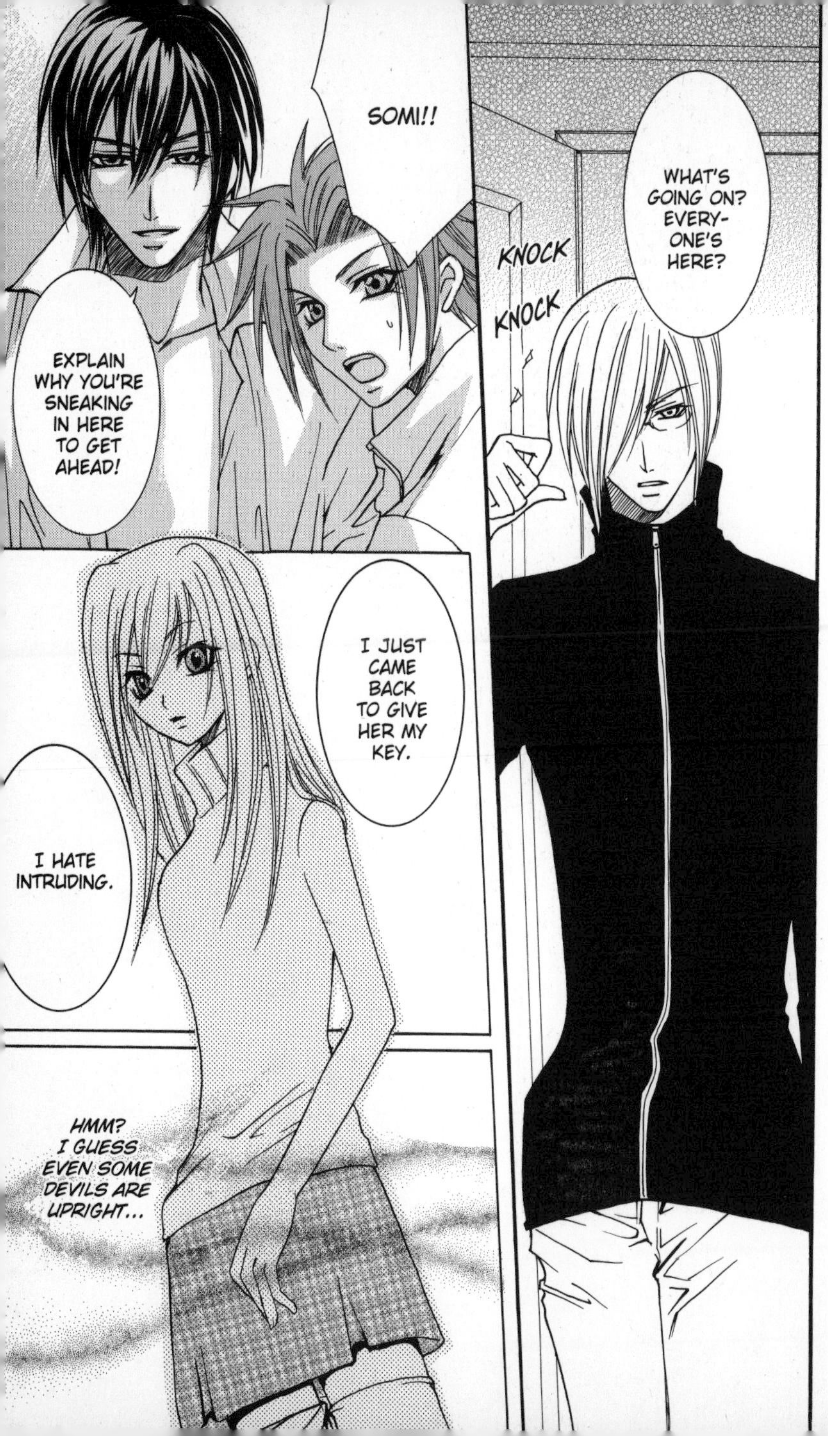
KNOCK
KNOCK
WHAT'S GOING ON? EVERY-ONE'S HERE?
SOMI!!
EXPLAIN WHY YOU'RE SNEAKING IN HERE TO GET AHEAD!
I JUST CAME BACK TO GIVE HER MY KEY.
I HATE INTRUDING.
HMM? I GUESS EVEN SOME DEVILS ARE UPRIGHT...

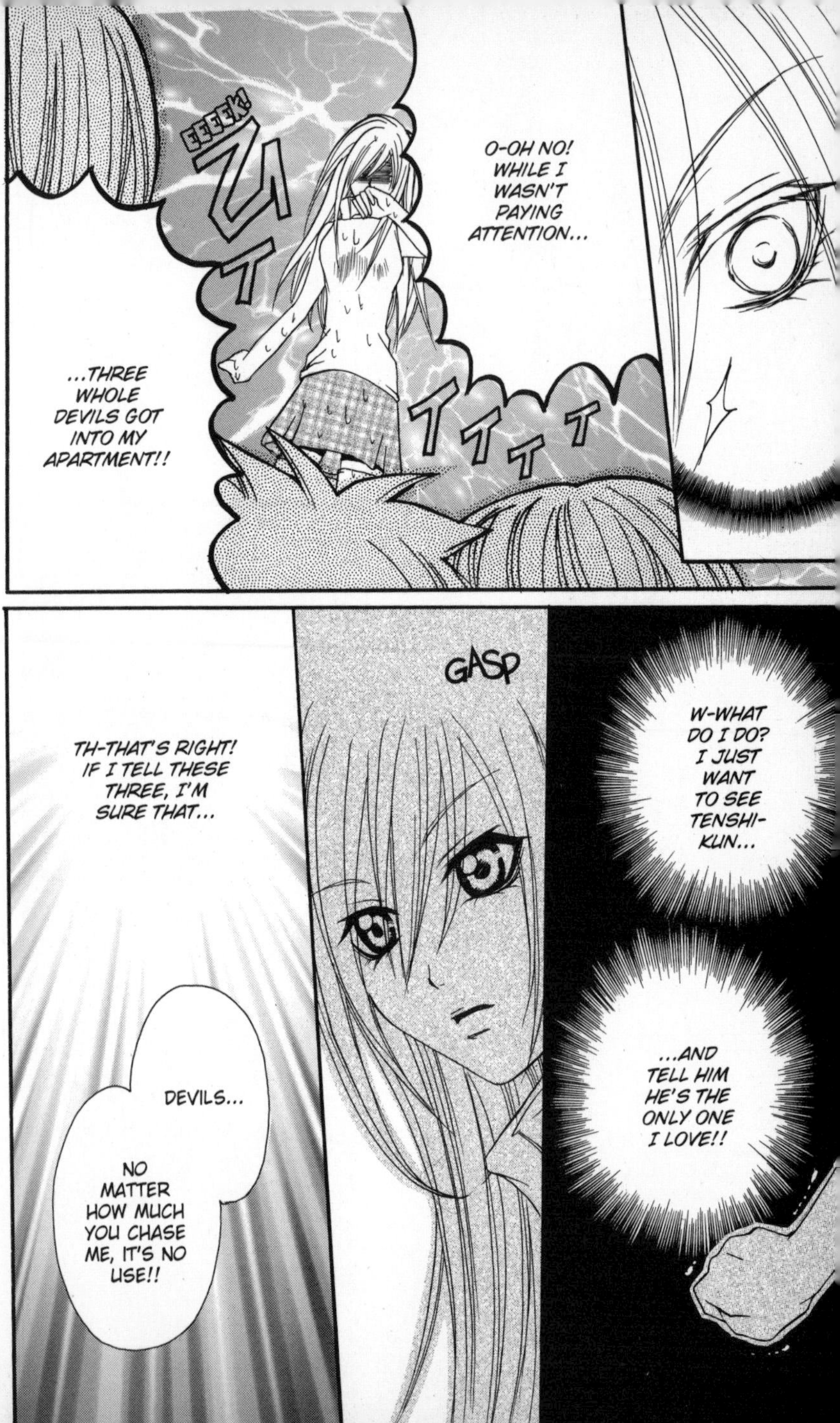
O-OH NO! WHILE I WASN'T PAYING ATTENTION...
EEEEK!
...THREE WHOLE DEVILS GOT INTO MY APARTMENT!!
GASP
W-WHAT DO I DO? I JUST WANT TO SEE TENSHI-KUN...
...AND TELL HIM HE'S THE ONLY ONE I LOVE!!
TH-THAT'S RIGHT! IF I TELL THESE THREE, I'M SURE THAT...
DEVILS...
NO MATTER HOW MUCH YOU CHASE ME, IT'S NO USE!!

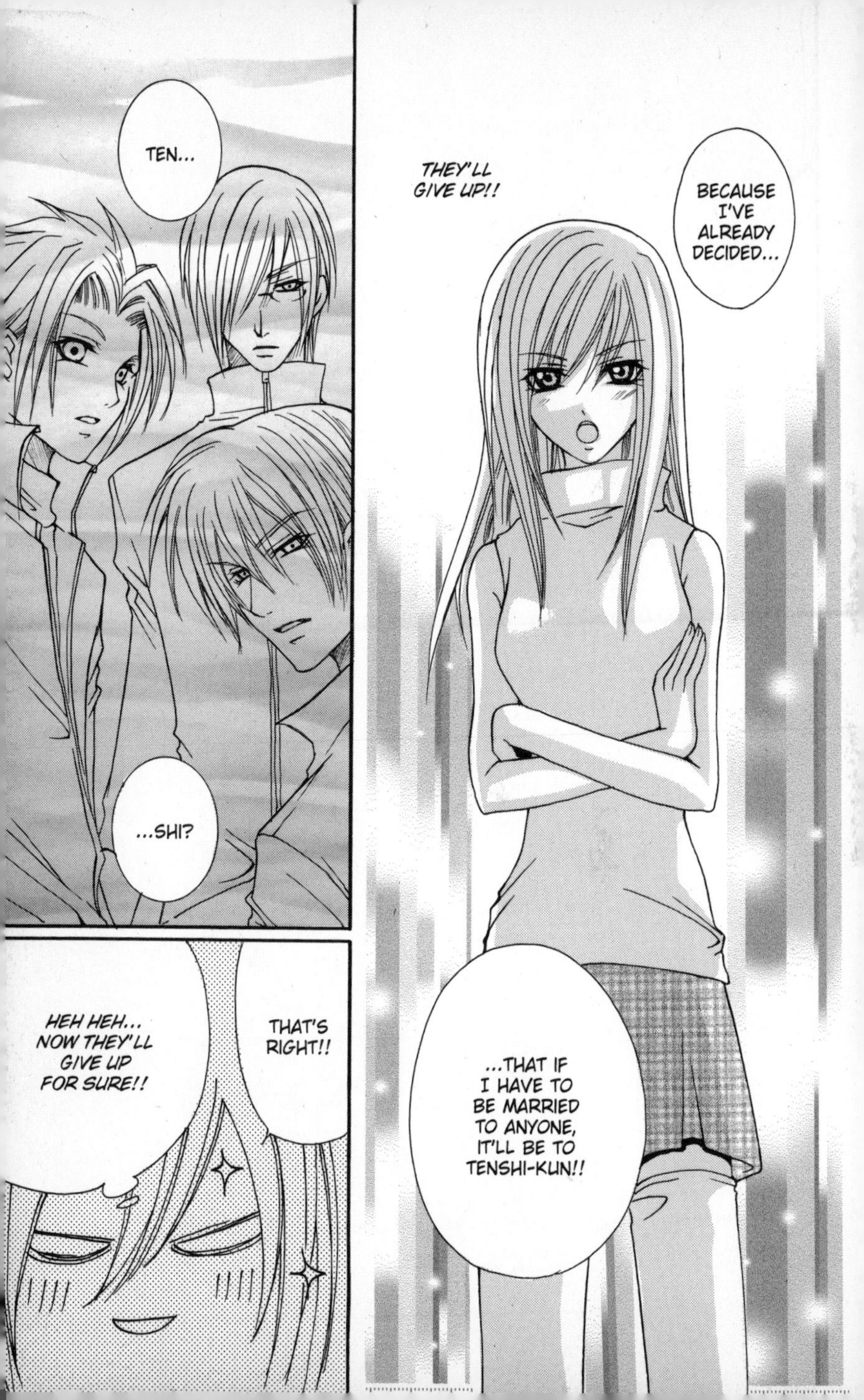
BECAUSE I'VE ALREADY DECIDED...
THEY'LL GIVE UP!!
...THAT IF I HAVE TO BE MARRIED TO ANYONE, IT'LL BE TO TENSHI-KUN!!
TEN...
...SHI?
THAT'S RIGHT!!
HEH HEH... NOW THEY'LL GIVE UP FOR SURE!!

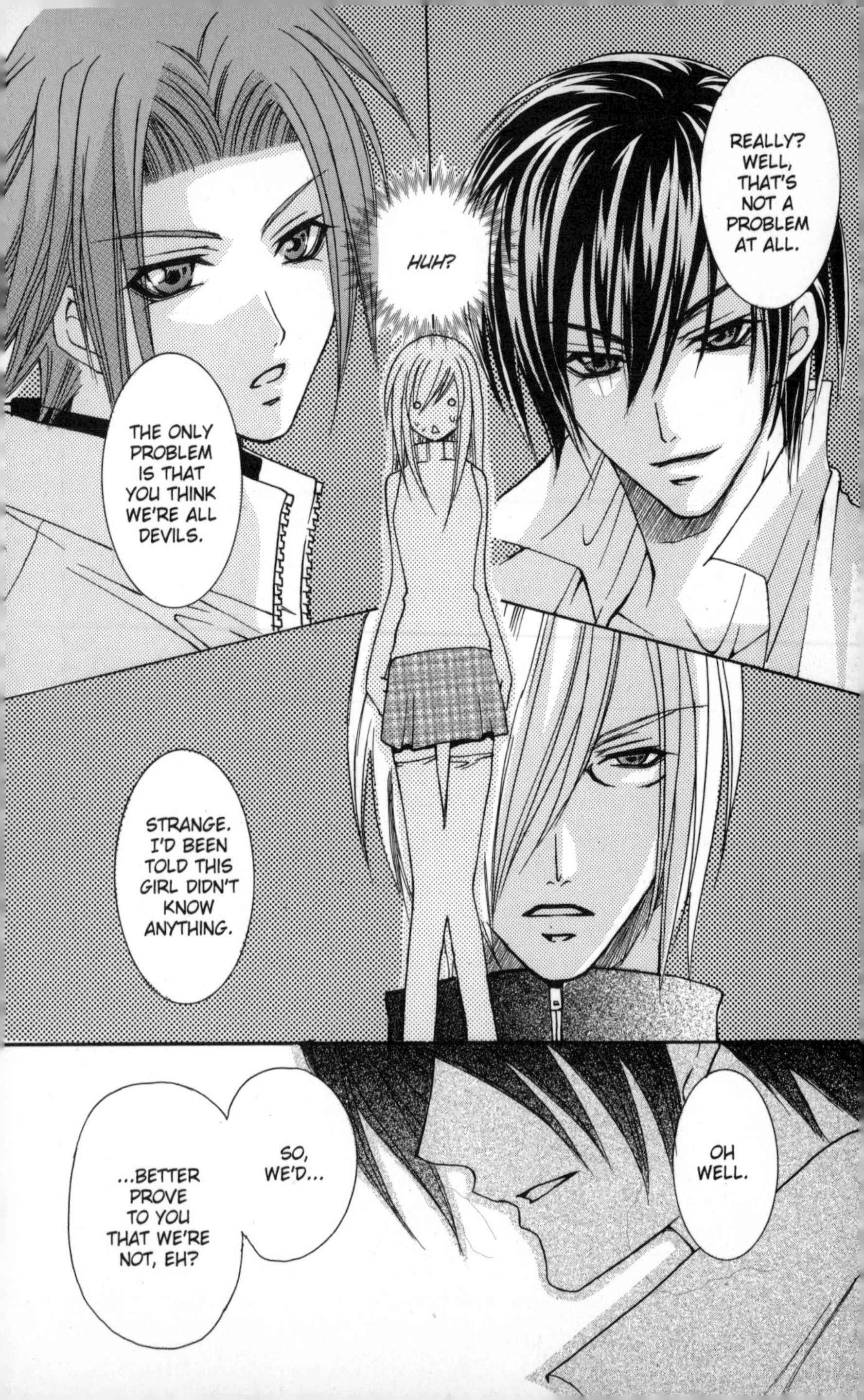
REALLY? WELL, THAT'S NOT A PROBLEM AT ALL.
HUH?
THE ONLY PROBLEM IS THAT YOU THINK WE'RE ALL DEVILS.
STRANGE. I'D BEEN TOLD THIS GIRL DIDN'T KNOW ANYTHING.
OH WELL.
SO, WE'D...
...BETTER PROVE TO YOU THAT WE'RE NOT, EH?

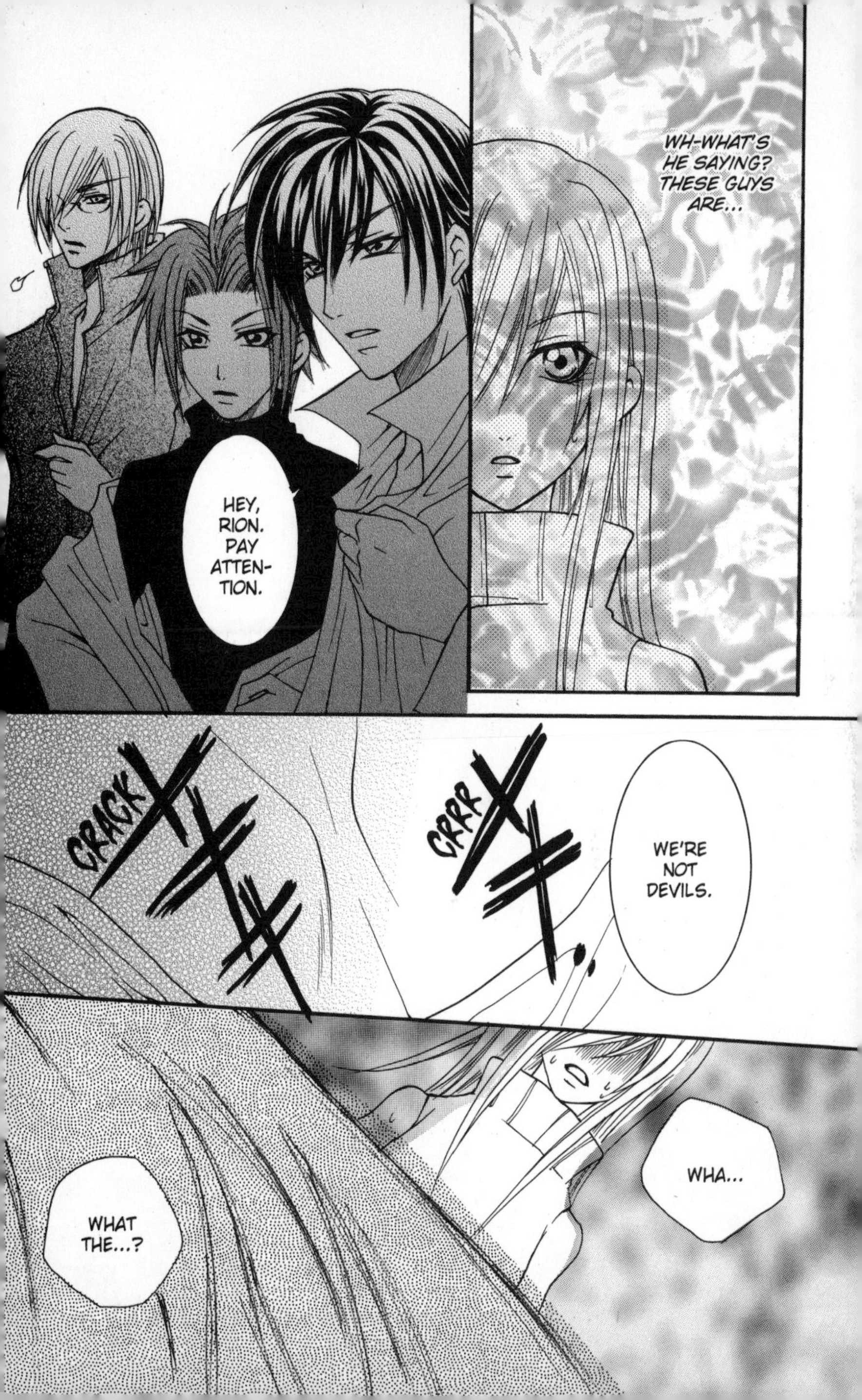
WH-WHAT'S HE SAYING? THESE GUYS ARE...
HEY, RION. PAY ATTEN-TION.
WE'RE NOT DEVILS.
CRRR
CRACK
WHA...
WHAT THE...?

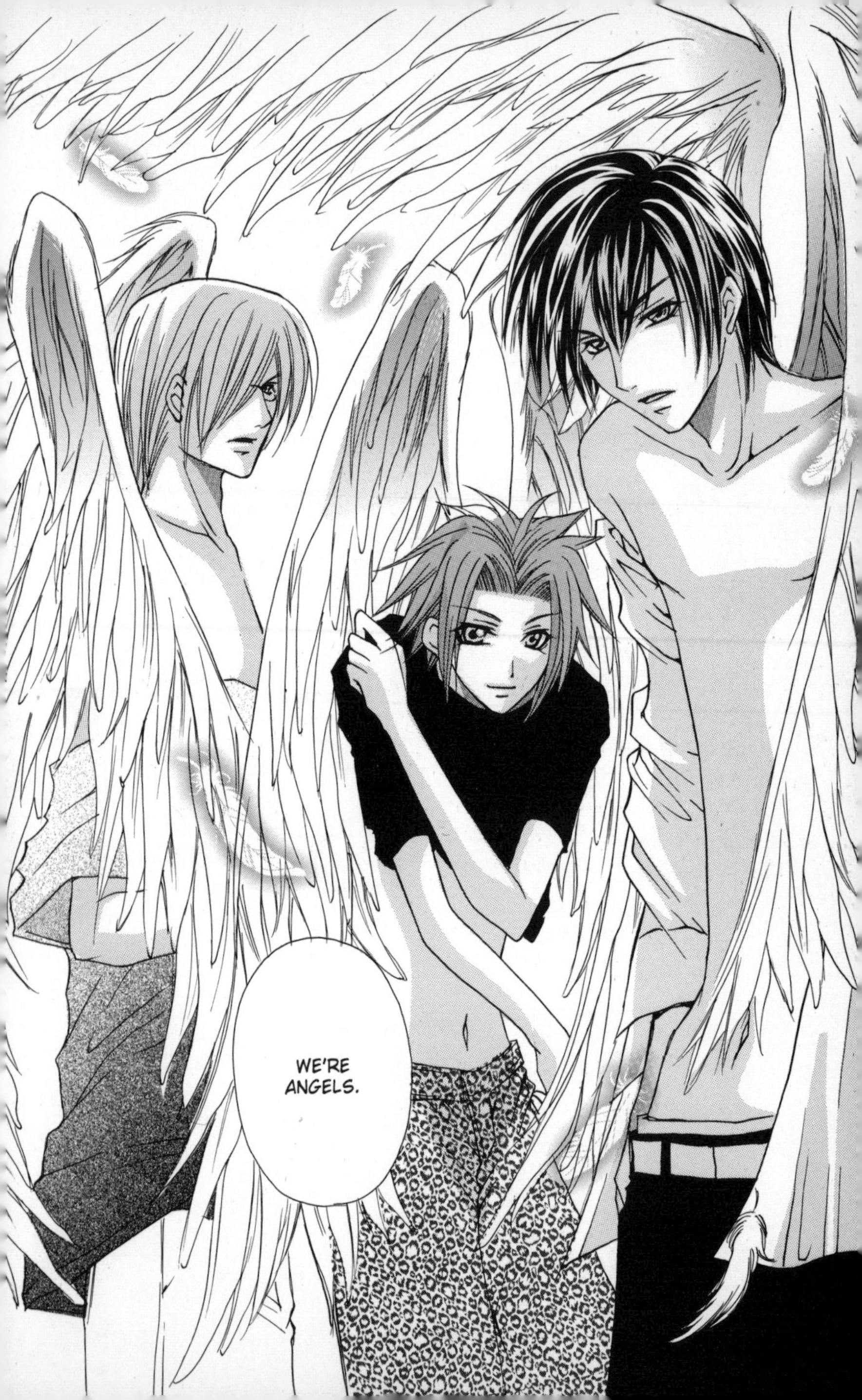
WE'RE ANGELS.

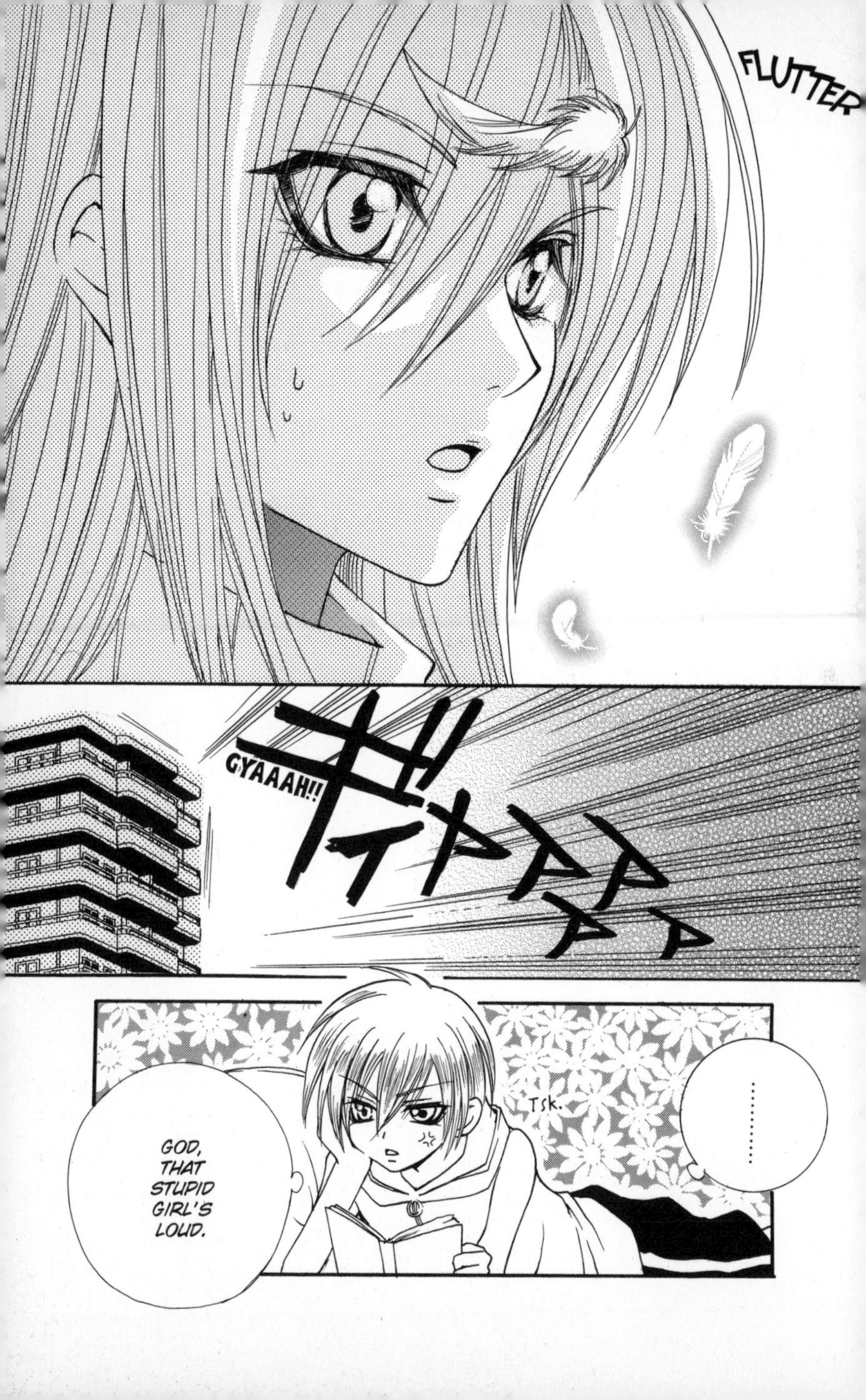
FLUTTER
GYAAAH!!
......
TSK.
GOD, THAT STUPID GIRL'S LOUD.

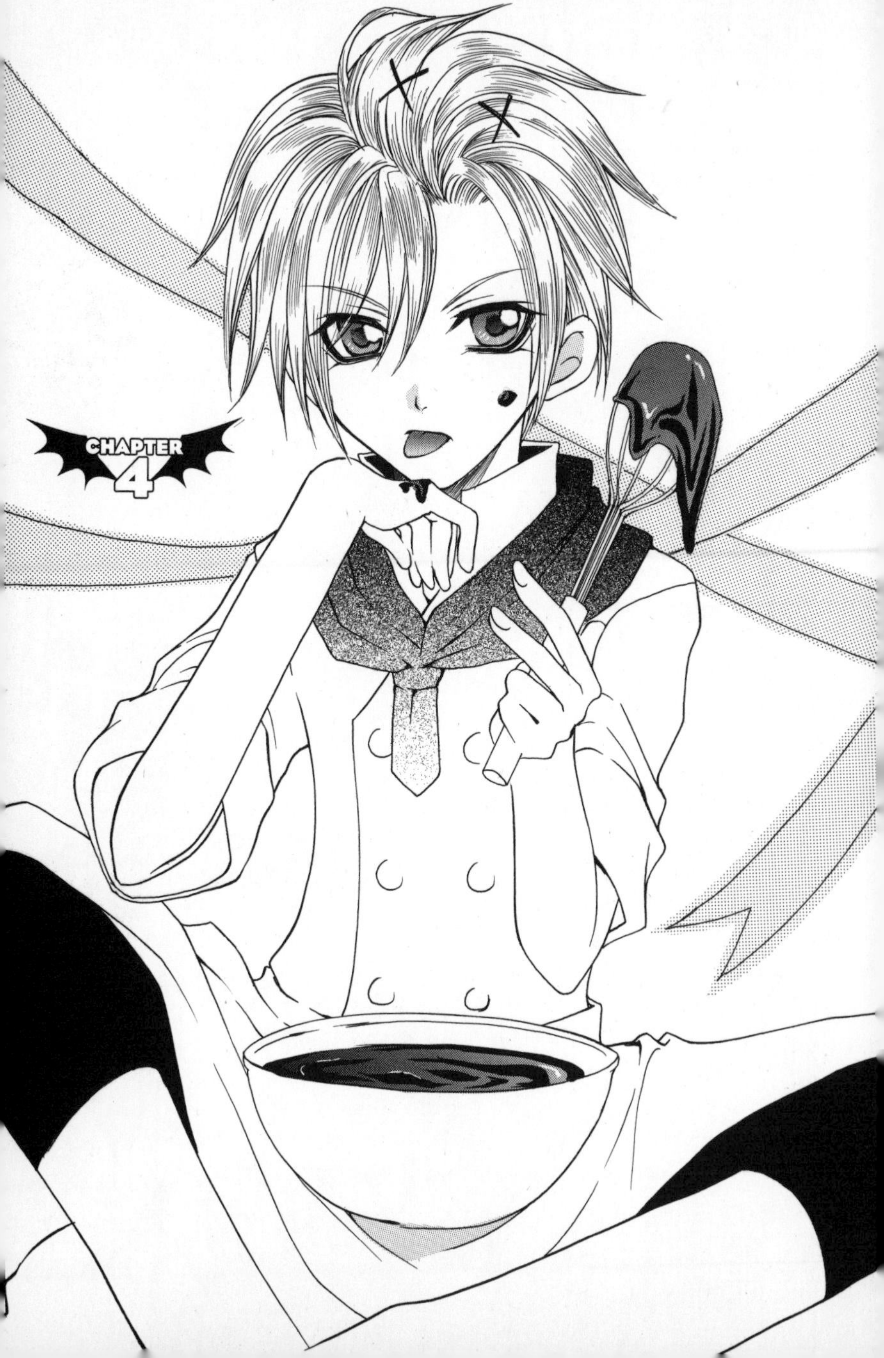
CHAPTER
4

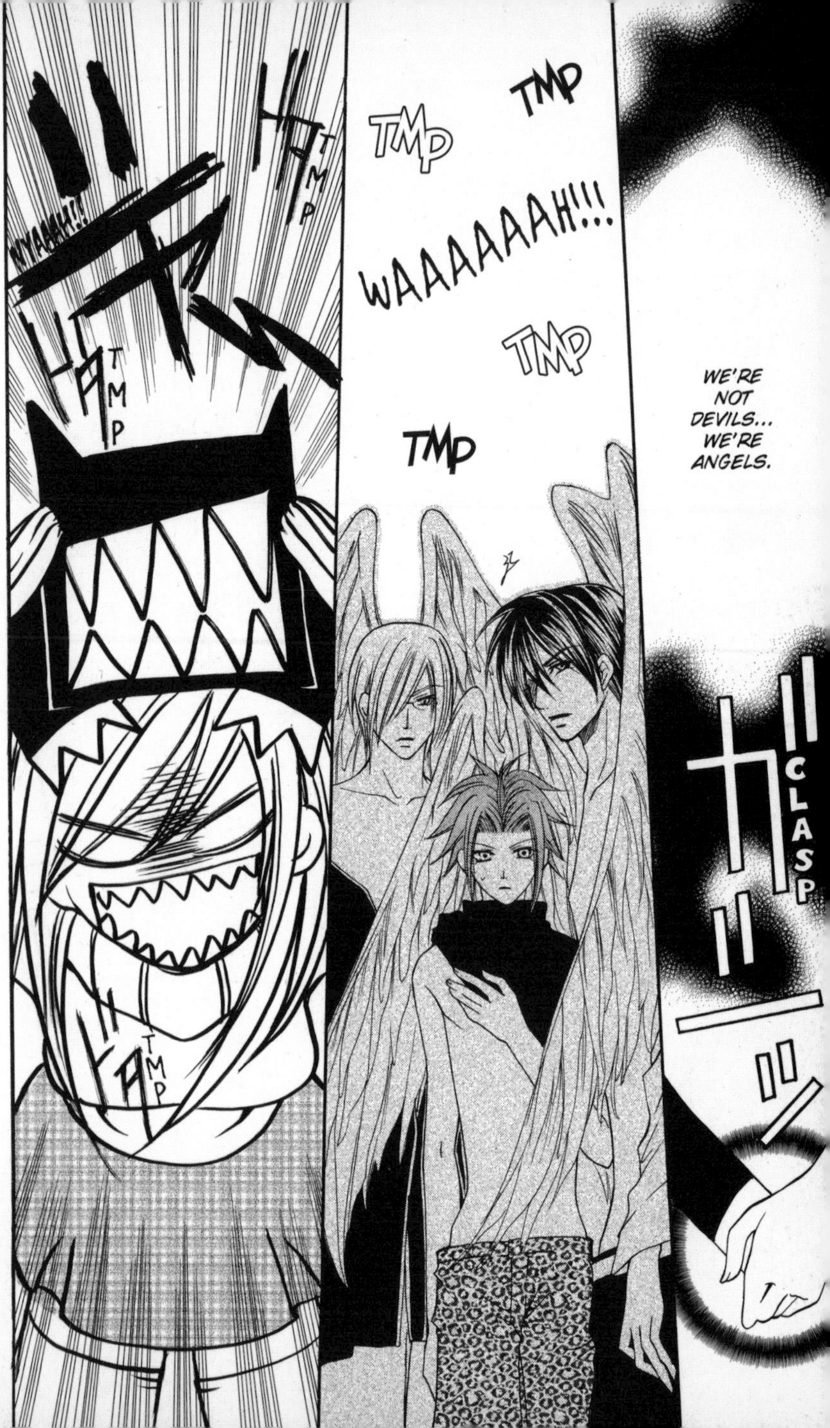
WE'RE NOT DEVILS... WE'RE ANGELS.
CLASP
TMP
TMP
WAAAAAAAH!!!
TMP
TMP
NYAAHH!!!
TMP
TMP
TMP

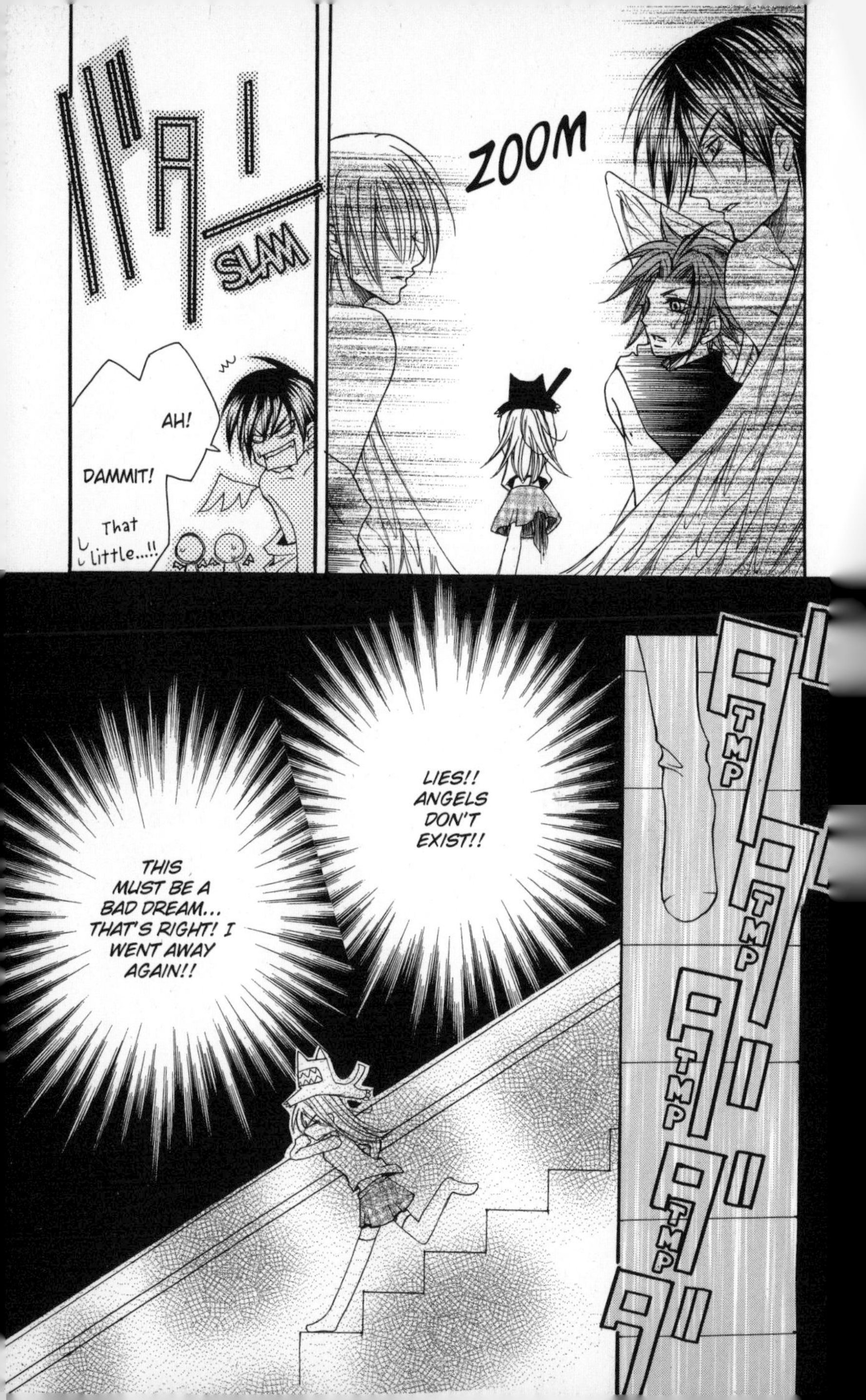
ZOOM
SLAM
AH!
DAMMIT!
That little...!!
LIES!! ANGELS DON'T EXIST!!
THIS MUST BE A BAD DREAM... THAT'S RIGHT! I WENT AWAY AGAIN!!
TMP
TMP
TMP
TMP

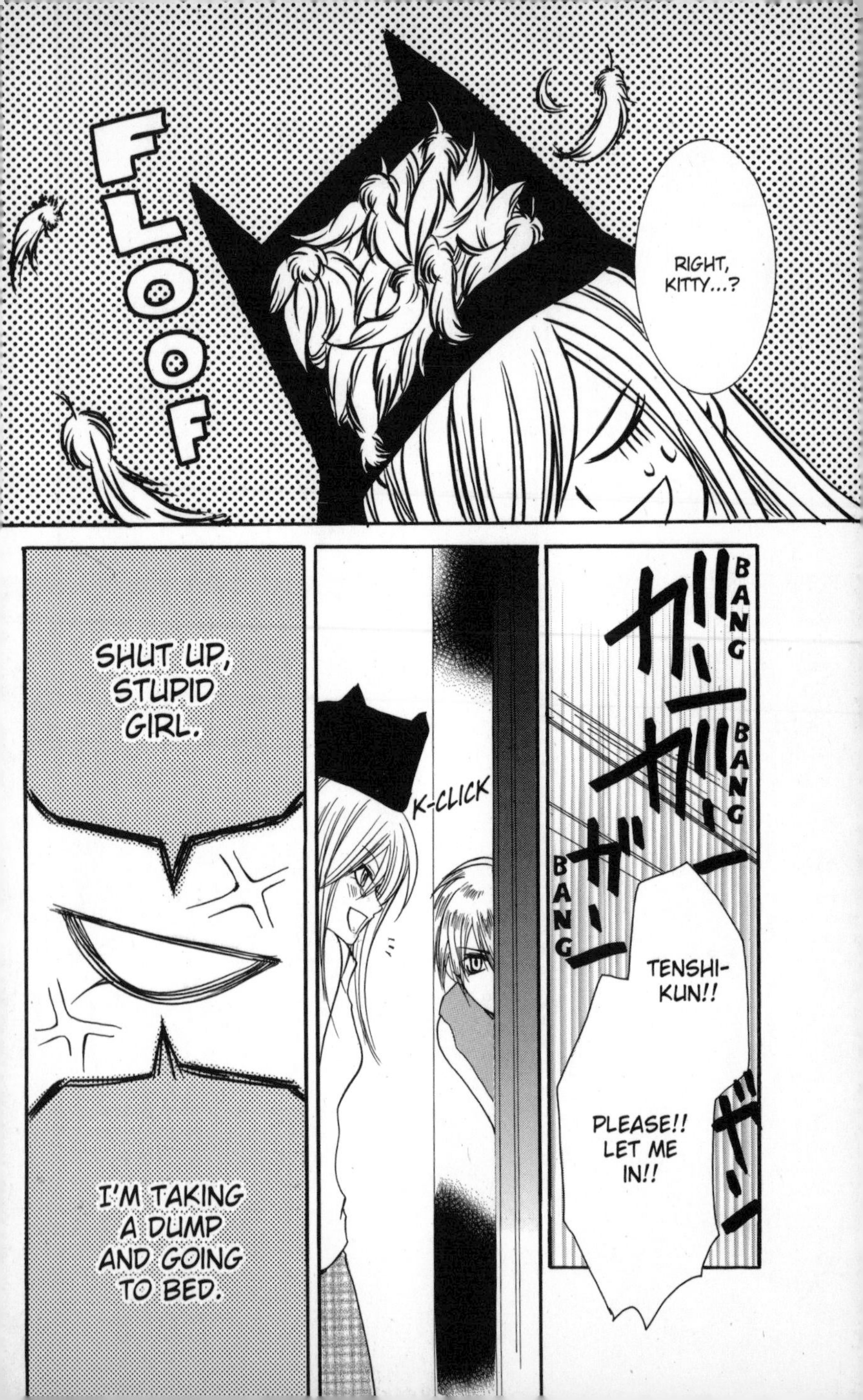
FLOOF
RIGHT, KITTY...?
BANG
BANG
BANG
TENSHI-KUN!!
PLEASE!! LET ME IN!!
K-CLICK
SHUT UP, STUPID GIRL.
I'M TAKING A DUMP AND GOING TO BED.

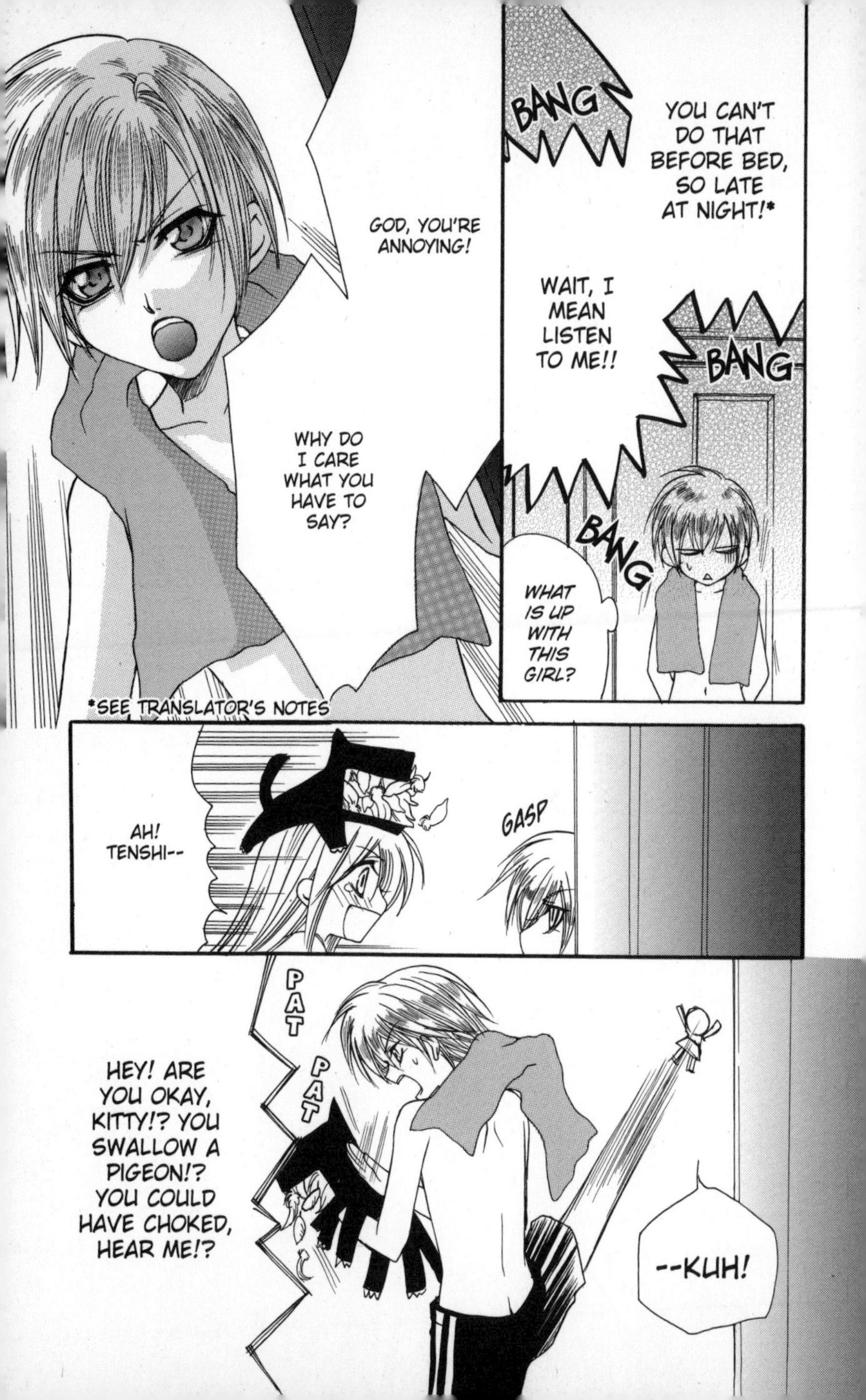
BANG
YOU CAN'T DO THAT BEFORE BED, SO LATE AT NIGHT!*
WAIT, I MEAN LISTEN TO ME!!
BANG
BANG
WHAT IS UP WITH THIS GIRL?
GOD, YOU'RE ANNOYING!
WHY DO I CARE WHAT YOU HAVE TO SAY?
GASP
AH! TENSHI--
--KUH!
PAT
PAT
HEY! ARE YOU OKAY, KITTY!? YOU SWALLOW A PIGEON!? YOU COULD HAVE CHOKED, HEAR ME!?

*SEE TRANSLATOR'S NOTES

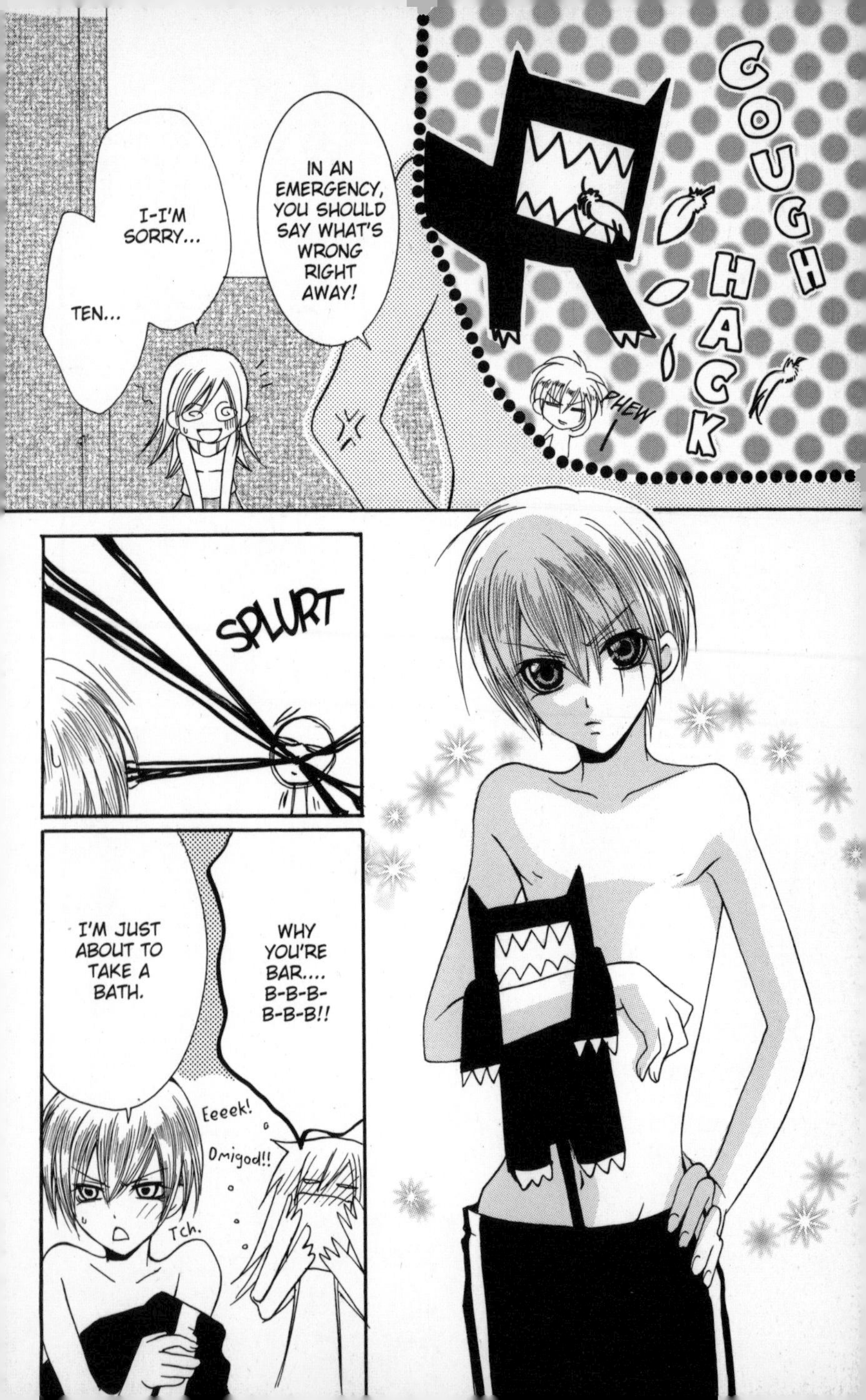
COUGH
HACK
PHEW
IN AN EMERGENCY, YOU SHOULD SAY WHAT'S WRONG RIGHT AWAY!
I-I'M SORRY...
TEN...
SPLURT
WHY YOU'RE BAR.... B-B-B-B-B-B!!
I'M JUST ABOUT TO TAKE A BATH.
Eeeek!
Omigod!!
Tch.

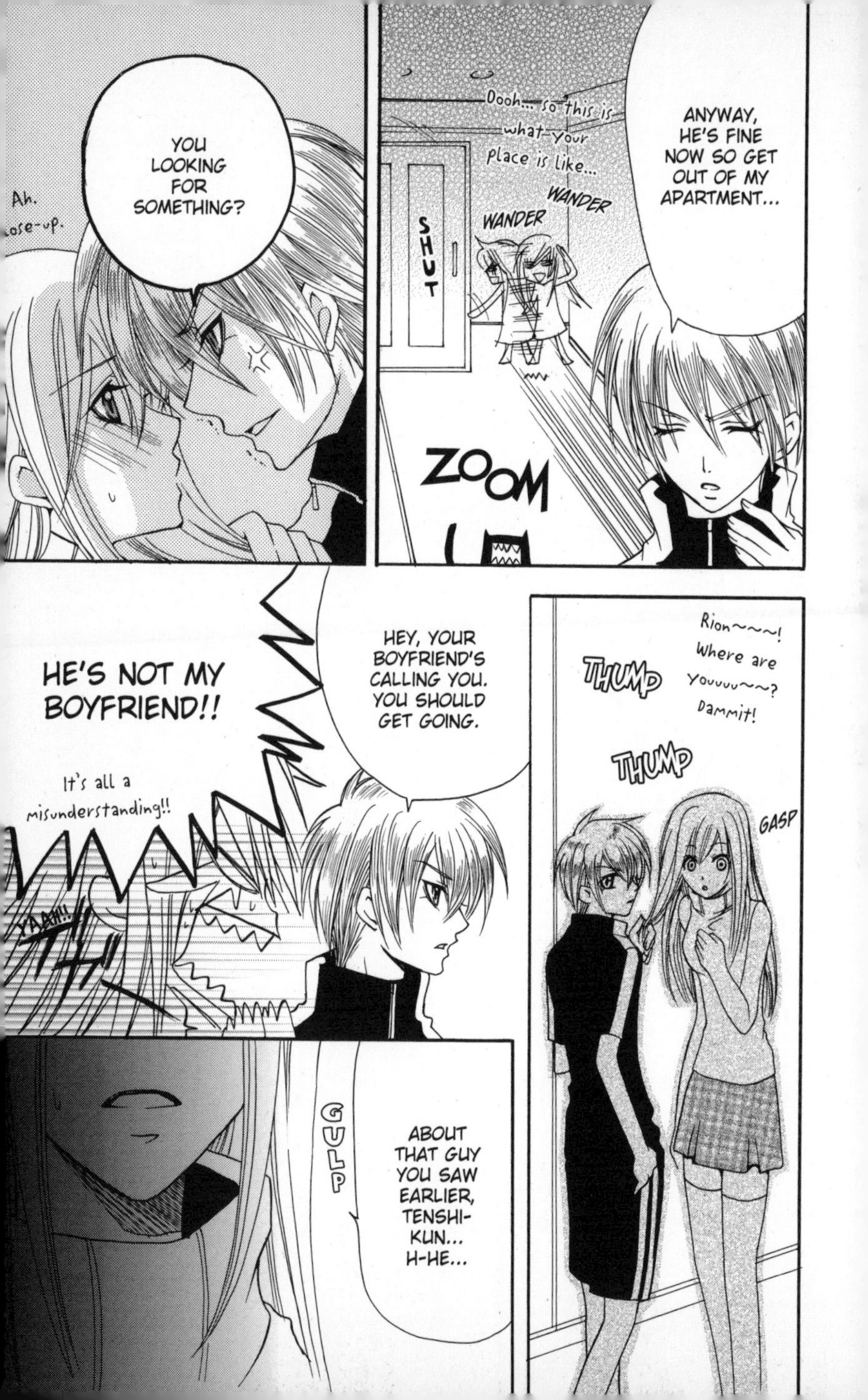
ANYWAY, HE'S FINE NOW SO GET OUT OF MY APARTMENT...
Dooh... so this is what your place is like...
WANDER
WANDER
SHUT
ZOOM
YOU LOOKING FOR SOMETHING?
Ah.
ose-up.
THUMP
Rion~~~! Where are Youuuu~~? Dammit!
THUMP
GASP
HEY, YOUR BOYFRIEND'S CALLING YOU. YOU SHOULD GET GOING.
HE'S NOT MY BOYFRIEND!!
It's all a misunderstanding!!
YAAH!!
GULP
ABOUT THAT GUY YOU SAW EARLIER, TENSHI-KUN... H-HE...

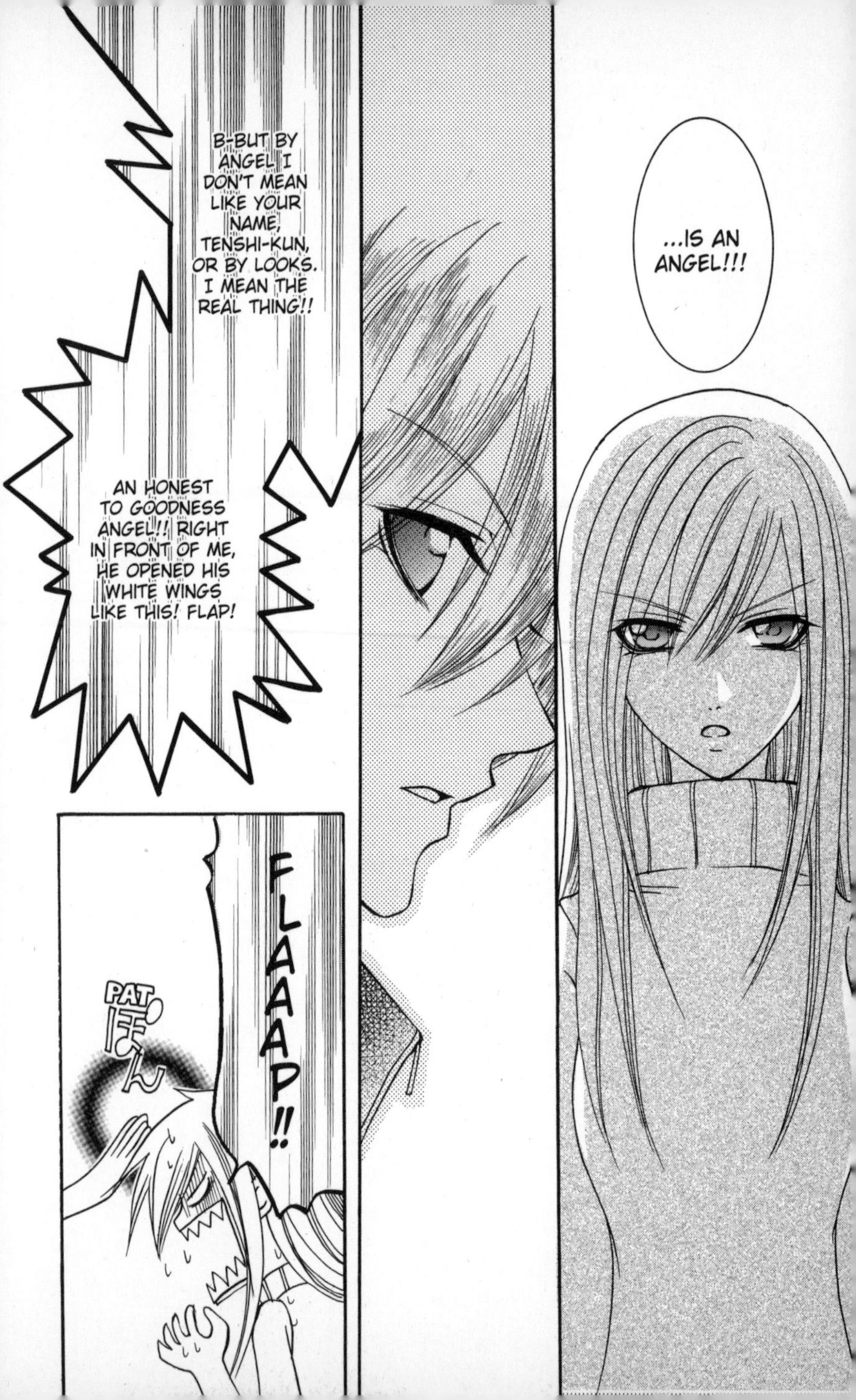

...IS AN ANGEL!!!
B-BUT BY ANGEL I DON'T MEAN LIKE YOUR NAME, TENSHI-KUN, OR BY LOOKS. I MEAN THE REAL THING!!
AN HONEST TO GOODNESS ANGEL!! RIGHT IN FRONT OF ME, HE OPENED HIS WHITE WINGS LIKE THIS! FLAP!
FLAAAAP!!
PAT
ぽん

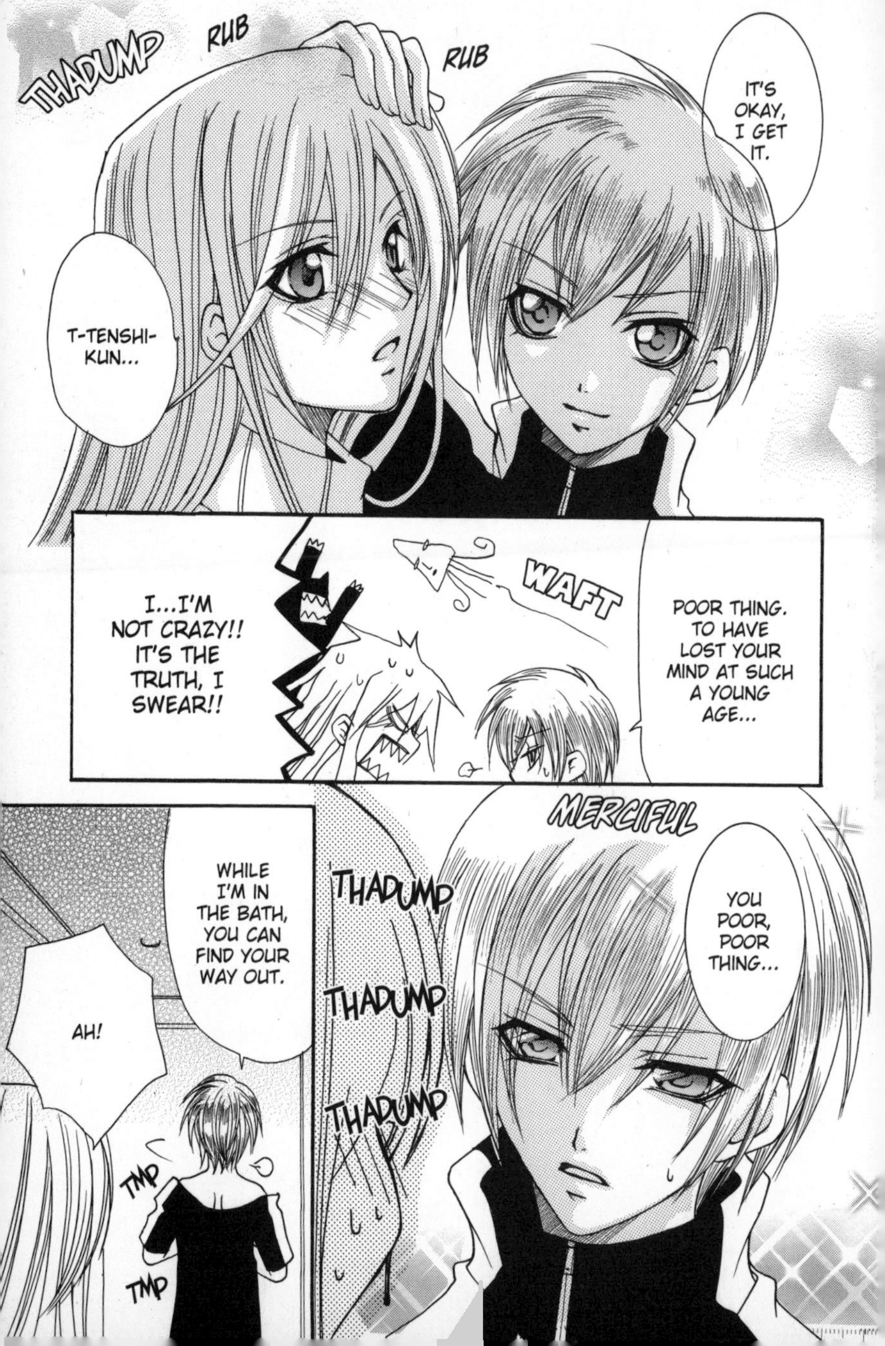
IT'S OKAY, I GET IT.
RUB
RUB
THADUMP
T-TENSHI-KUN...
POOR THING. TO HAVE LOST YOUR MIND AT SUCH A YOUNG AGE...
WAFT
I...I'M NOT CRAZY!! IT'S THE TRUTH, I SWEAR!!
MERCIFUL
YOU POOR, POOR THING...
THADUMP
THADUMP
THADUMP
WHILE I'M IN THE BATH, YOU CAN FIND YOUR WAY OUT.
AH!
TMP
TMP

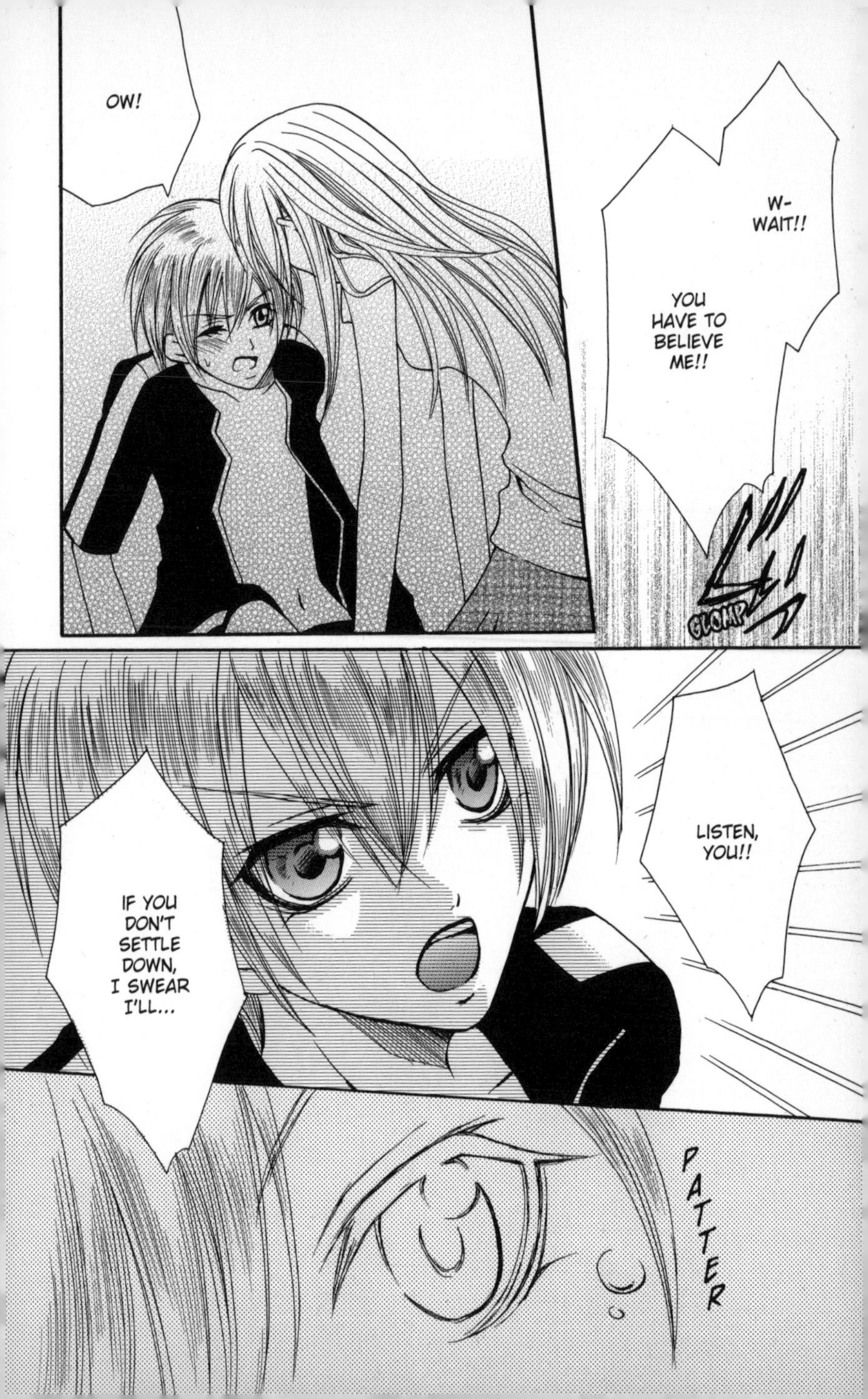
W-
WAIT!!
YOU HAVE TO BELIEVE ME!!
GLOMP
OW!
LISTEN, YOU!!
IF YOU DON'T SETTLE DOWN, I SWEAR I'LL...
PATTER

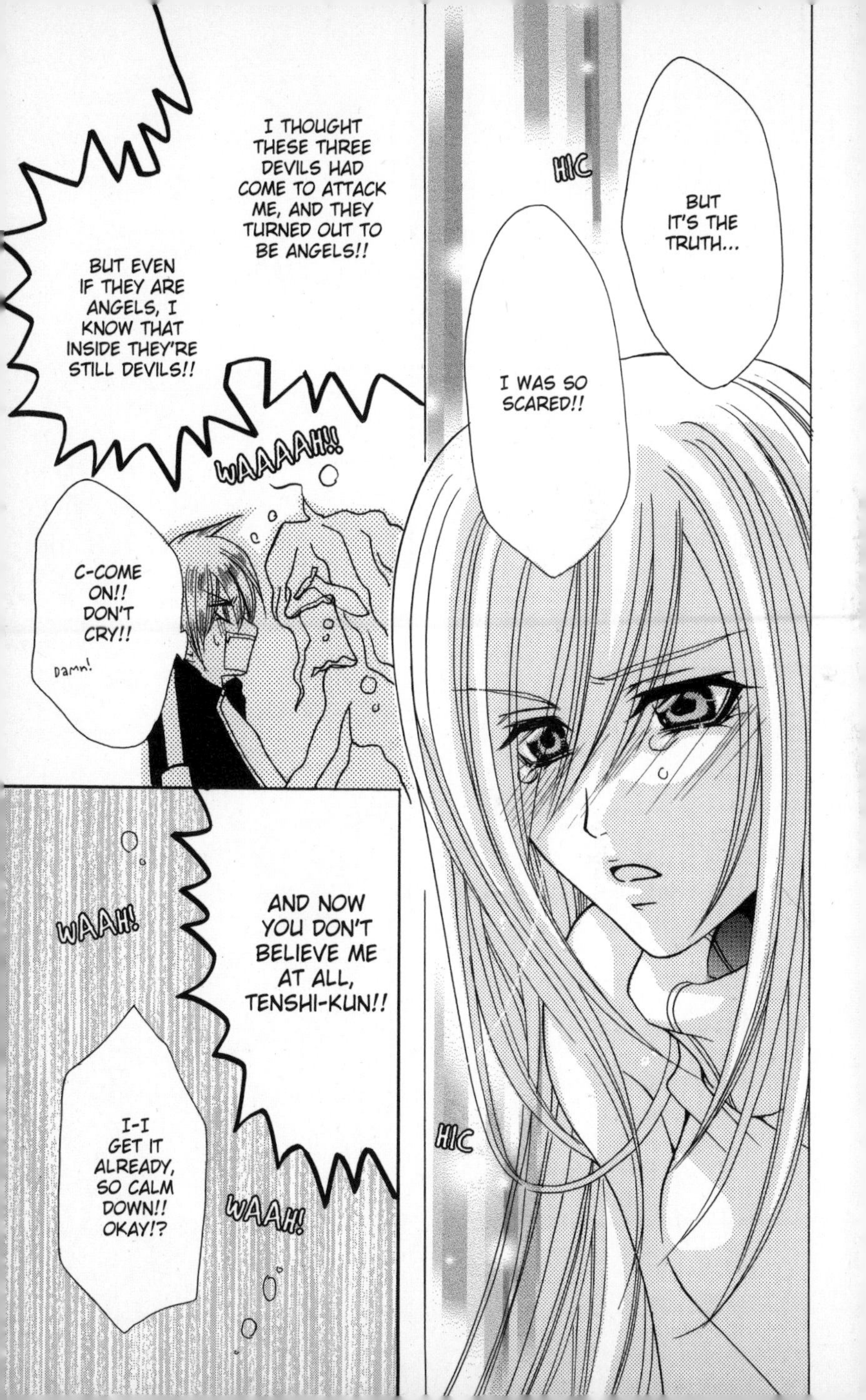
HIC
BUT IT'S THE TRUTH...
I WAS SO SCARED!!
I THOUGHT THESE THREE DEVILS HAD COME TO ATTACK ME, AND THEY TURNED OUT TO BE ANGELS!!
BUT EVEN IF THEY ARE ANGELS, I KNOW THAT INSIDE THEY'RE STILL DEVILS!!
WAAAAH!!
C-COME ON!! DON'T CRY!!
Damn!
WAAH!
AND NOW YOU DON'T BELIEVE ME AT ALL, TENSHI-KUN!!
HIC
WAAH!
I-I GET IT ALREADY, SO CALM DOWN!! OKAY!?

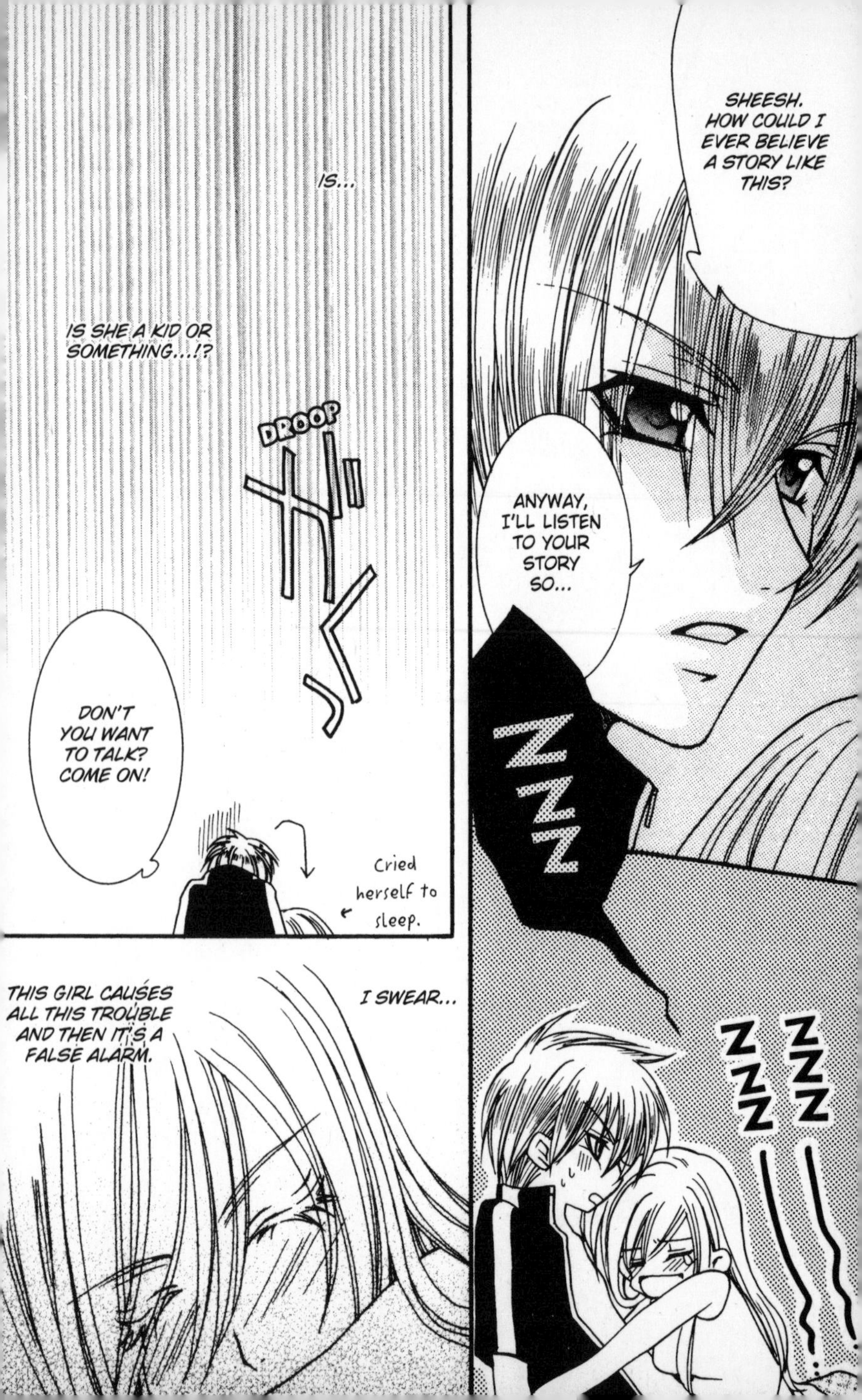

SHEESH. HOW COULD I EVER BELIEVE A STORY LIKE THIS?
ANYWAY, I'LL LISTEN TO YOUR STORY SO...
NNN
ZZZ
ZZZ
IS...
IS SHE A KID OR SOMETHING...!?
DROOP
DON'T YOU WANT TO TALK? COME ON!
Cried herself to sleep.
I SWEAR...
THIS GIRL CAUSES ALL THIS TROUBLE AND THEN IT'S A FALSE ALARM.

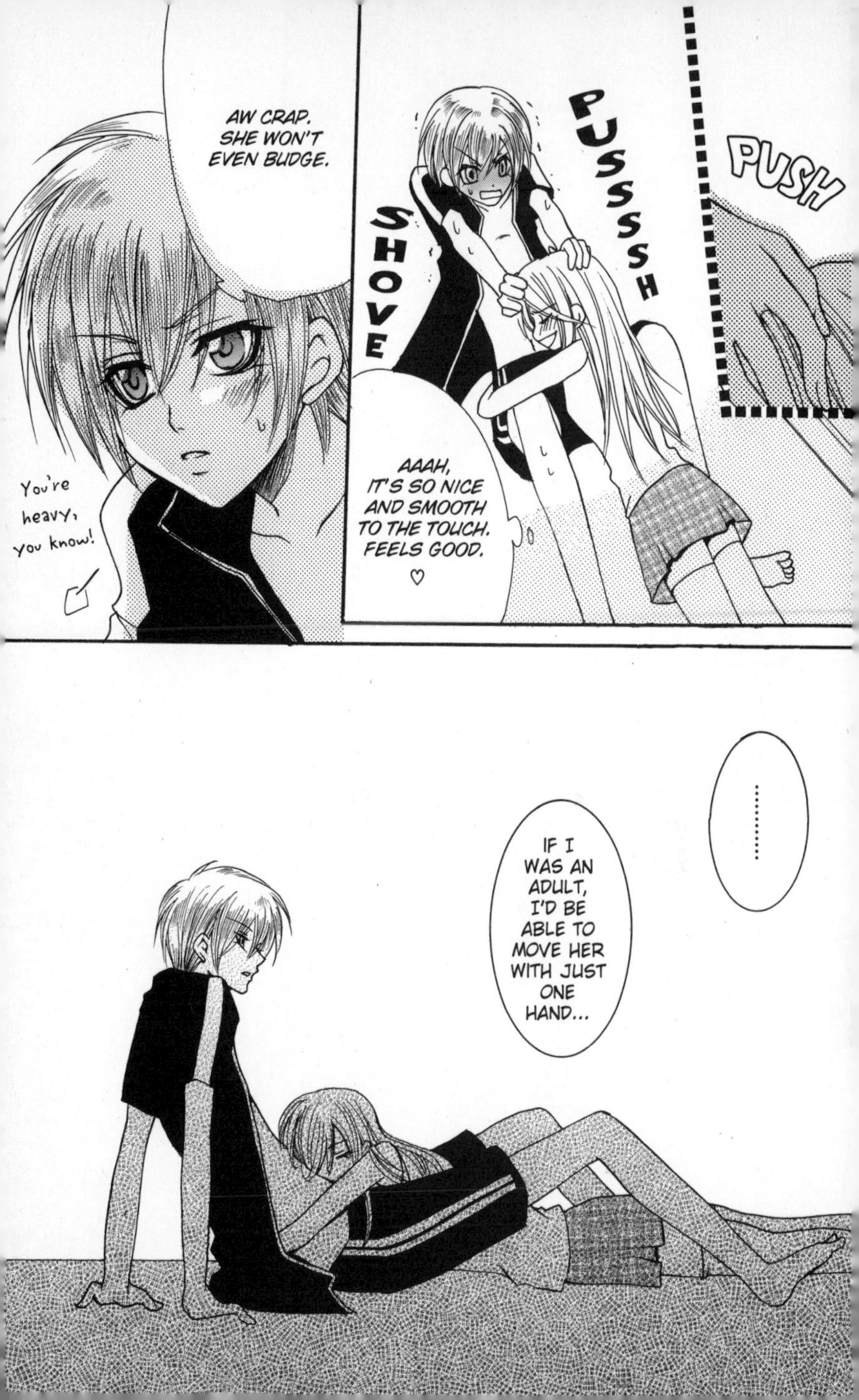
PUSH
PUSSSSH
SHOVE
AAAH, IT'S SO NICE AND SMOOTH TO THE TOUCH. FEELS GOOD. ♡
AW CRAP. SHE WON'T EVEN BUDGE.
You're heavy, you know!
....
IF I WAS AN ADULT, I'D BE ABLE TO MOVE HER WITH JUST ONE HAND...

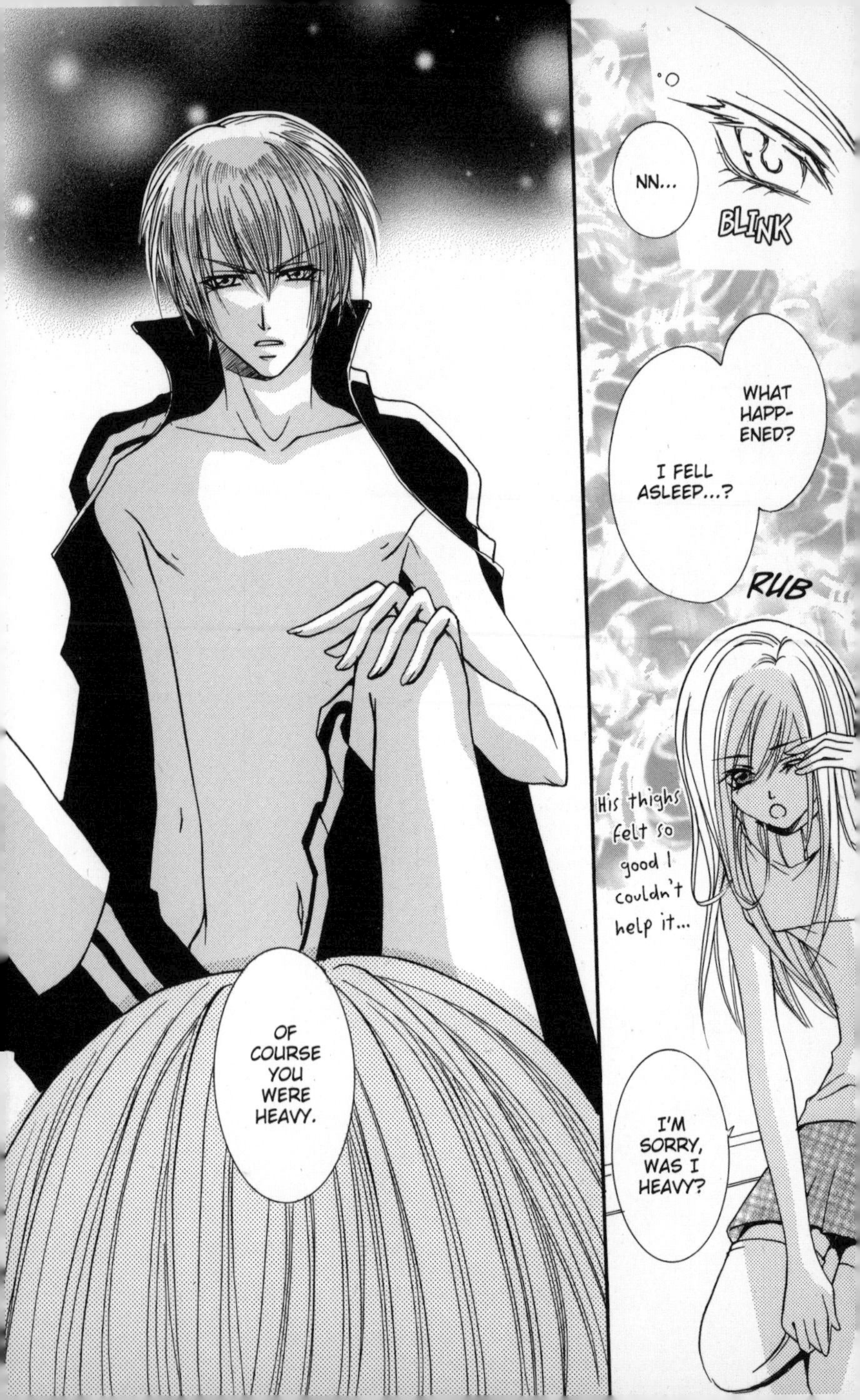
NN...
BLINK
WHAT HAPPENED?
I FELL ASLEEP...?
RUB
His thighs felt so good I couldn't help it...
I'M SORRY, WAS I HEAVY?
OF COURSE YOU WERE HEAVY.

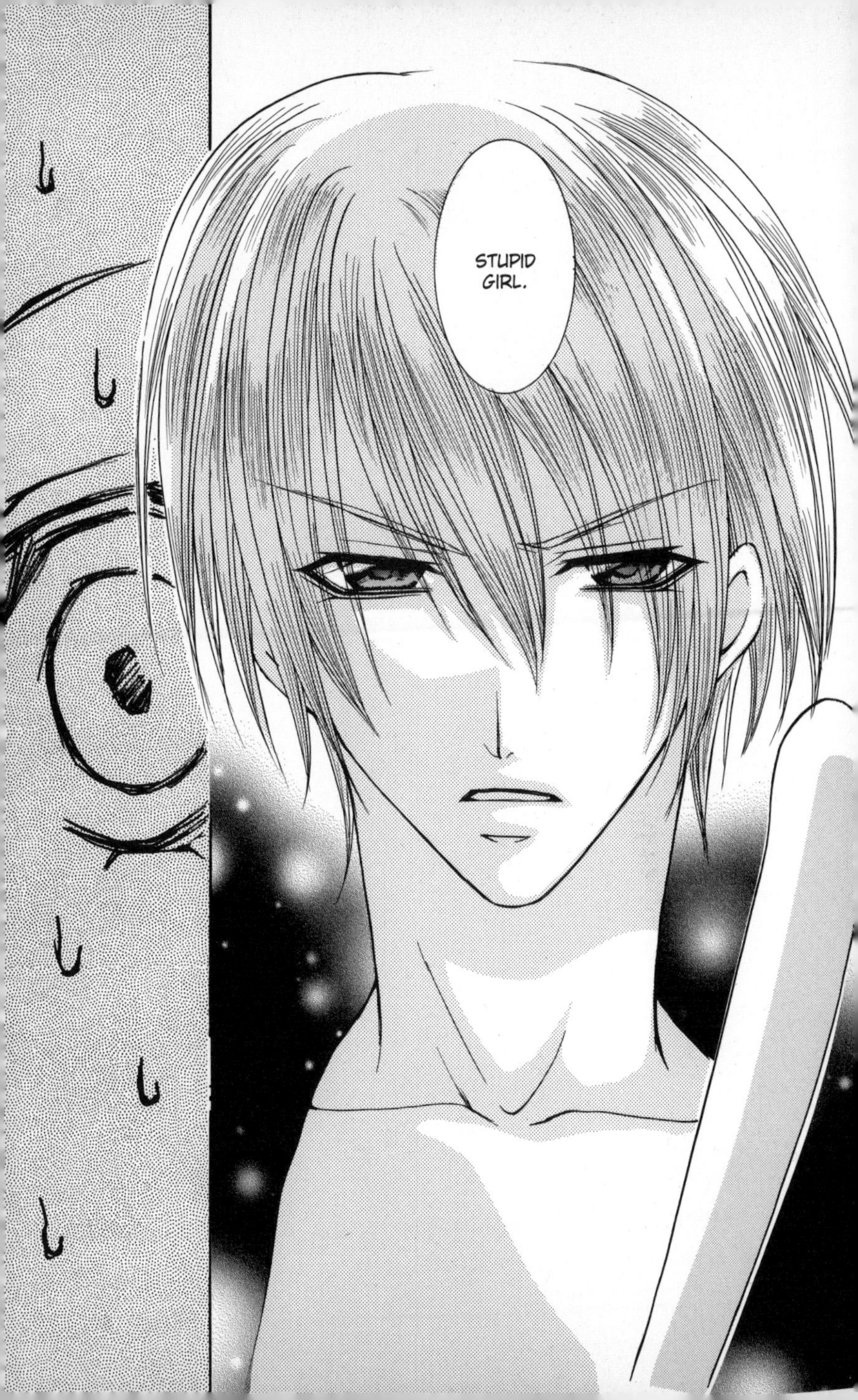
STUPID GIRL.

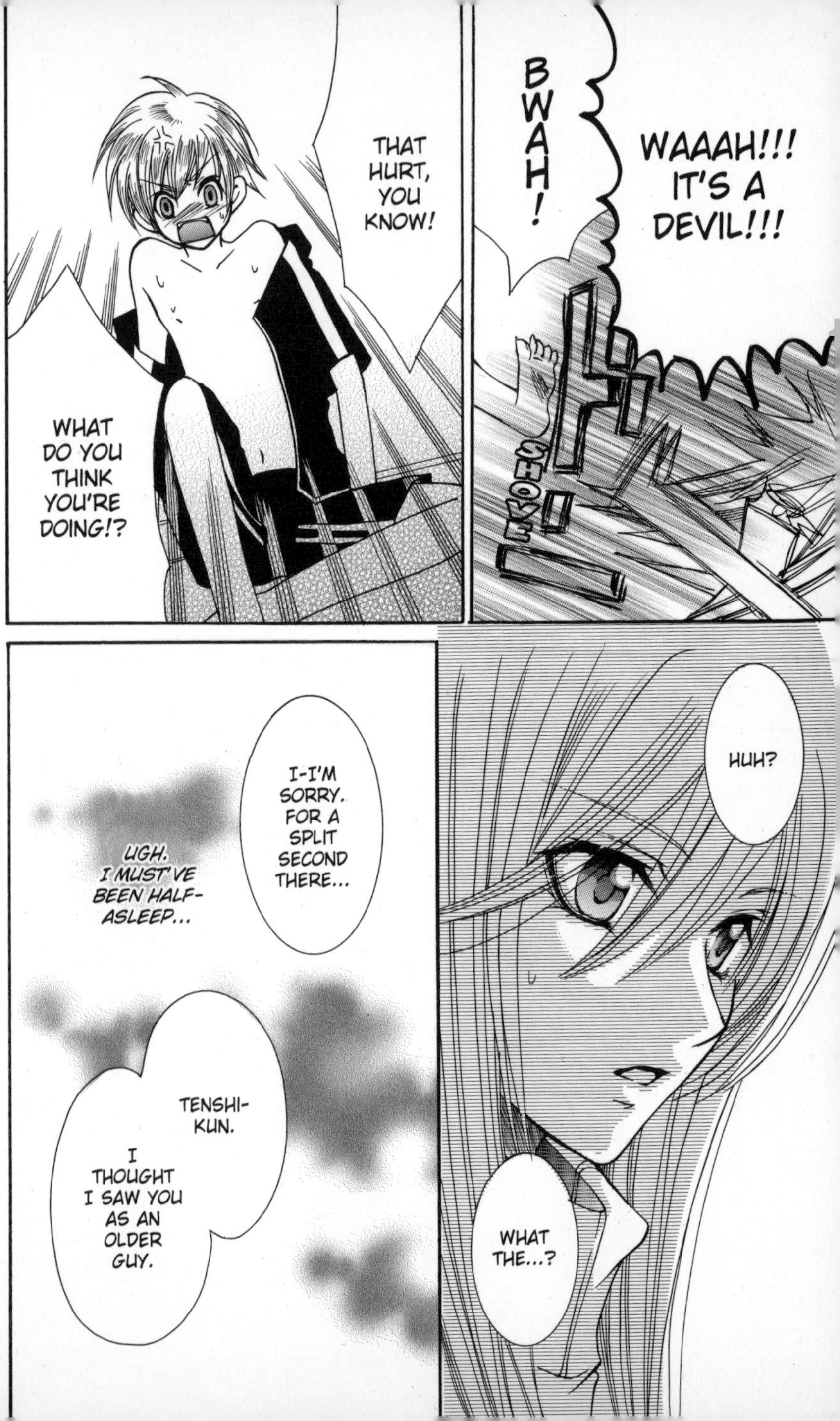
WAAAH!!! IT'S A DEVIL!!!
BWAH!
SHOVE
THAT HURT, YOU KNOW!
WHAT DO YOU THINK YOU'RE DOING!?
HUH?
WHAT THE...?
I-I'M SORRY. FOR A SPLIT SECOND THERE...
UGH. I MUST'VE BEEN HALF-ASLEEP...
TENSHI-KUN.
I THOUGHT I SAW YOU AS AN OLDER GUY.

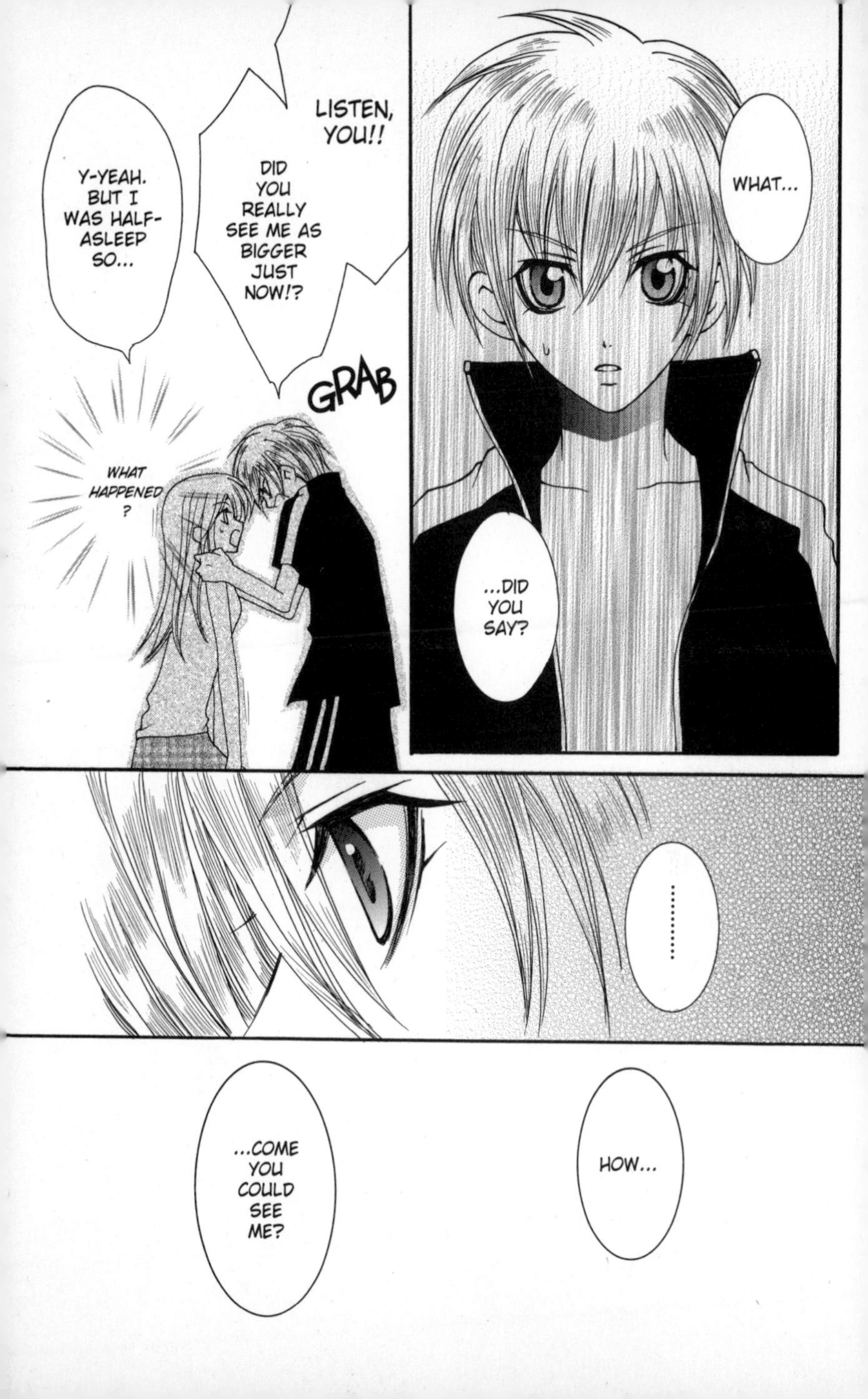
WHAT...
...DID YOU SAY?
LISTEN, YOU!!
DID YOU REALLY SEE ME AS BIGGER JUST NOW!?
GRAB
Y-YEAH. BUT I WAS HALF-ASLEEP SO...
WHAT HAPPENED?
......
HOW...
...COME YOU COULD SEE ME?

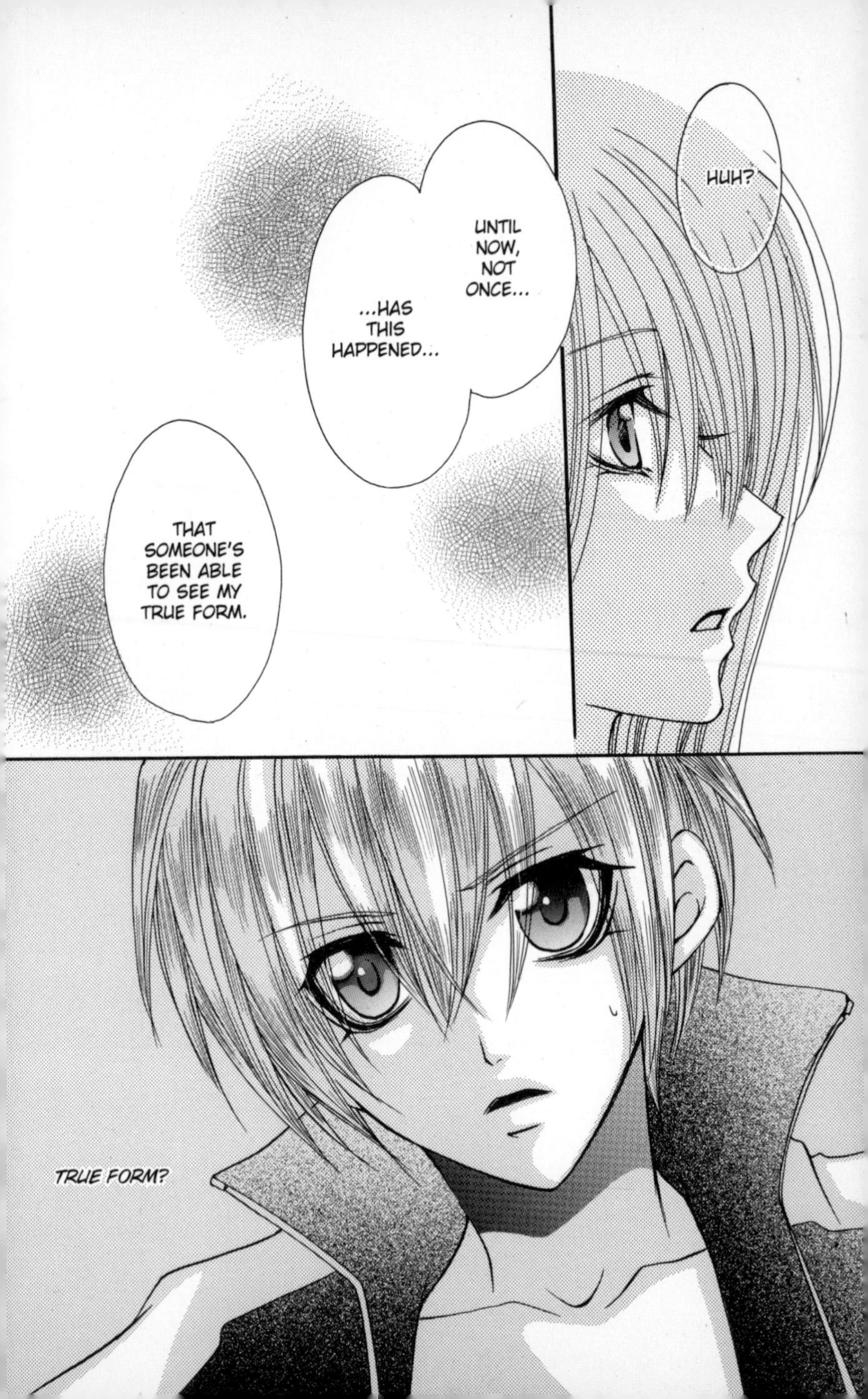
HUH?
UNTIL NOW, NOT ONCE...
...HAS THIS HAPPENED...
THAT SOMEONE'S BEEN ABLE TO SEE MY TRUE FORM.
TRUE FORM?

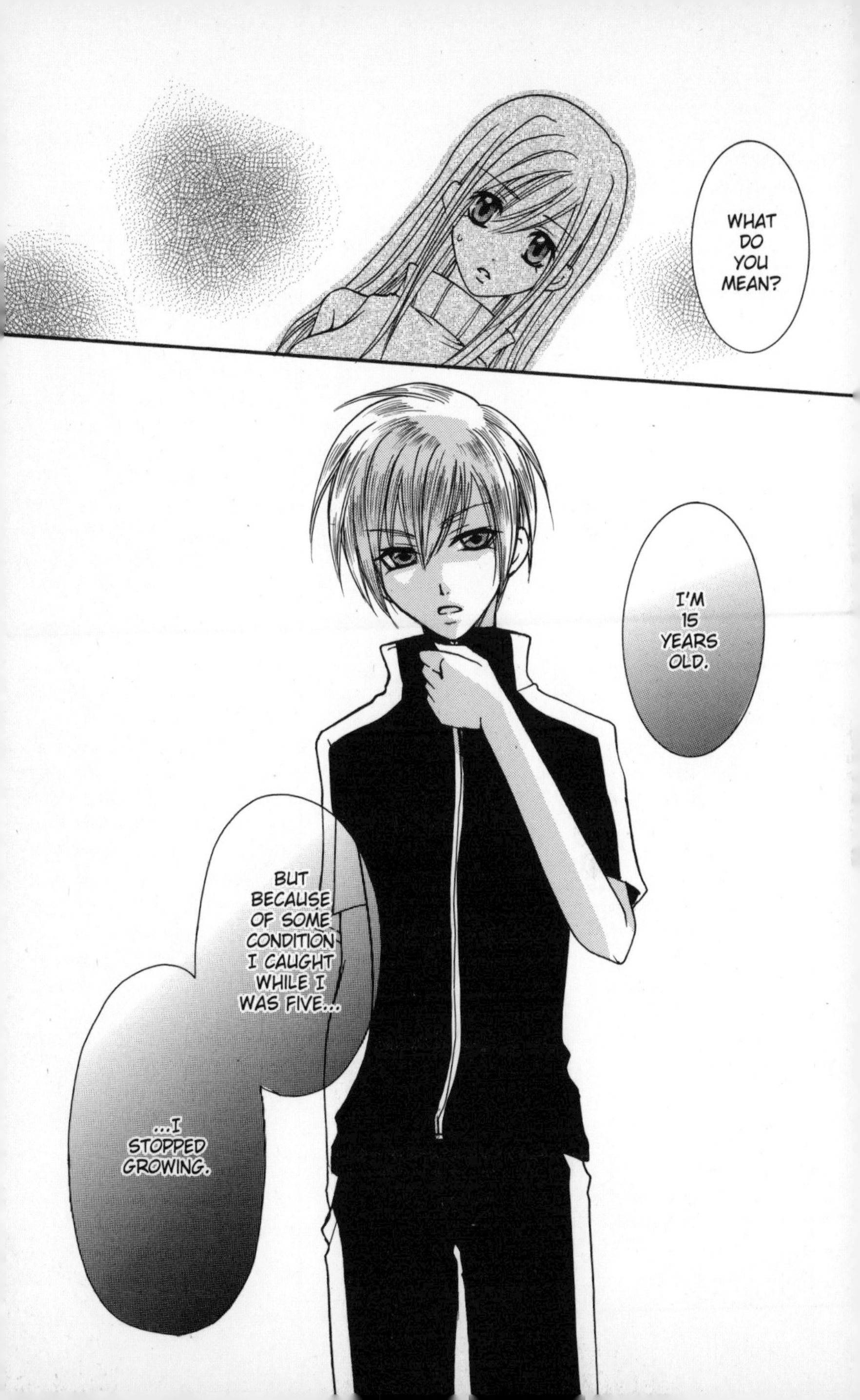
WHAT DO YOU MEAN?
I'M 15 YEARS OLD.
BUT BECAUSE OF SOME CONDITION I CAUGHT WHILE I WAS FIVE...
...I STOPPED GROWING.

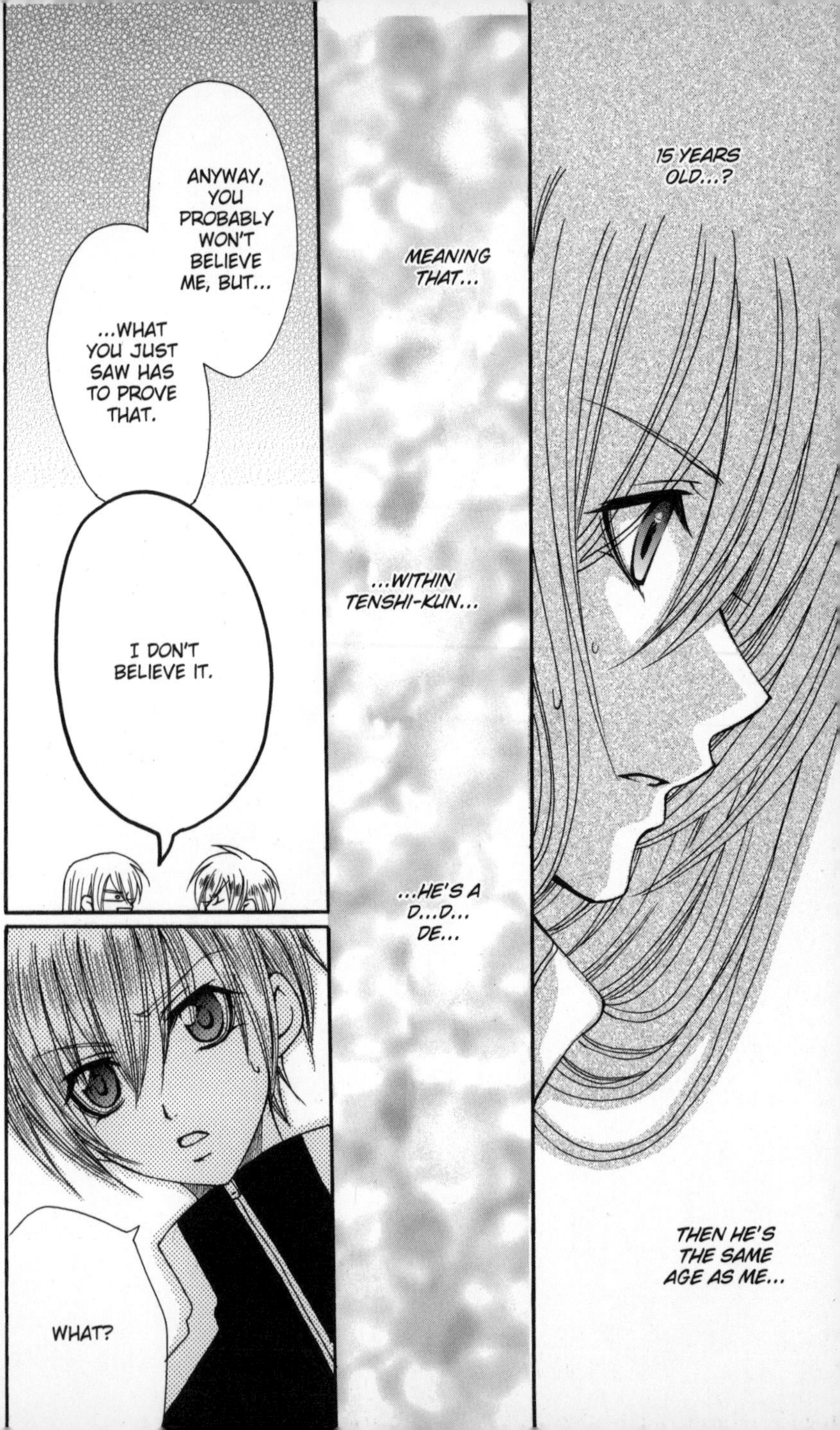
15 YEARS OLD...?
MEANING THAT...
...WITHIN TENSHI-KUN...
...HE'S A D...D... DE...
THEN HE'S THE SAME AGE AS ME...
ANYWAY, YOU PROBABLY WON'T BELIEVE ME, BUT...
...WHAT YOU JUST SAW HAS TO PROVE THAT.
I DON'T BELIEVE IT.
WHAT?

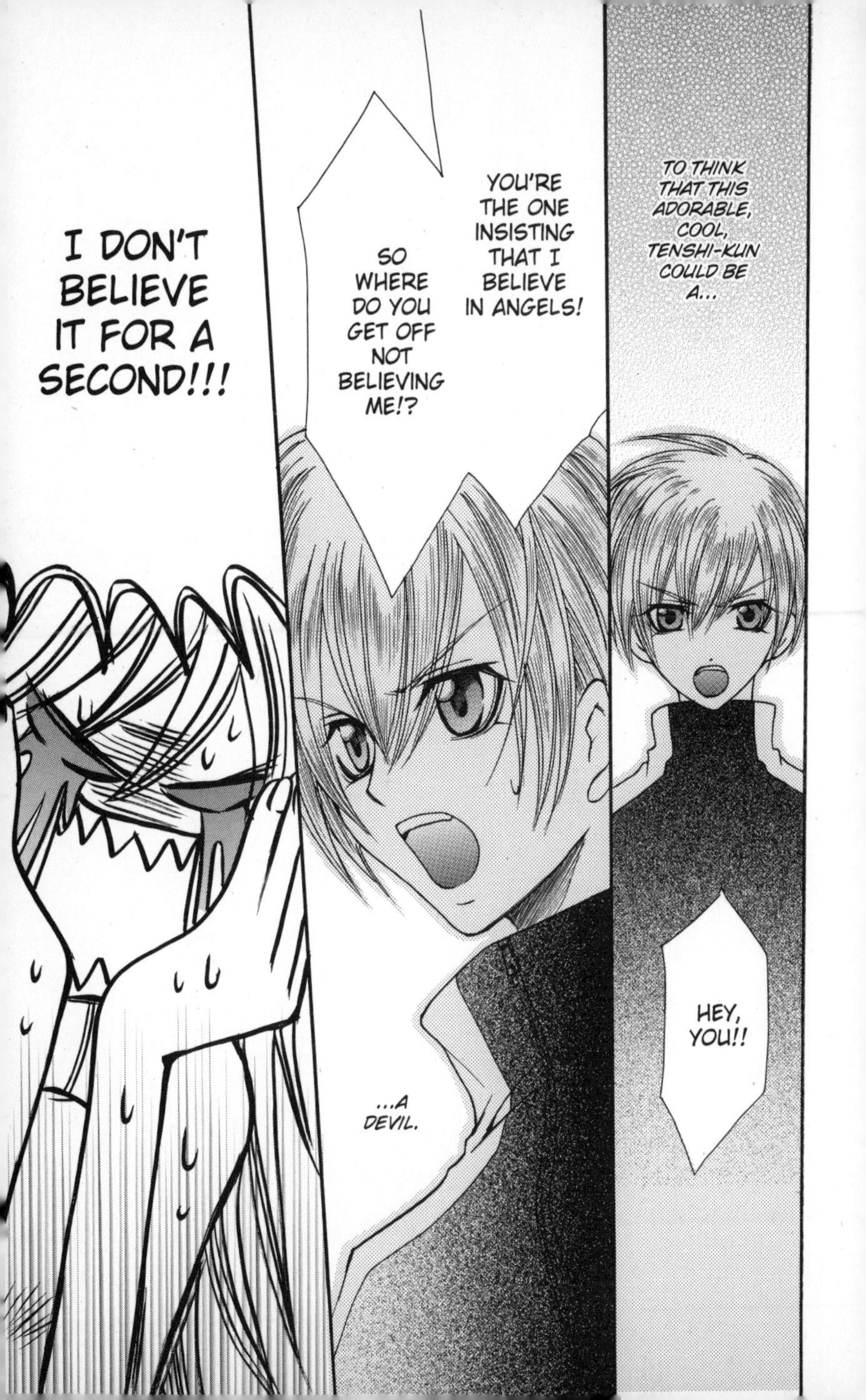
TO THINK THAT THIS ADORABLE, COOL, TENSHI-KUN COULD BE A...
HEY, YOU!!
...A DEVIL.
YOU'RE THE ONE INSISTING THAT I BELIEVE IN ANGELS!
SO WHERE DO YOU GET OFF NOT BELIEVING ME!?
I DON'T BELIEVE IT FOR A SECOND!!!

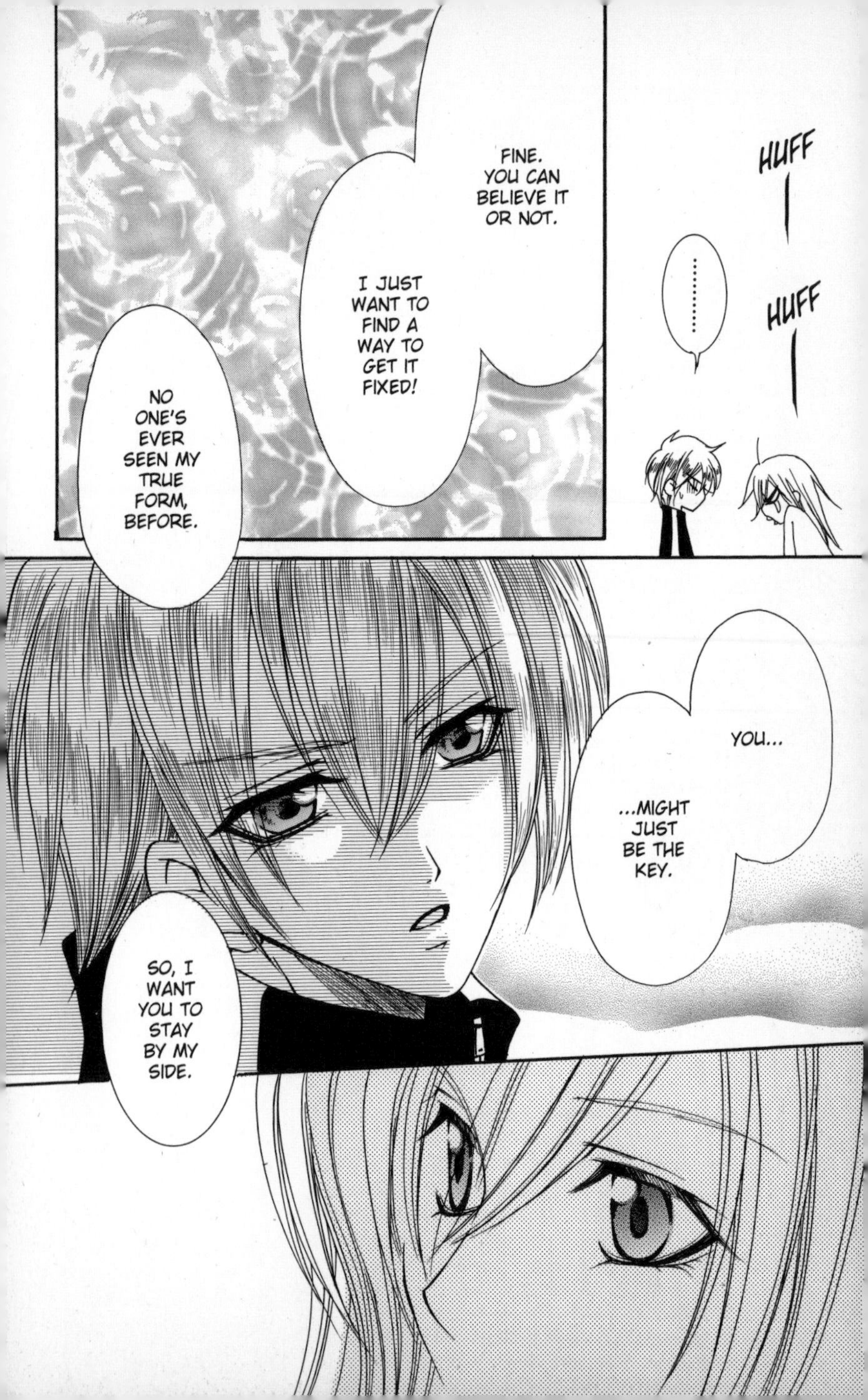
HUFF
HUFF
......
FINE. YOU CAN BELIEVE IT OR NOT.
I JUST WANT TO FIND A WAY TO GET IT FIXED!
NO ONE'S EVER SEEN MY TRUE FORM, BEFORE.
YOU...
...MIGHT JUST BE THE KEY.
SO, I WANT YOU TO STAY BY MY SIDE.

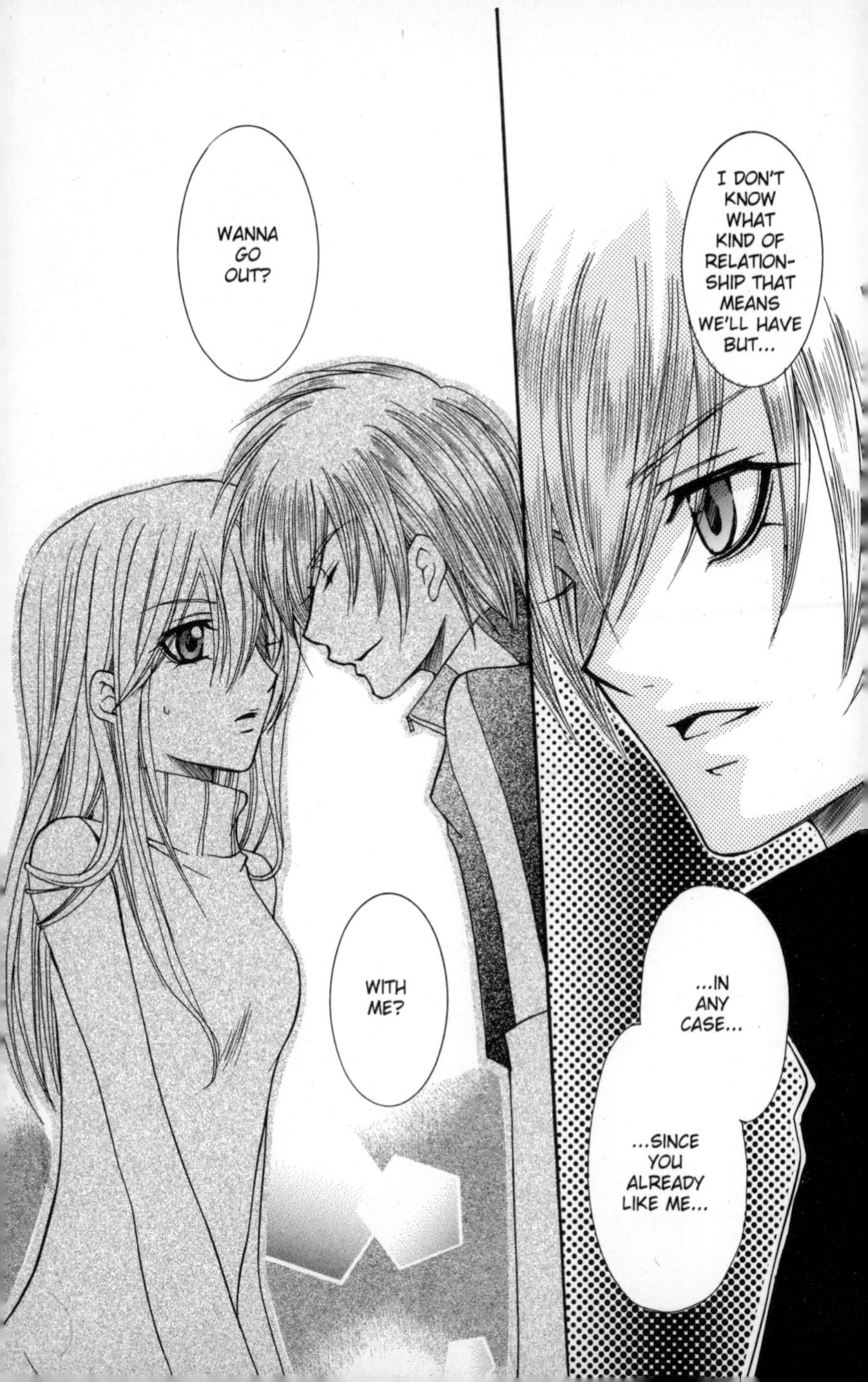
I DON'T KNOW WHAT KIND OF RELATION-SHIP THAT MEANS WE'LL HAVE BUT...
...IN ANY CASE...
...SINCE YOU ALREADY LIKE ME...
WANNA GO OUT?
WITH ME?

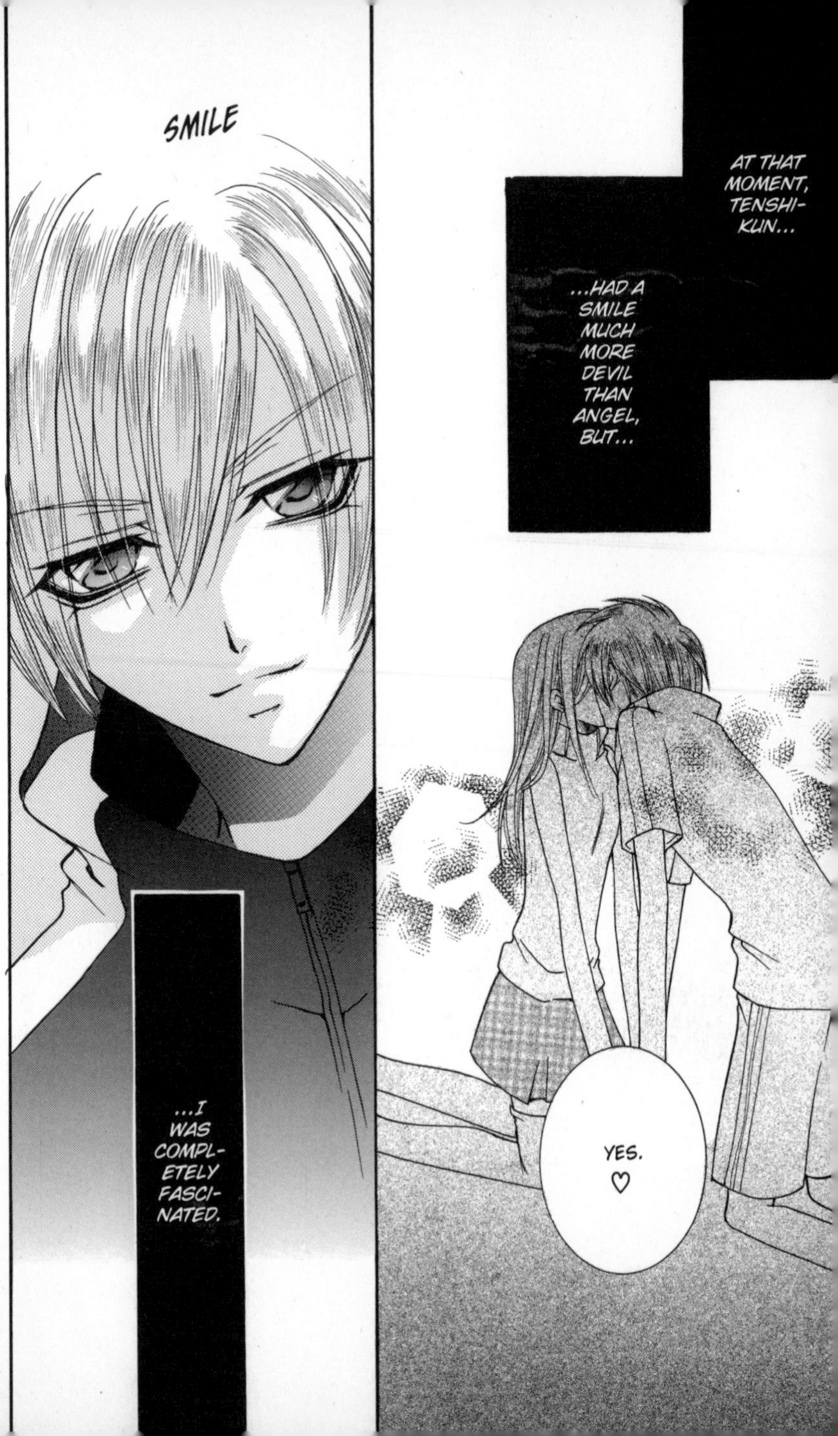

AT THAT MOMENT, TENSHI-KUN...
...HAD A SMILE MUCH MORE DEVIL THAN ANGEL, BUT...
YES. ♡
SMILE
...I WAS COMPLETELY FASCINATED.

Chibi Angel Chibi Devil (2)

◀ Chibi Wind Version ▶

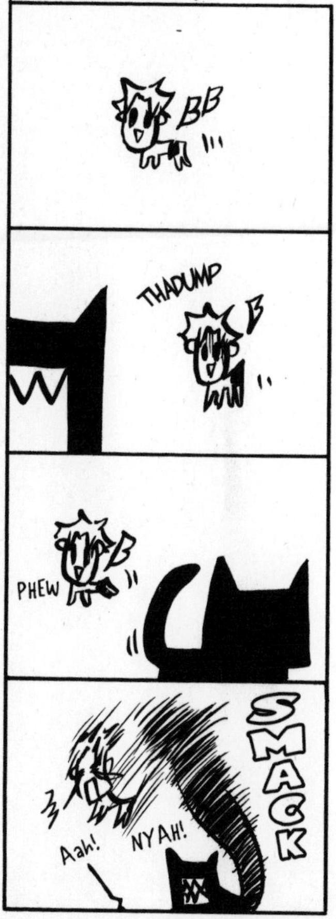

BB
THADUMP
B
PHEW
B
SMACK
Aah!
NYAH!

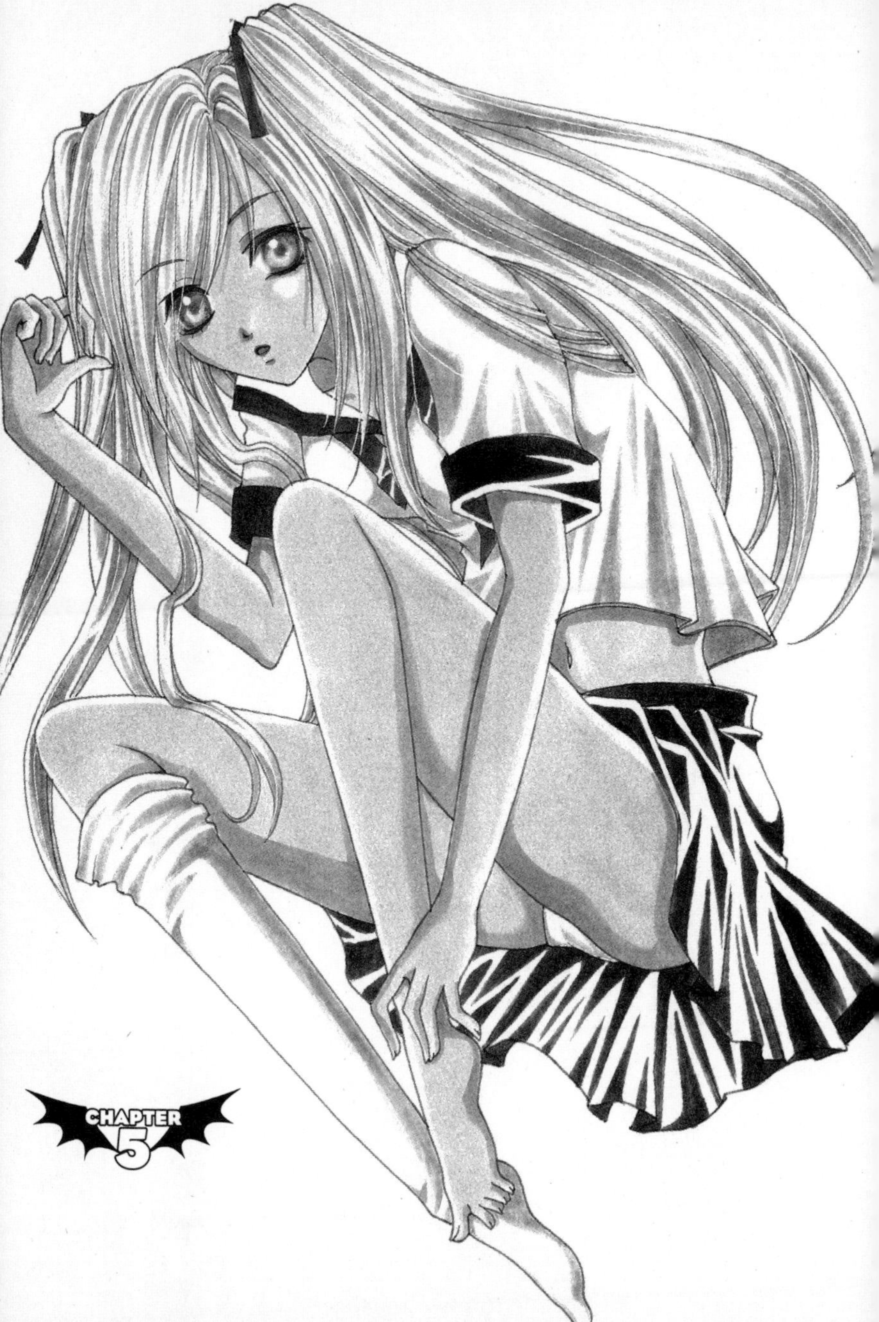
CHAPTER
5

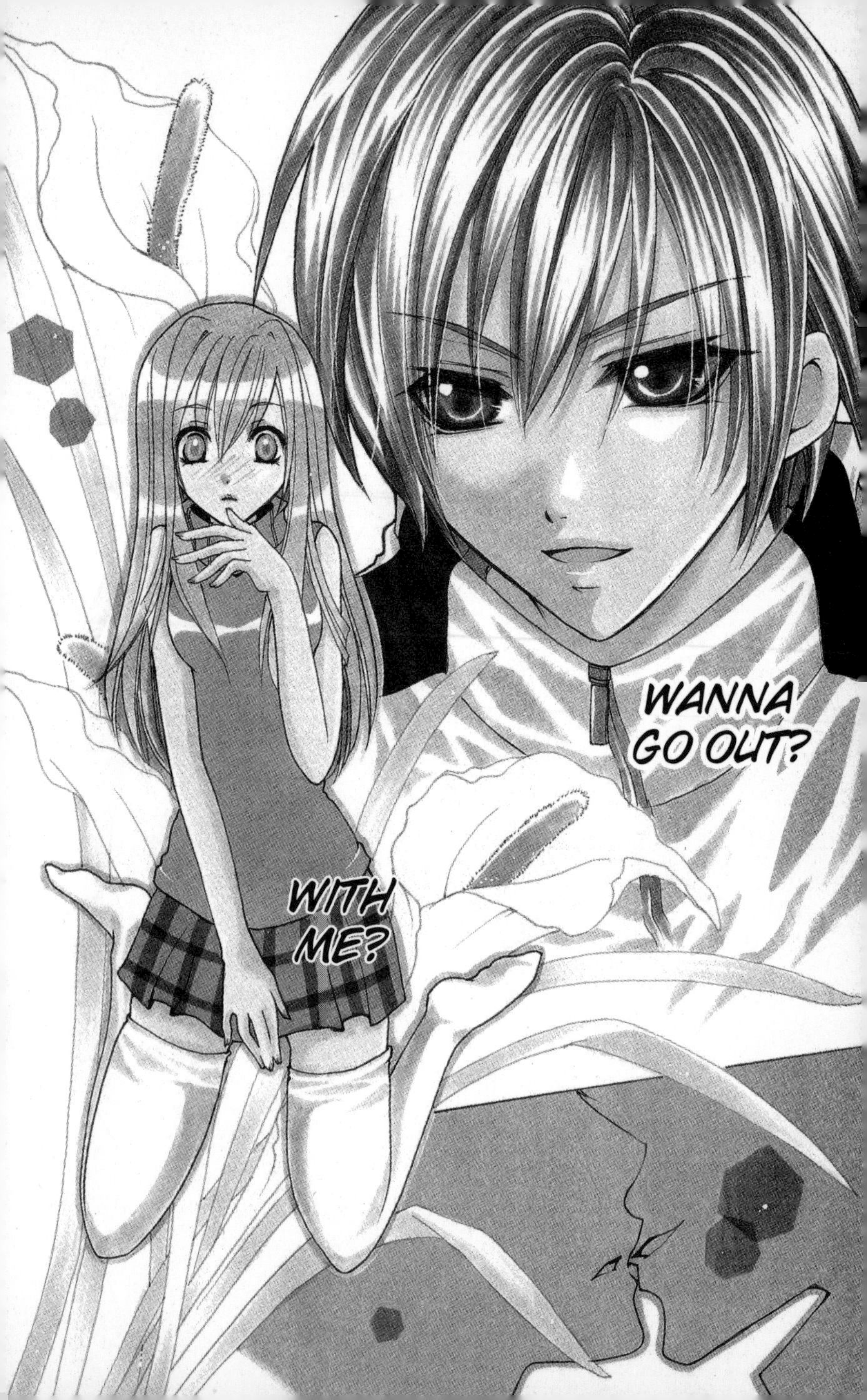
WANNA GO OUT?
WITH ME?

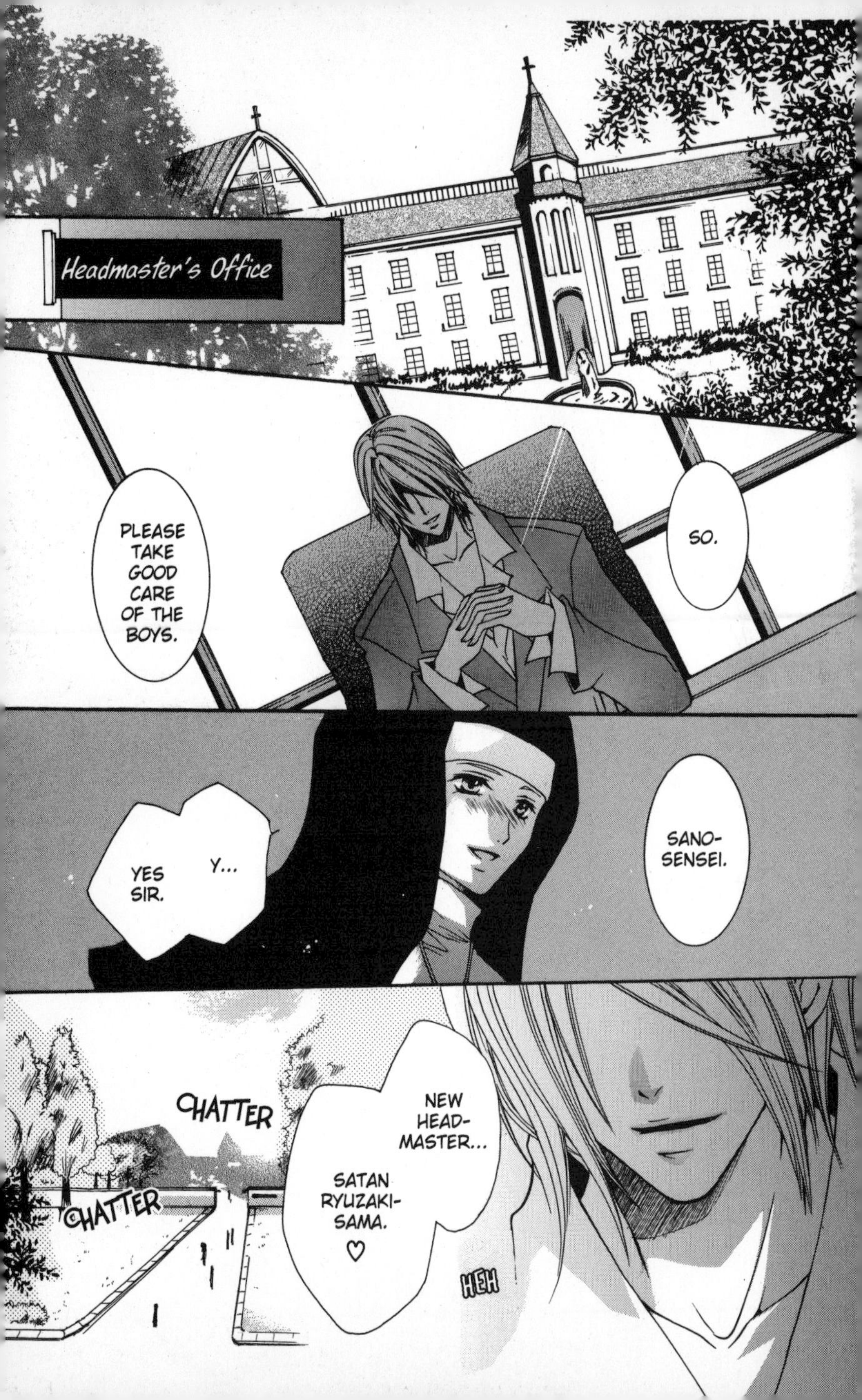
Headmaster's Office
SO.
PLEASE TAKE GOOD CARE OF THE BOYS.
SANO-SENSEI.
Y... YES SIR.
HEH
NEW HEAD-MASTER... SATAN RYUZAKI-SAMA. ♡
CHATTER
CHATTER

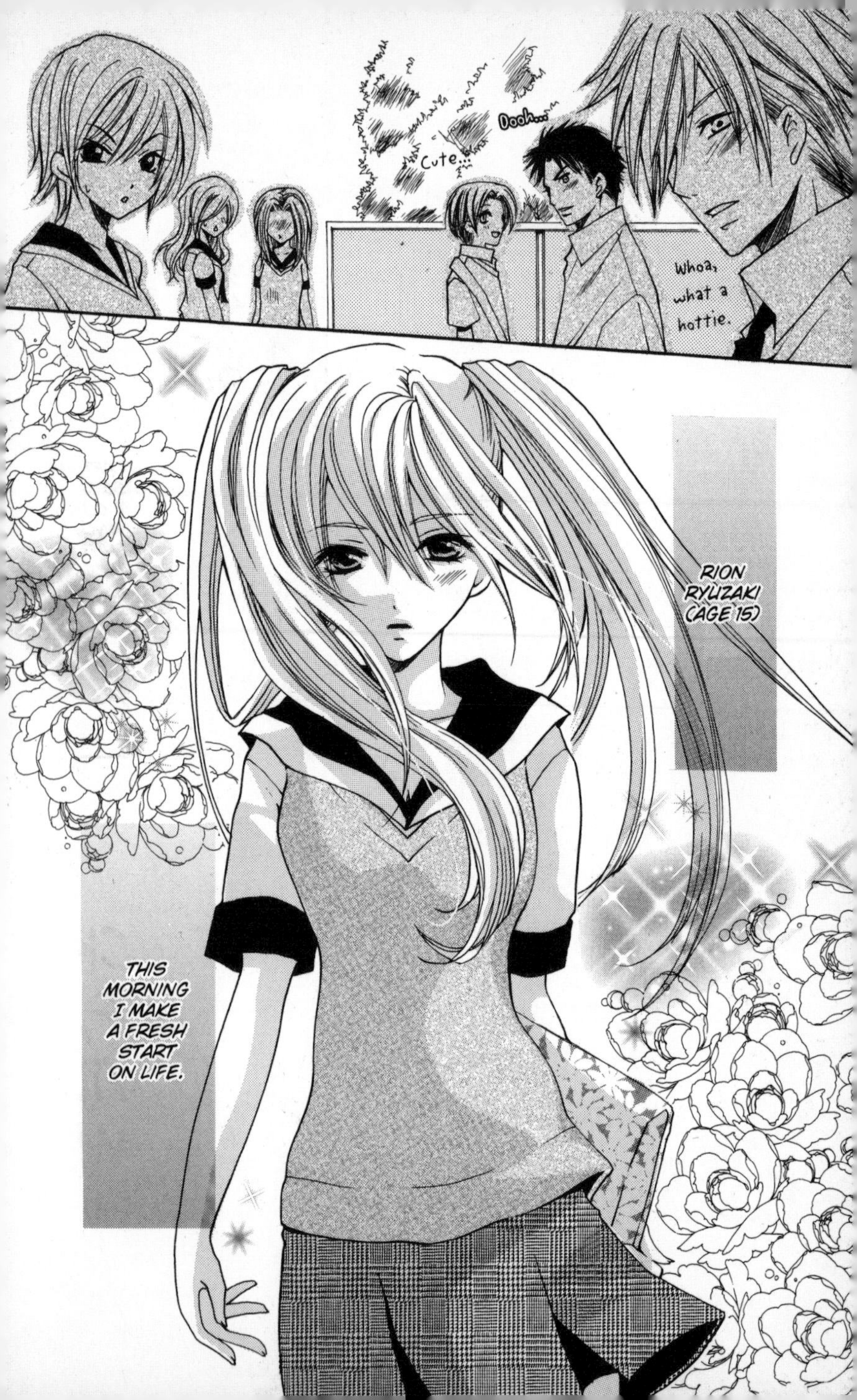
Whoa, what a hottie.
Oooh...
Cute...
RION RYUZAKI (AGE 15)
THIS MORNING I MAKE A FRESH START ON LIFE.

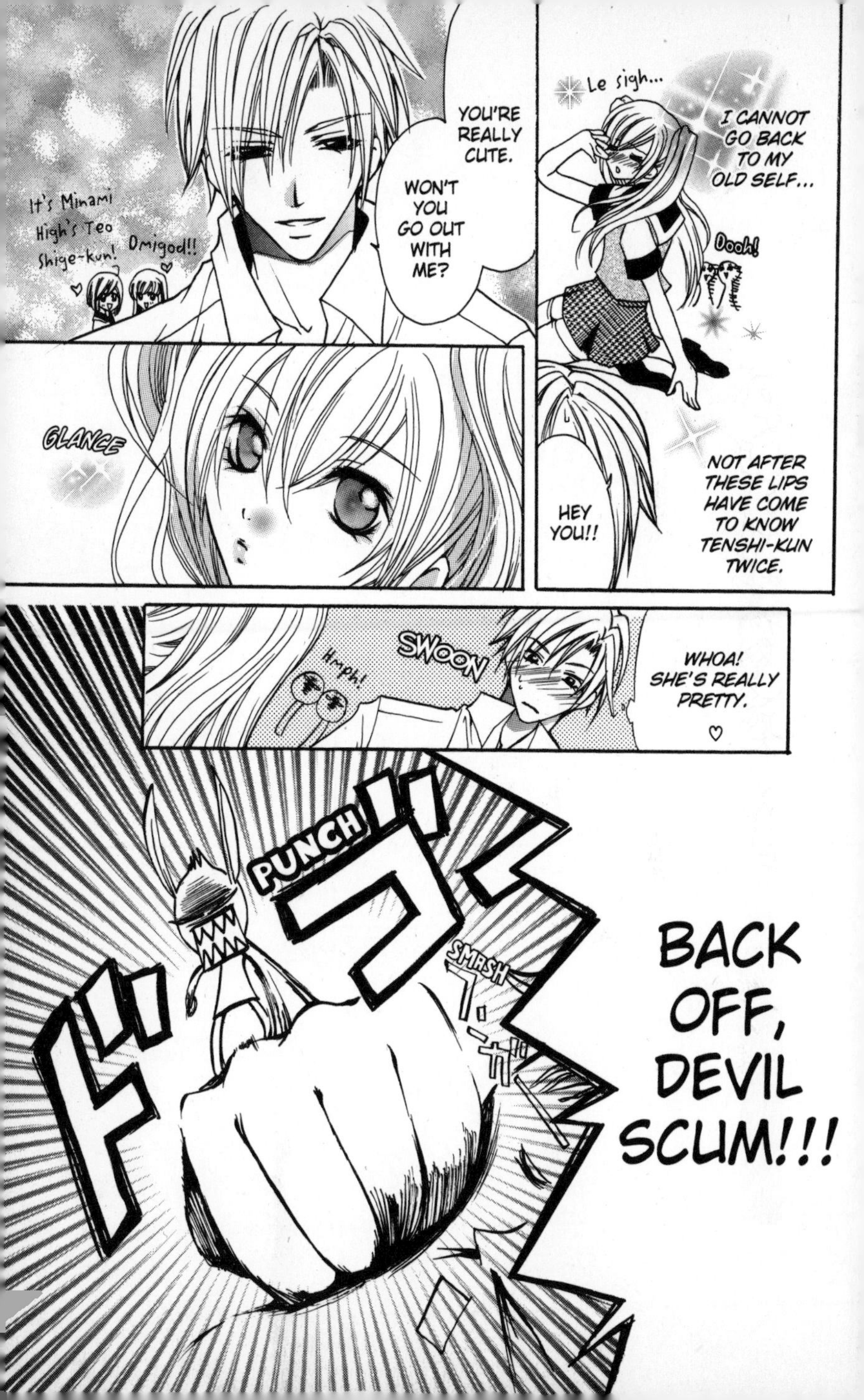
It's Minami High's Teo Shige-kun!
Omigod!!
YOU'RE REALLY CUTE.
WON'T YOU GO OUT WITH ME?
Le sigh...
I CANNOT GO BACK TO MY OLD SELF...
Oooh!
NOT AFTER THESE LIPS HAVE COME TO KNOW TENSHI-KUN TWICE.
HEY YOU!!
GLANCE
SWOON
Hmph!
WHOA! SHE'S REALLY PRETTY.
PUNCH
SMASH
BACK OFF, DEVIL SCUM!!!

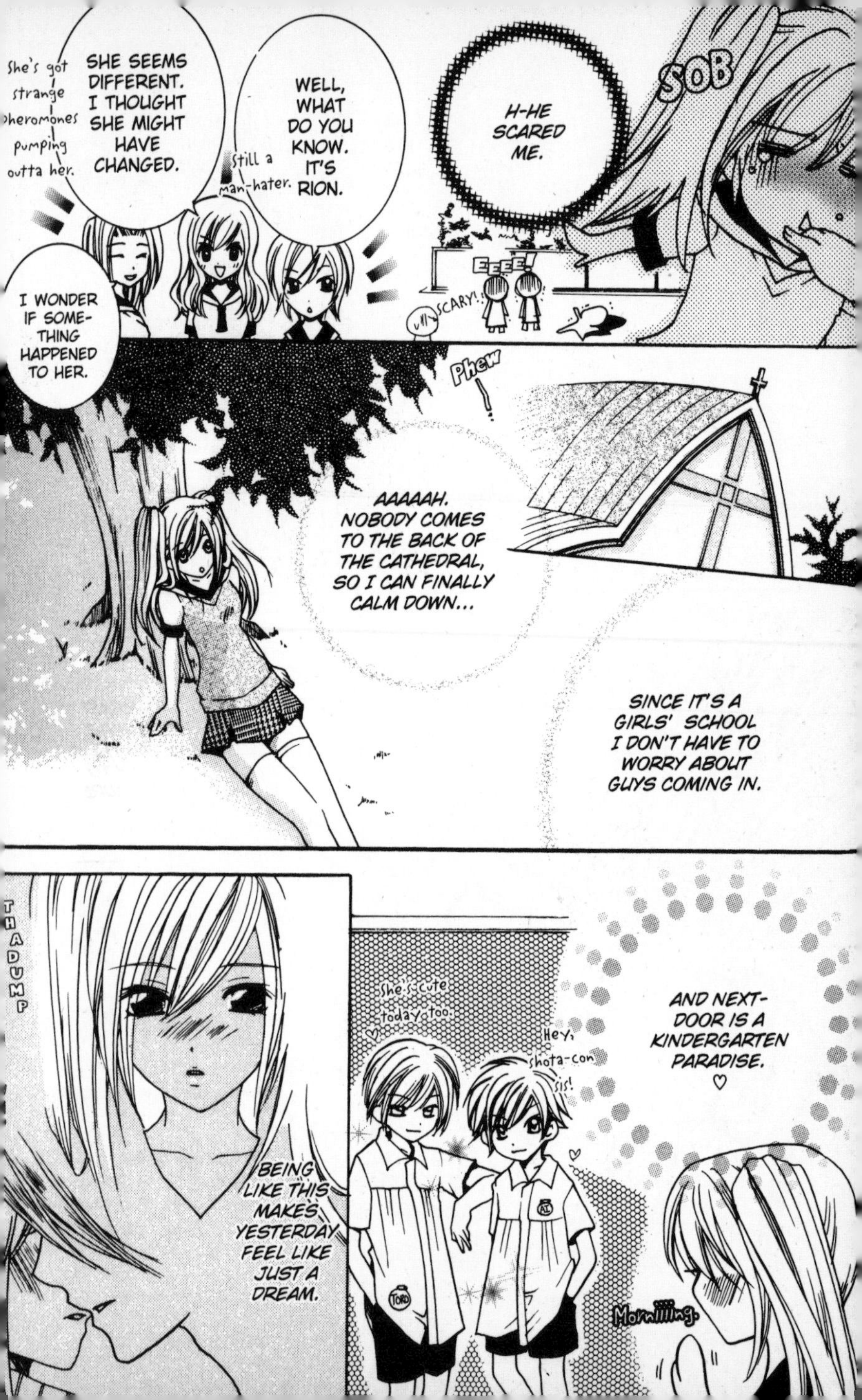
SOB
H-HE SCARED ME.
EEEE!
SCARY!
WELL, WHAT DO YOU KNOW. IT'S RION.
Still a man-hater.
SHE SEEMS DIFFERENT. I THOUGHT SHE MIGHT HAVE CHANGED.
She's got strange heromones pumping outta her.
I WONDER IF SOME-THING HAPPENED TO HER.
Phew
AAAAAH. NOBODY COMES TO THE BACK OF THE CATHEDRAL, SO I CAN FINALLY CALM DOWN...
SINCE IT'S A GIRLS' SCHOOL I DON'T HAVE TO WORRY ABOUT GUYS COMING IN.
AND NEXT-DOOR IS A KINDERGARTEN PARADISE. ♡
She's cute today, too.
Hey, shota-con sis!
Morniiing.
THADUMP
BEING LIKE THIS MAKES YESTERDAY FEEL LIKE JUST A DREAM.

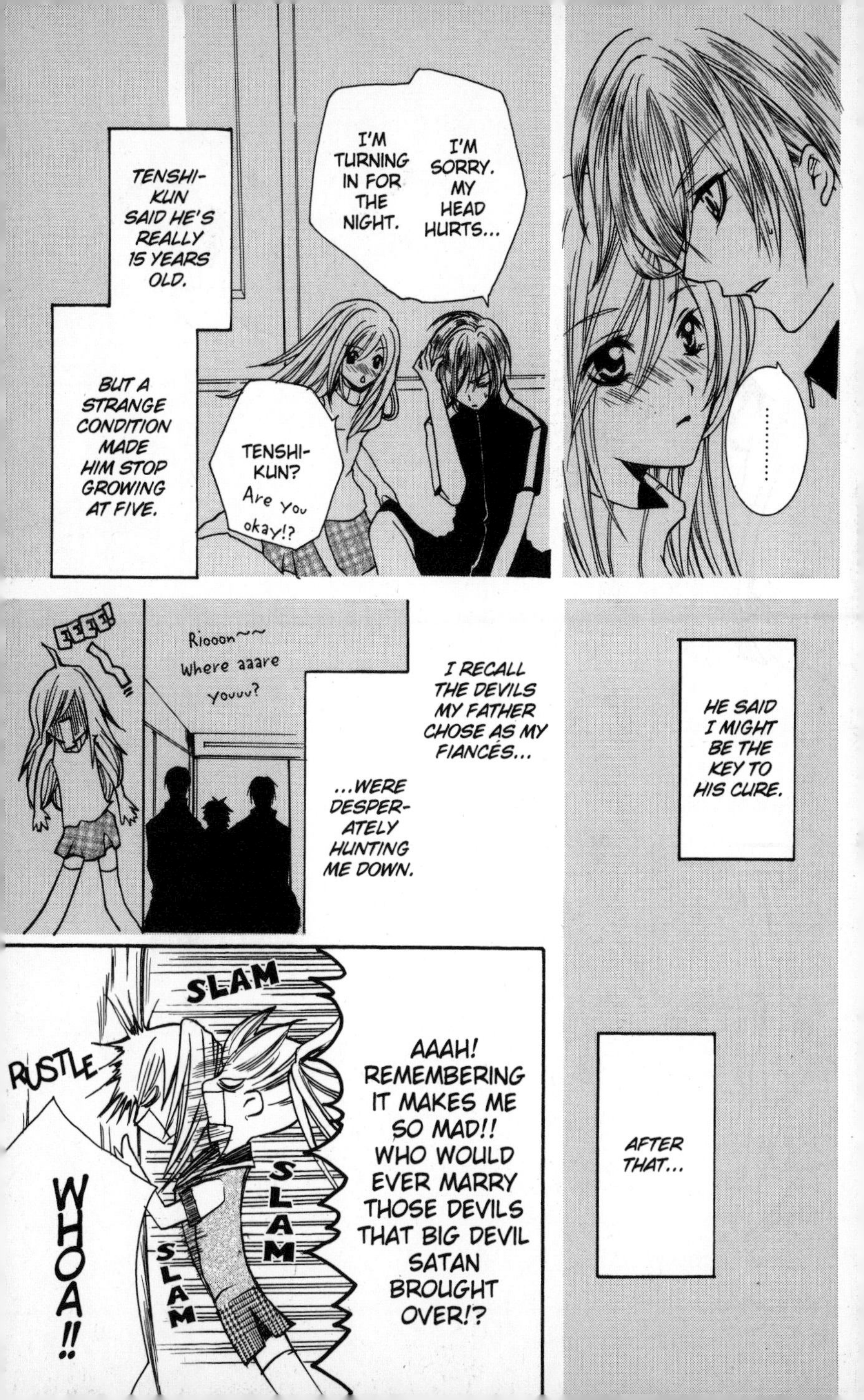

TENSHI-KUN SAID HE'S REALLY 15 YEARS OLD.
BUT A STRANGE CONDITION MADE HIM STOP GROWING AT FIVE.
TENSHI-KUN? Are you okay!?
I'M SORRY. MY HEAD HURTS...
I'M TURNING IN FOR THE NIGHT.
......
HE SAID I MIGHT BE THE KEY TO HIS CURE.
AFTER THAT...
I RECALL THE DEVILS MY FATHER CHOSE AS MY FIANCÉS...
...WERE DESPERATELY HUNTING ME DOWN.
Riooon~~ Where aaare youuu?
AAAH! REMEMBERING IT MAKES ME SO MAD!! WHO WOULD EVER MARRY THOSE DEVILS THAT BIG DEVIL SATAN BROUGHT OVER!?
SLAM
SLAM
SLAM
RUSTLE
WHOA!!

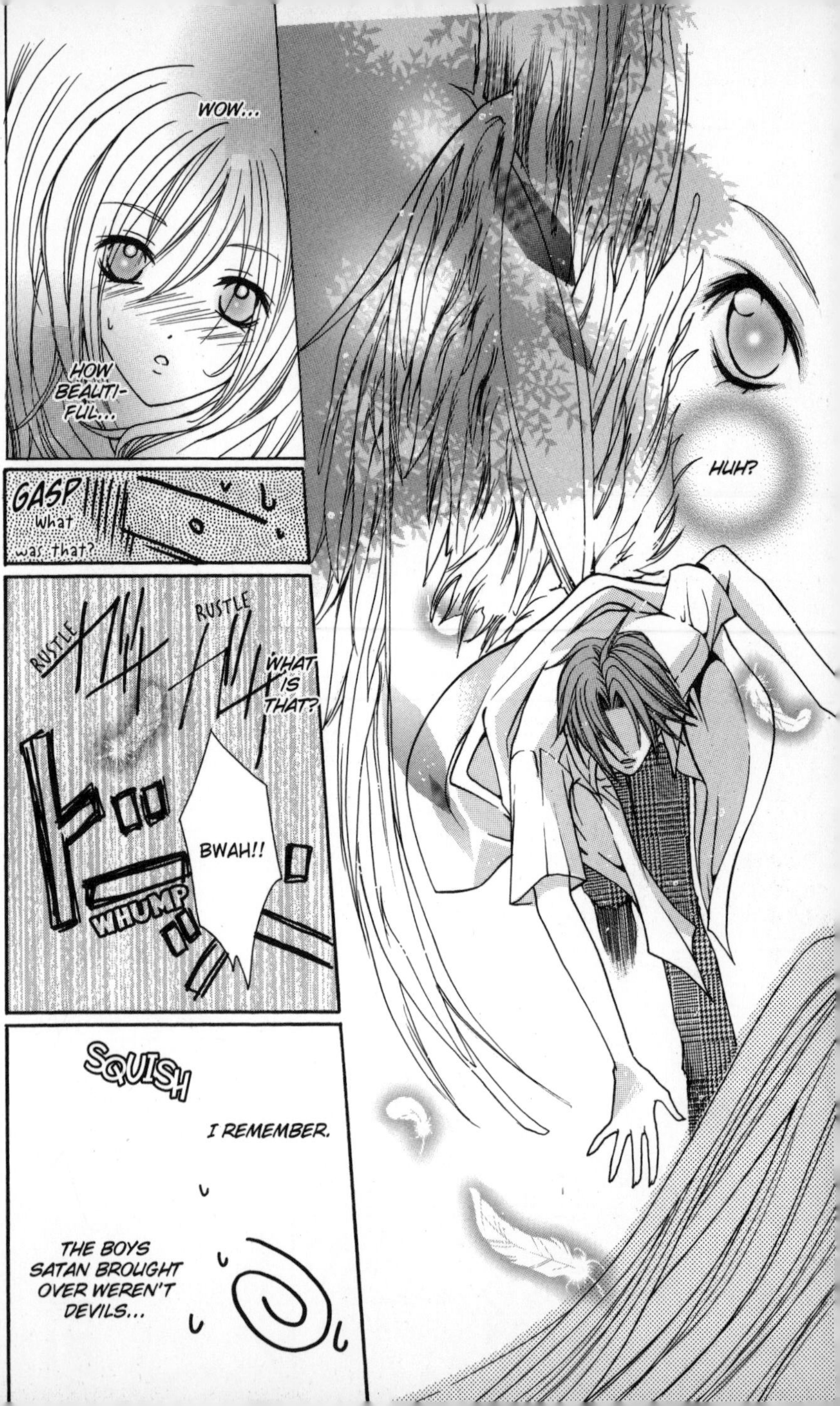
HUH?
WOW...
HOW BEAUTI-FUL...
GASP
what was that?
RUSTLE
RUSTLE
WHAT IS THAT?
BWAH!!
WHUMP
SQUISH
I REMEMBER.
THE BOYS SATAN BROUGHT OVER WEREN'T DEVILS...

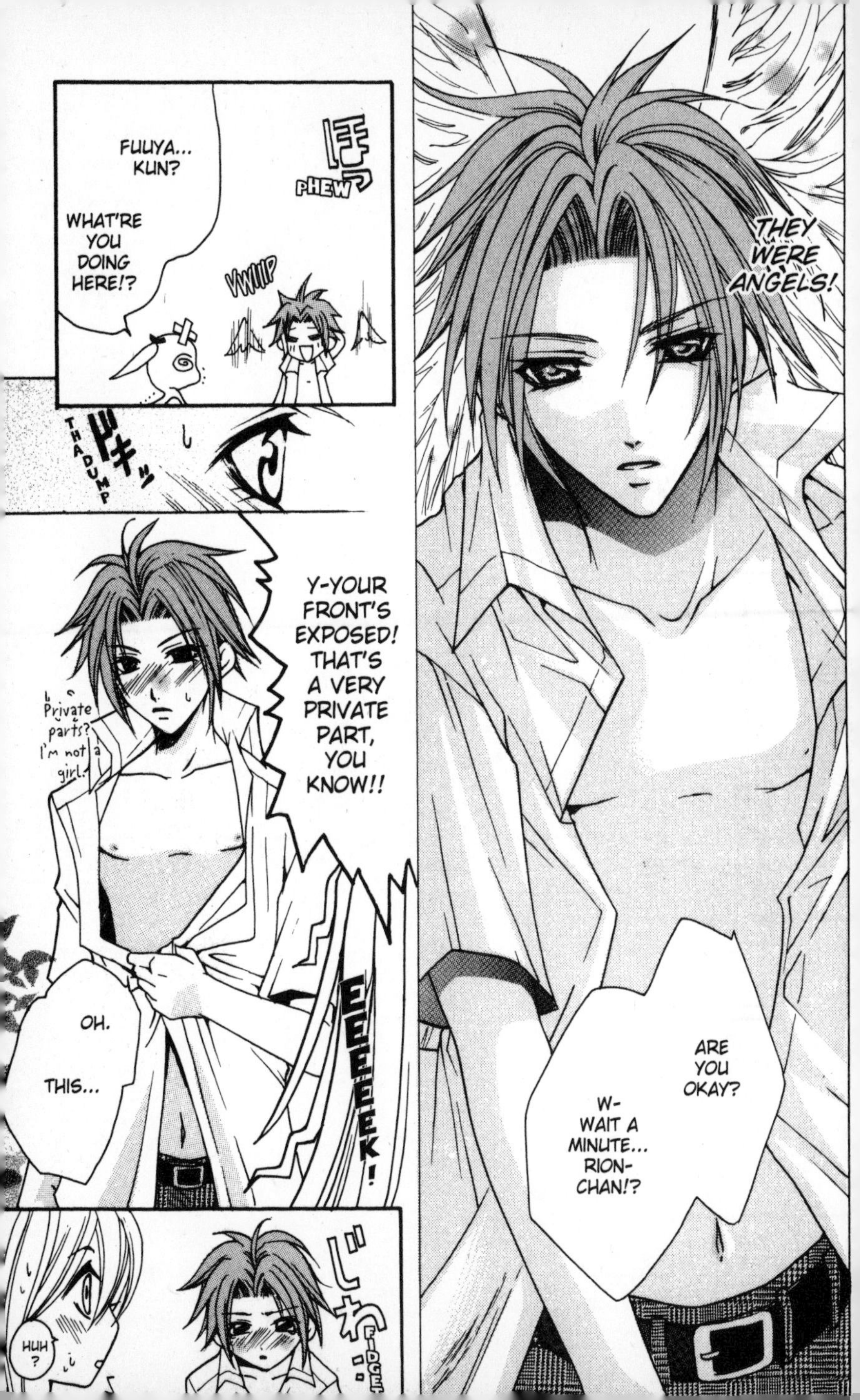
THEY WERE ANGELS!
ARE YOU OKAY?
W-WAIT A MINUTE... RION-CHAN!?
FUUYA... KUN?
WHAT'RE YOU DOING HERE!?
PHEW
VWIIIP
THADUMP
Y-YOUR FRONT'S EXPOSED! THAT'S A VERY PRIVATE PART, YOU KNOW!!
EEEEEEEK!
OH.
THIS...
Private parts? I'm not a girl.
FIDGET
HUH?

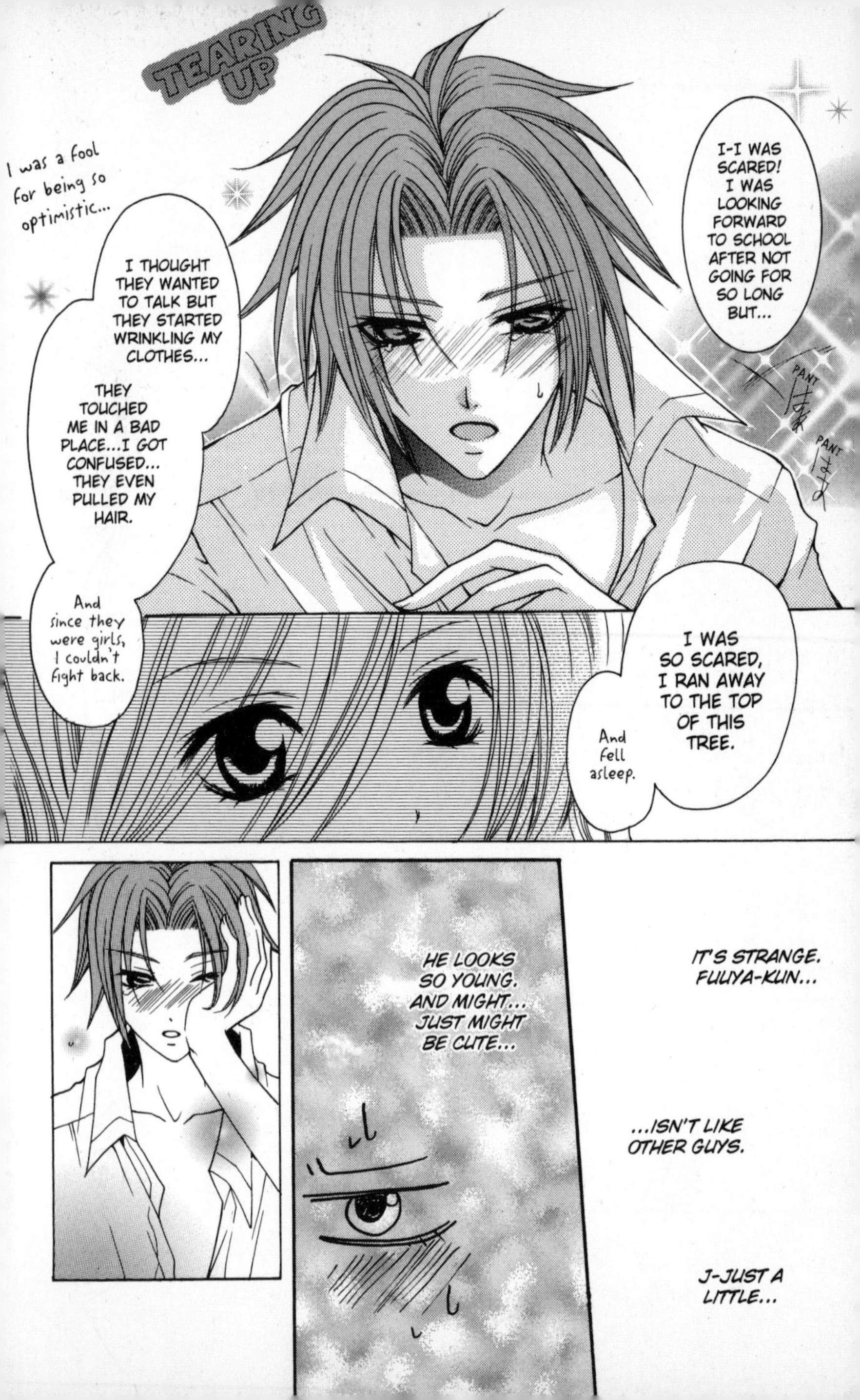
TEARING UP
I-I WAS SCARED! I WAS LOOKING FORWARD TO SCHOOL AFTER NOT GOING FOR SO LONG BUT...
PANT
PANT
I THOUGHT THEY WANTED TO TALK BUT THEY STARTED WRINKLING MY CLOTHES...
THEY TOUCHED ME IN A BAD PLACE...I GOT CONFUSED... THEY EVEN PULLED MY HAIR.
I was a fool for being so optimistic...
I WAS SO SCARED, I RAN AWAY TO THE TOP OF THIS TREE.
And fell asleep.
And since they were girls, I couldn't fight back.
IT'S STRANGE. FUUYA-KUN...
...ISN'T LIKE OTHER GUYS.
J-JUST A LITTLE...
HE LOOKS SO YOUNG. AND MIGHT... JUST MIGHT BE CUTE...

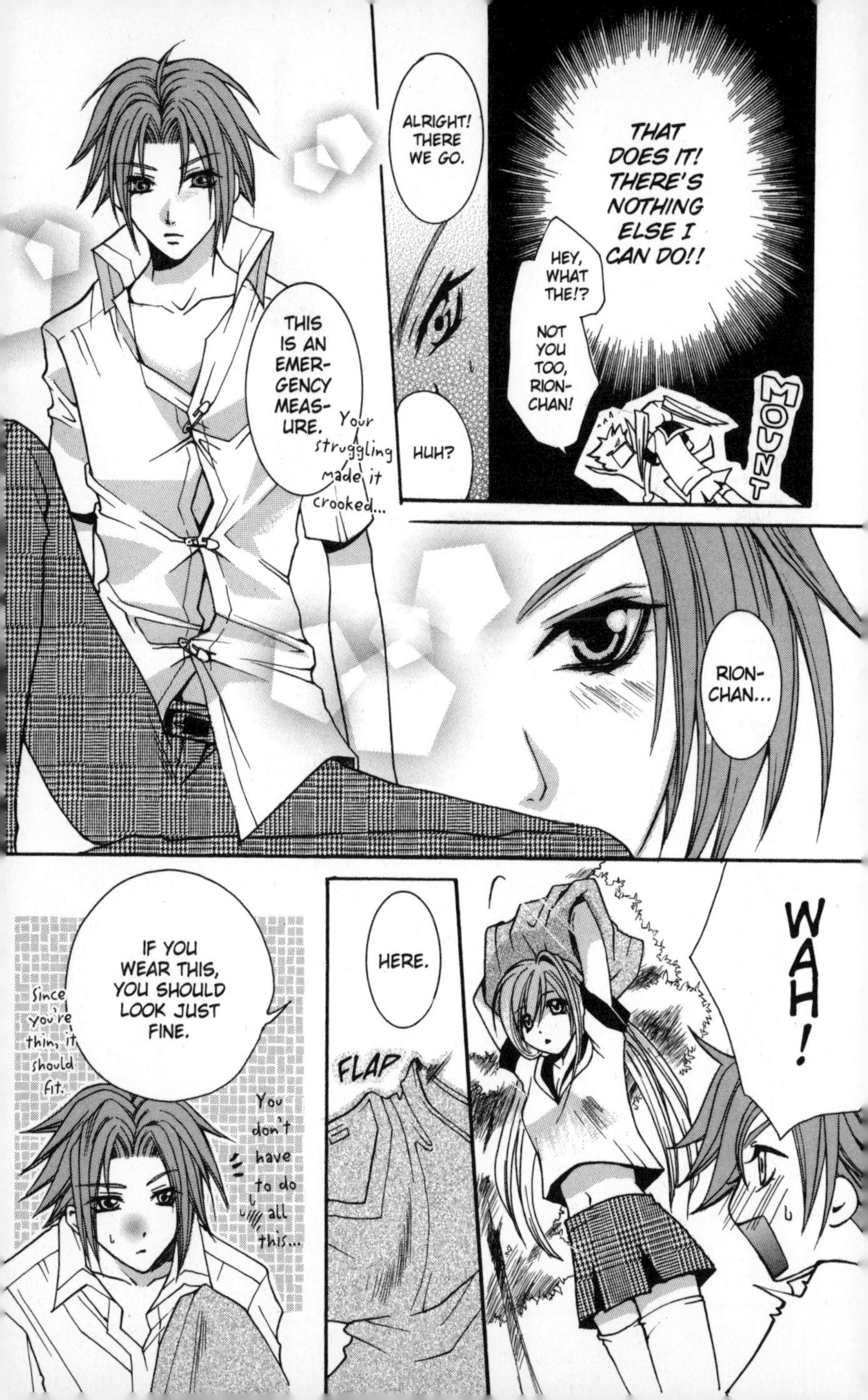
THAT DOES IT! THERE'S NOTHING ELSE I CAN DO!!
HEY, WHAT THE!?
NOT YOU TOO, RION-CHAN!
MOUNT
ALRIGHT! THERE WE GO.
HUH?
THIS IS AN EMER-GENCY MEAS-URE.
Your struggling made it crooked...
RION-CHAN...
WAH!
HERE.
FLAP
IF YOU WEAR THIS, YOU SHOULD LOOK JUST FINE.
Since you're thin, it should fit.
You don't have to do all this...

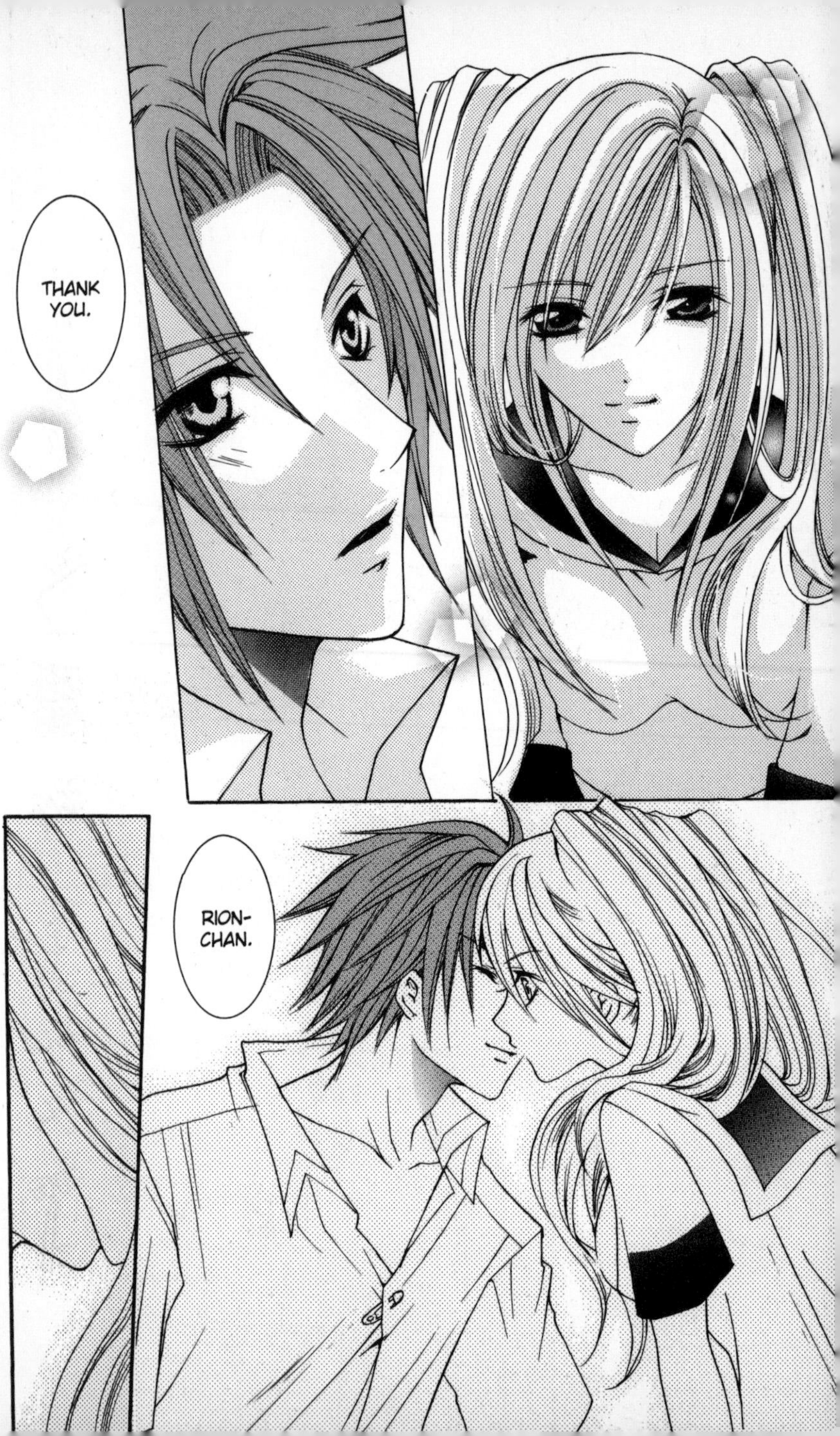
THANK YOU.
RION-CHAN.

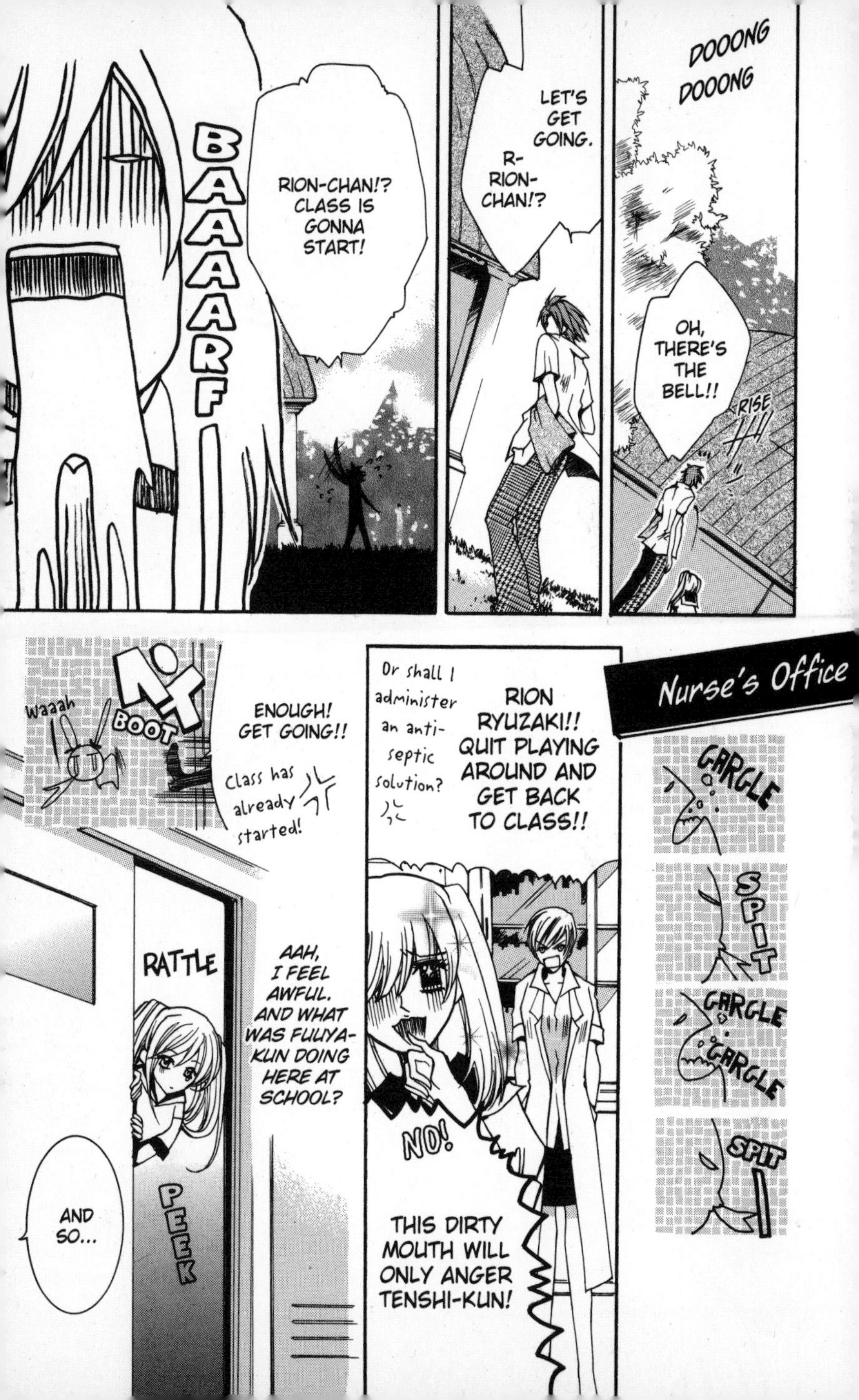
DOOONG
DOOONG
OH, THERE'S THE BELL!!
RISE
LET'S GET GOING.
R-RION-CHAN!?
RION-CHAN!? CLASS IS GONNA START!
BAAAAARF
Nurse's Office
GARGLE
SPIT
GARGLE
GARGLE
SPIT
RION RYUZAKI!! QUIT PLAYING AROUND AND GET BACK TO CLASS!!
Or shall I administer an anti-septic solution?
ENOUGH! GET GOING!!
Class has already started!
BOOT
waaah
NO!
THIS DIRTY MOUTH WILL ONLY ANGER TENSHI-KUN!
AAH, I FEEL AWFUL. AND WHAT WAS FUUYA-KUN DOING HERE AT SCHOOL?
RATTLE
PEEK
AND SO...

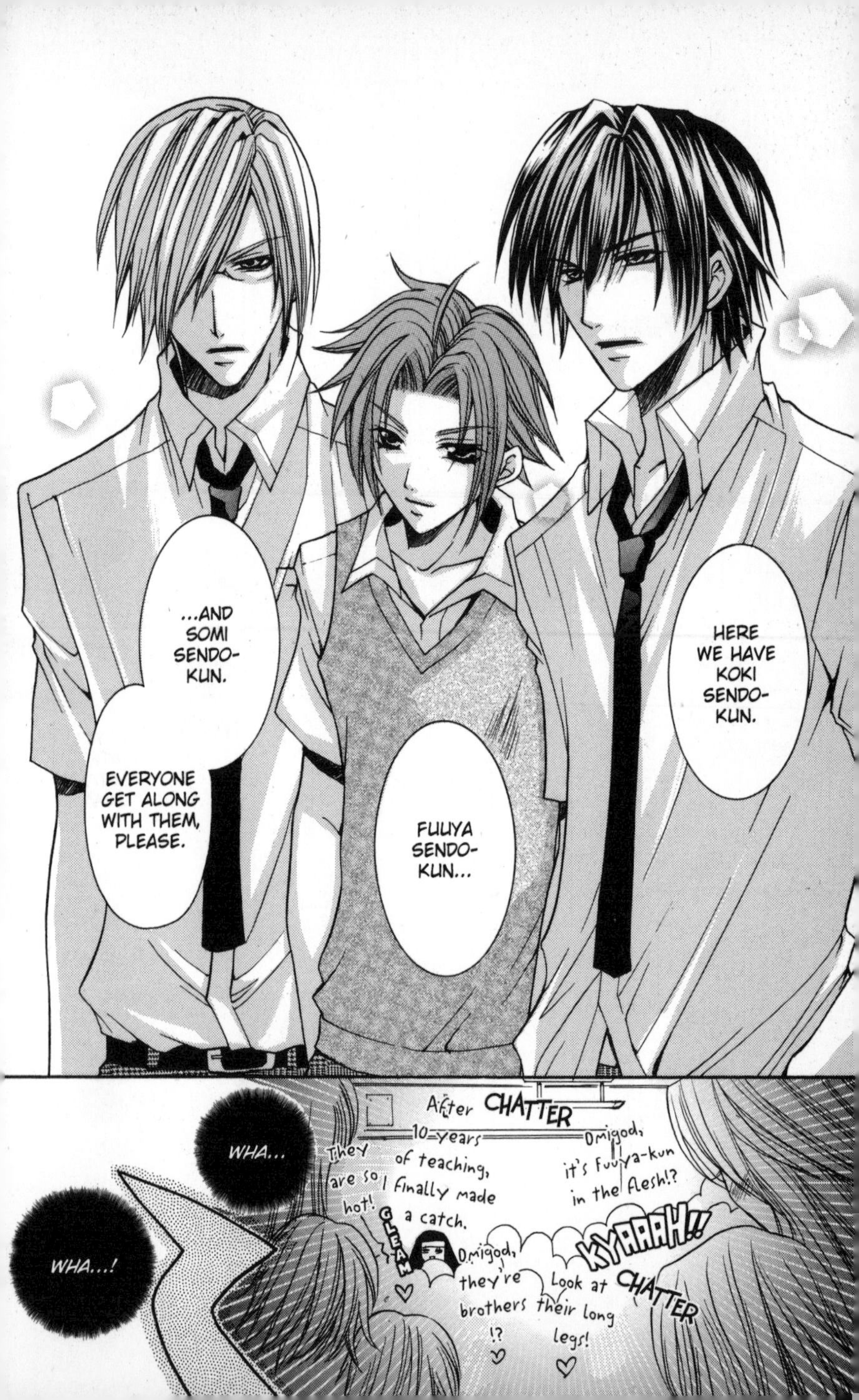
HERE WE HAVE KOKI SENDO-KUN.
FUUYA SENDO-KUN...
...AND SOMI SENDO-KUN.
EVERYONE GET ALONG WITH THEM, PLEASE.
Omigod, it's Fuuya-kun in the flesh!?
KYAAAH!!
CHATTER
Look at their long legs!
Omigod, they're brothers!?
After 10 years of teaching, I finally made a catch.
GLEAM
CHATTER
They are so hot!
WHA...
WHA...!

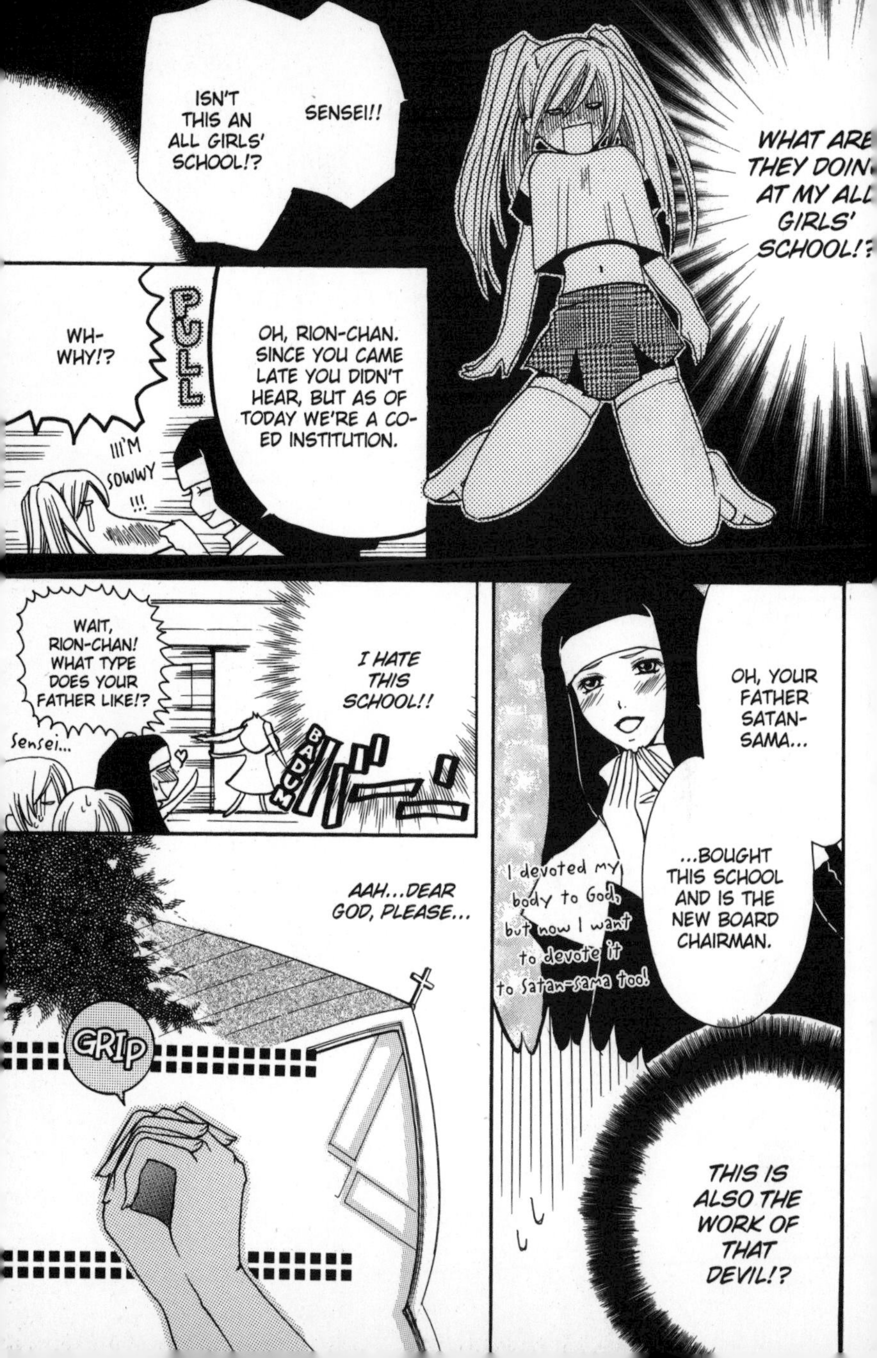
WHAT ARE THEY DOIN AT MY ALL GIRLS' SCHOOL!?
SENSEI!!
ISN'T THIS AN ALL GIRLS' SCHOOL!?
OH, RION-CHAN. SINCE YOU CAME LATE YOU DIDN'T HEAR, BUT AS OF TODAY WE'RE A CO-ED INSTITUTION.
PULL
WH-WHY!?
III'M SOWWY!!!
OH, YOUR FATHER SATAN-SAMA...
...BOUGHT THIS SCHOOL AND IS THE NEW BOARD CHAIRMAN.
I devoted my body to God, but now I want to devote it to Satan-sama too!
I HATE THIS SCHOOL!!
BADUM
WAIT, RION-CHAN! WHAT TYPE DOES YOUR FATHER LIKE!?
Sensei...
THIS IS ALSO THE WORK OF THAT DEVIL!?
AAH...DEAR GOD, PLEASE...
GRIP

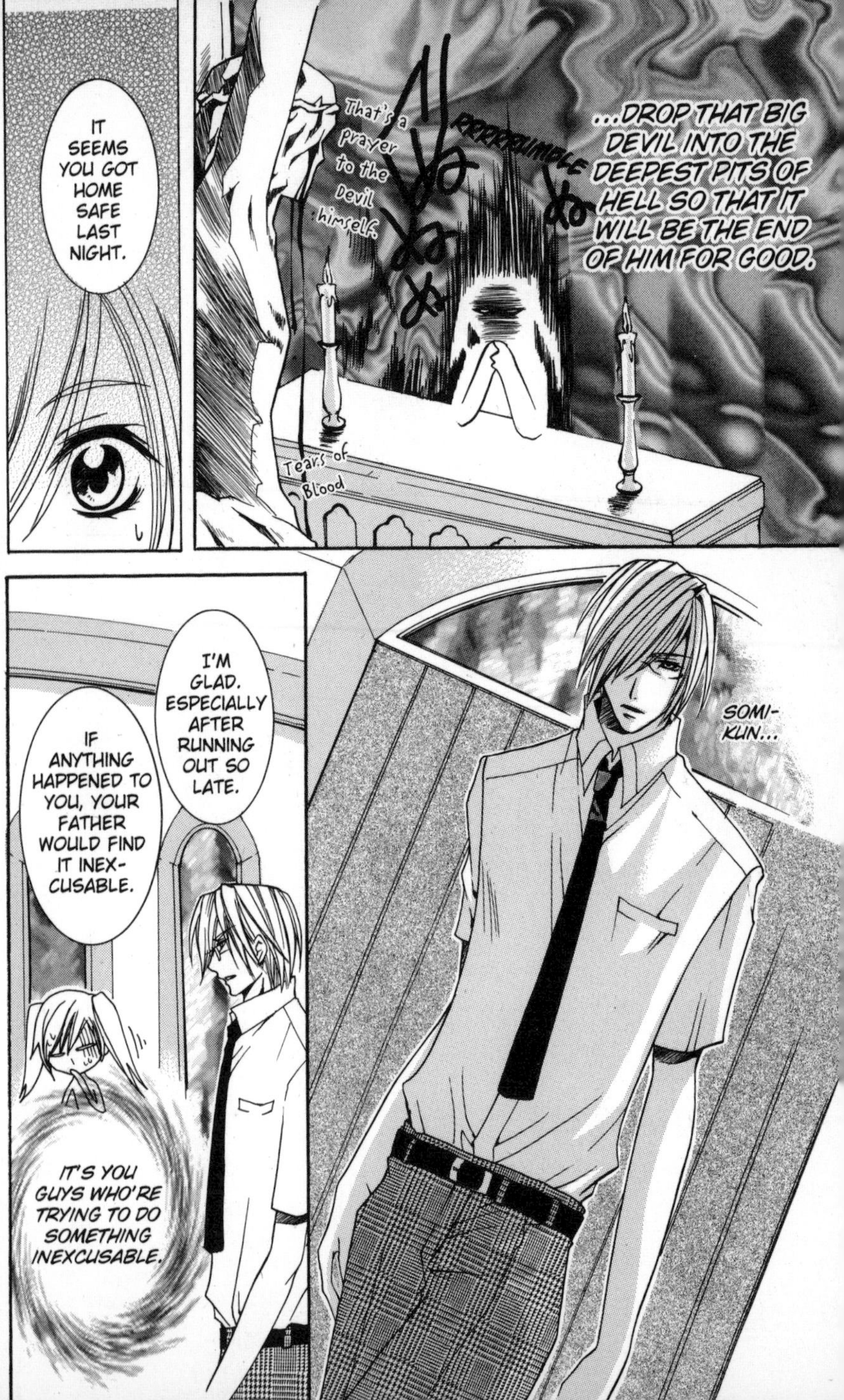
...DROP THAT BIG DEVIL INTO THE DEEPEST PITS OF HELL SO THAT IT WILL BE THE END OF HIM FOR GOOD.
RRRRRUMBLE
That's a prayer to the Devil himself.
Tears of Blood
IT SEEMS YOU GOT HOME SAFE LAST NIGHT.
SOMI-KUN...
I'M GLAD. ESPECIALLY AFTER RUNNING OUT SO LATE.
IF ANYTHING HAPPENED TO YOU, YOUR FATHER WOULD FIND IT INEXCUSABLE.
IT'S YOU GUYS WHO'RE TRYING TO DO SOMETHING INEXCUSABLE.

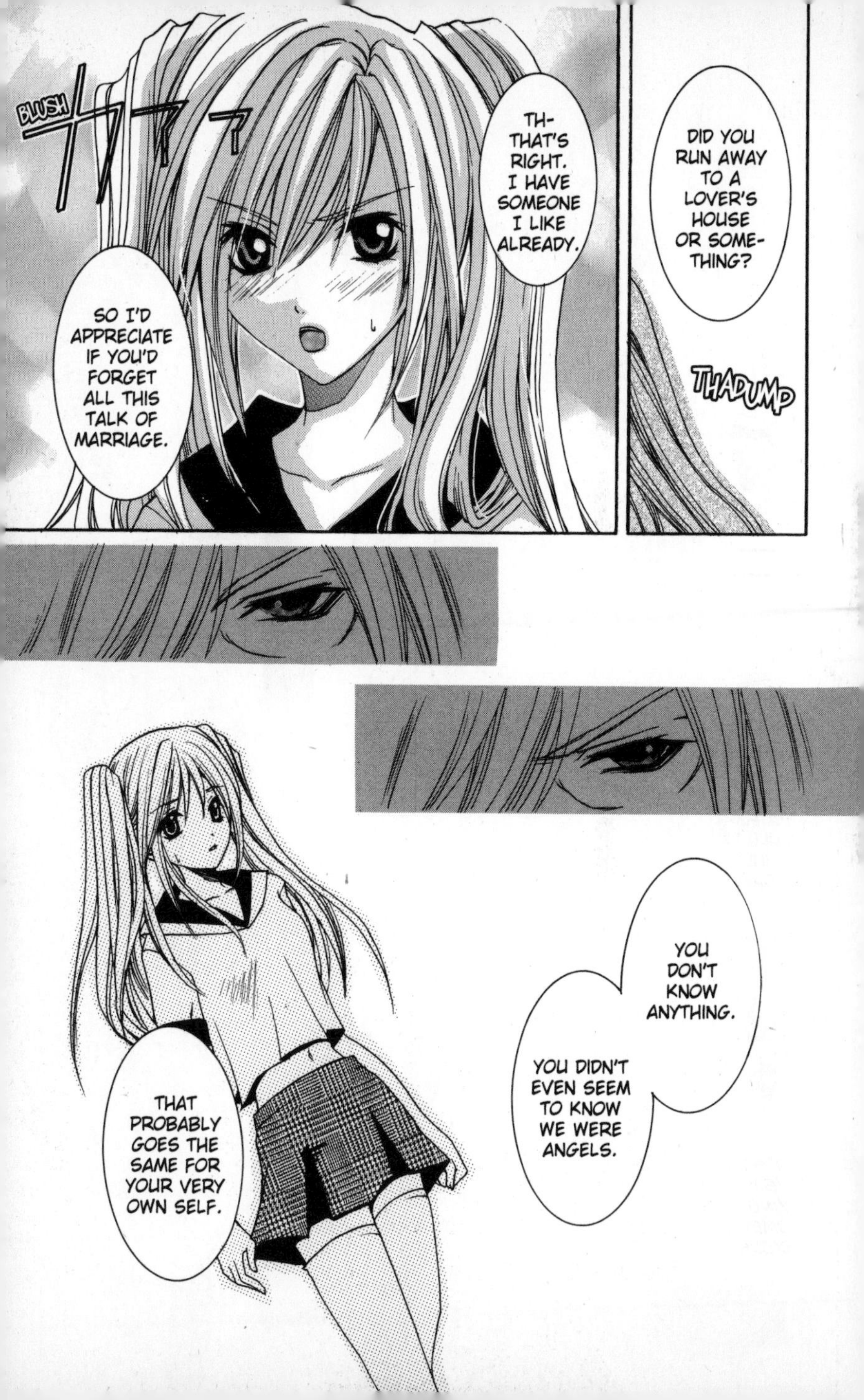
DID YOU RUN AWAY TO A LOVER'S HOUSE OR SOME-THING?
THADUMP
TH-THAT'S RIGHT. I HAVE SOMEONE I LIKE ALREADY.
BLUSH
SO I'D APPRECIATE IF YOU'D FORGET ALL THIS TALK OF MARRIAGE.
YOU DON'T KNOW ANYTHING.
YOU DIDN'T EVEN SEEM TO KNOW WE WERE ANGELS.
THAT PROBABLY GOES THE SAME FOR YOUR VERY OWN SELF.

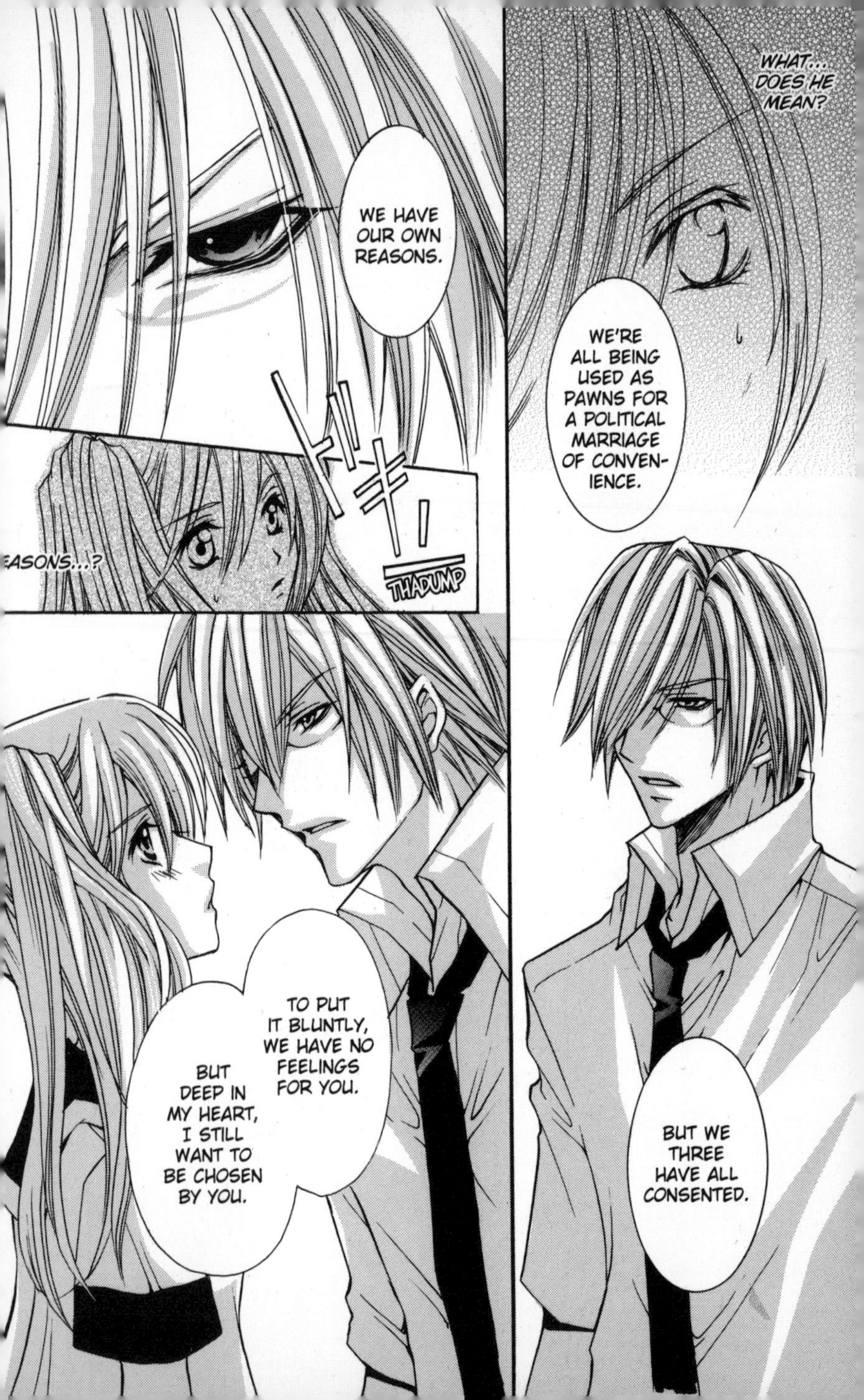
WHAT... DOES HE MEAN?
WE'RE ALL BEING USED AS PAWNS FOR A POLITICAL MARRIAGE OF CONVEN-IENCE.
WE HAVE OUR OWN REASONS.
EASONS...?
THADUMP
BUT WE THREE HAVE ALL CONSENTED.
TO PUT IT BLUNTLY, WE HAVE NO FEELINGS FOR YOU.
BUT DEEP IN MY HEART, I STILL WANT TO BE CHOSEN BY YOU.

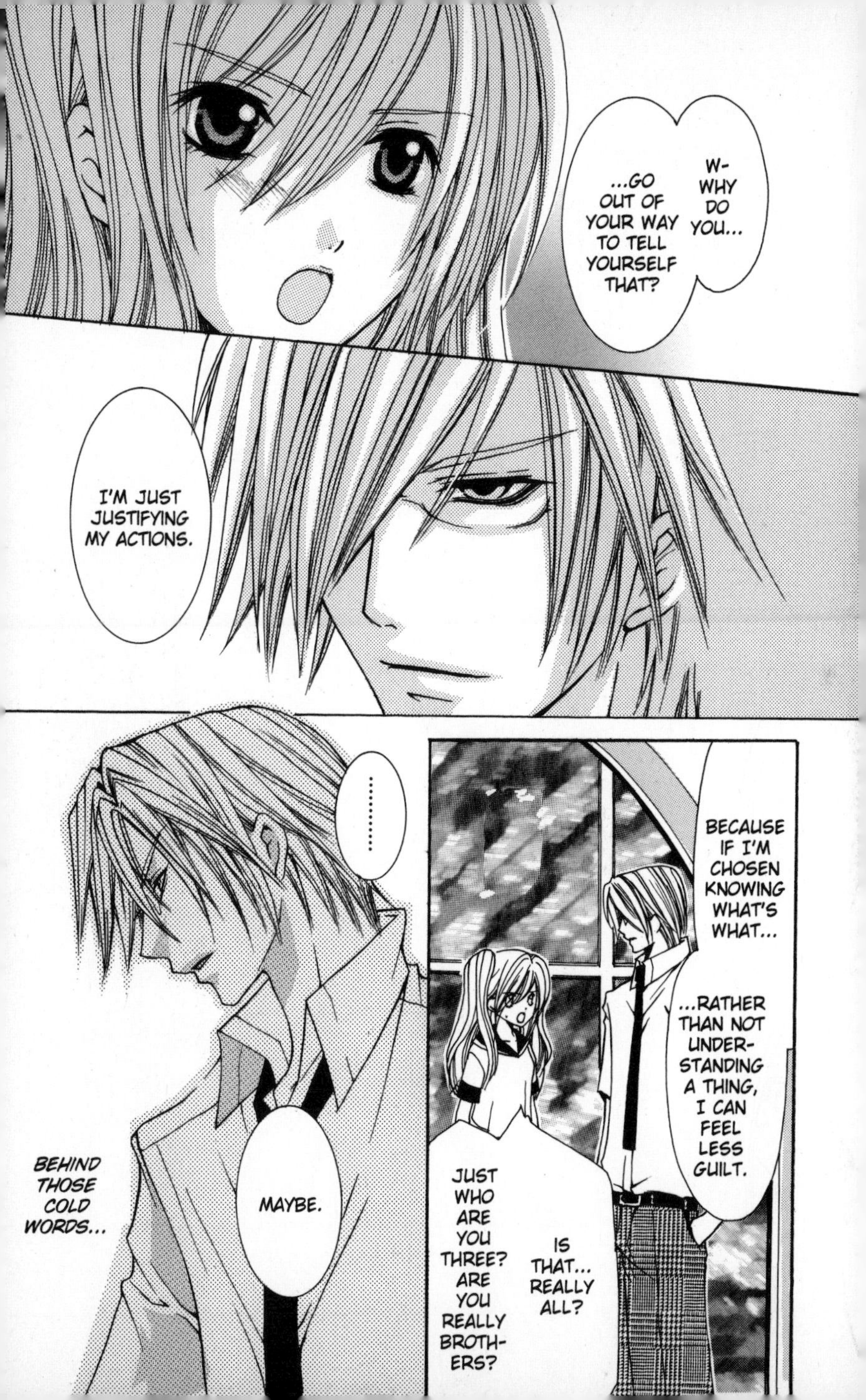
W-WHY DO YOU...
...GO OUT OF YOUR WAY TO TELL YOURSELF THAT?
I'M JUST JUSTIFYING MY ACTIONS.
BECAUSE IF I'M CHOSEN KNOWING WHAT'S WHAT...
...RATHER THAN NOT UNDER-STANDING A THING, I CAN FEEL LESS GUILT.
IS THAT... REALLY ALL?
JUST WHO ARE YOU THREE? ARE YOU REALLY BROTHER-S?
......
MAYBE.
BEHIND THOSE COLD WORDS...

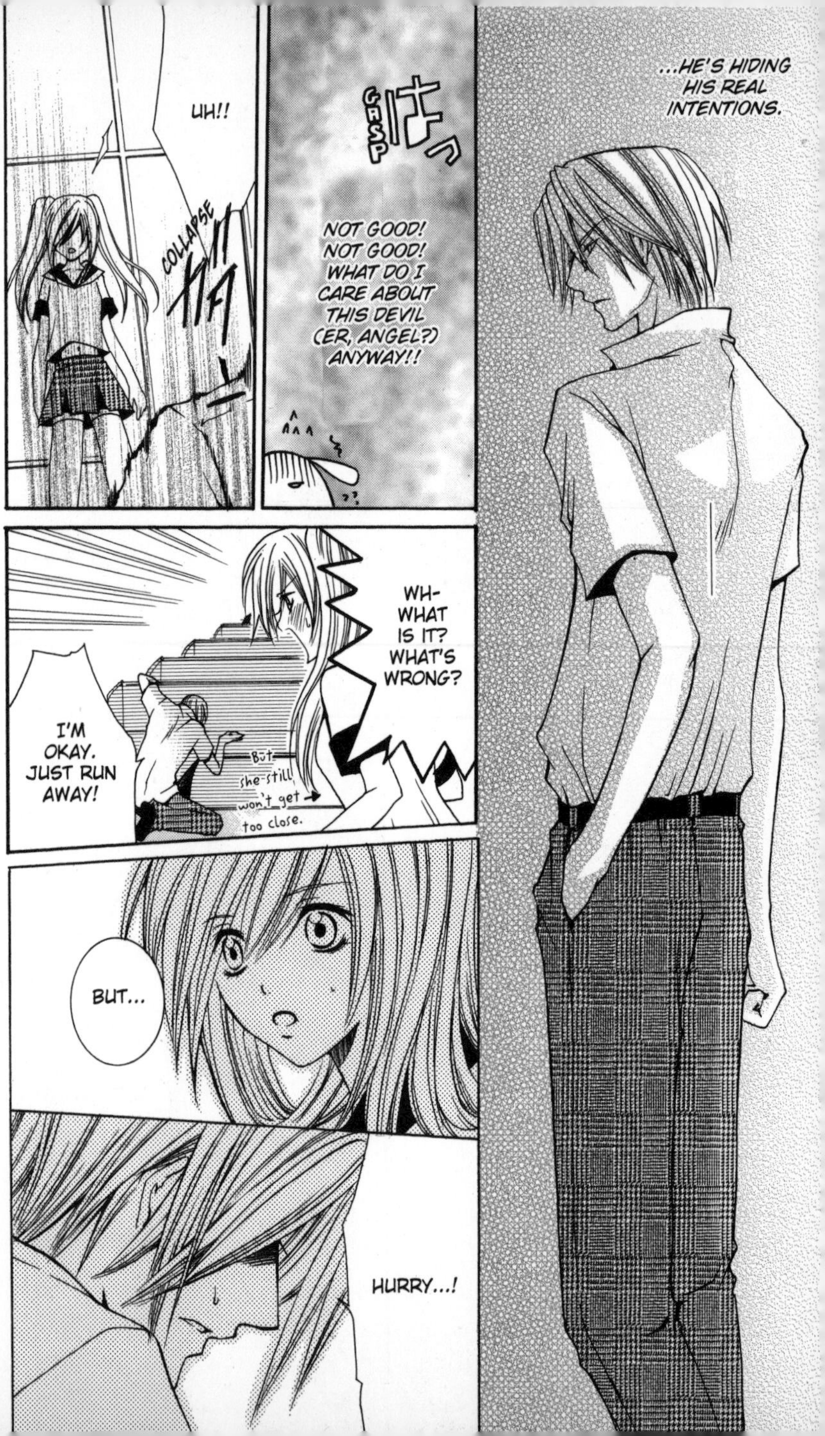
...HE'S HIDING HIS REAL INTENTIONS.
GASP
NOT GOOD! NOT GOOD! WHAT DO I CARE ABOUT THIS DEVIL (ER, ANGEL?) ANYWAY!!
UH!!
COLLAPSE
WH- WHAT IS IT? WHAT'S WRONG?
I'M OKAY. JUST RUN AWAY!
But she still won't get too close.
BUT...
HURRY...!

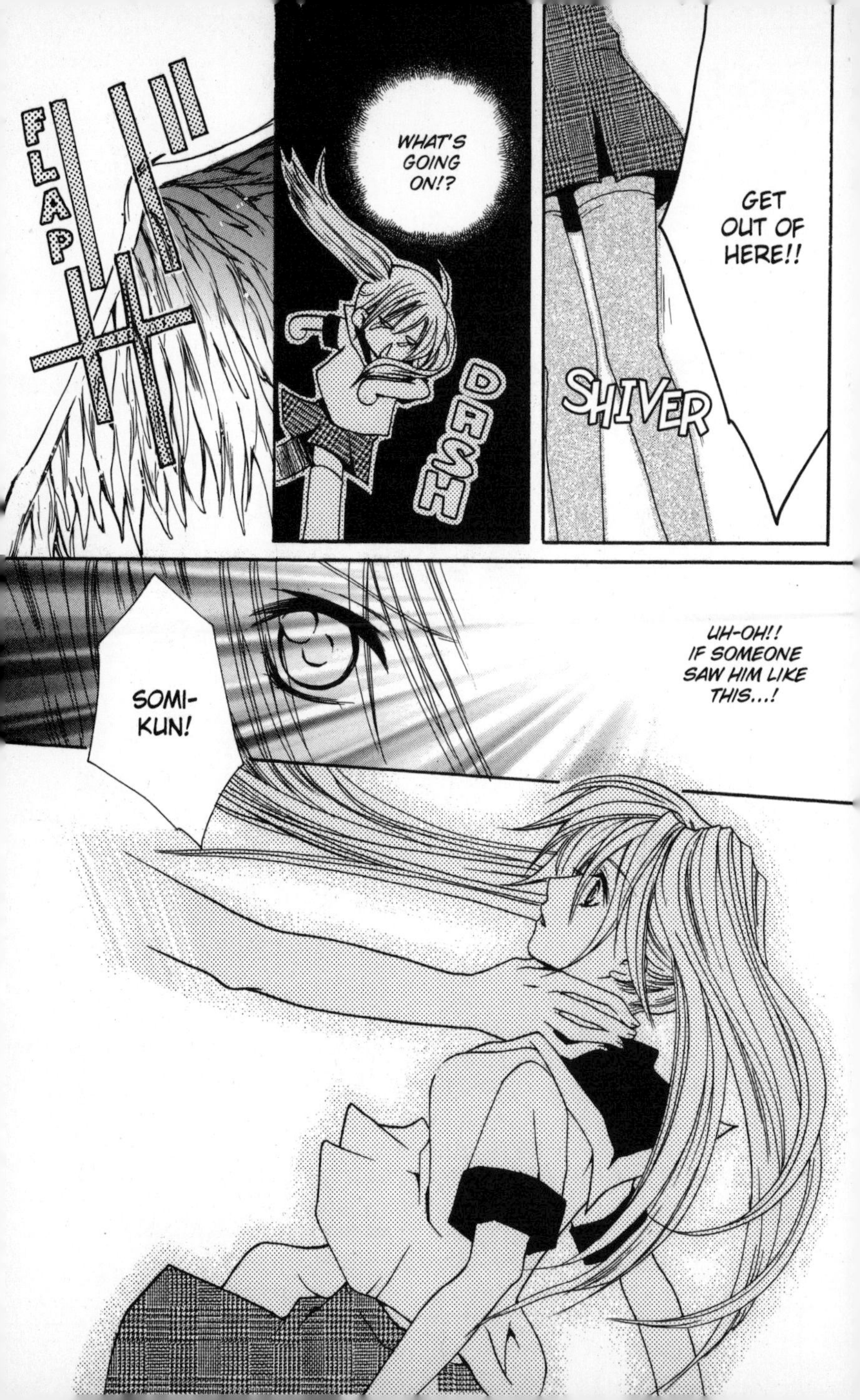
GET OUT OF HERE!!
SHIVER
WHAT'S GOING ON!?
DASH
FLAP
UH-OH!! IF SOMEONE SAW HIM LIKE THIS...!
SOMI-KUN!

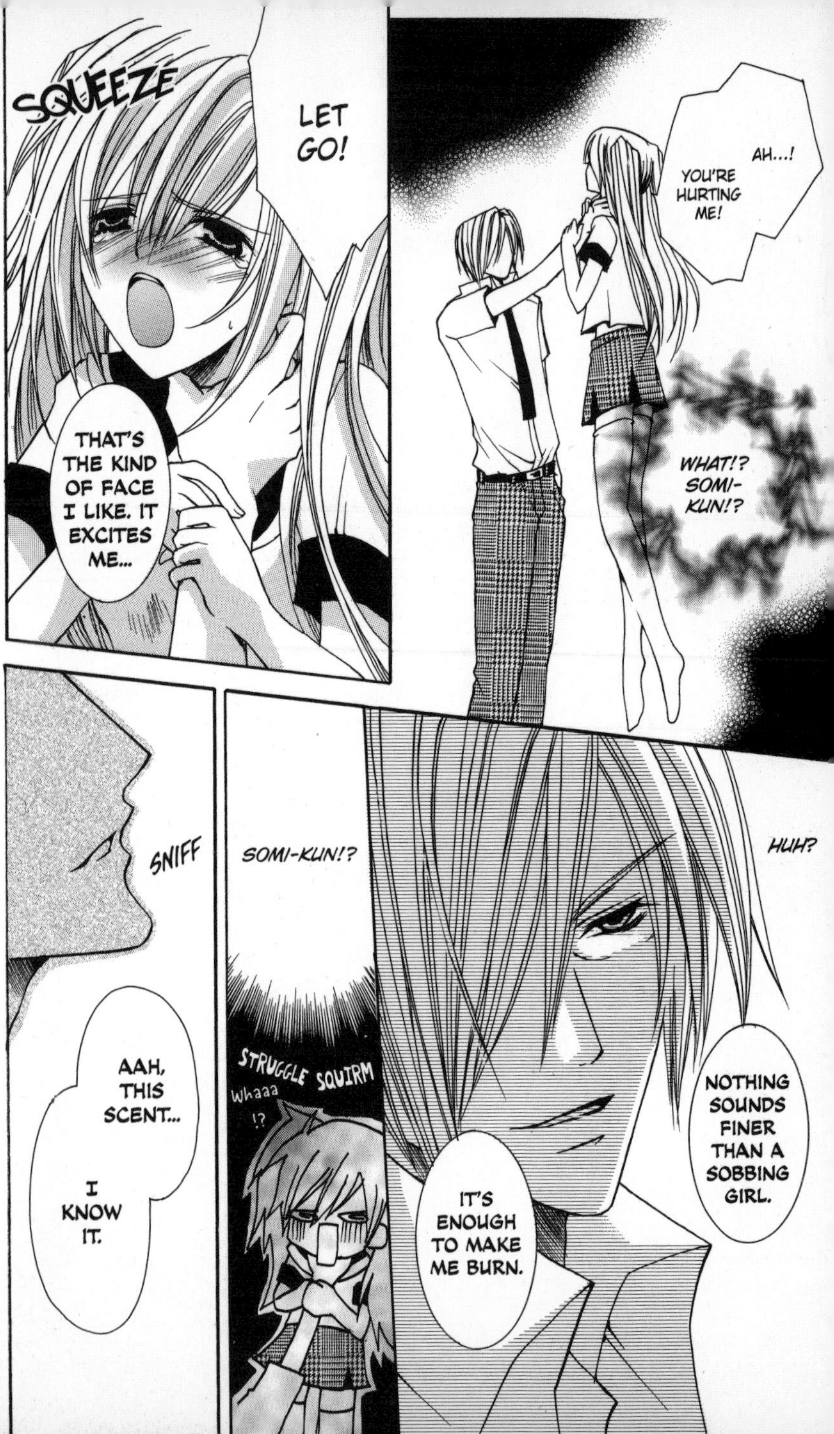
AH...!
YOU'RE HURTING ME!
WHAT!? SOMI-KUN!?
LET GO!
SQUEEZE
THAT'S THE KIND OF FACE I LIKE. IT EXCITES ME...
HUH?
NOTHING SOUNDS FINER THAN A SOBBING GIRL.
IT'S ENOUGH TO MAKE ME BURN.
SOMI-KUN!?
STRUGGLE SQUIRM
Whaaa !?
SNIFF
AAH, THIS SCENT...
I KNOW IT.

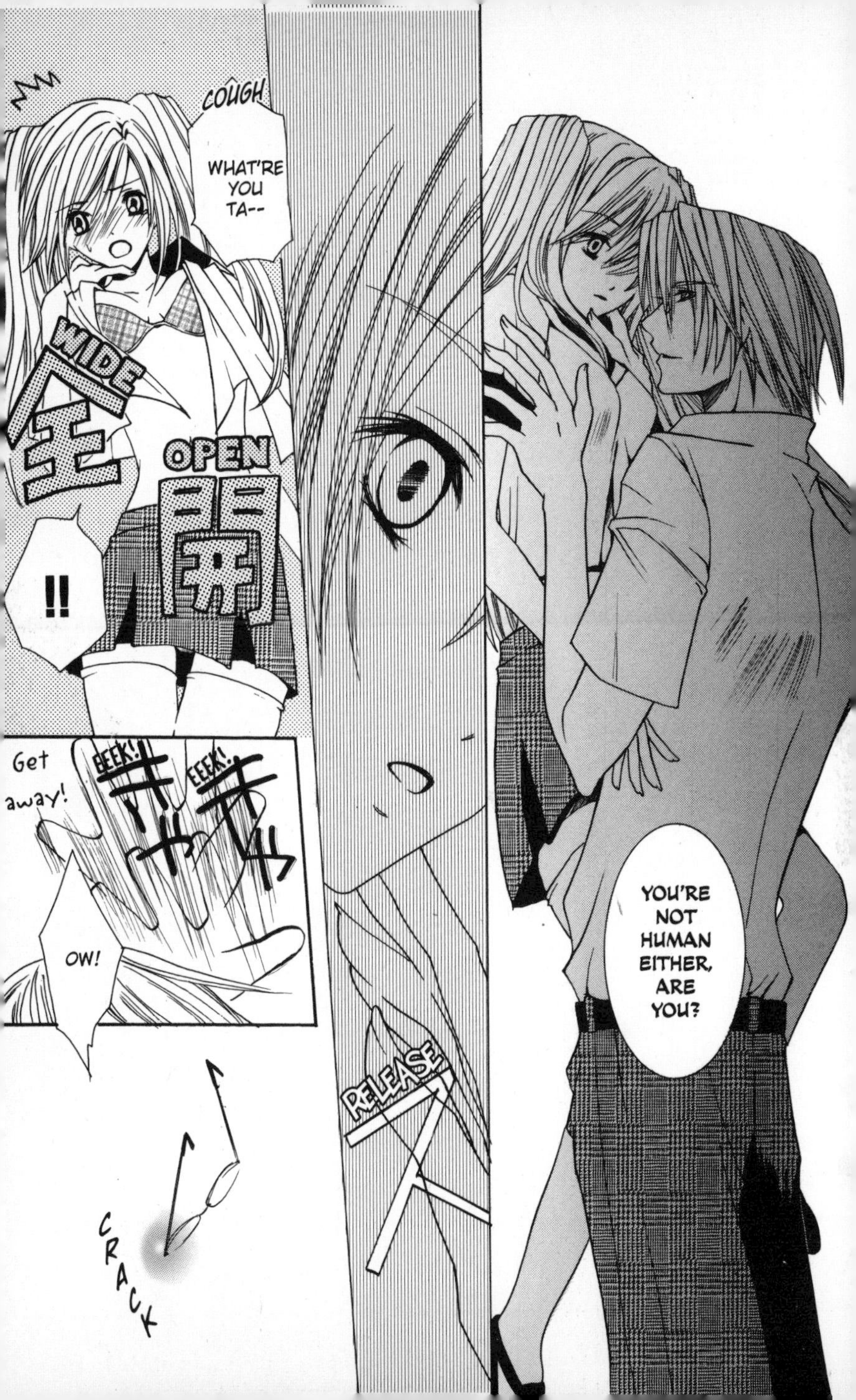
YOU'RE NOT HUMAN EITHER, ARE YOU?
RELEASE
COUGH
WHAT'RE YOU TA--
WIDE
OPEN
!!
Get away!
EEEK!
EEEK!
OW!
CRACK

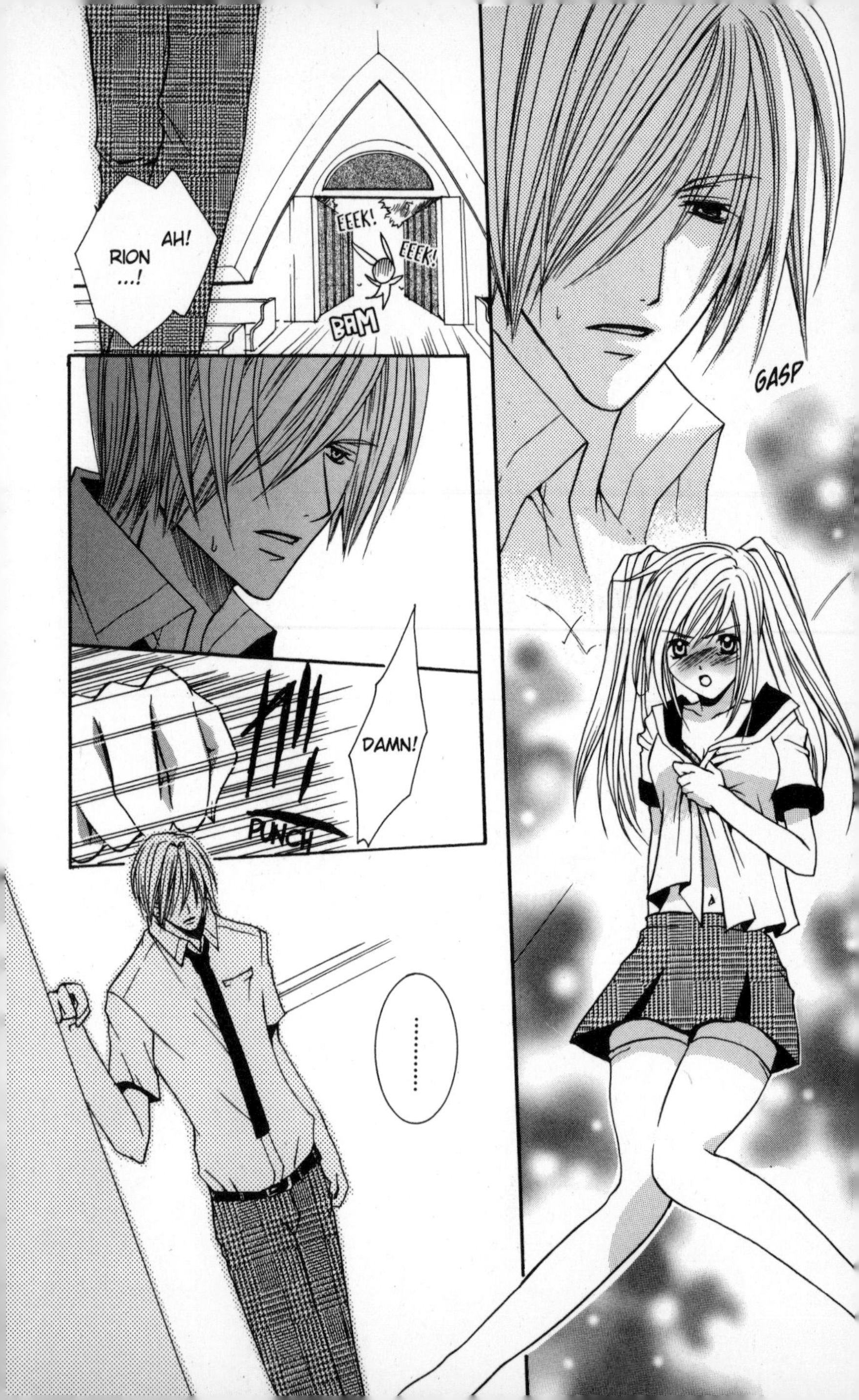
GASP
AH! RION ...!
EEEK!
EEEK!
BAM
DAMN!
PUNCH
....

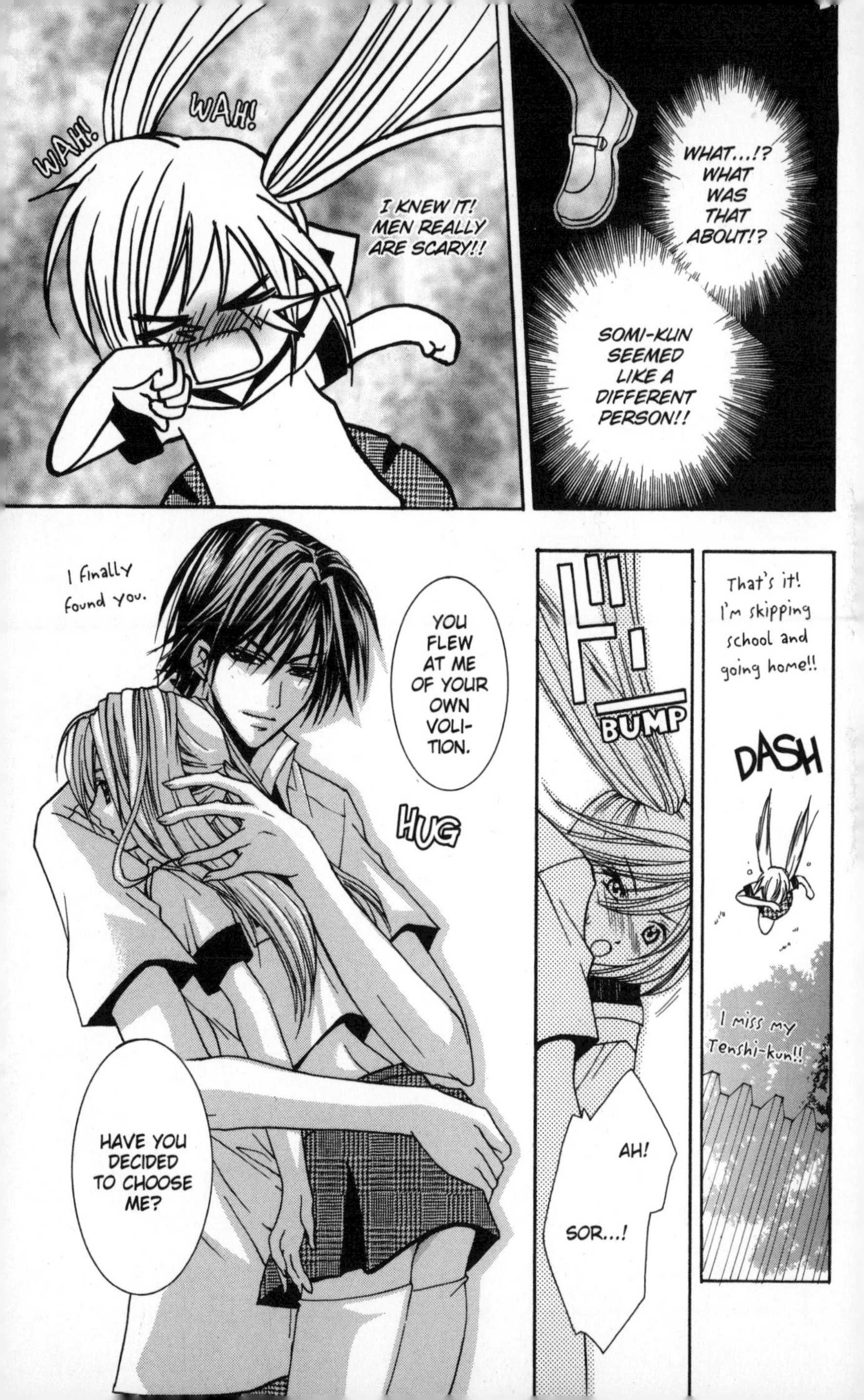
WHAT...!? WHAT WAS THAT ABOUT!?
SOMI-KUN SEEMED LIKE A DIFFERENT PERSON!!
WAH!
WAH!
I KNEW IT! MEN REALLY ARE SCARY!!
That's it! I'm skipping school and going home!!
DASH
I miss my Tenshi-kun!!
BUMP
AH!
SOR...!
I finally found you.
YOU FLEW AT ME OF YOUR OWN VOLI-TION.
HUG
HAVE YOU DECIDED TO CHOOSE ME?

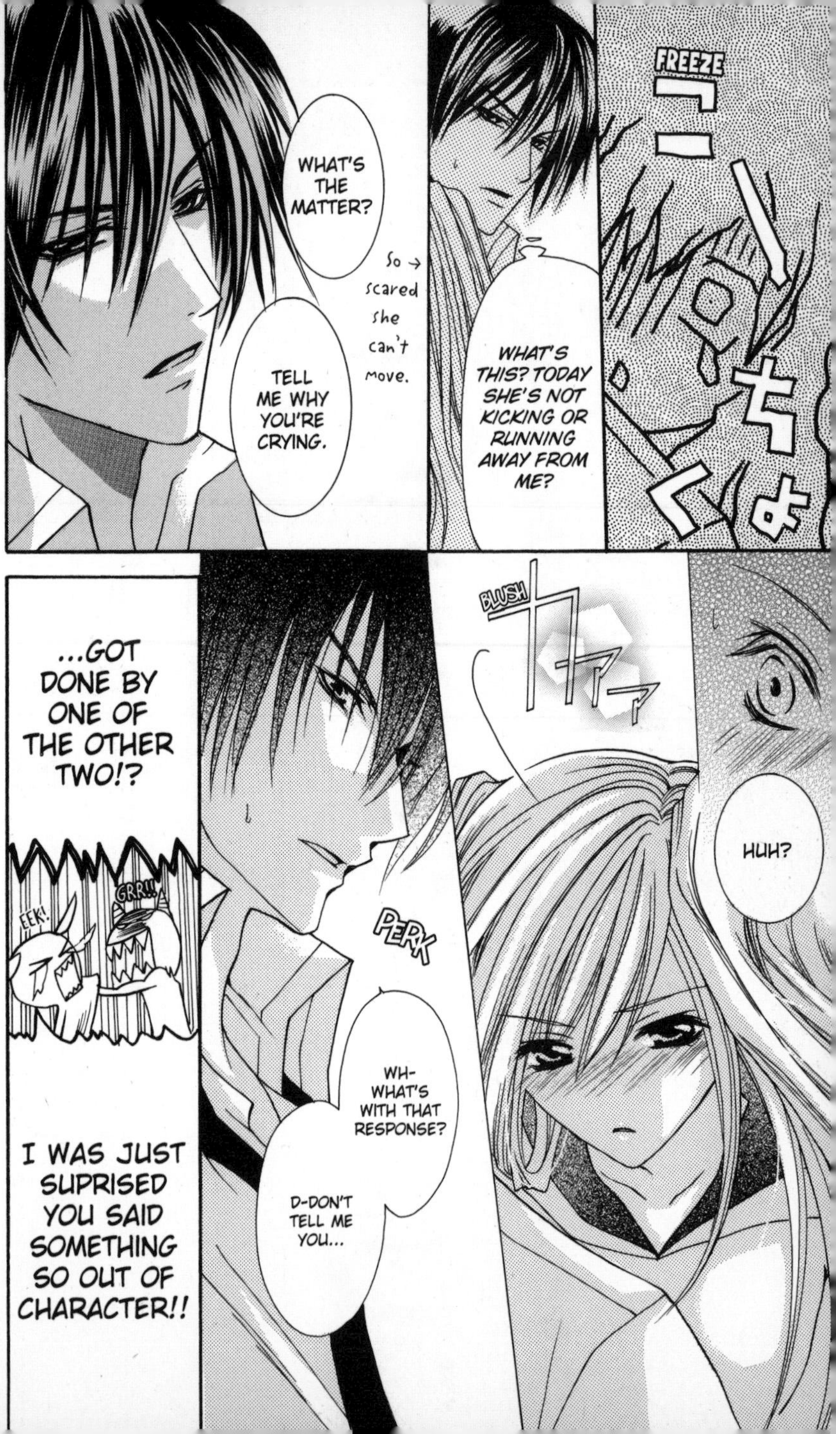

FREEZE
So → scared she can't move.
WHAT'S THIS? TODAY SHE'S NOT KICKING OR RUNNING AWAY FROM ME?
WHAT'S THE MATTER?
TELL ME WHY YOU'RE CRYING.
BLUSH
HUH?
PERK
WH- WHAT'S WITH THAT RESPONSE?
D-DON'T TELL ME YOU...
...GOT DONE BY ONE OF THE OTHER TWO!?
EEK!
GRR!!
I WAS JUST SUPRISED YOU SAID SOMETHING SO OUT OF CHARACTER!!

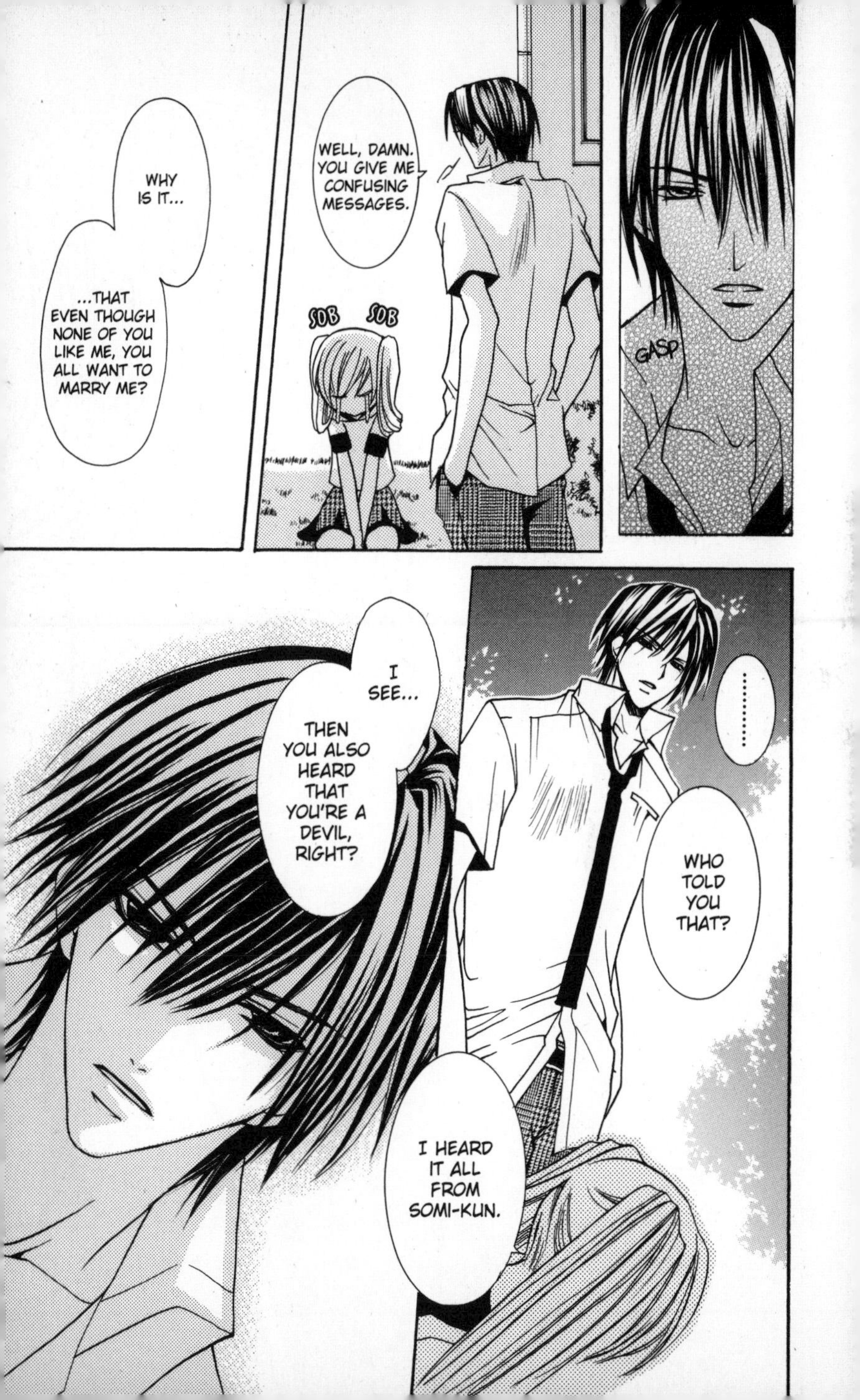
GASP
WELL, DAMN. YOU GIVE ME CONFUSING MESSAGES.
SOB SOB
WHY IS IT...
...THAT EVEN THOUGH NONE OF YOU LIKE ME, YOU ALL WANT TO MARRY ME?
....
WHO TOLD YOU THAT?
I HEARD IT ALL FROM SOMI-KUN.
I SEE...
THEN YOU ALSO HEARD THAT YOU'RE A DEVIL, RIGHT?

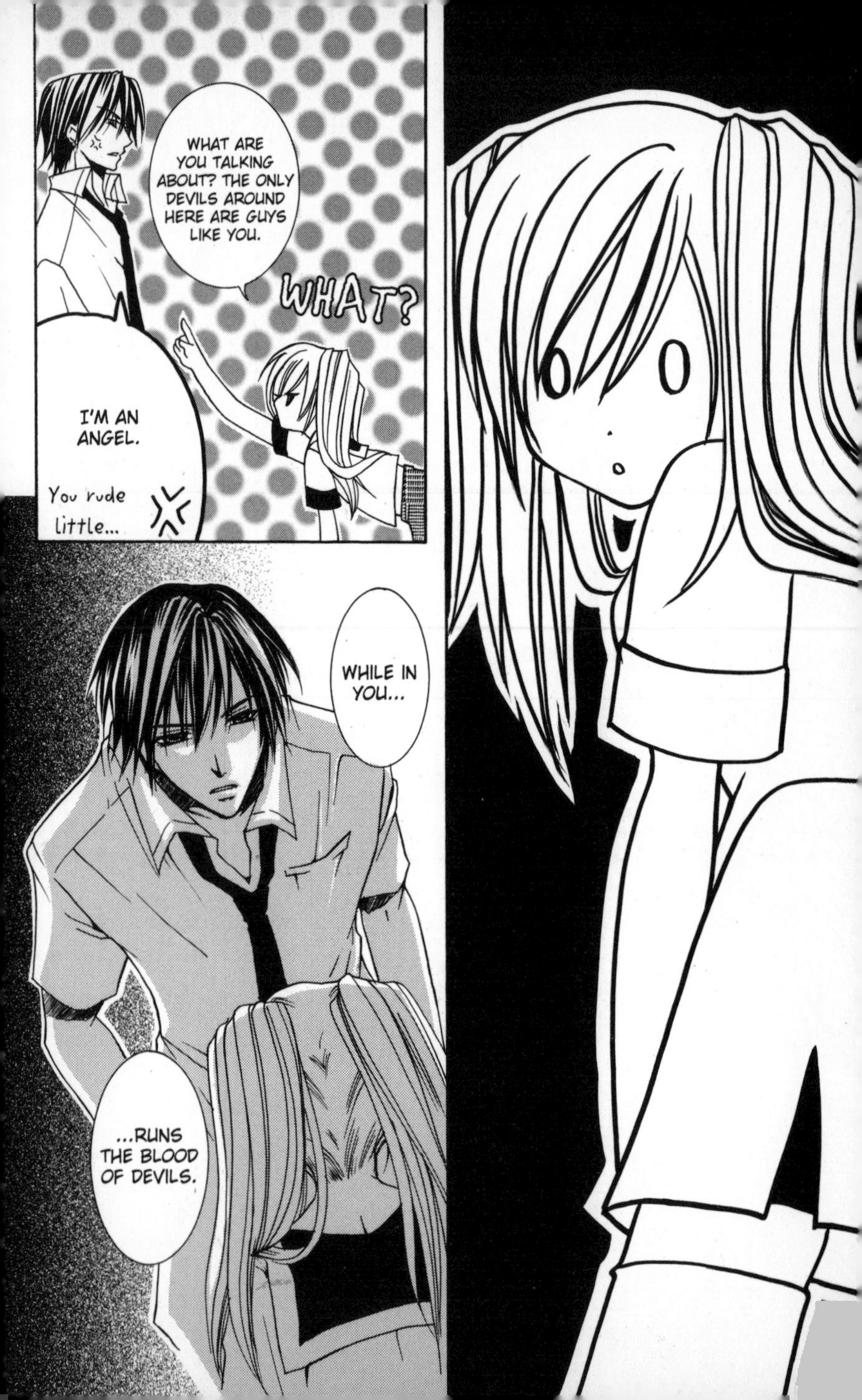
WHAT ARE YOU TALKING ABOUT? THE ONLY DEVILS AROUND HERE ARE GUYS LIKE YOU.
WHAT?
I'M AN ANGEL.
You rude little...
WHILE IN YOU...
...RUNS THE BLOOD OF DEVILS.

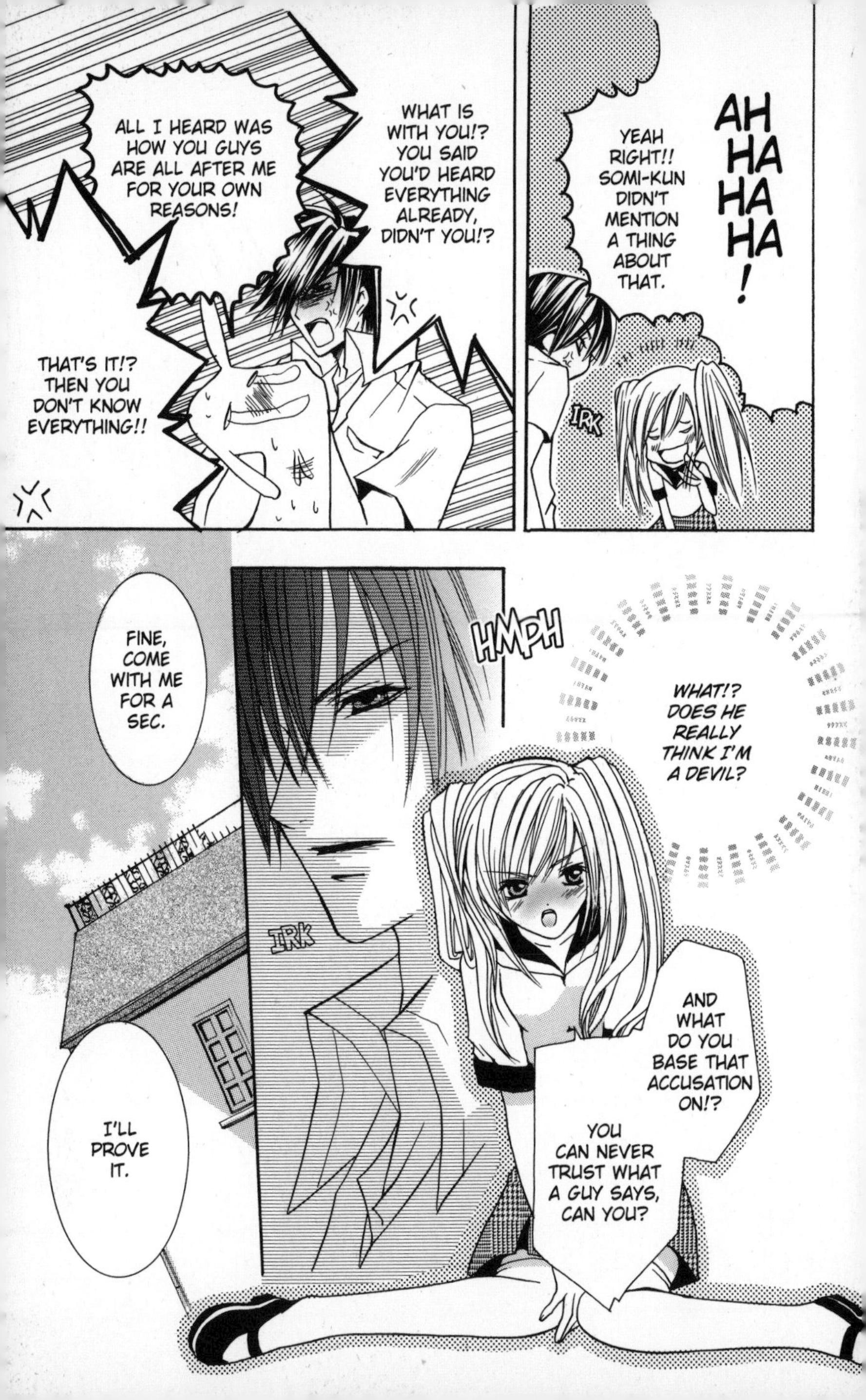
AH HA HA HA!
YEAH RIGHT!! SOMI-KUN DIDN'T MENTION A THING ABOUT THAT.
IRK
WHAT IS WITH YOU!? YOU SAID YOU'D HEARD EVERYTHING ALREADY, DIDN'T YOU!?
ALL I HEARD WAS HOW YOU GUYS ARE ALL AFTER ME FOR YOUR OWN REASONS!
THAT'S IT!? THEN YOU DON'T KNOW EVERYTHING!!
HMPH
WHAT!? DOES HE REALLY THINK I'M A DEVIL?
AND WHAT DO YOU BASE THAT ACCUSATION ON!?
YOU CAN NEVER TRUST WHAT A GUY SAYS, CAN YOU?
IRK
FINE, COME WITH ME FOR A SEC.
I'LL PROVE IT.

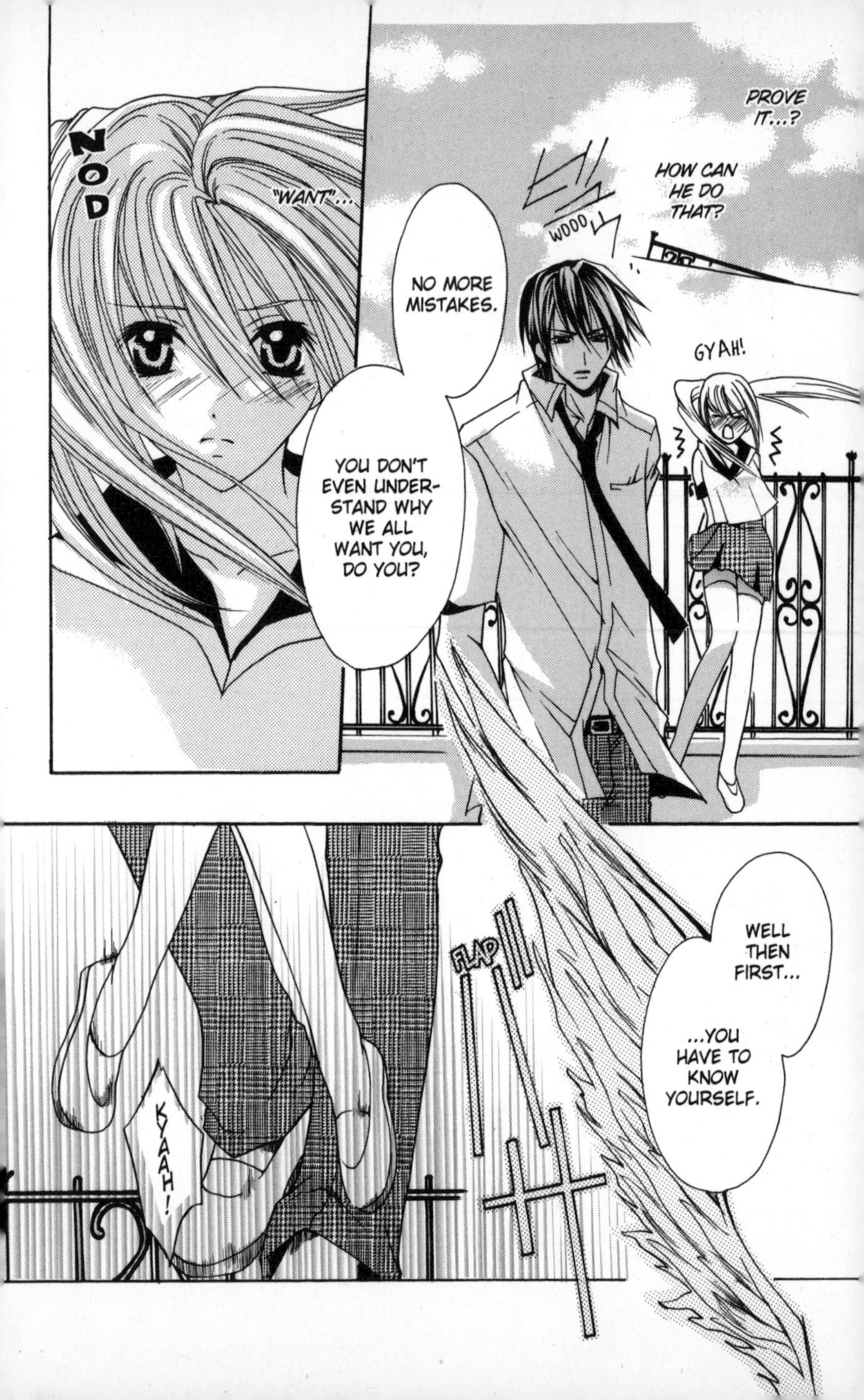
PROVE IT...?
HOW CAN HE DO THAT?
WOOO
NO MORE MISTAKES.
GYAH!
YOU DON'T EVEN UNDER-STAND WHY WE ALL WANT YOU, DO YOU?
NOD
"WANT"...
WELL THEN FIRST...
...YOU HAVE TO KNOW YOURSELF.
FLAP
KYAAH!

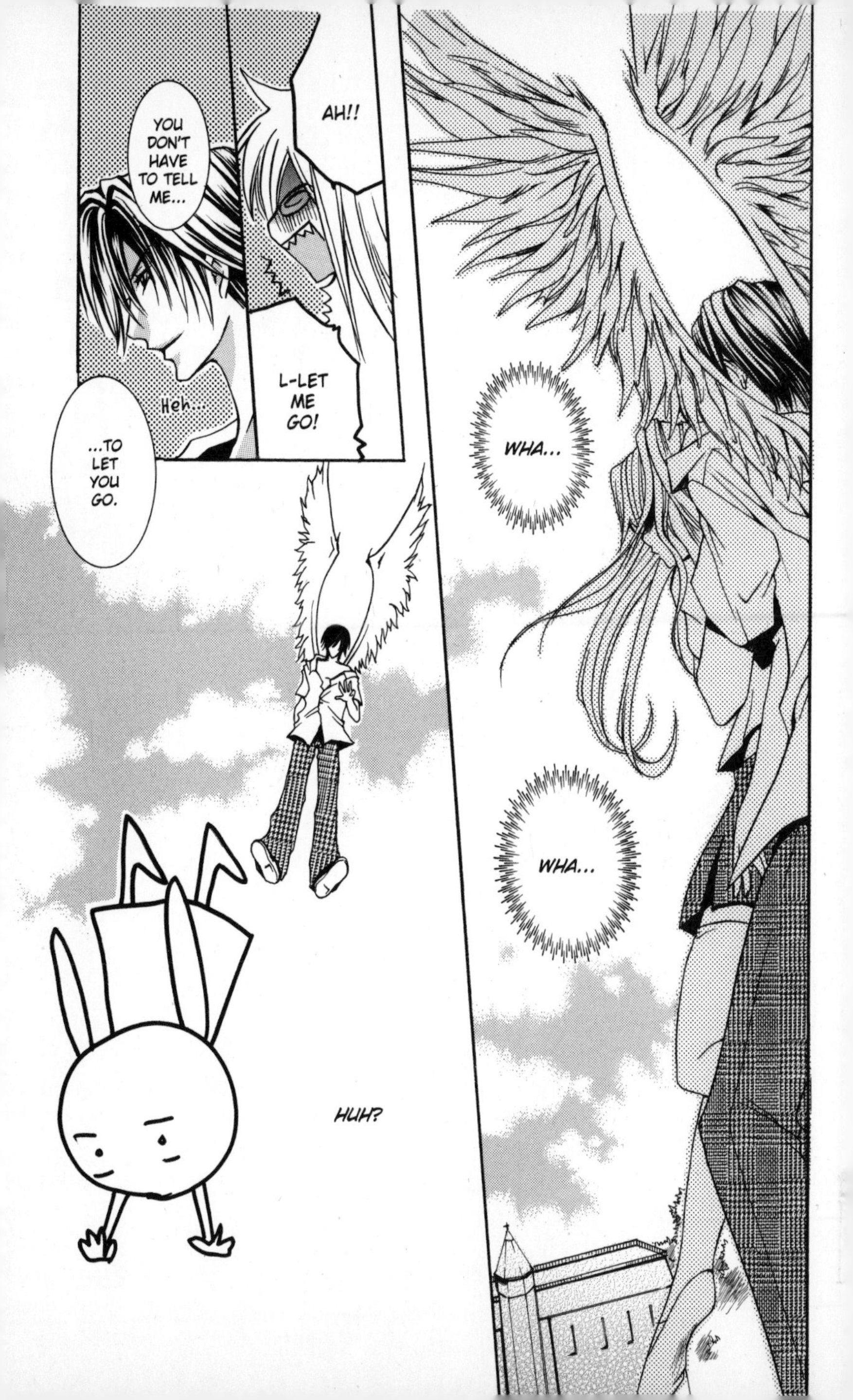
AH!!
YOU DON'T HAVE TO TELL ME...
L-LET ME GO!
Heh...
...TO LET YOU GO.
WHA...
WHA...
HUH?

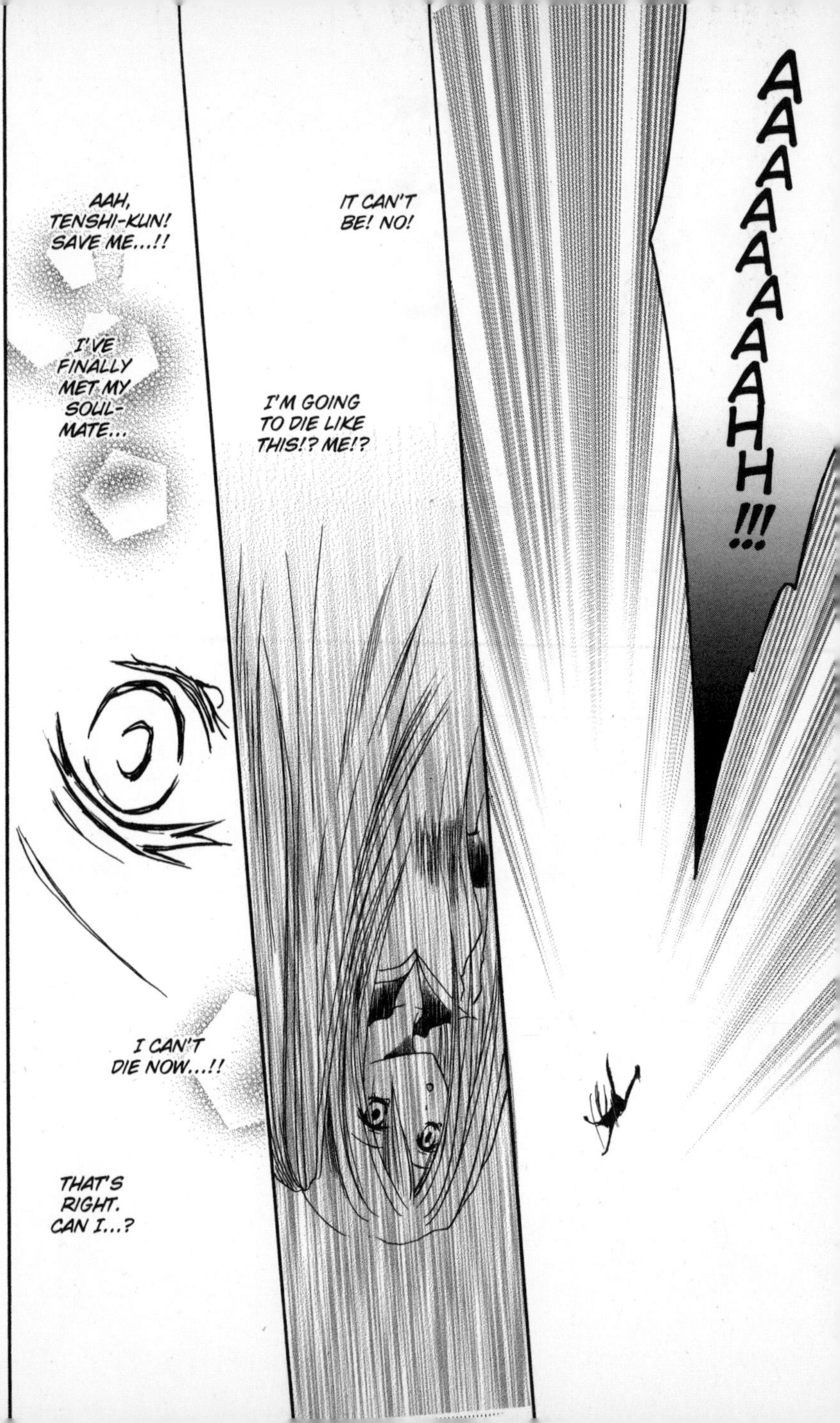
AAAAAAAAHH!!!
IT CAN'T BE! NO!
I'M GOING TO DIE LIKE THIS!? ME!?
AAH, TENSHI-KUN! SAVE ME...!!
I'VE FINALLY MET MY SOUL-MATE...
I CAN'T DIE NOW...!!
THAT'S RIGHT. CAN I...?

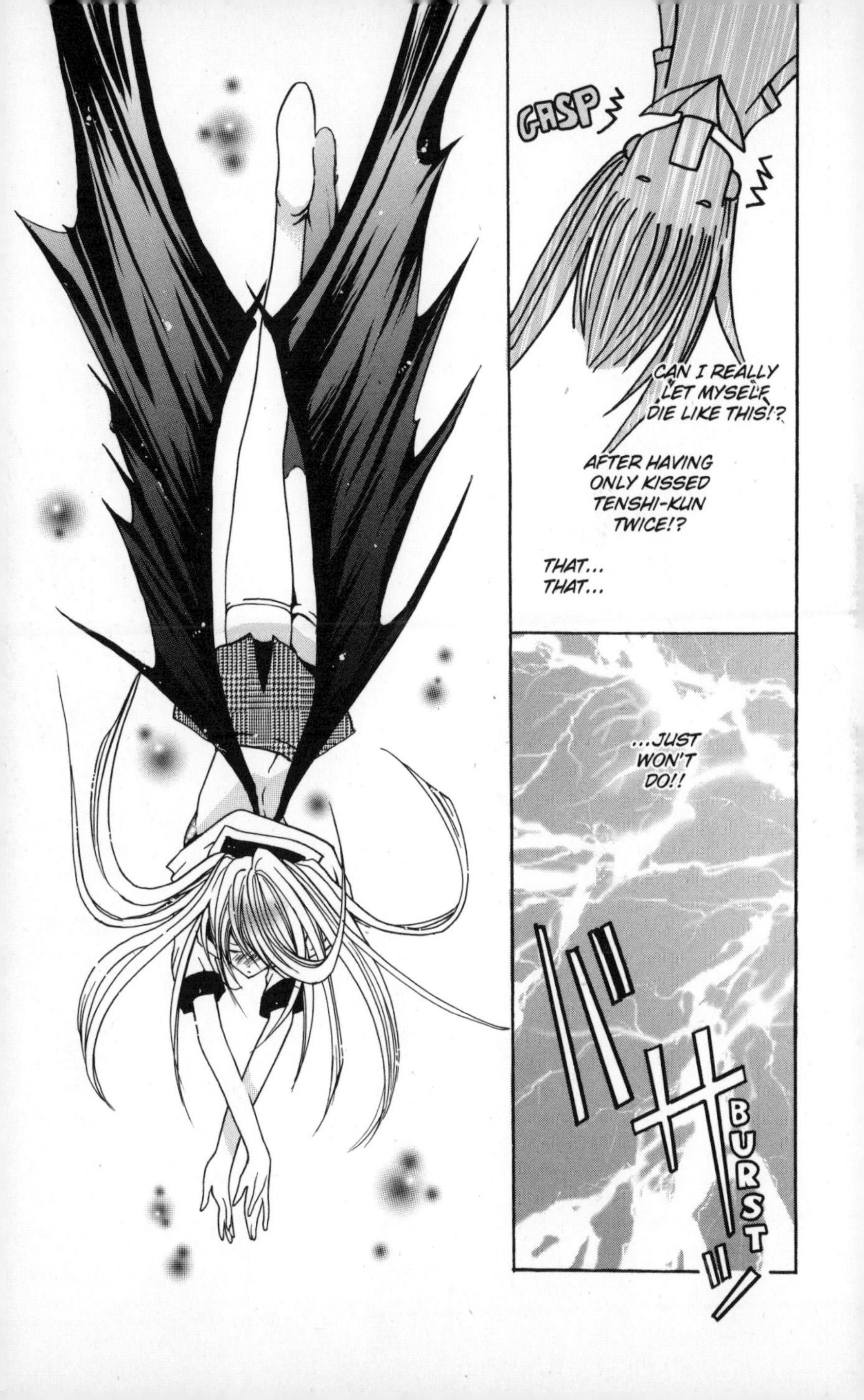
GASP
CAN I REALLY LET MYSELF DIE LIKE THIS!?
AFTER HAVING ONLY KISSED TENSHI-KUN TWICE!?
THAT... THAT...
...JUST WON'T DO!!
BURST

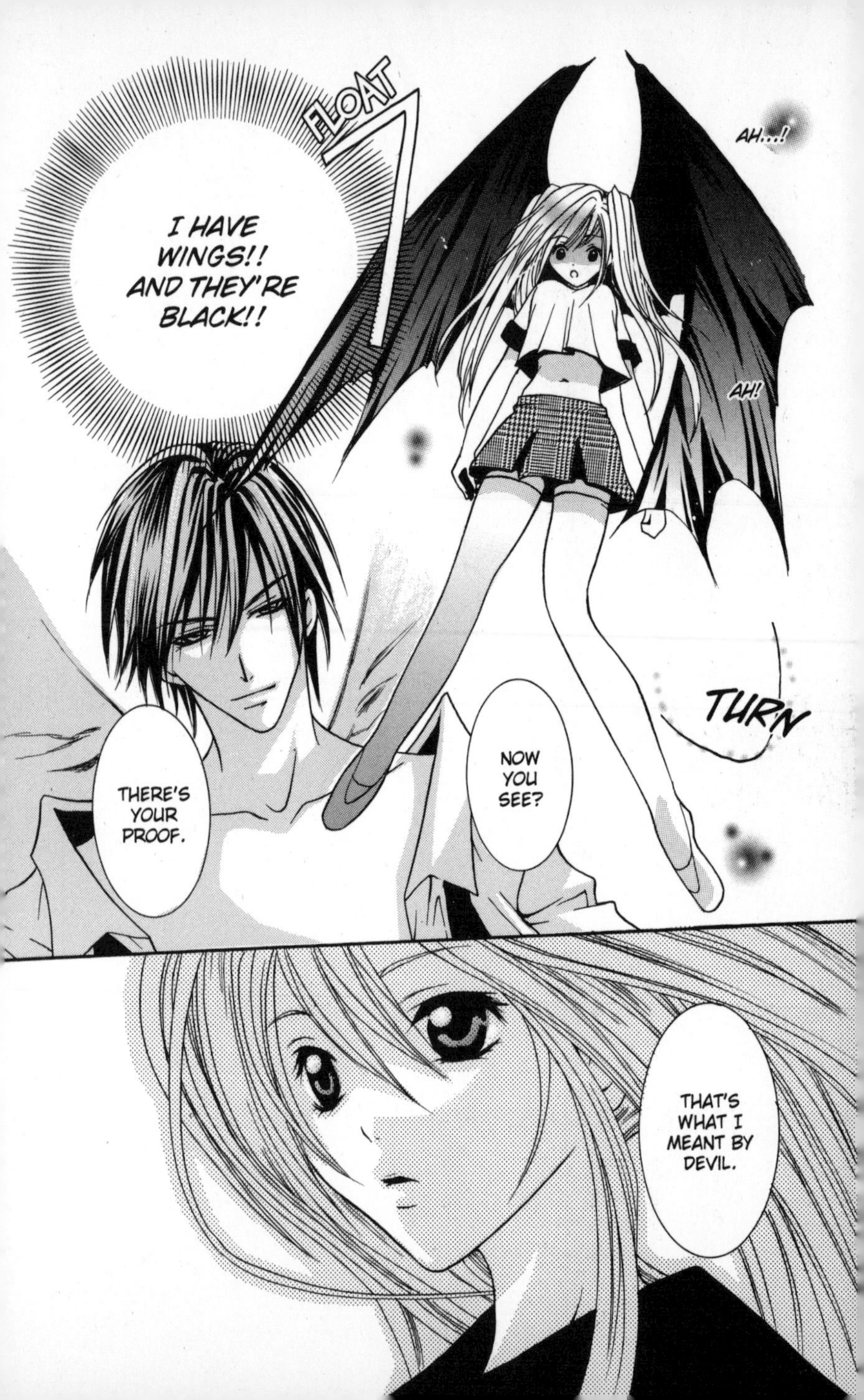
AH...!
FLOAT
I HAVE WINGS!! AND THEY'RE BLACK!!
AH!
TURN
NOW YOU SEE?
THERE'S YOUR PROOF.
THAT'S WHAT I MEANT BY DEVIL.

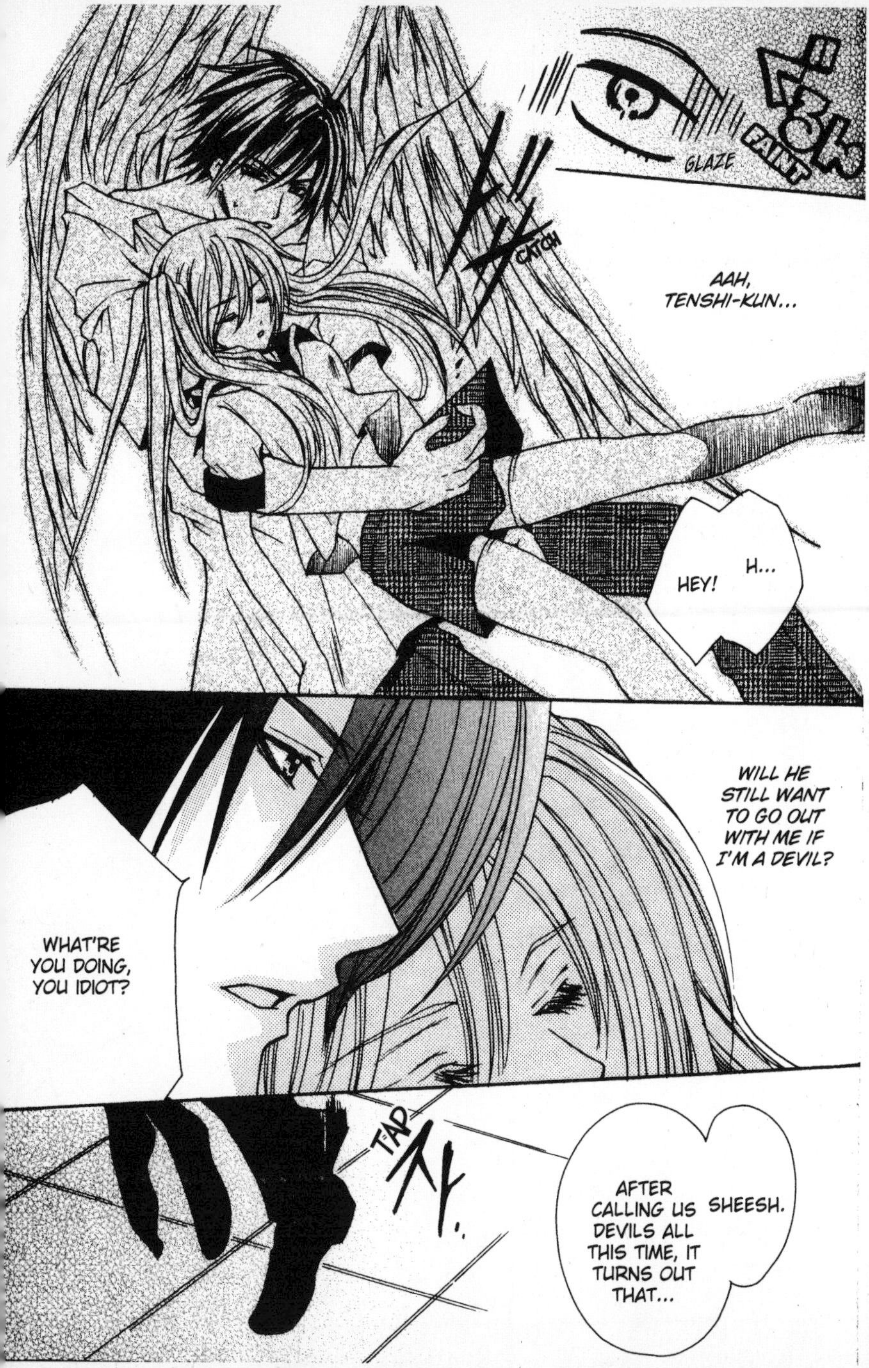
FAINT
GLAZE
CATCH
AAH, TENSHI-KUN...
H... HEY!
WILL HE STILL WANT TO GO OUT WITH ME IF I'M A DEVIL?
WHAT'RE YOU DOING, YOU IDIOT?
TAP
SHEESH. AFTER CALLING US DEVILS ALL THIS TIME, IT TURNS OUT THAT...

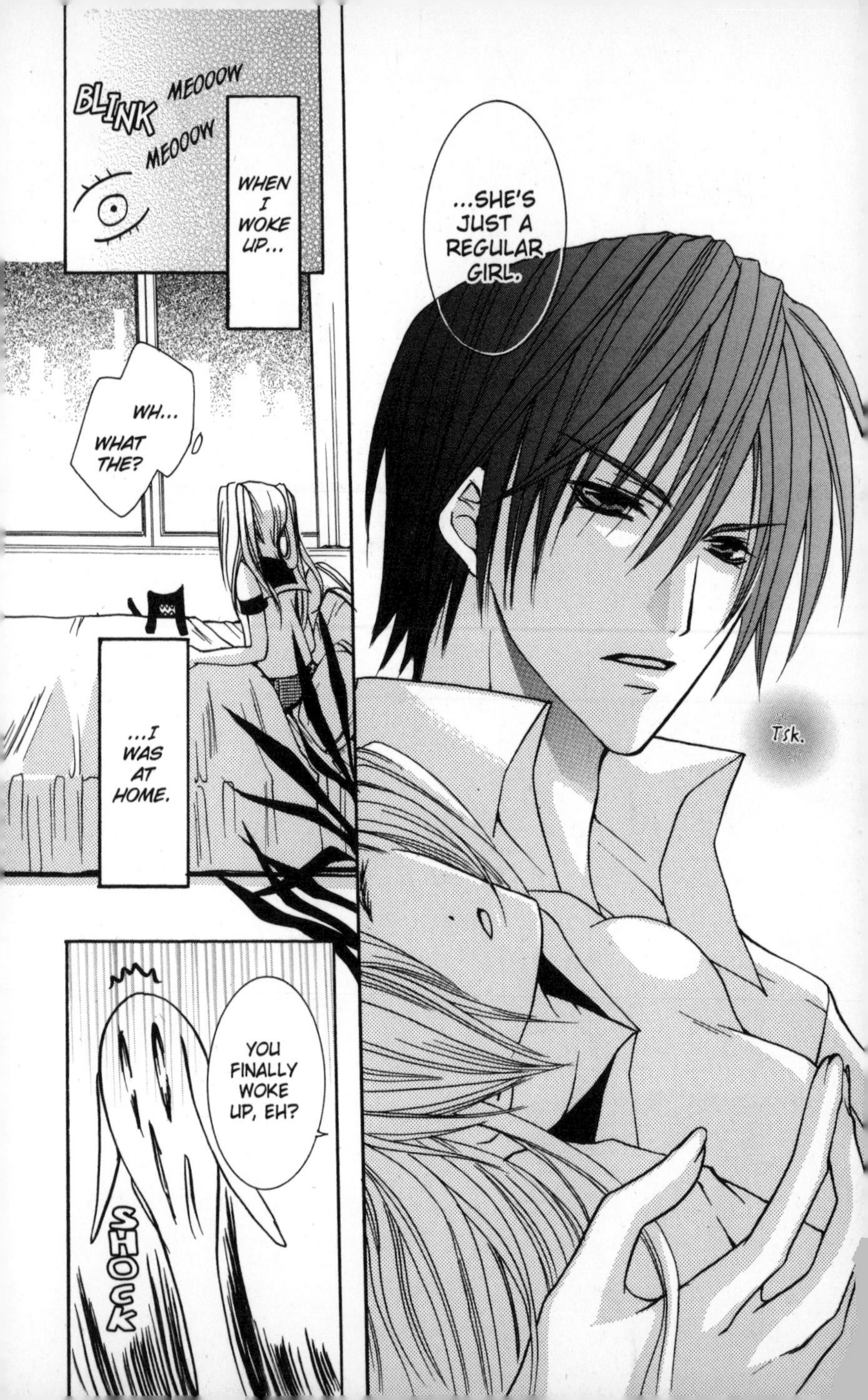
...SHE'S JUST A REGULAR GIRL.
Tsk.
BLINK
MEOOOW
MEOOOW
WHEN I WOKE UP...
WH... WHAT THE?
...I WAS AT HOME.
YOU FINALLY WOKE UP, EH?
SHOCK

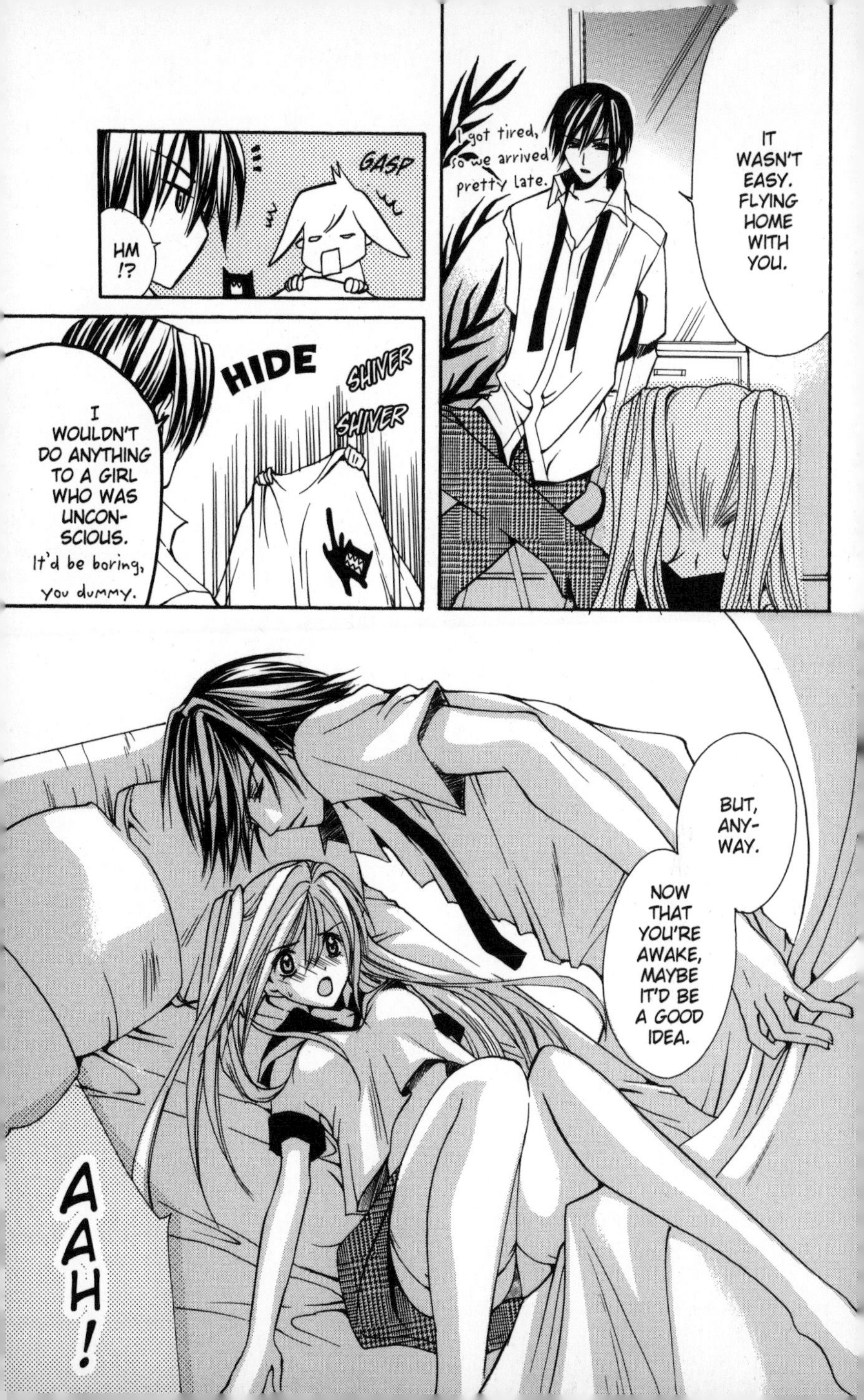
IT WASN'T EASY. FLYING HOME WITH YOU.
I got tired, so we arrived pretty late.
GASP
HM !?
HIDE
SHIVER
SHIVER
I WOULDN'T DO ANYTHING TO A GIRL WHO WAS UNCON- SCIOUS.
It'd be boring, you dummy.
BUT, ANY- WAY.
NOW THAT YOU'RE AWAKE, MAYBE IT'D BE A GOOD IDEA.
AAH!

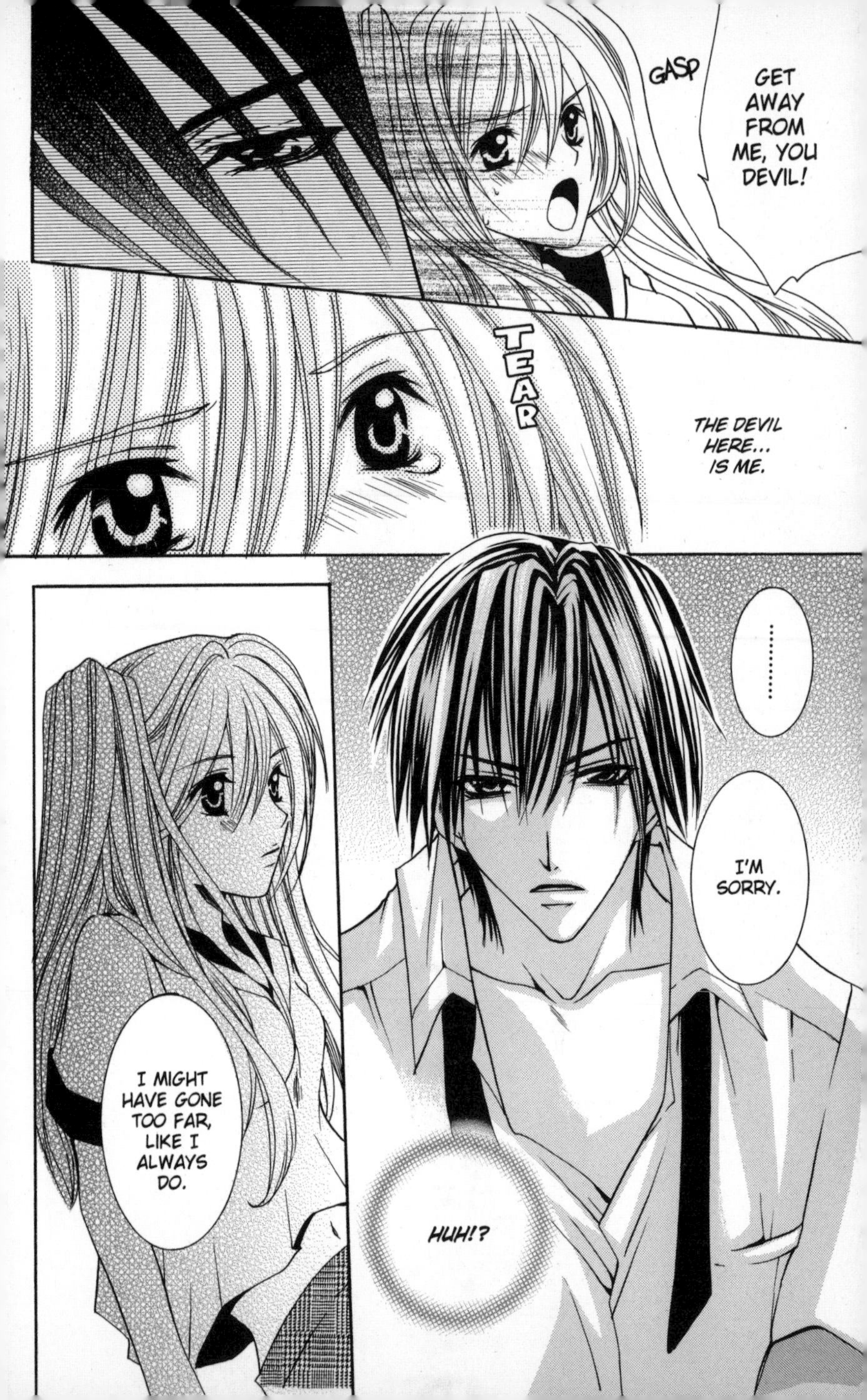
GET AWAY FROM ME, YOU DEVIL!
GASP
TEAR
THE DEVIL HERE... IS ME.
......
I'M SORRY.
HUH!?
I MIGHT HAVE GONE TOO FAR, LIKE I ALWAYS DO.

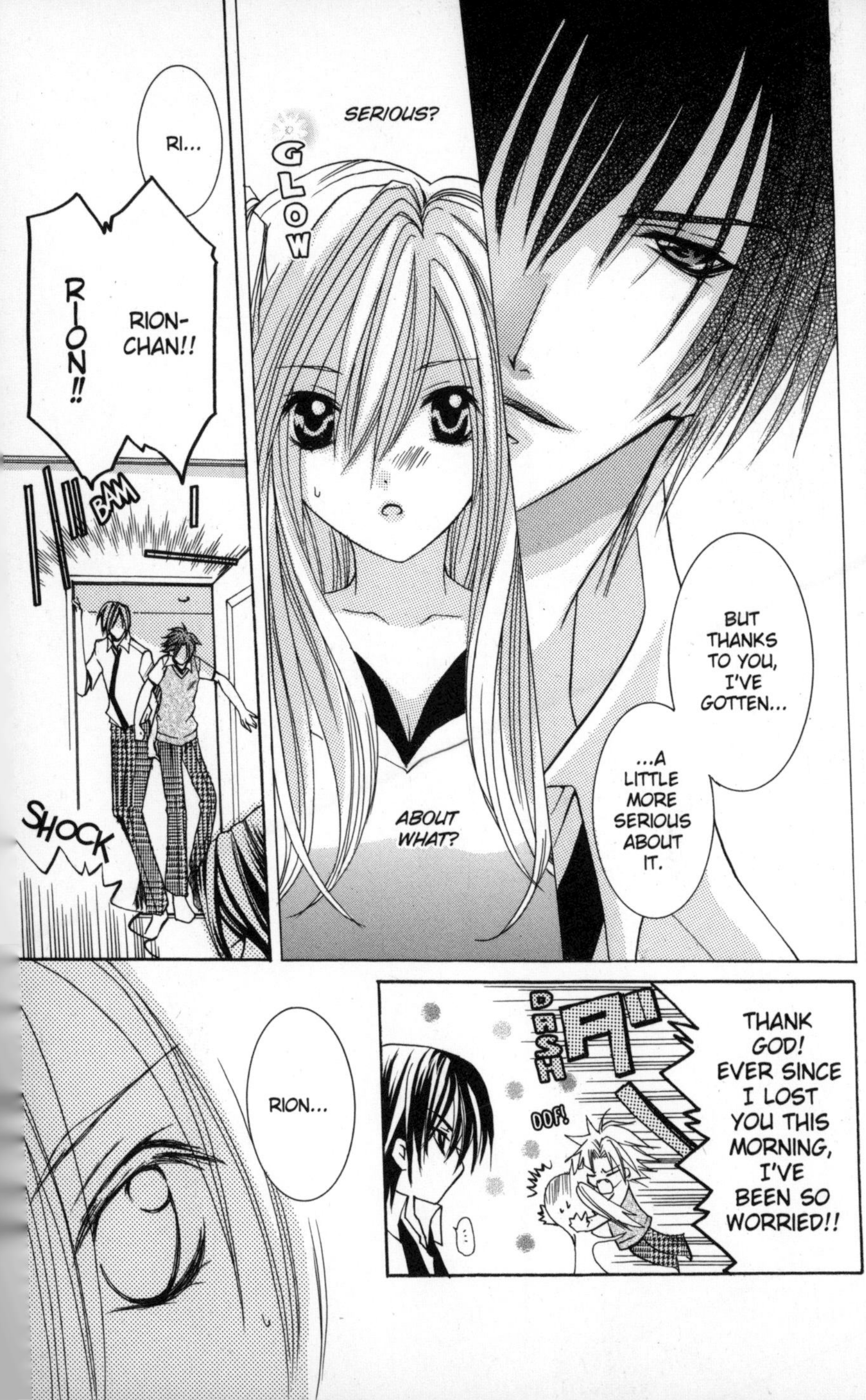
BUT THANKS TO YOU, I'VE GOTTEN...
...A LITTLE MORE SERIOUS ABOUT IT.
ABOUT WHAT?
SERIOUS?
GLOW
RI...
RION-CHAN!!
RION!!
BAM
SHOCK
THANK GOD! EVER SINCE I LOST YOU THIS MORNING, I'VE BEEN SO WORRIED!!
DASH
DOF!
RION...

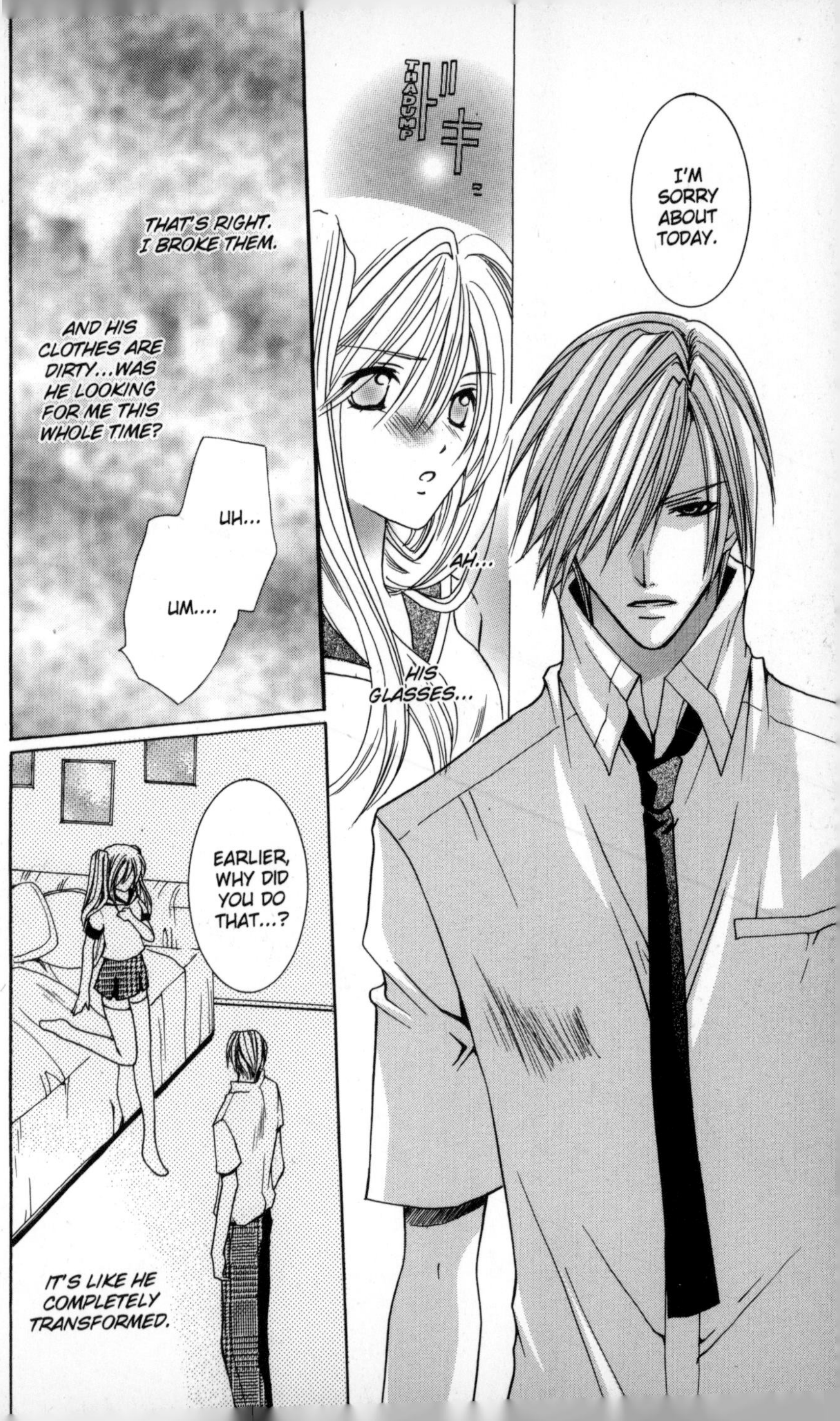
I'M SORRY ABOUT TODAY.
THADUMP
AH...
HIS GLASSES...
THAT'S RIGHT. I BROKE THEM.
AND HIS CLOTHES ARE DIRTY...WAS HE LOOKING FOR ME THIS WHOLE TIME?
UH...
UM....
EARLIER, WHY DID YOU DO THAT...?
IT'S LIKE HE COMPLETELY TRANSFORMED.

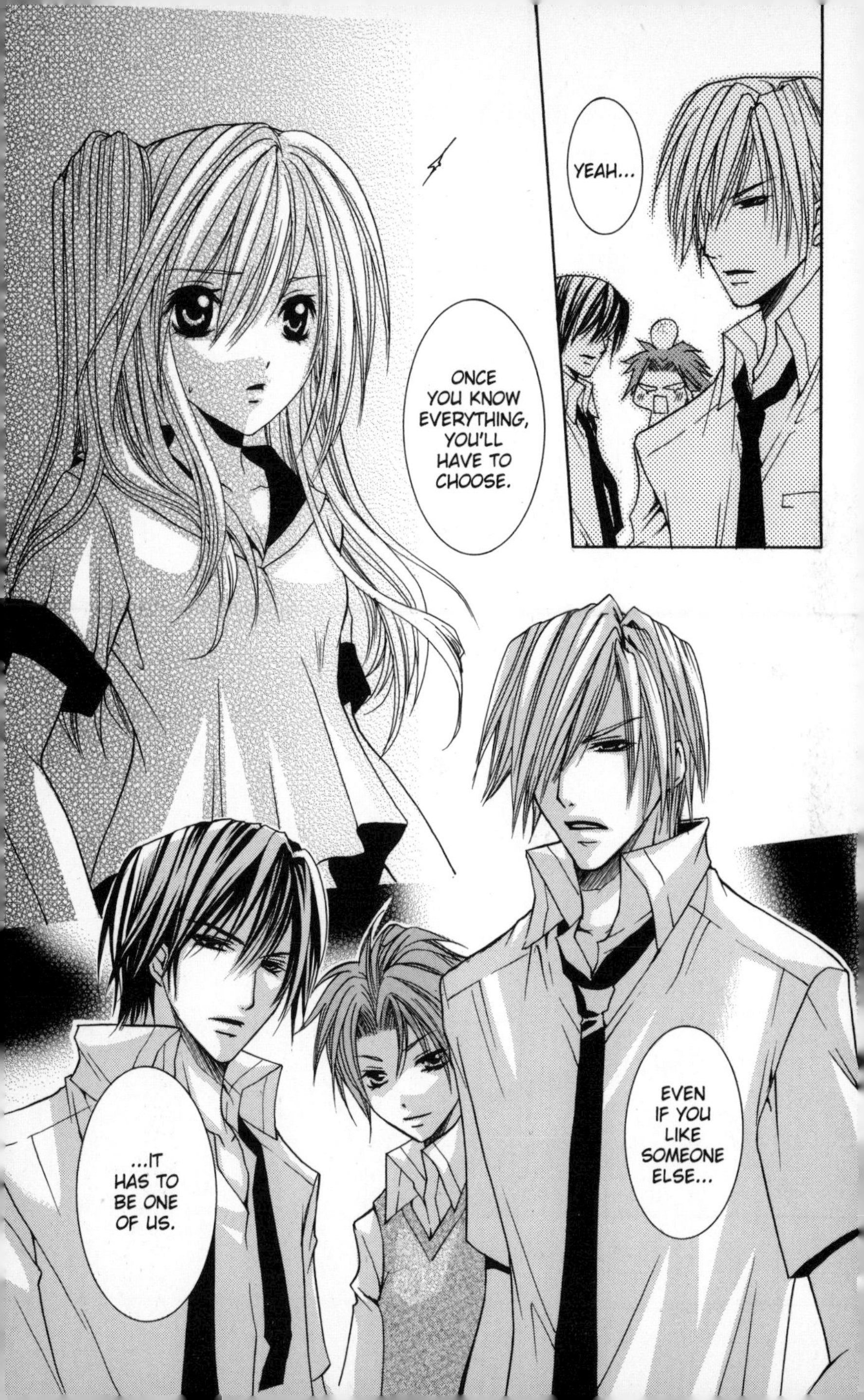
YEAH...
ONCE YOU KNOW EVERYTHING, YOU'LL HAVE TO CHOOSE.
EVEN IF YOU LIKE SOMEONE ELSE...
...IT HAS TO BE ONE OF US.

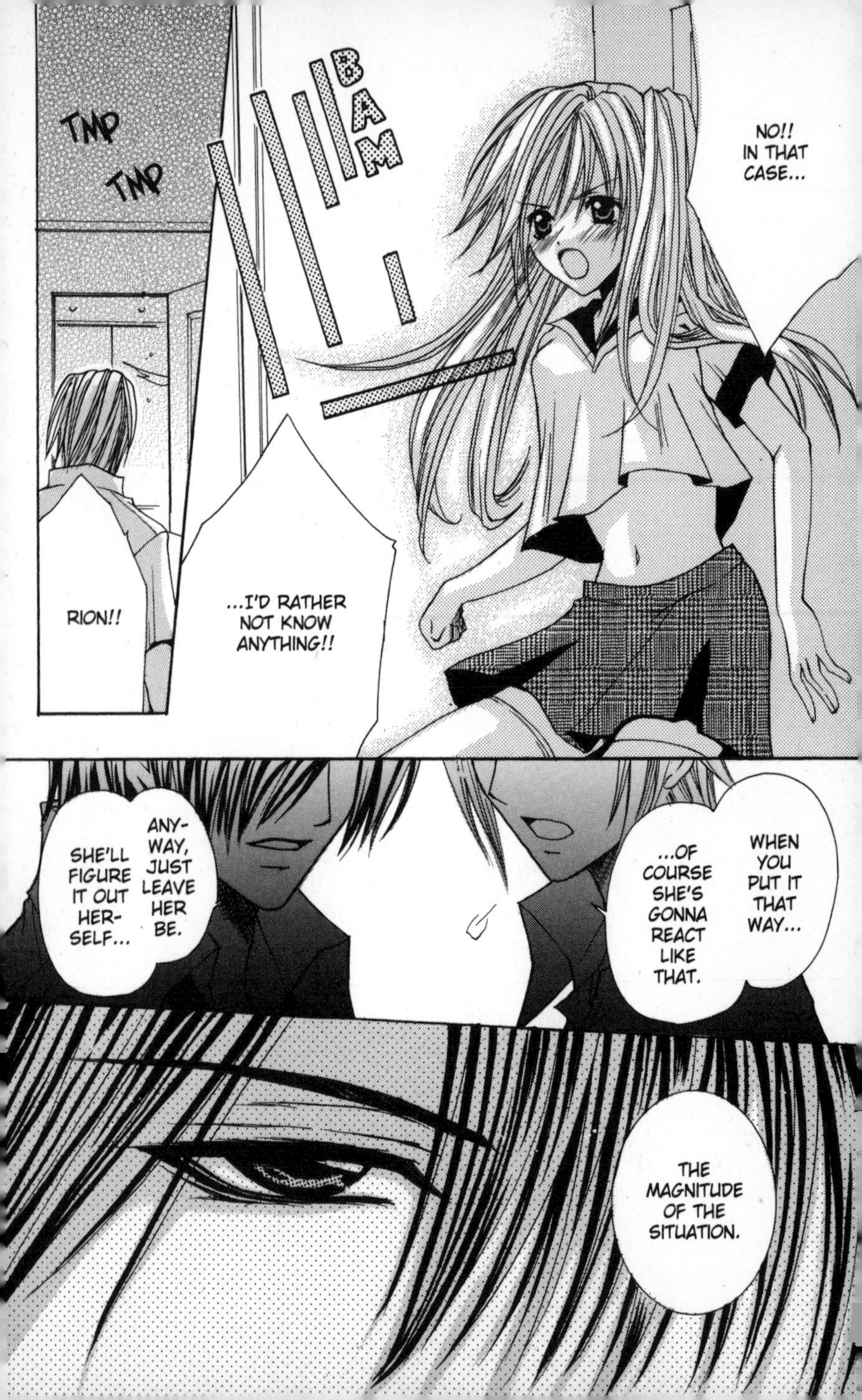
NO!! IN THAT CASE...
BAM
TMP TMP
...I'D RATHER NOT KNOW ANYTHING!!
RION!!
WHEN YOU PUT IT THAT WAY...
...OF COURSE SHE'S GONNA REACT LIKE THAT.
ANY-WAY, JUST LEAVE HER BE.
SHE'LL FIGURE IT OUT HER-SELF...
THE MAGNITUDE OF THE SITUATION.

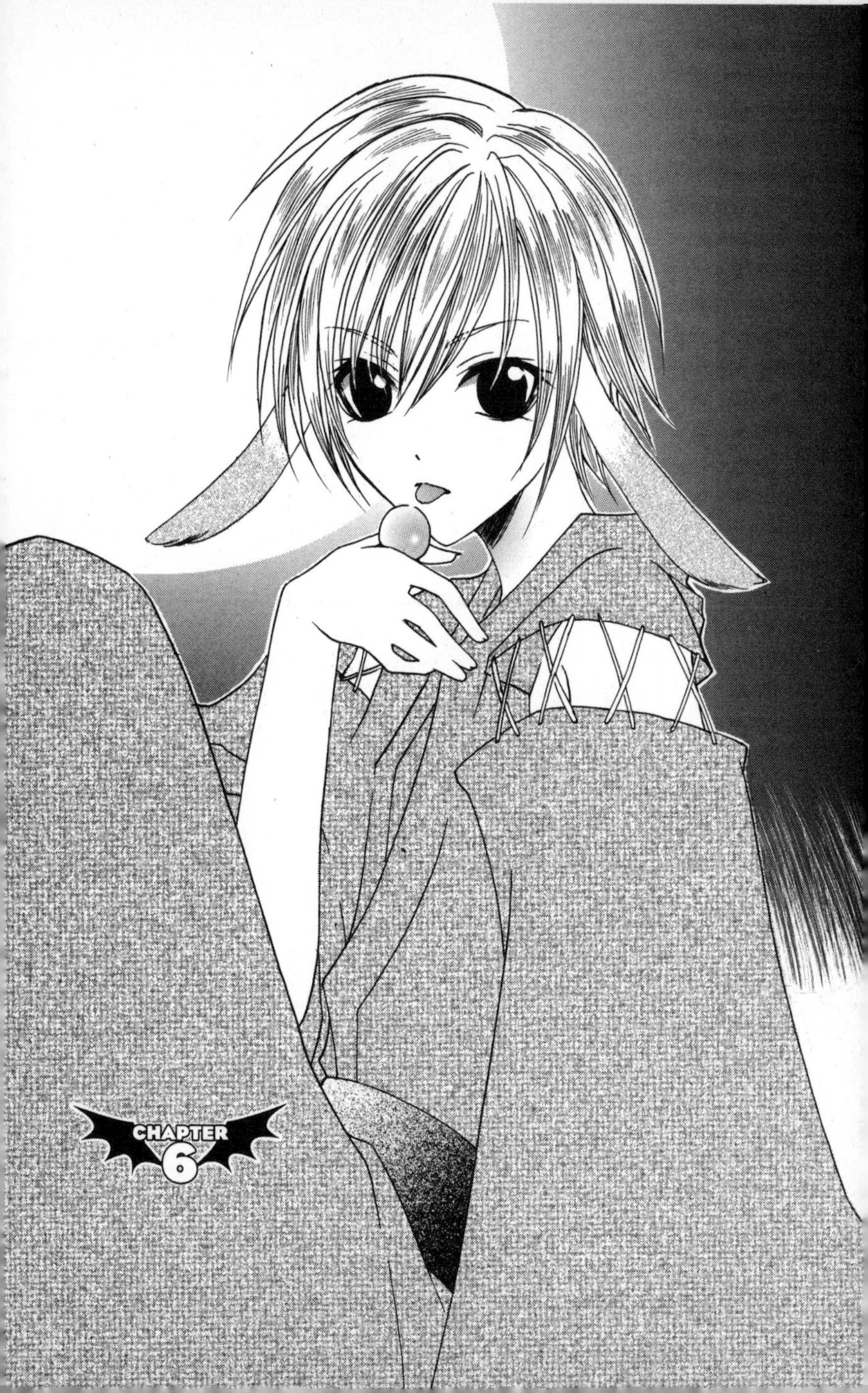
CHAPTER
6

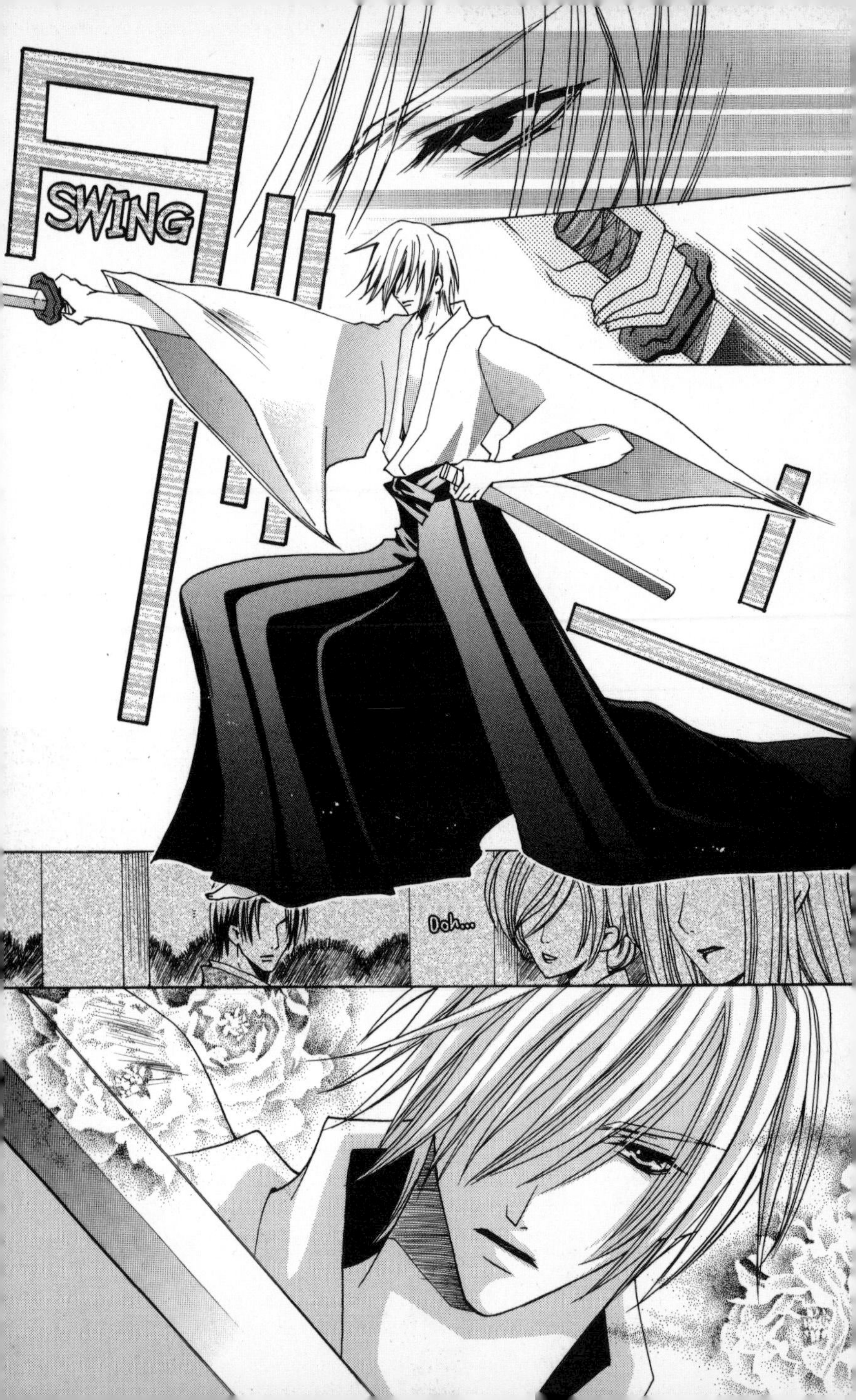
SWING
Ooh...

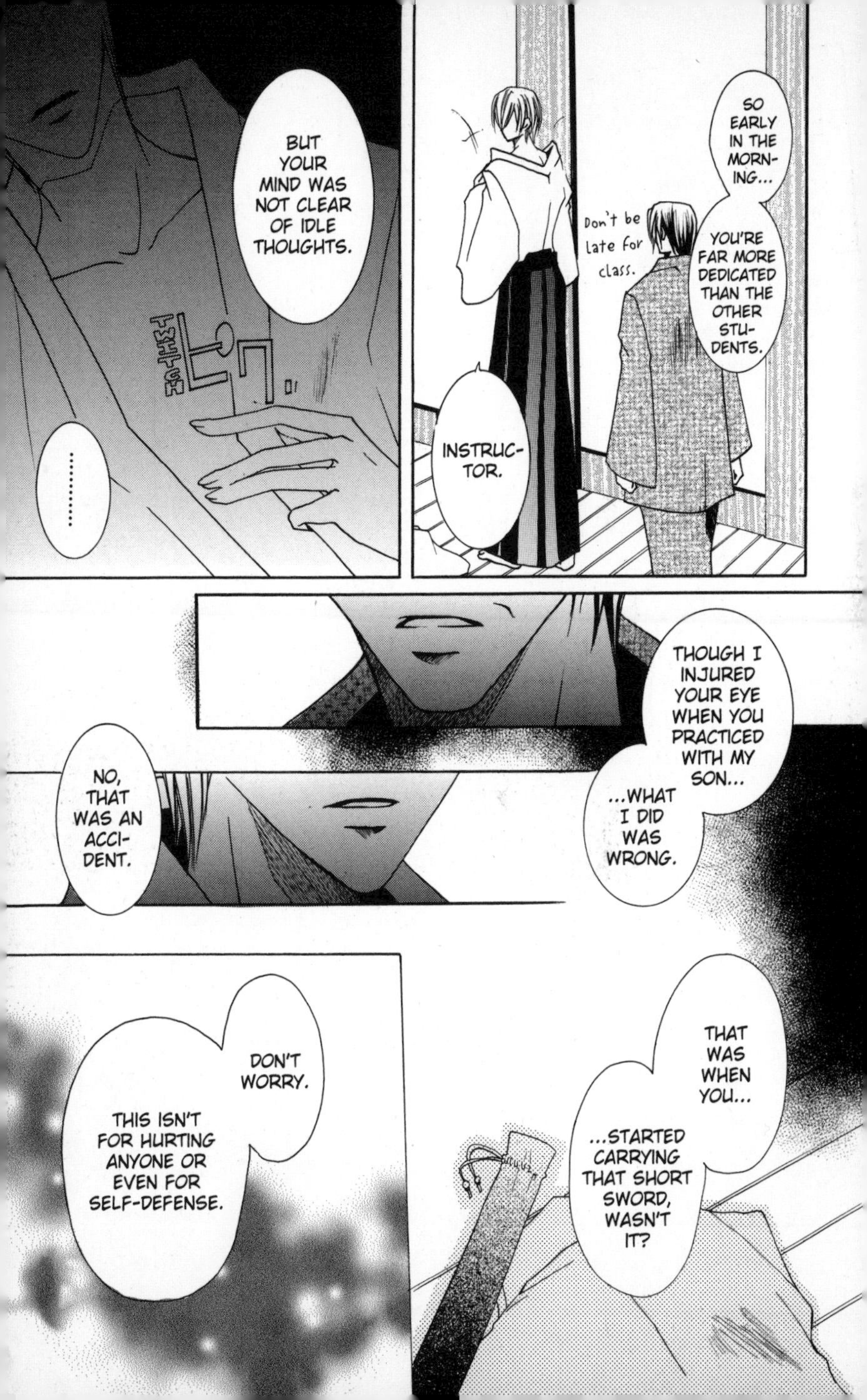
SO EARLY IN THE MORNING...
YOU'RE FAR MORE DEDICATED THAN THE OTHER STUDENTS.
Don't be late for class.
INSTRUCTOR.
BUT YOUR MIND WAS NOT CLEAR OF IDLE THOUGHTS.
TWITCH
......
THOUGH I INJURED YOUR EYE WHEN YOU PRACTICED WITH MY SON...
...WHAT I DID WAS WRONG.
NO, THAT WAS AN ACCIDENT.
THAT WAS WHEN YOU...
...STARTED CARRYING THAT SHORT SWORD, WASN'T IT?
DON'T WORRY.
THIS ISN'T FOR HURTING ANYONE OR EVEN FOR SELF-DEFENSE.

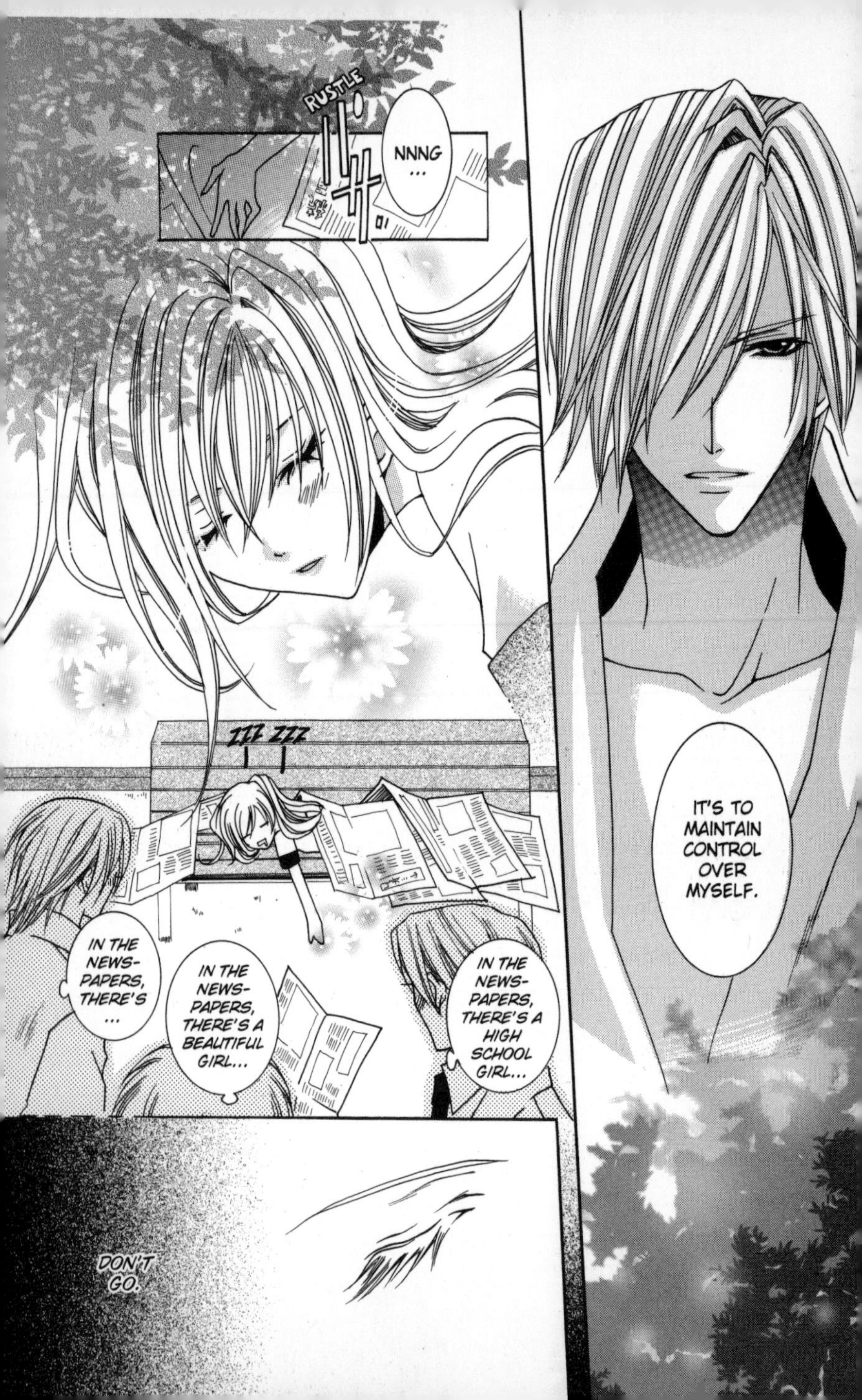
IT'S TO MAINTAIN CONTROL OVER MYSELF.
RUSTLE
NNNG ...
ZZZ ZZZ
IN THE NEWS-PAPERS, THERE'S A HIGH SCHOOL GIRL...
IN THE NEWS-PAPERS, THERE'S A BEAUTIFUL GIRL...
IN THE NEWS-PAPERS, THERE'S ...
DON'T GO.

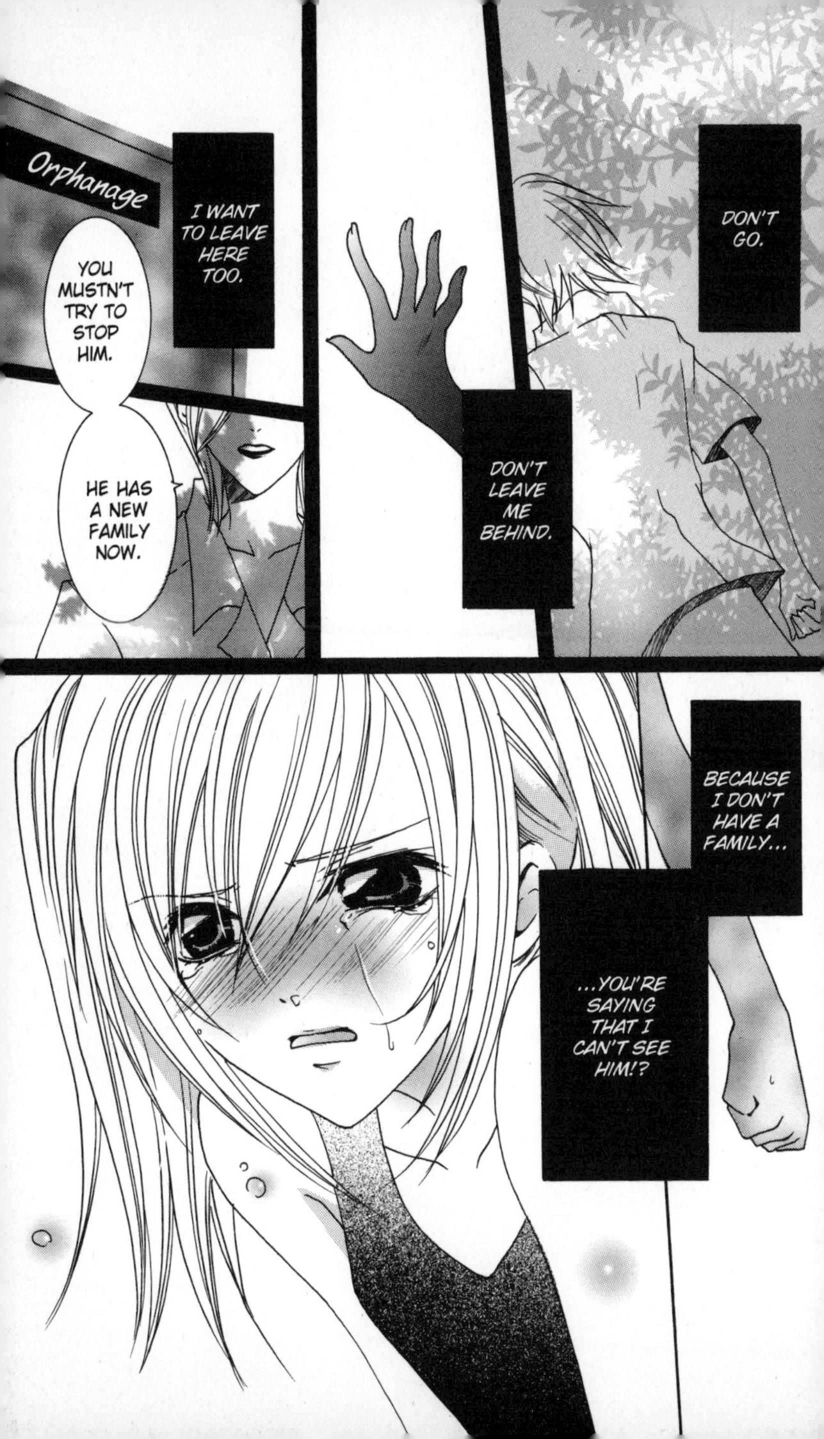
DON'T GO.
DON'T LEAVE ME BEHIND.
I WANT TO LEAVE HERE TOO.
Orphanage
YOU MUSTN'T TRY TO STOP HIM.
HE HAS A NEW FAMILY NOW.
BECAUSE I DON'T HAVE A FAMILY...
...YOU'RE SAYING THAT I CAN'T SEE HIM!?

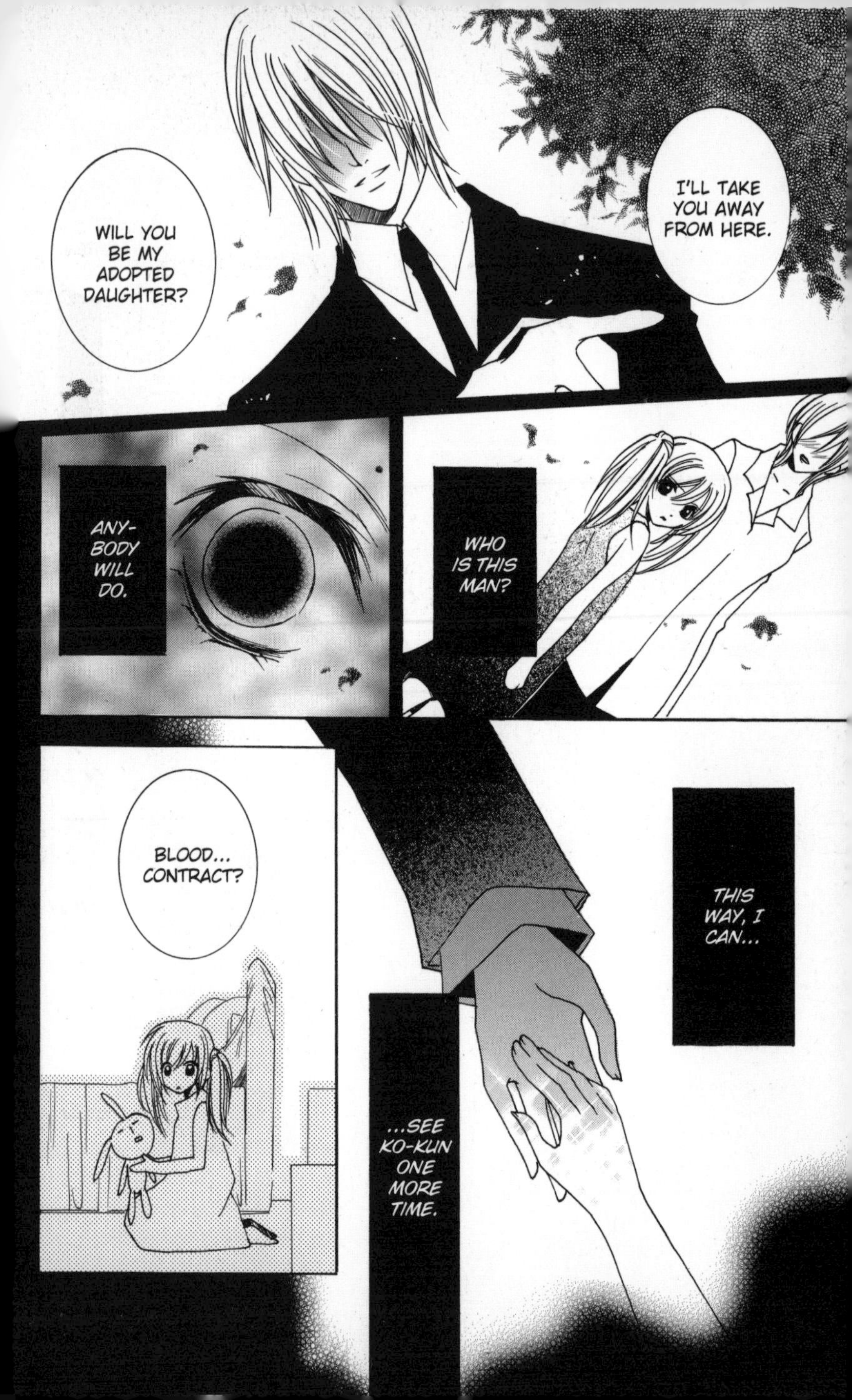

I'LL TAKE YOU AWAY FROM HERE.
WILL YOU BE MY ADOPTED DAUGHTER?
WHO IS THIS MAN?
ANY-BODY WILL DO.
THIS WAY, I CAN...
...SEE KO-KUN ONE MORE TIME.
BLOOD... CONTRACT?

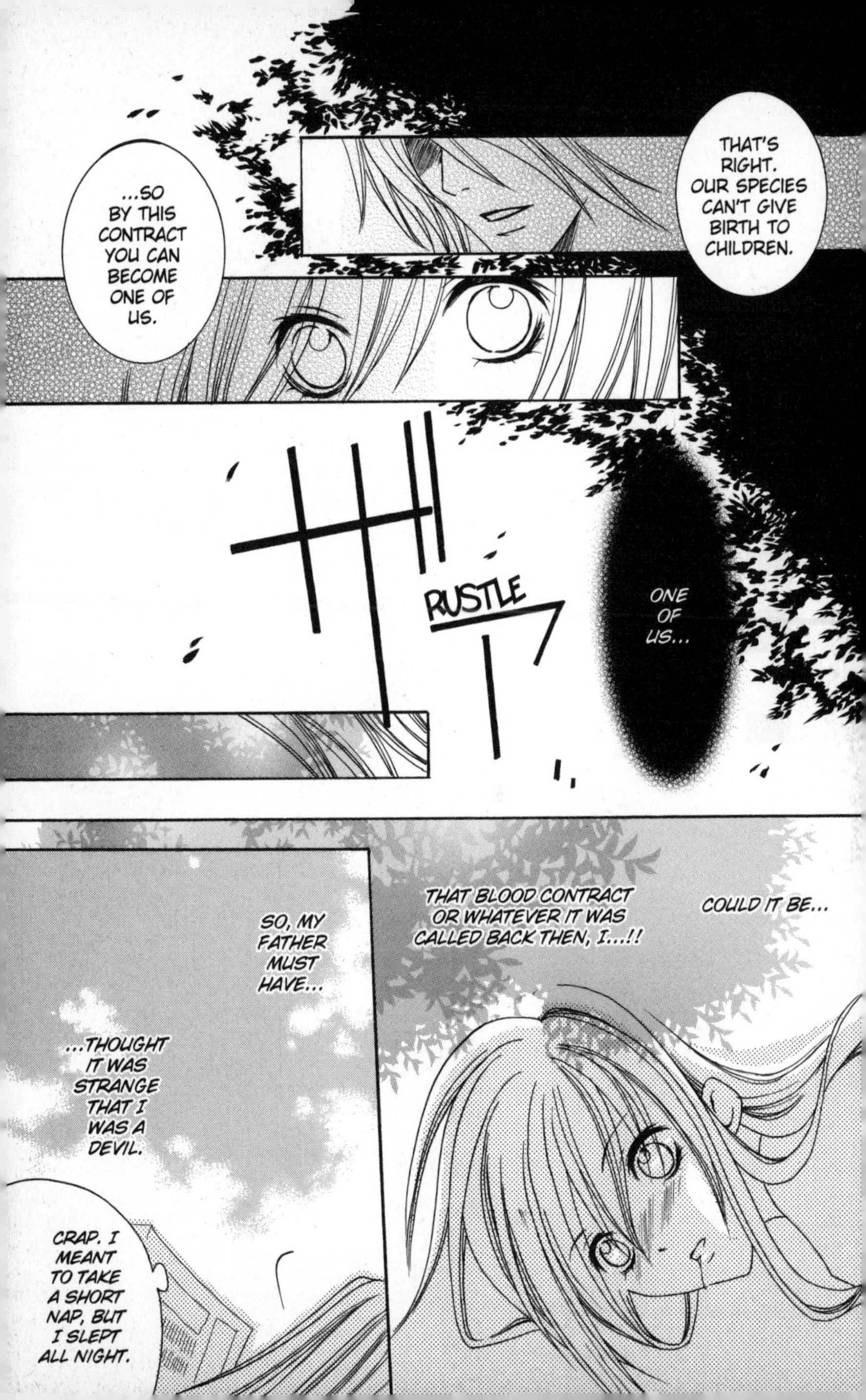
THAT'S RIGHT. OUR SPECIES CAN'T GIVE BIRTH TO CHILDREN.
...SO BY THIS CONTRACT YOU CAN BECOME ONE OF US.
RUSTLE
ONE OF US...
COULD IT BE...
THAT BLOOD CONTRACT OR WHATEVER IT WAS CALLED BACK THEN, I...!!
SO, MY FATHER MUST HAVE...
...THOUGHT IT WAS STRANGE THAT I WAS A DEVIL.
CRAP. I MEANT TO TAKE A SHORT NAP, BUT I SLEPT ALL NIGHT.

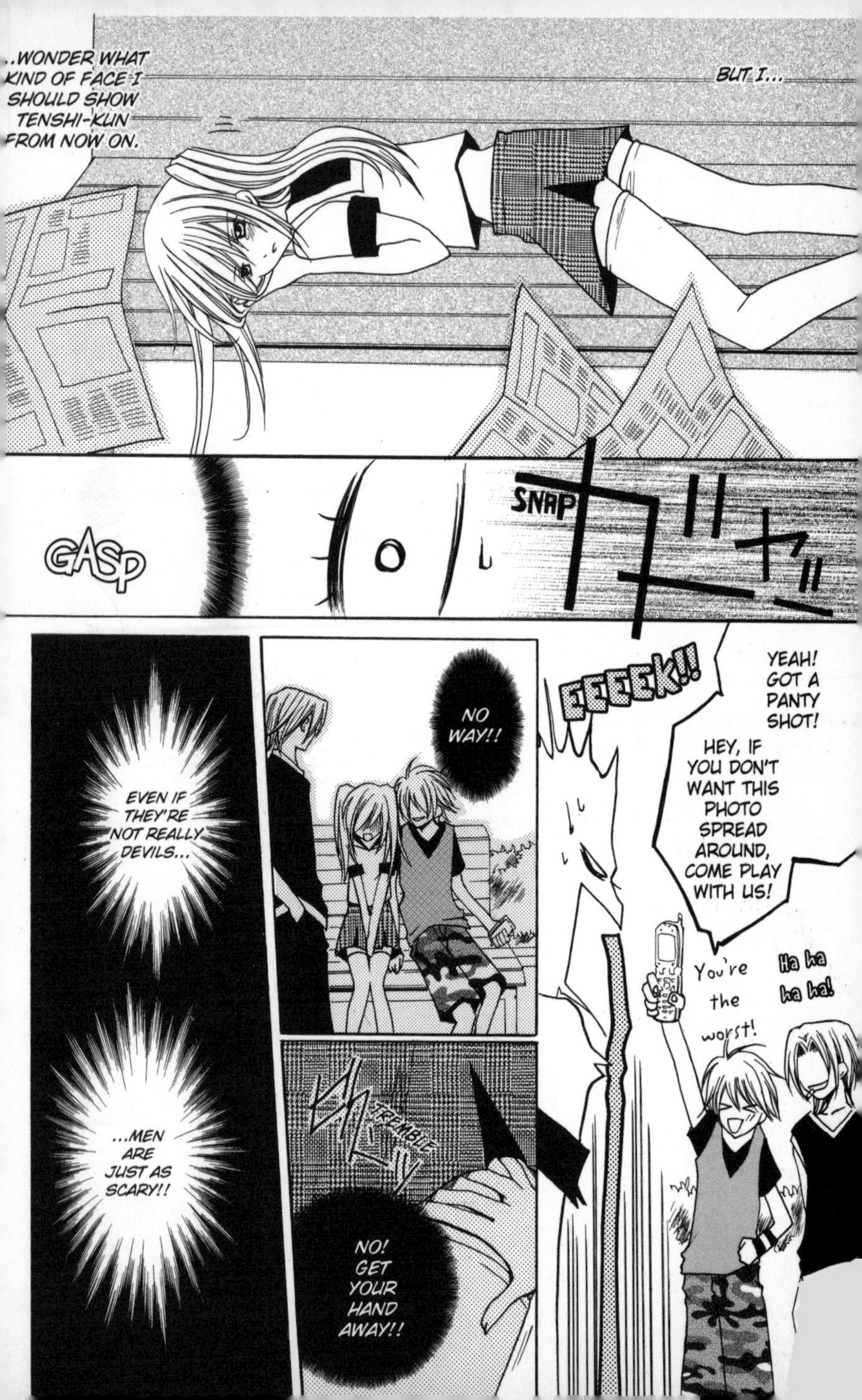
BUT I...
..WONDER WHAT KIND OF FACE I SHOULD SHOW TENSHI-KUN FROM NOW ON.
SNAP
GASP
YEAH! GOT A PANTY SHOT!
HEY, IF YOU DON'T WANT THIS PHOTO SPREAD AROUND, COME PLAY WITH US!
EEEEK!!
You're the worst!
Ha ha ha ha!
NO WAY!!
TREMBLE
NO! GET YOUR HAND AWAY!!
EVEN IF THEY'RE NOT REALLY DEVILS...
...MEN ARE JUST AS SCARY!!

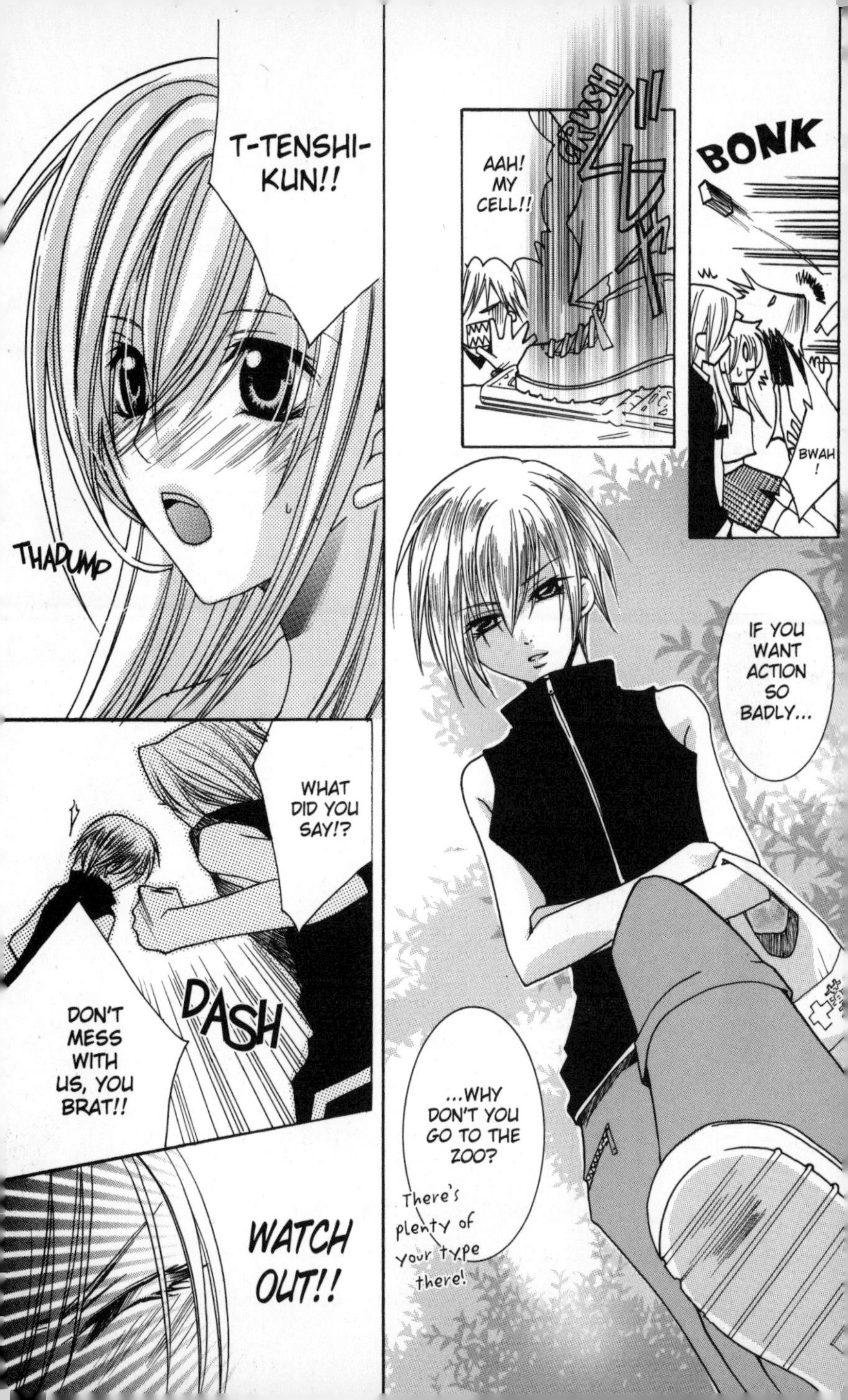
BONK
BWAH!
CRUSH
AAH! MY CELL!!
IF YOU WANT ACTION SO BADLY...
...WHY DON'T YOU GO TO THE ZOO?
There's plenty of your type there!
T-TENSHI-KUN!!
THADUMP
WHAT DID YOU SAY!?
DON'T MESS WITH US, YOU BRAT!!
DASH
WATCH OUT!!

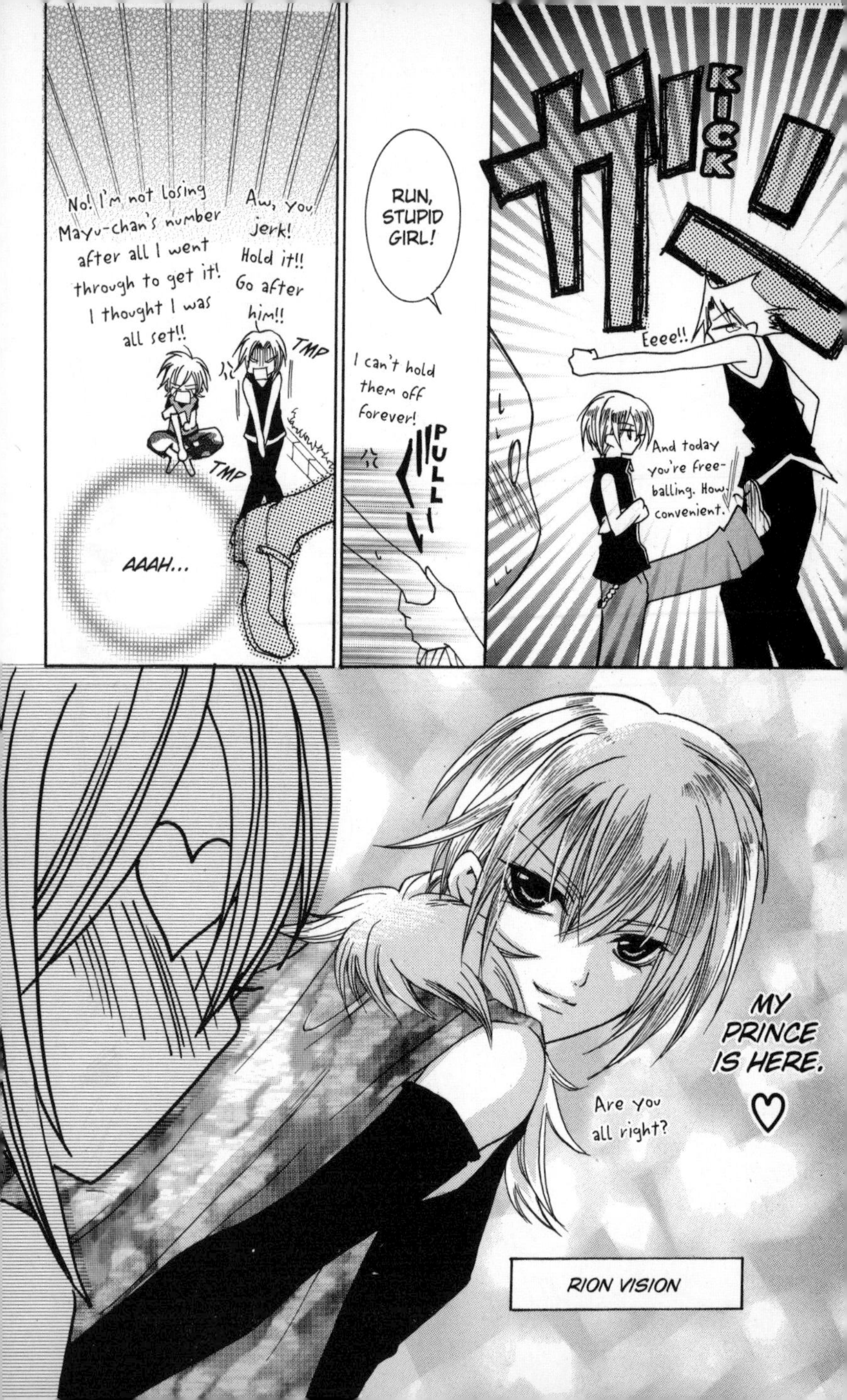
KICK
Eeee!!
And today you're free-balling. How convenient.
RUN, STUPID GIRL!
I can't hold them off forever!
PULL
Aw, you jerk! Hold it!! Go after him!!
No! I'm not losing Mayu-chan's number after all I went through to get it! I thought I was all set!!
TMP
TMP
AAAH...
MY PRINCE IS HERE. ♥
Are you all right?
RION VISION

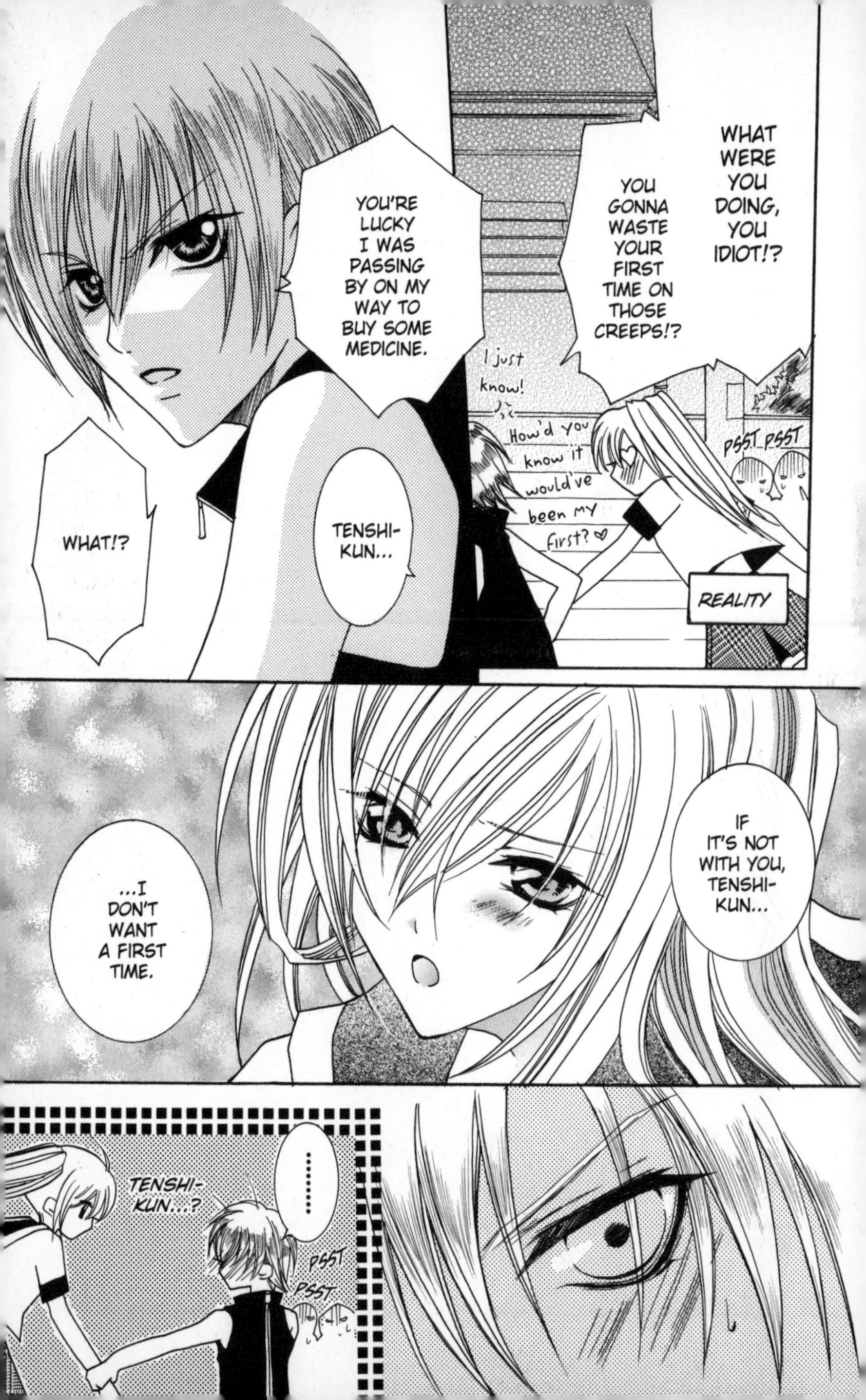
WHAT WERE YOU DOING, YOU IDIOT!?
YOU GONNA WASTE YOUR FIRST TIME ON THOSE CREEPS!?
I just know!
How'd you know it would've been my first?
PSST PSST
REALITY
YOU'RE LUCKY I WAS PASSING BY ON MY WAY TO BUY SOME MEDICINE.
TENSHI-KUN...
WHAT!?
IF IT'S NOT WITH YOU, TENSHI-KUN...
...I DON'T WANT A FIRST TIME.
......
TENSHI-KUN...?
PSST PSST

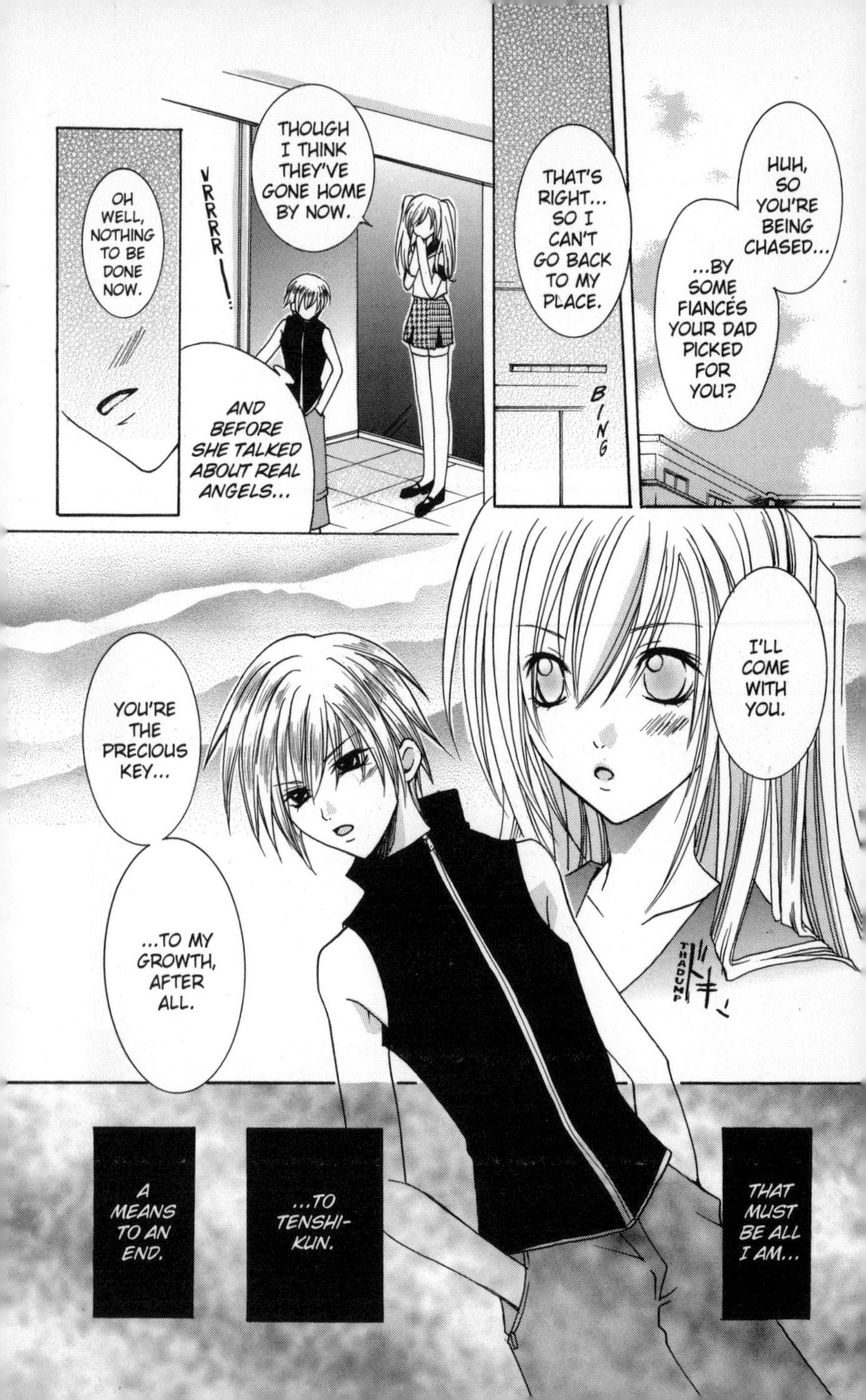
HUH, SO YOU'RE BEING CHASED...
...BY SOME FIANCÉS YOUR DAD PICKED FOR YOU?
BING
THAT'S RIGHT... SO I CAN'T GO BACK TO MY PLACE.
THOUGH I THINK THEY'VE GONE HOME BY NOW.
VRRRR!
AND BEFORE SHE TALKED ABOUT REAL ANGELS...
OH WELL, NOTHING TO BE DONE NOW.
I'LL COME WITH YOU.
THADUMP
YOU'RE THE PRECIOUS KEY...
...TO MY GROWTH, AFTER ALL.
THAT MUST BE ALL I AM...
...TO TENSHI-KUN.
A MEANS TO AN END.

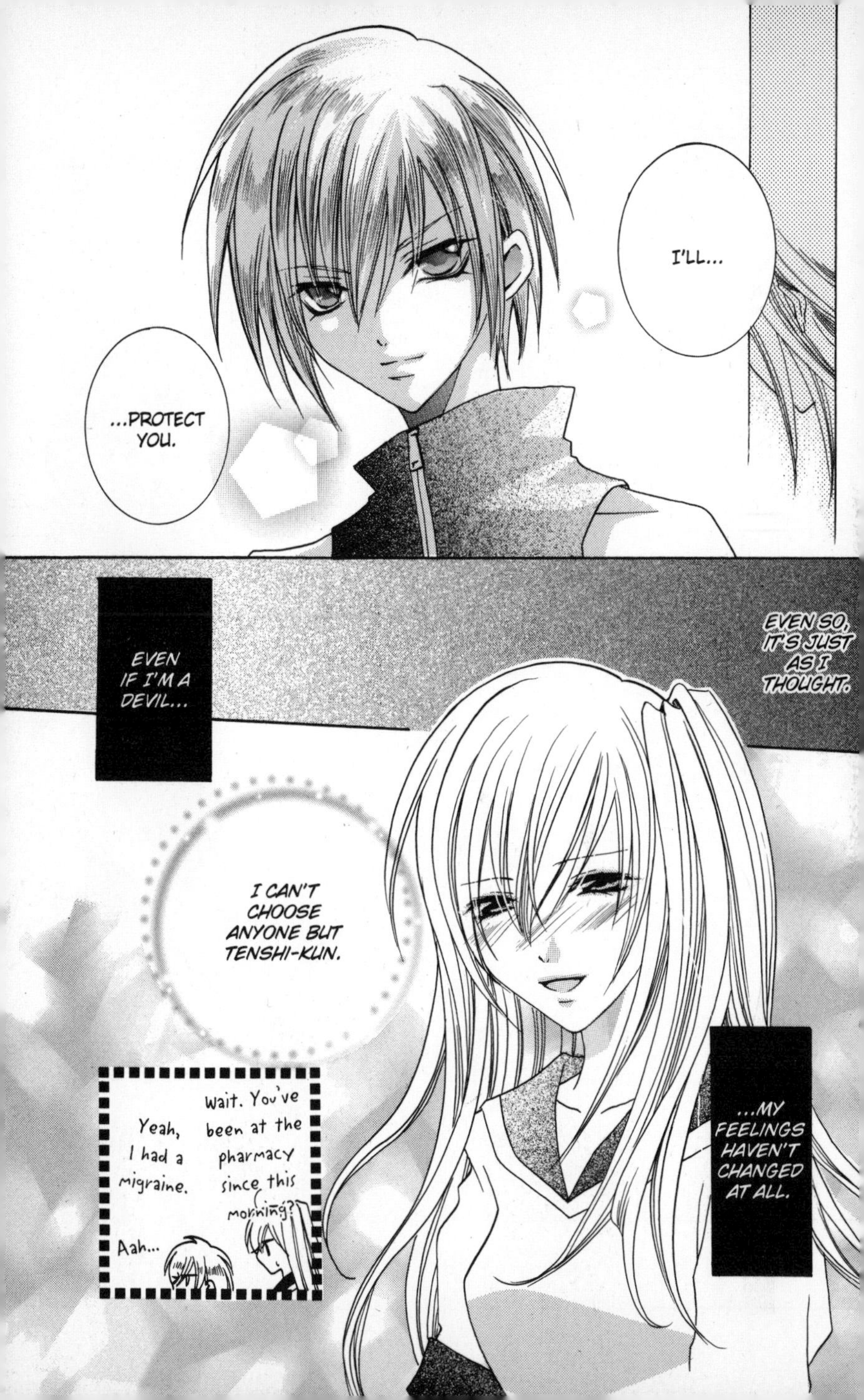
I'LL...
...PROTECT YOU.
EVEN SO, IT'S JUST AS I THOUGHT.
EVEN IF I'M A DEVIL...
I CAN'T CHOOSE ANYONE BUT TENSHI-KUN.
...MY FEELINGS HAVEN'T CHANGED AT ALL.
Wait. You've been at the pharmacy since this morning?
Yeah, I had a migraine.
Aah...

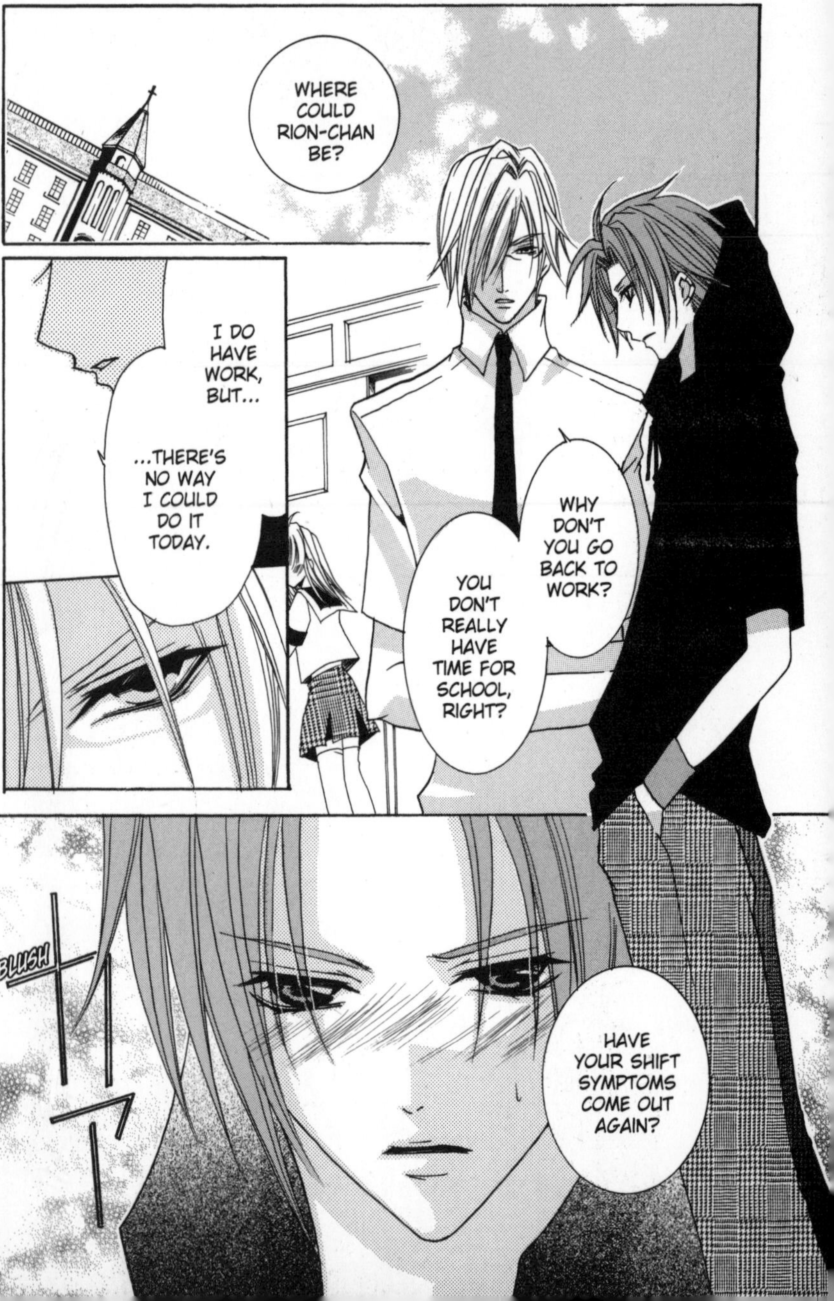
WHERE COULD RION-CHAN BE?
WHY DON'T YOU GO BACK TO WORK?
YOU DON'T REALLY HAVE TIME FOR SCHOOL, RIGHT?
I DO HAVE WORK, BUT...
...THERE'S NO WAY I COULD DO IT TODAY.
BLUSH
HAVE YOUR SHIFT SYMPTOMS COME OUT AGAIN?

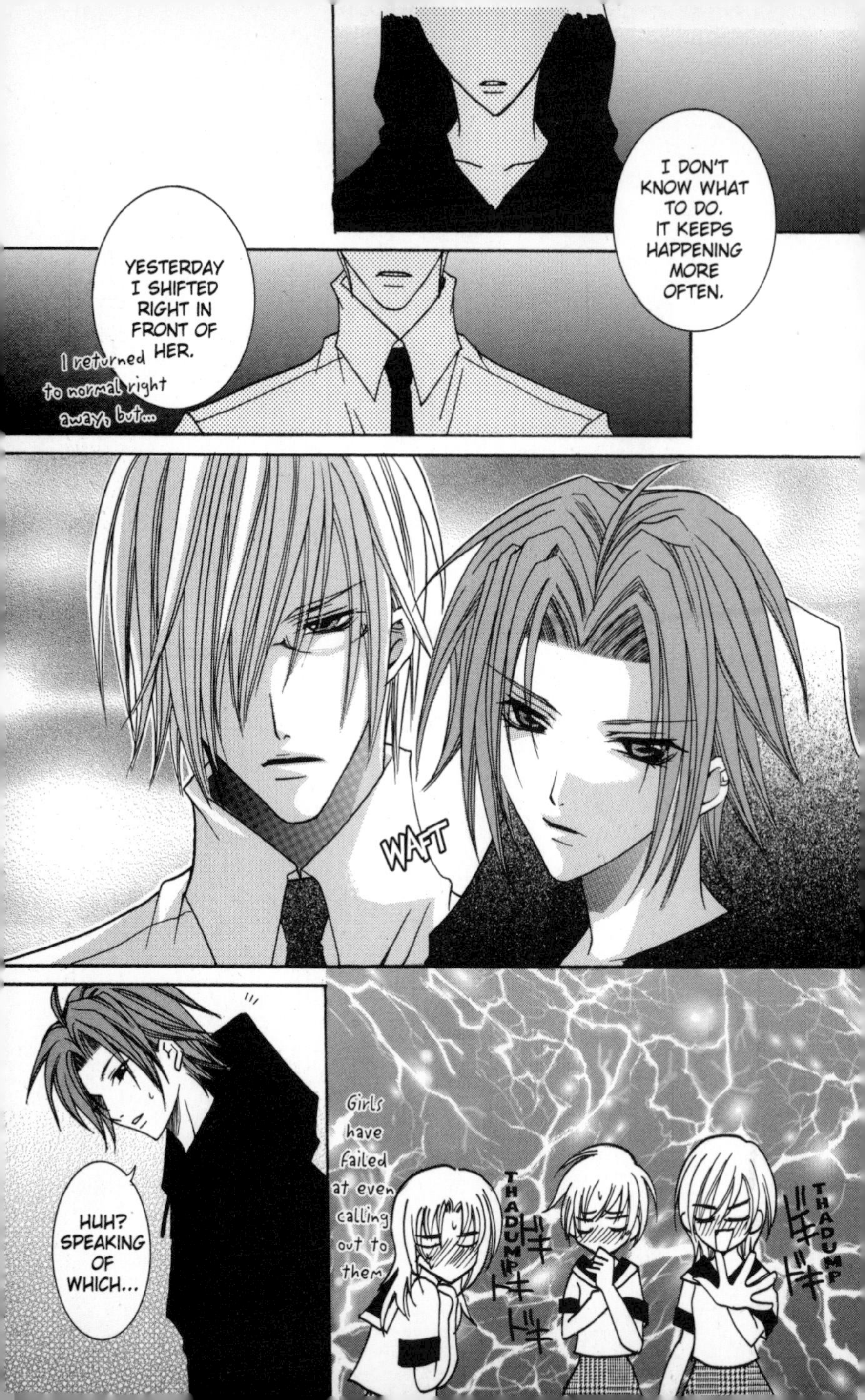
I DON'T KNOW WHAT TO DO. IT KEEPS HAPPENING MORE OFTEN.
YESTERDAY I SHIFTED RIGHT IN FRONT OF HER.
I returned to normal right away, but...
WAFT
Girls have failed at even calling out to them
THADUMP
THADUMP
HUH? SPEAKING OF WHICH...

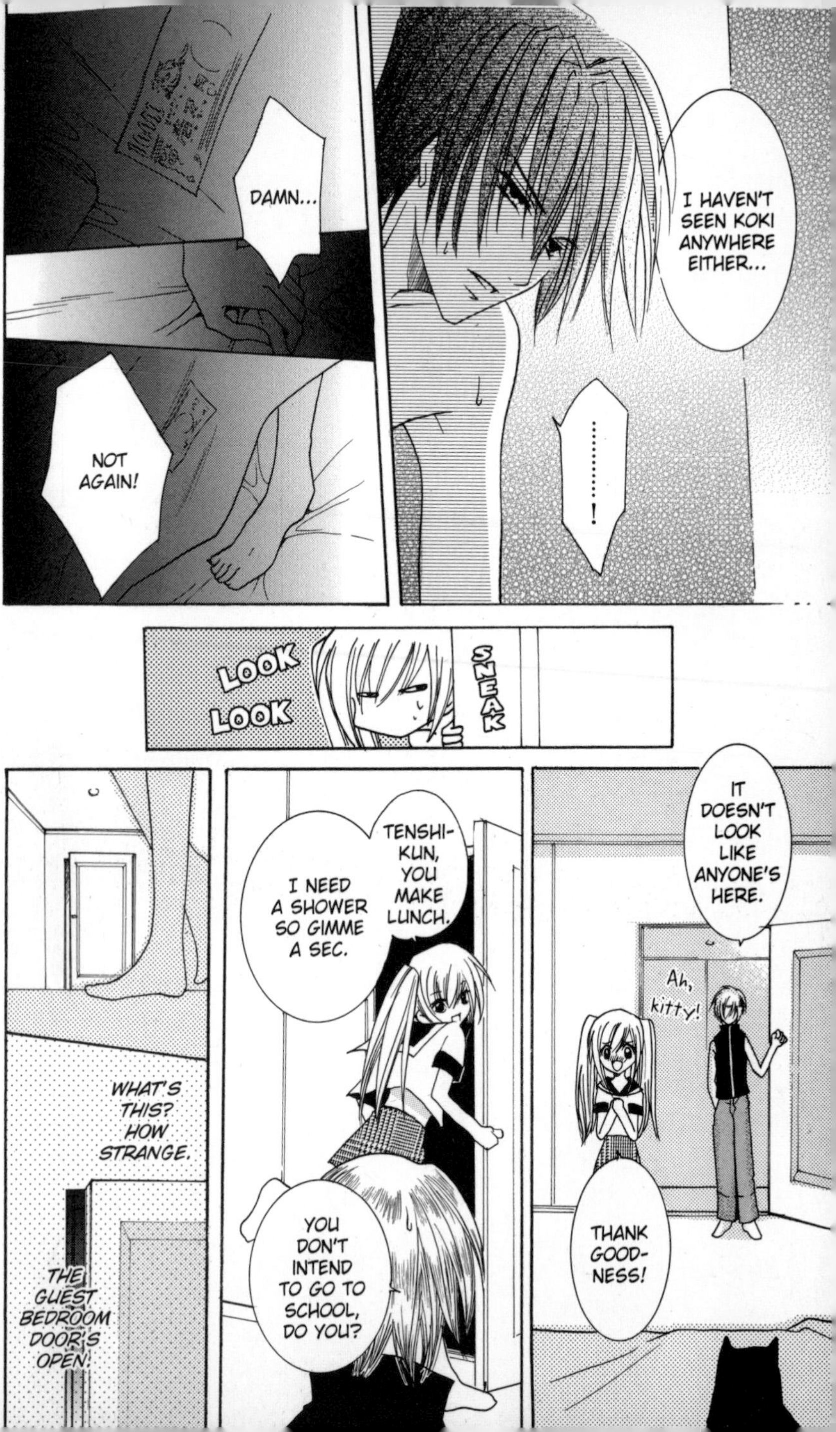
I HAVEN'T SEEN KOKI ANYWHERE EITHER...
......!
DAMN...
NOT AGAIN!
SNEAK
LOOK LOOK
IT DOESN'T LOOK LIKE ANYONE'S HERE.
Ah, kitty!
THANK GOOD-NESS!
TENSHI-KUN, YOU MAKE LUNCH.
I NEED A SHOWER SO GIMME A SEC.
YOU DON'T INTEND TO GO TO SCHOOL, DO YOU?
WHAT'S THIS? HOW STRANGE.
THE GUEST BEDROOM DOOR'S OPEN.

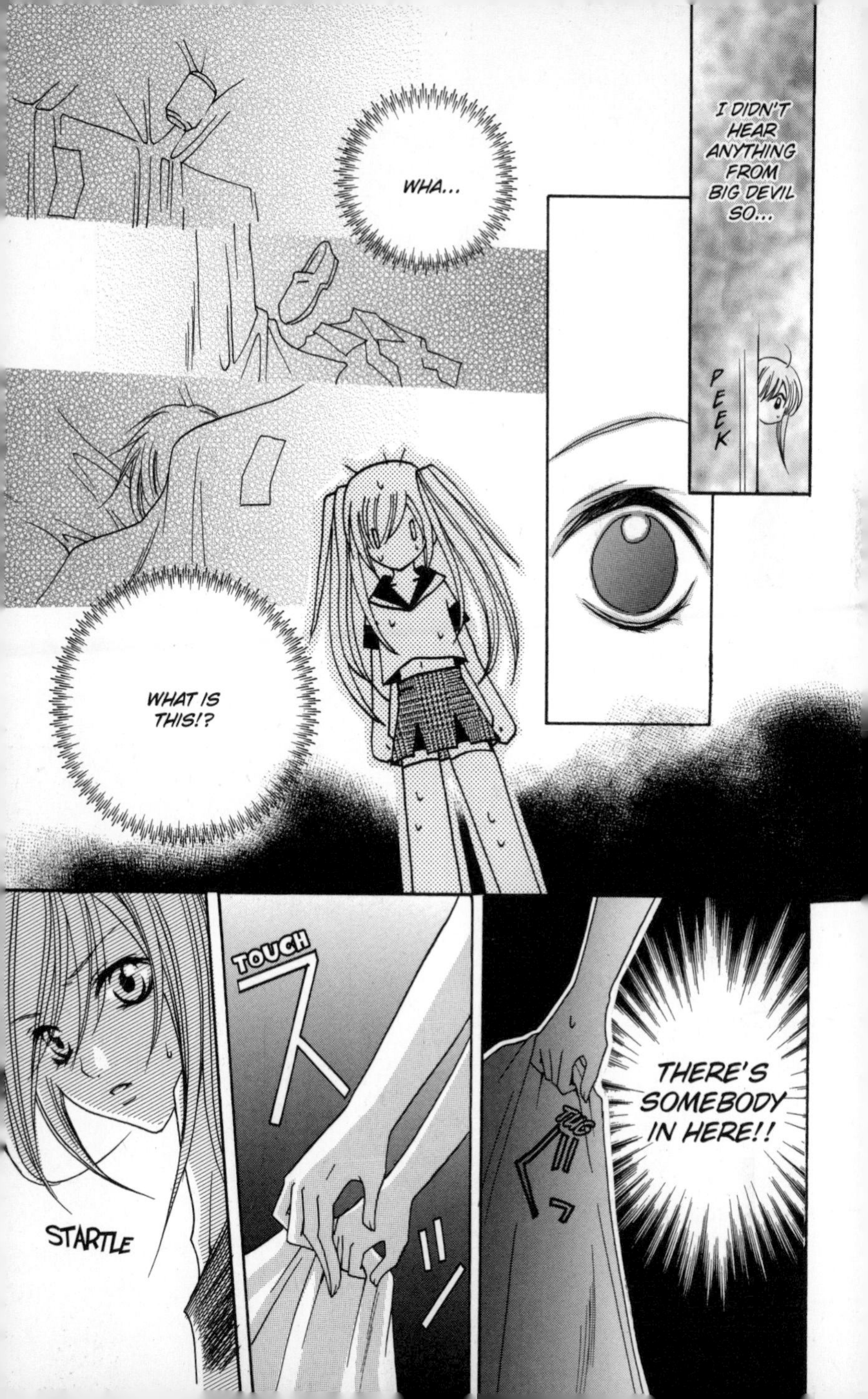
I DIDN'T HEAR ANYTHING FROM BIG DEVIL SO...
PEEK
WHA...
WHAT IS THIS!?
THERE'S SOMEBODY IN HERE!!
TUG
TOUCH
STARTLE

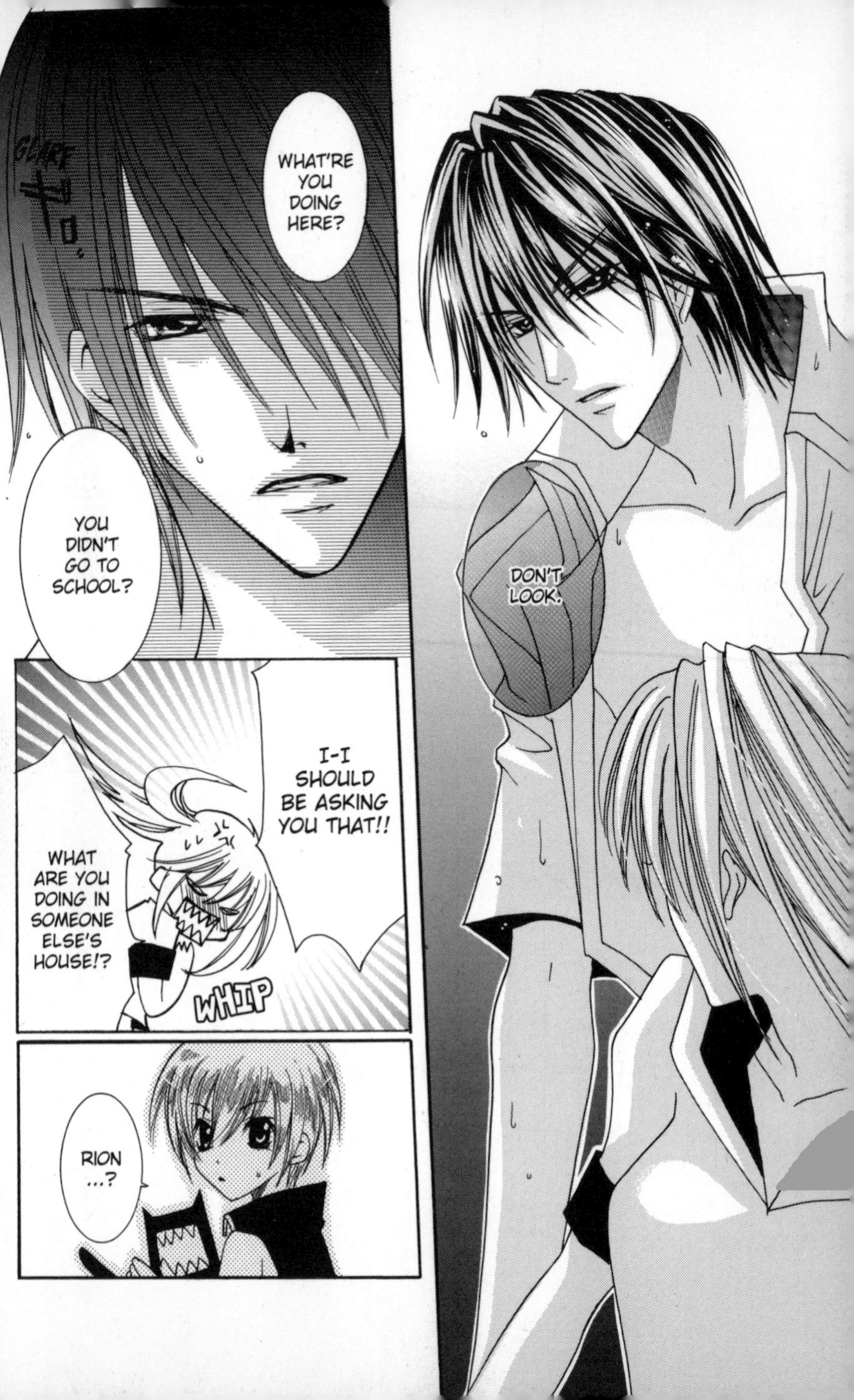
DON'T LOOK.
WHAT'RE YOU DOING HERE?
GLARE
YOU DIDN'T GO TO SCHOOL?
I-I SHOULD BE ASKING YOU THAT!!
WHAT ARE YOU DOING IN SOMEONE ELSE'S HOUSE!?
WHIP
RION ...?

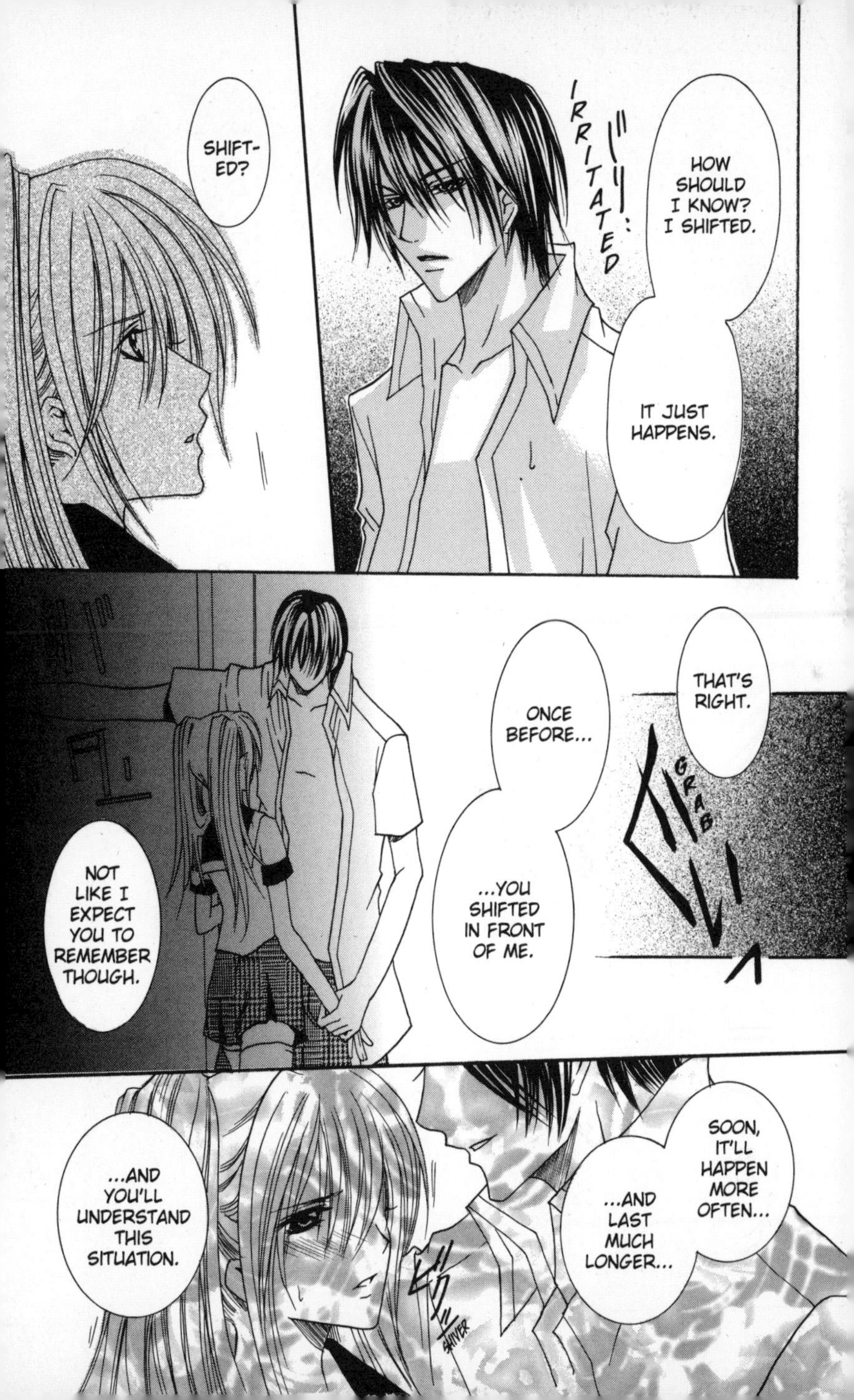
IRRITATED
HOW SHOULD I KNOW? I SHIFTED.
IT JUST HAPPENS.
SHIFT-ED?
THAT'S RIGHT.
GRAB
ONCE BEFORE...
...YOU SHIFTED IN FRONT OF ME.
NOT LIKE I EXPECT YOU TO REMEMBER THOUGH.
SOON, IT'LL HAPPEN MORE OFTEN...
...AND LAST MUCH LONGER...
SHIVER
...AND YOU'LL UNDERSTAND THIS SITUATION.

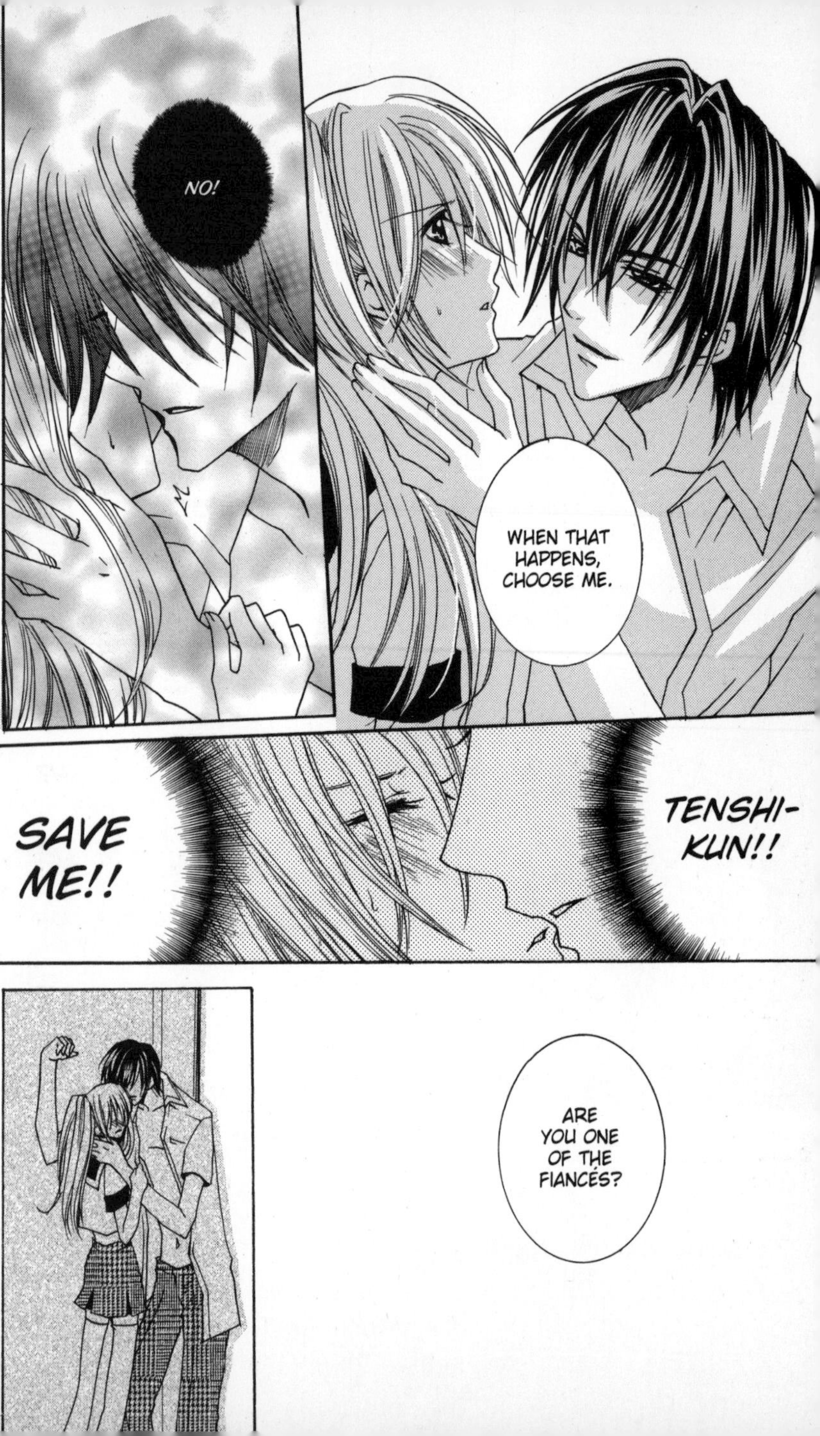
WHEN THAT HAPPENS, CHOOSE ME.
NO!
TENSHI-KUN!!
SAVE ME!!
ARE YOU ONE OF THE FIANCÉS?

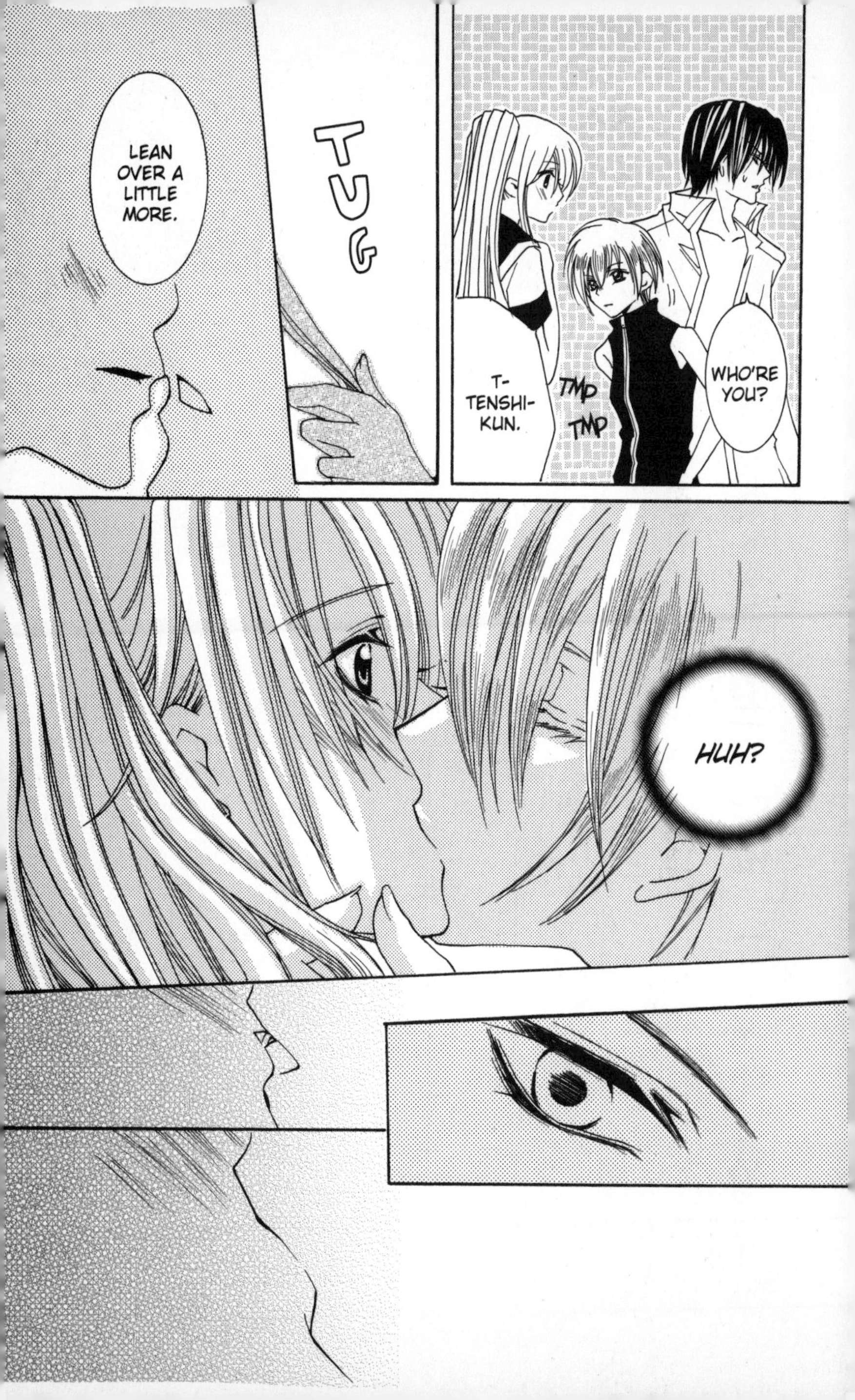
WHO'RE YOU?
TMP TMP
T-TENSHI-KUN.
TUG
LEAN OVER A LITTLE MORE.
HUH?

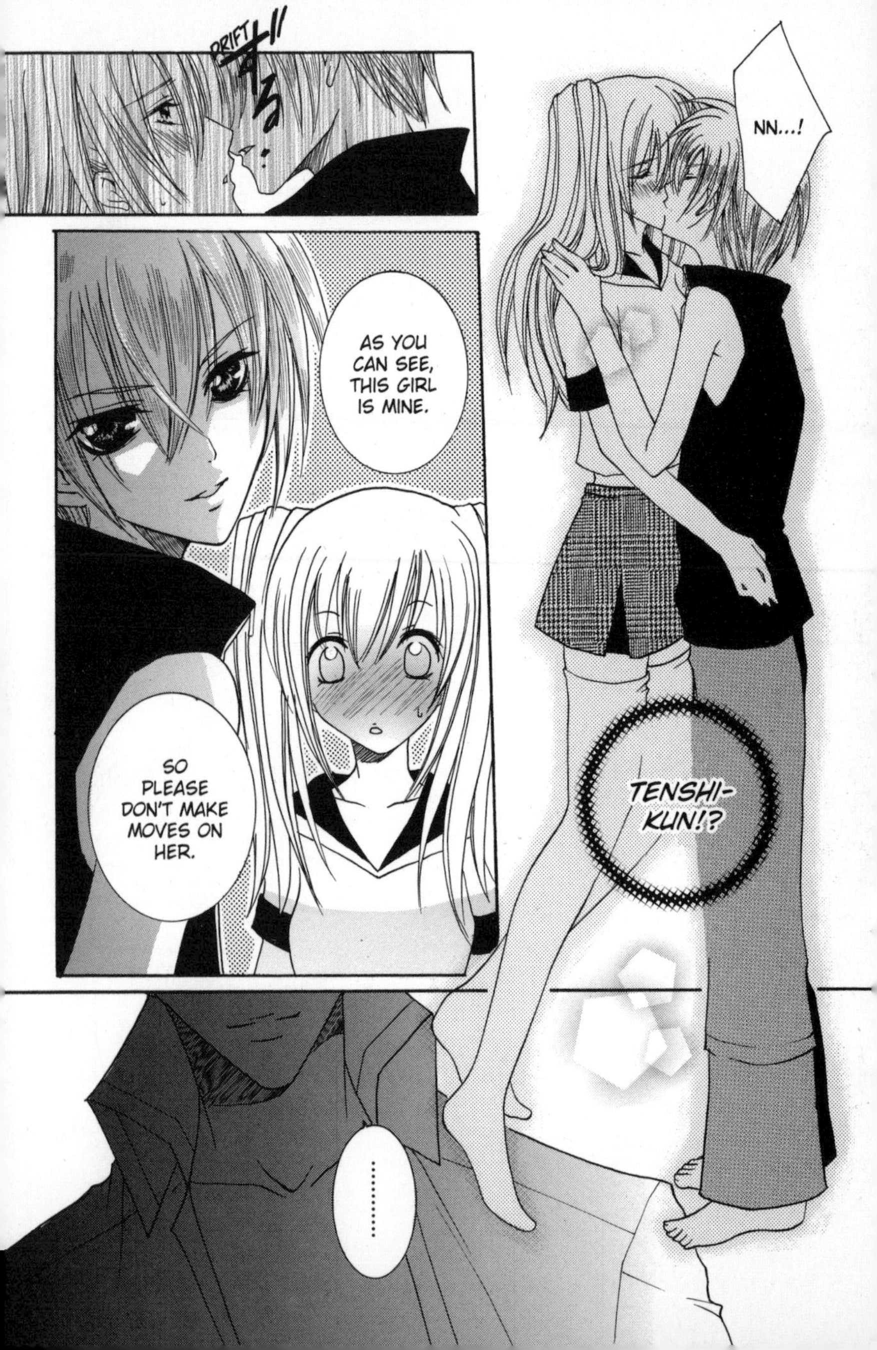
NN...!
DRIFT
AS YOU CAN SEE, THIS GIRL IS MINE.
SO PLEASE DON'T MAKE MOVES ON HER.
TENSHI-KUN!?
......

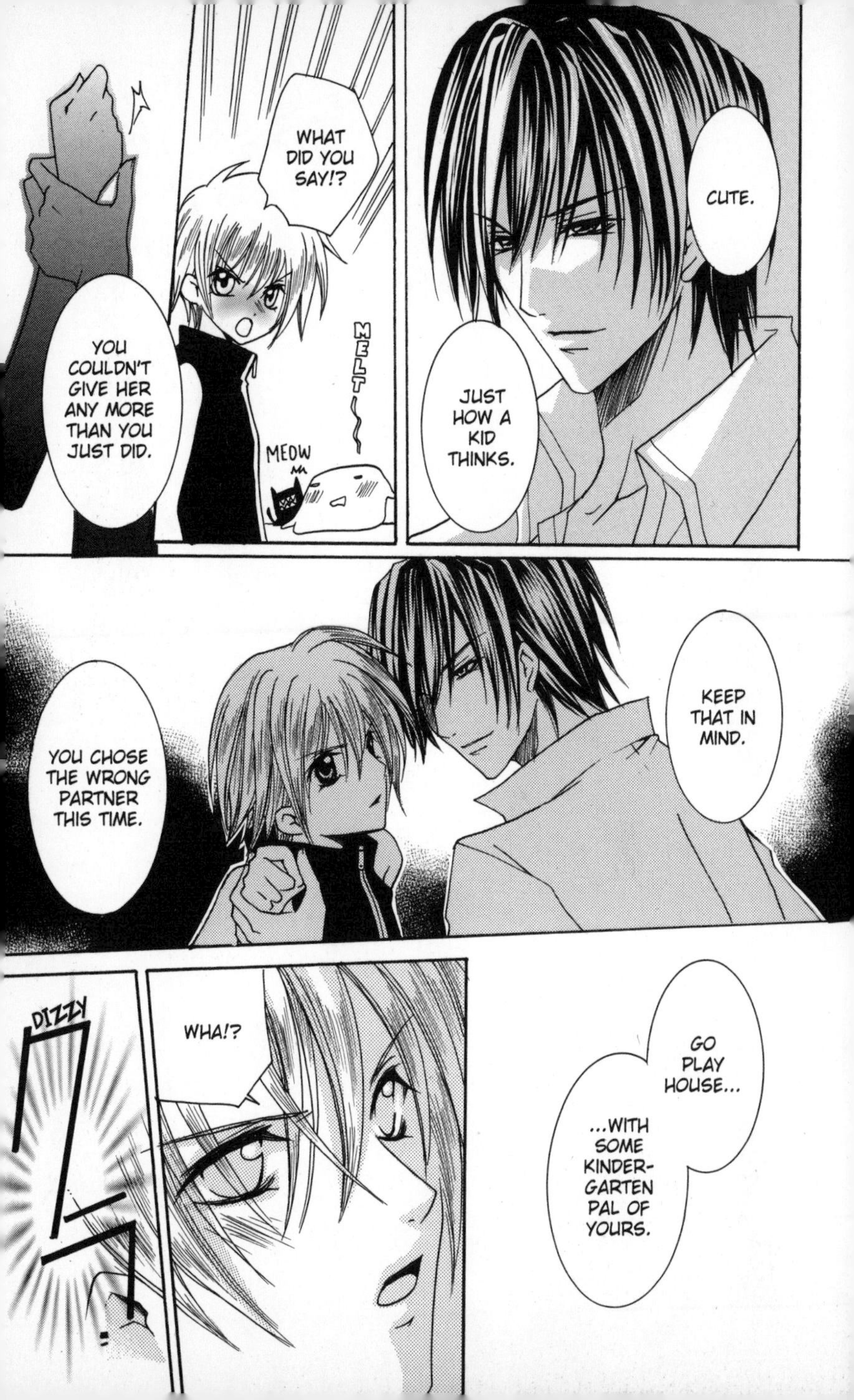
CUTE.
JUST HOW A KID THINKS.
WHAT DID YOU SAY!?
MELT
MEOW
YOU COULDN'T GIVE HER ANY MORE THAN YOU JUST DID.
KEEP THAT IN MIND.
YOU CHOSE THE WRONG PARTNER THIS TIME.
GO PLAY HOUSE...
...WITH SOME KINDER-GARTEN PAL OF YOURS.
WHA!?
DIZZY

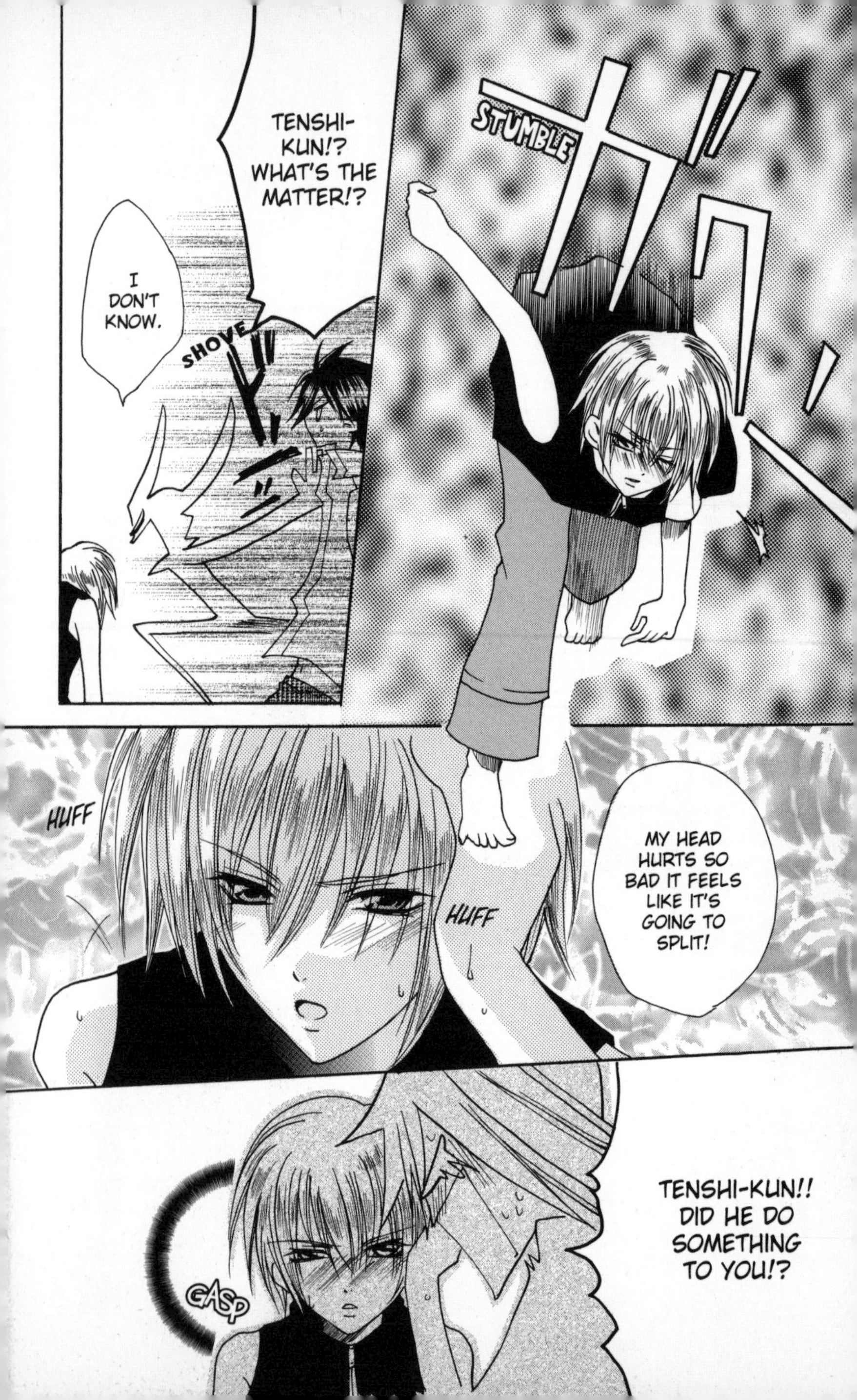
STUMBLE
TENSHI-KUN!? WHAT'S THE MATTER!?
I DON'T KNOW.
SHOVE
HUFF
HUFF
MY HEAD HURTS SO BAD IT FEELS LIKE IT'S GOING TO SPLIT!
TENSHI-KUN!! DID HE DO SOMETHING TO YOU!?
GASP

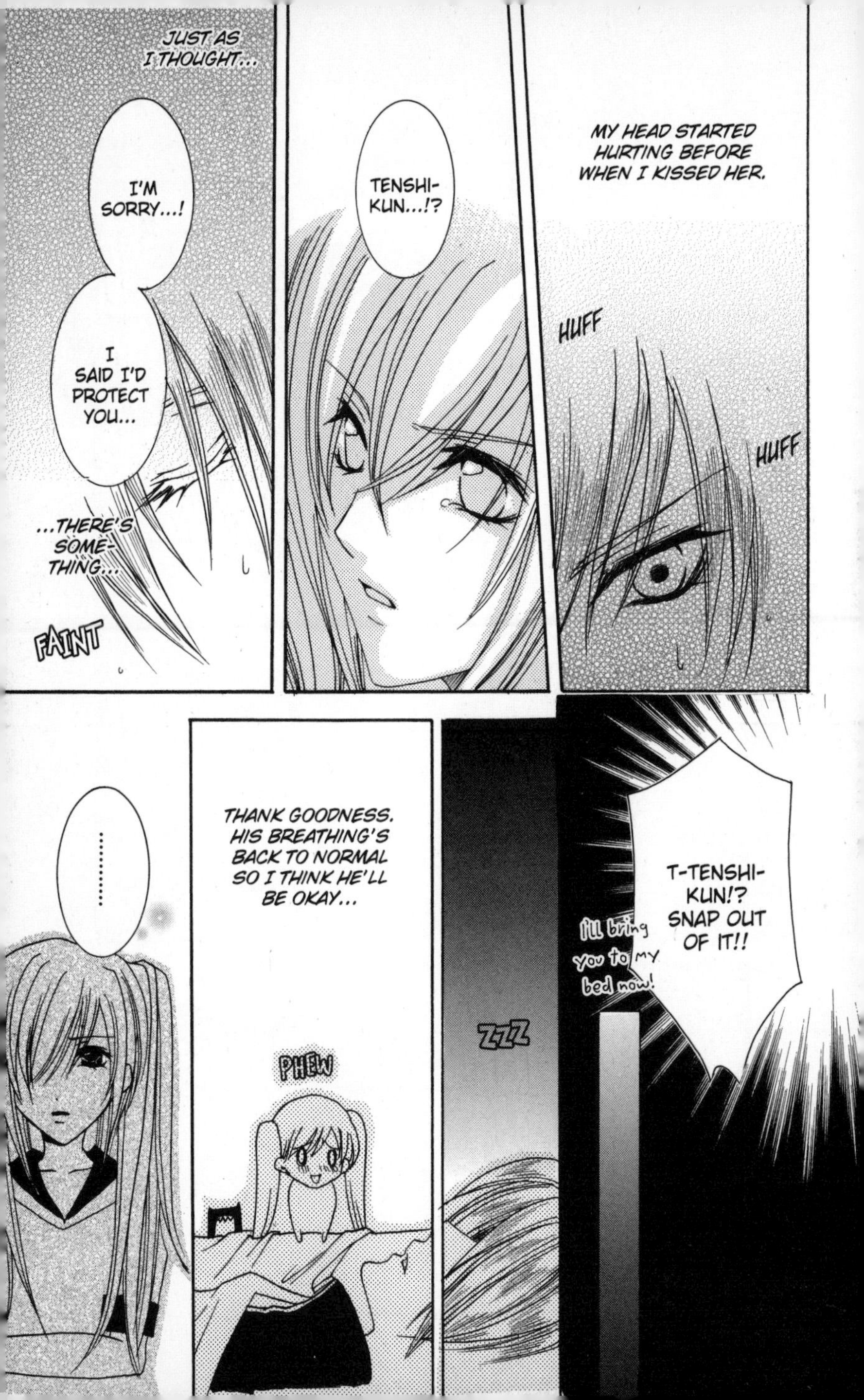
MY HEAD STARTED HURTING BEFORE WHEN I KISSED HER.
HUFF
HUFF
TENSHI-KUN...!?
JUST AS I THOUGHT...
I'M SORRY...!
I SAID I'D PROTECT YOU...
...THERE'S SOME-THING...
FAINT
T-TENSHI-KUN!? SNAP OUT OF IT!!
I'll bring you to my bed now!
ZZZ
THANK GOODNESS. HIS BREATHING'S BACK TO NORMAL SO I THINK HE'LL BE OKAY...
PHEW
......

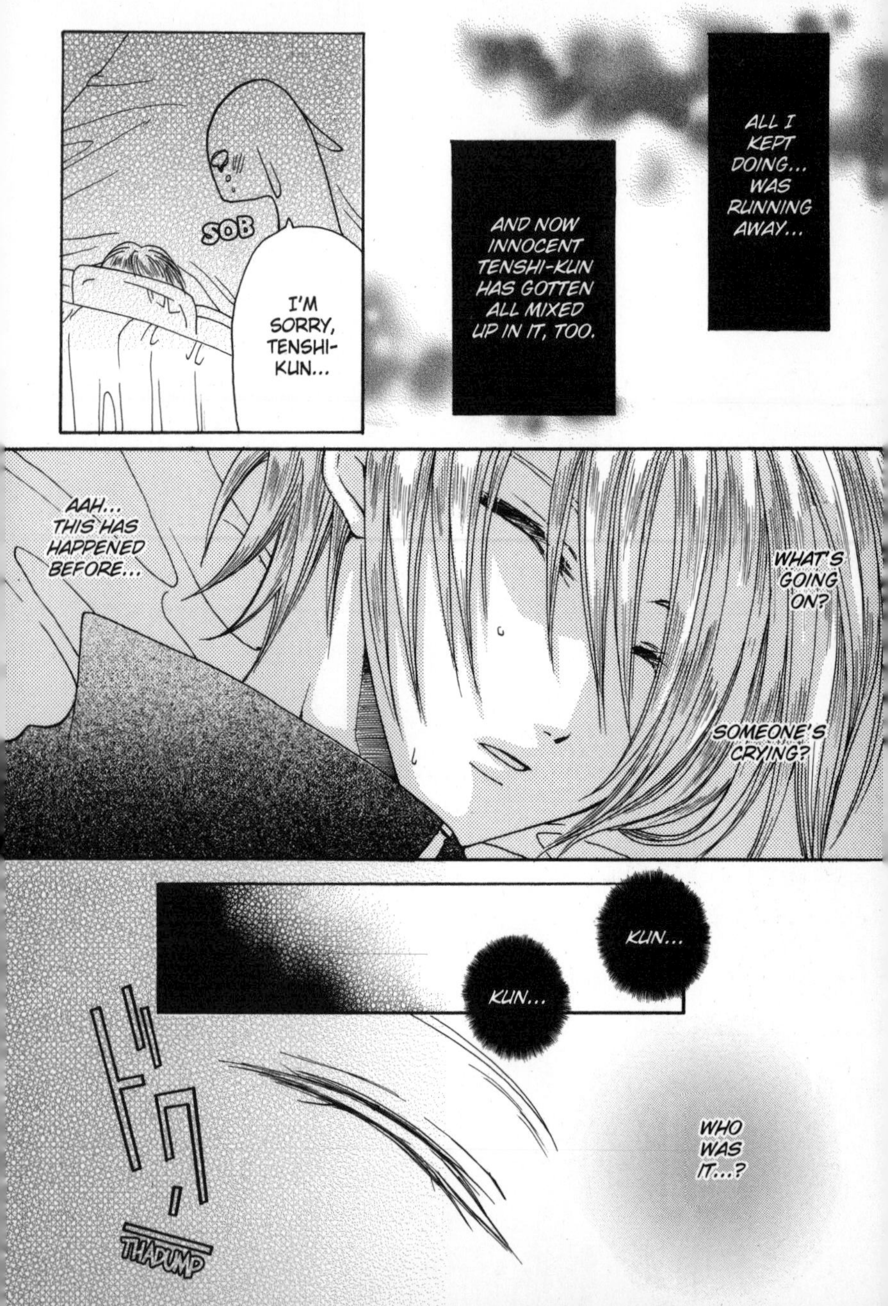
ALL I KEPT DOING... WAS RUNNING AWAY...
AND NOW INNOCENT TENSHI-KUN HAS GOTTEN ALL MIXED UP IN IT, TOO.
SOB
I'M SORRY, TENSHI-KUN...
WHAT'S GOING ON?
SOMEONE'S CRYING?
AAH... THIS HAS HAPPENED BEFORE...
KUN...
KUN...
WHO WAS IT...?
THADUMP

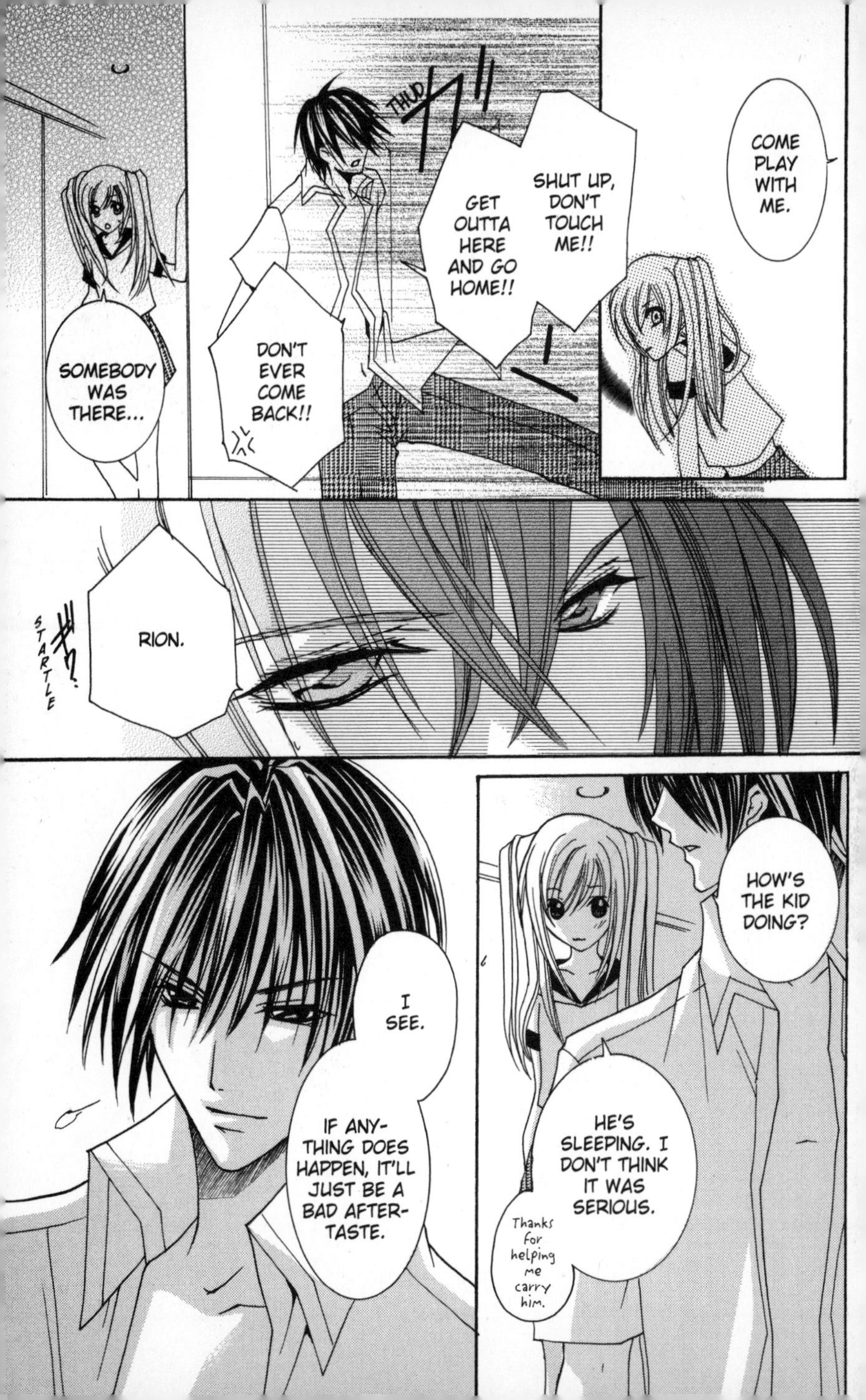
COME PLAY WITH ME.
THUD
SHUT UP, DON'T TOUCH ME!!
GET OUTTA HERE AND GO HOME!!
DON'T EVER COME BACK!!
SOMEBODY WAS THERE...
RION.
STARTLE
HOW'S THE KID DOING?
HE'S SLEEPING. I DON'T THINK IT WAS SERIOUS.
Thanks for helping me carry him.
I SEE.
IF ANYTHING DOES HAPPEN, IT'LL JUST BE A BAD AFTER-TASTE.

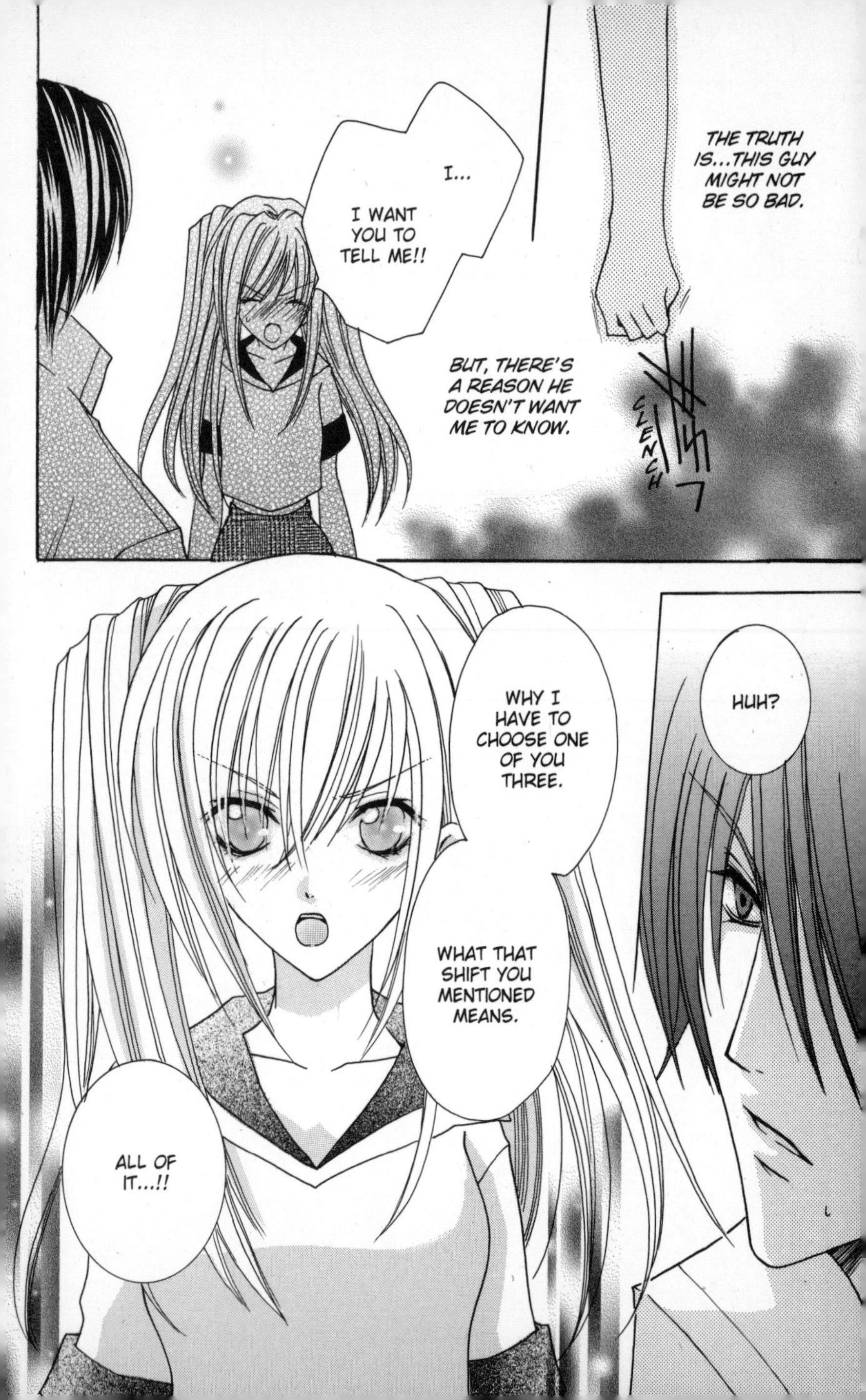
THE TRUTH IS...THIS GUY MIGHT NOT BE SO BAD.
CLENCH
BUT, THERE'S A REASON HE DOESN'T WANT ME TO KNOW.
I...
I WANT YOU TO TELL ME!!
HUH?
WHY I HAVE TO CHOOSE ONE OF YOU THREE.
WHAT THAT SHIFT YOU MENTIONED MEANS.
ALL OF IT...!!

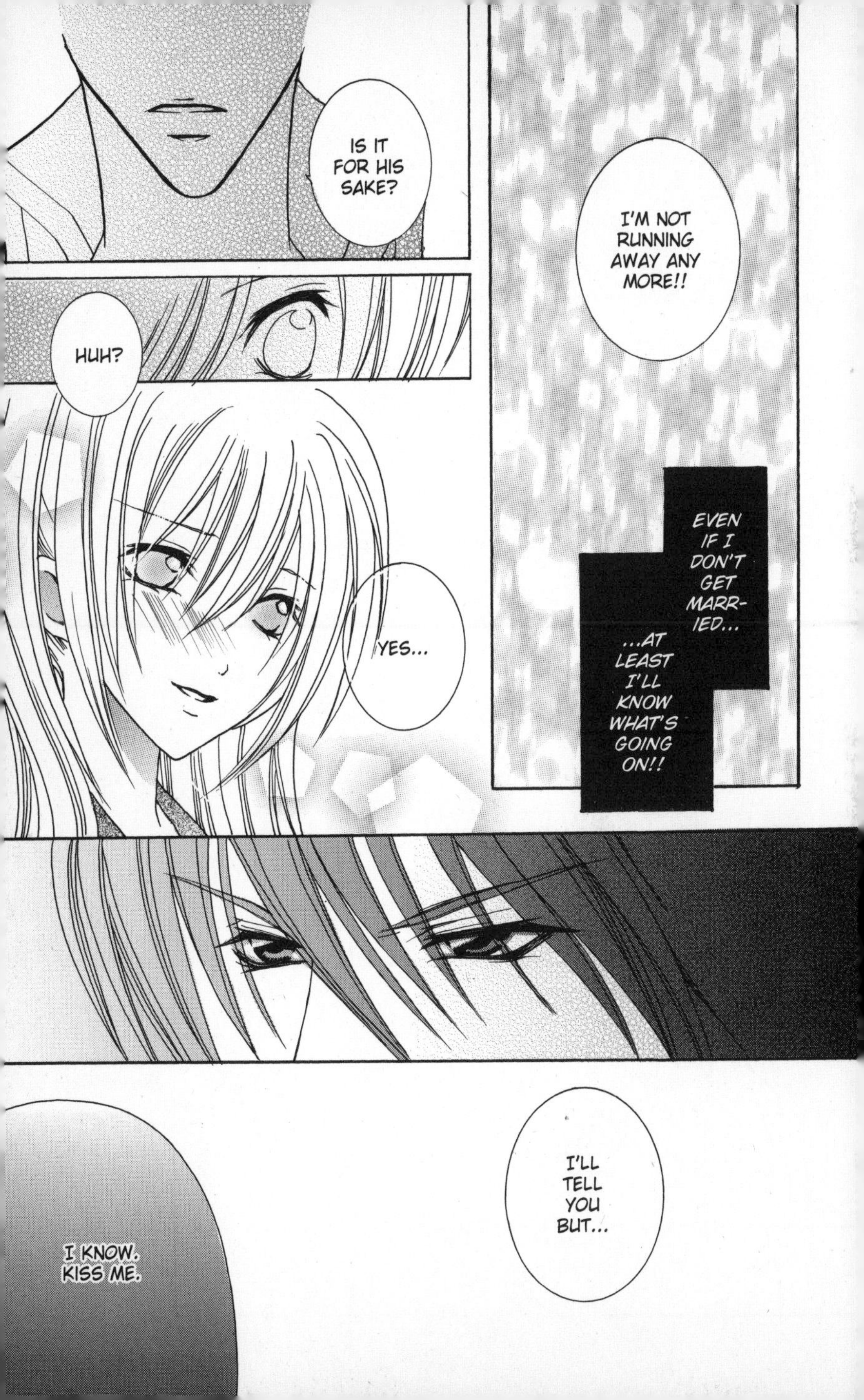
I'M NOT RUNNING AWAY ANY MORE!!
EVEN IF I DON'T GET MARRIED...
...AT LEAST I'LL KNOW WHAT'S GOING ON!!
IS IT FOR HIS SAKE?
HUH?
YES...
I'LL TELL YOU BUT...
I KNOW. KISS ME.

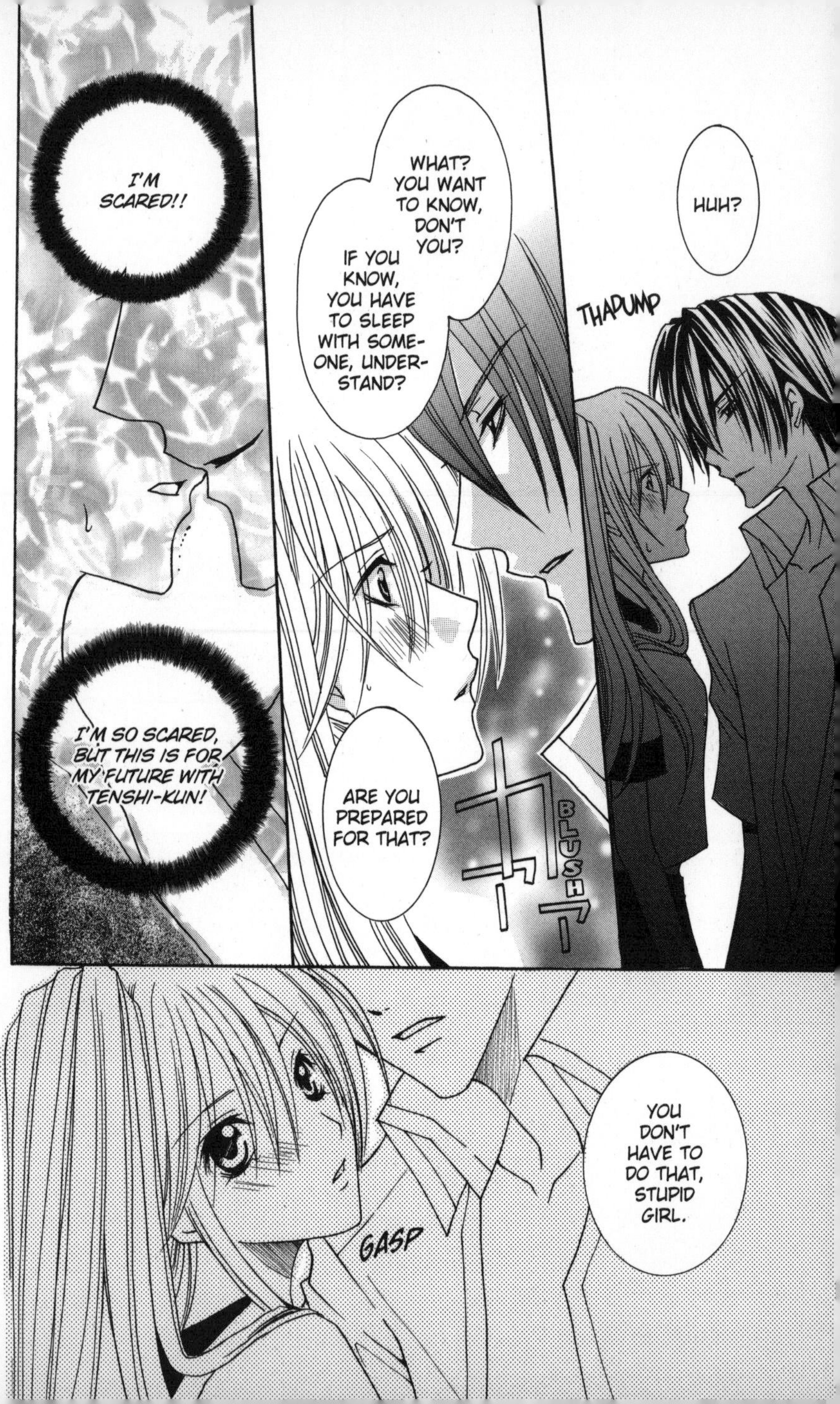
HUH?
THAPUMP
WHAT? YOU WANT TO KNOW, DON'T YOU?
IF YOU KNOW, YOU HAVE TO SLEEP WITH SOME-ONE, UNDER-STAND?
ARE YOU PREPARED FOR THAT?
BLUSH
I'M SCARED!!
I'M SO SCARED, BUT THIS IS FOR MY FUTURE WITH TENSHI-KUN!
YOU DON'T HAVE TO DO THAT, STUPID GIRL.
GASP

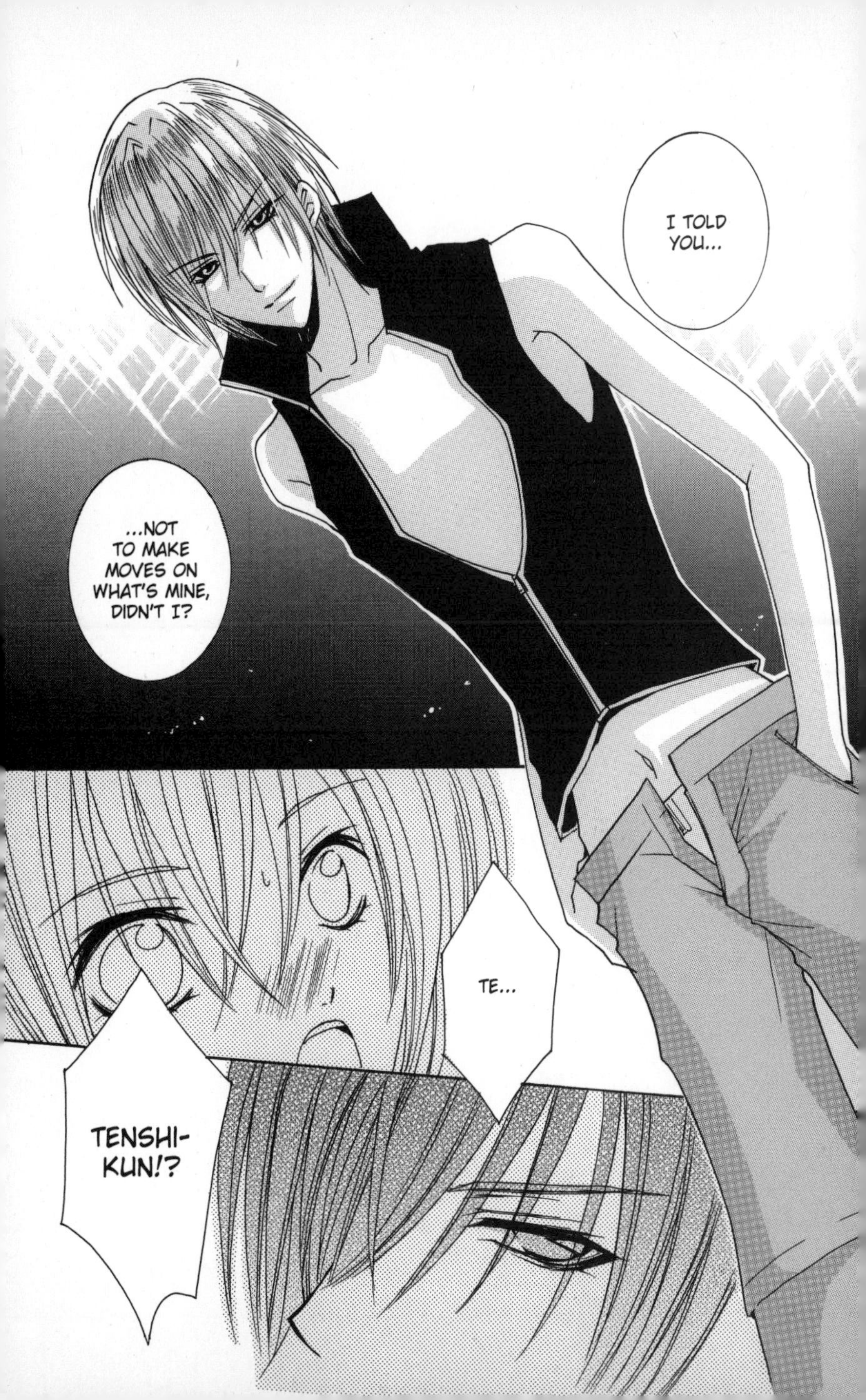
I TOLD YOU...
...NOT TO MAKE MOVES ON WHAT'S MINE, DIDN'T I?
TE...
TENSHI-KUN!?

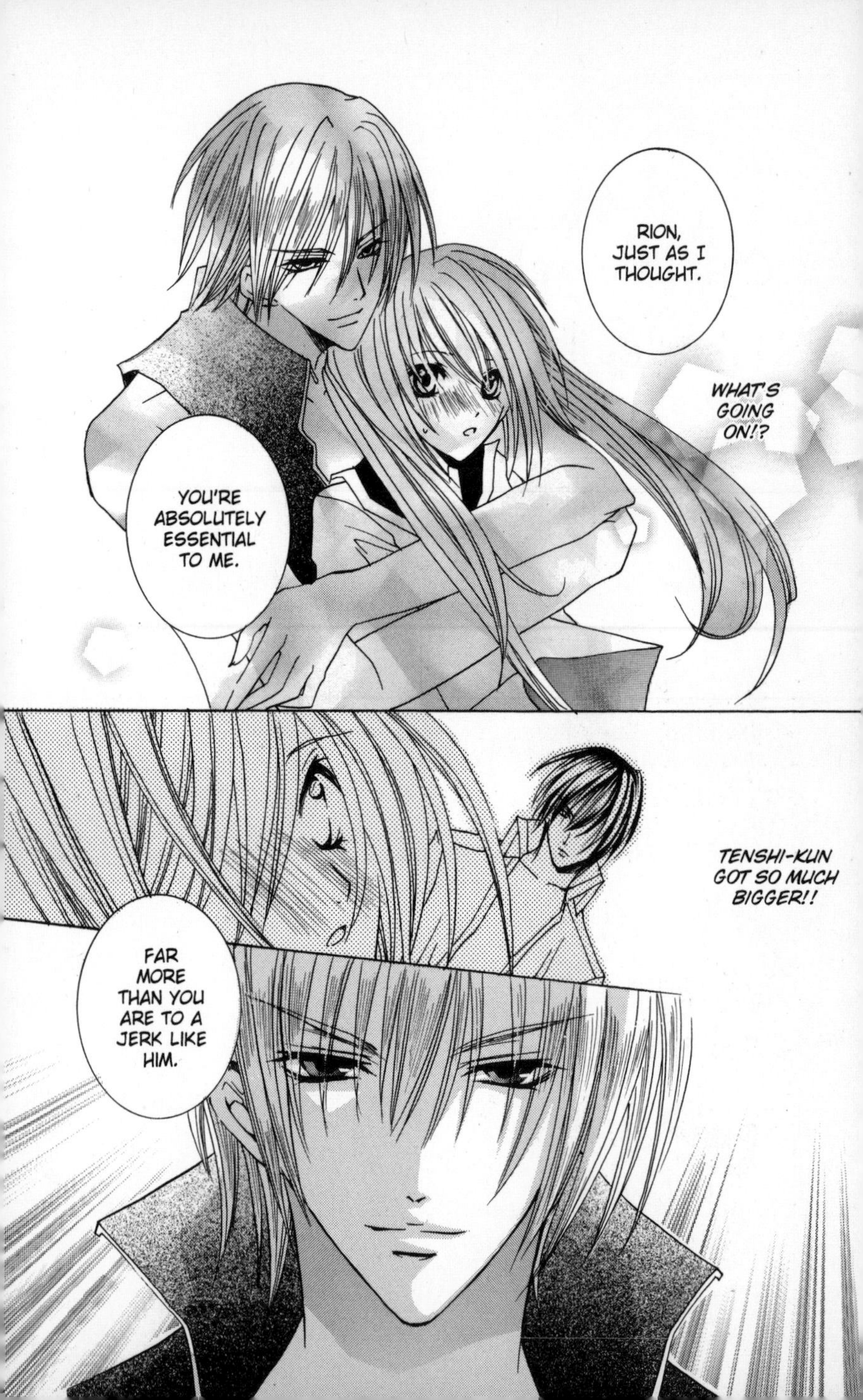

RION, JUST AS I THOUGHT.
WHAT'S GOING ON!?
YOU'RE ABSOLUTELY ESSENTIAL TO ME.
TENSHI-KUN GOT SO MUCH BIGGER!!
FAR MORE THAN YOU ARE TO A JERK LIKE HIM.

Chibi Angel Chibi Devil (3)

Chibi Water Version

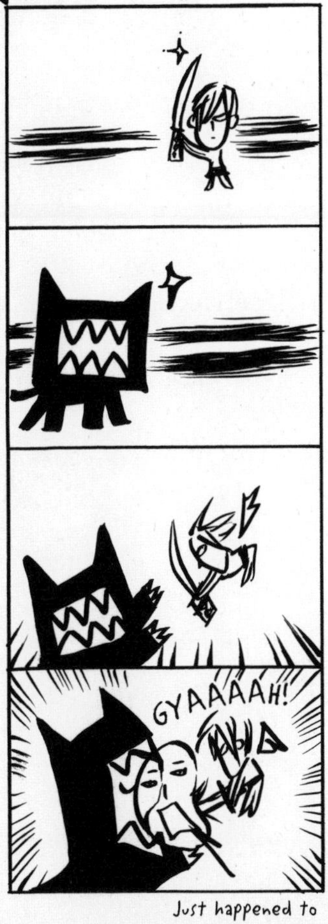
GYAAAAH!

Just happened to be passing by.

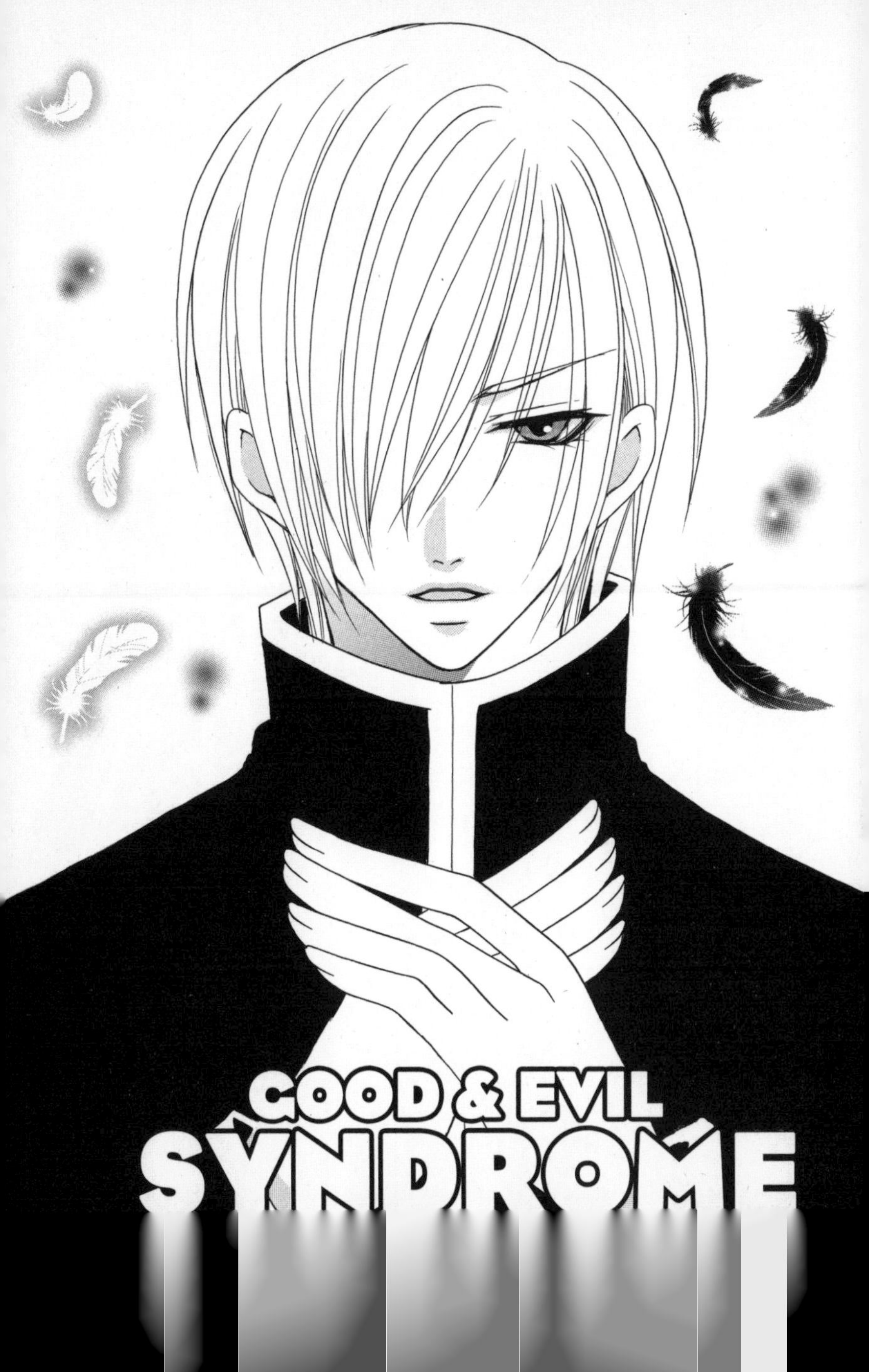
GOOD & EVIL
SYNDROME

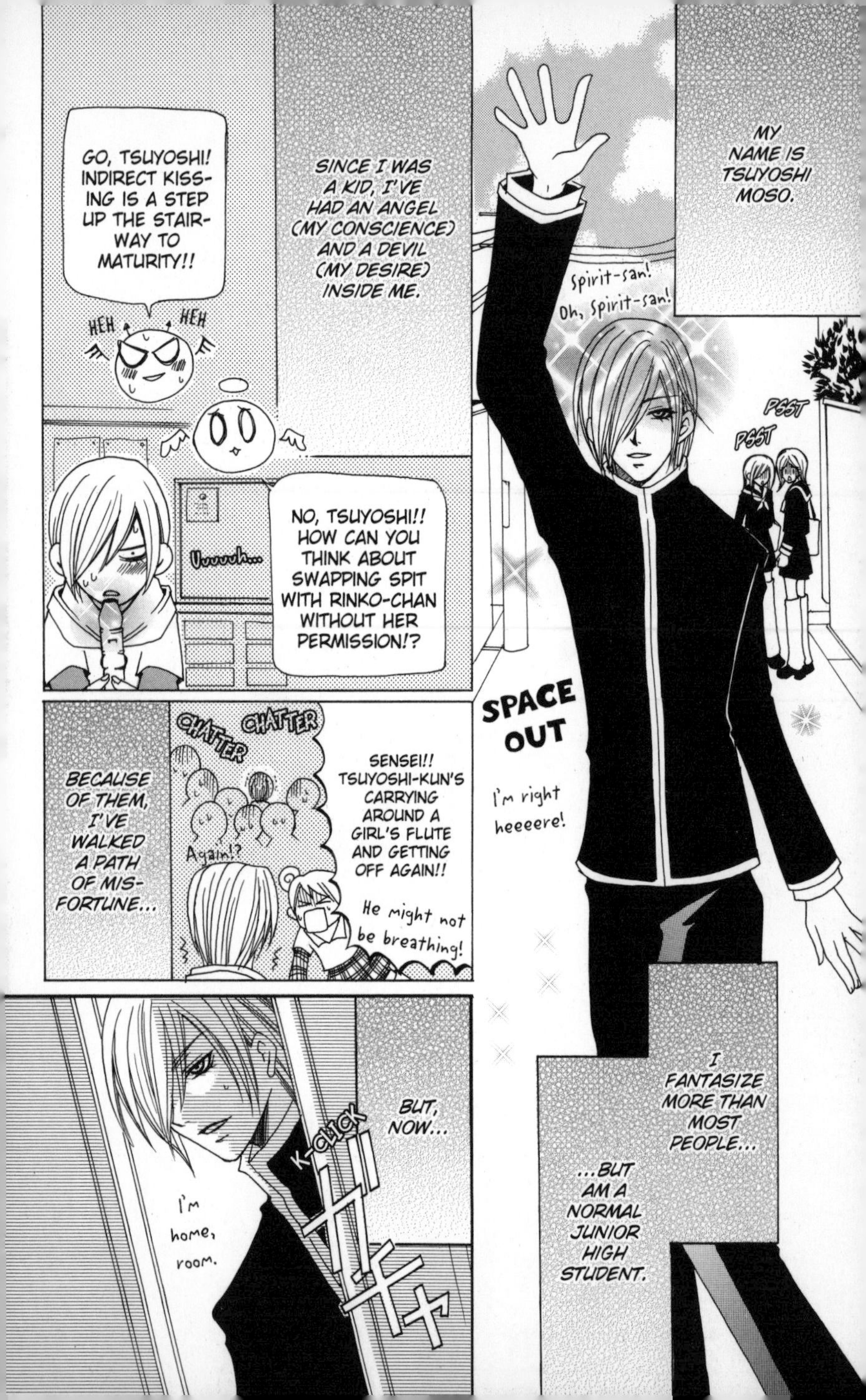
MY NAME IS TSUYOSHI MOSO.
Spirit-san! Oh, Spirit-san!
PSST
PSST
SPACE OUT
I'm right heeeere!
I FANTASIZE MORE THAN MOST PEOPLE...
...BUT AM A NORMAL JUNIOR HIGH STUDENT.
SINCE I WAS A KID, I'VE HAD AN ANGEL (MY CONSCIENCE) AND A DEVIL (MY DESIRE) INSIDE ME.
GO, TSUYOSHI! INDIRECT KISSING IS A STEP UP THE STAIRWAY TO MATURITY!!
HEH HEH
NO, TSUYOSHI!! HOW CAN YOU THINK ABOUT SWAPPING SPIT WITH RINKO-CHAN WITHOUT HER PERMISSION!?
Uuuuuh...
CHATTER CHATTER
SENSEI!! TSUYOSHI-KUN'S CARRYING AROUND A GIRL'S FLUTE AND GETTING OFF AGAIN!!
Again!?
He might not be breathing!
BECAUSE OF THEM, I'VE WALKED A PATH OF MISFORTUNE...
BUT, NOW...
K-CLICK
I'm home, room.

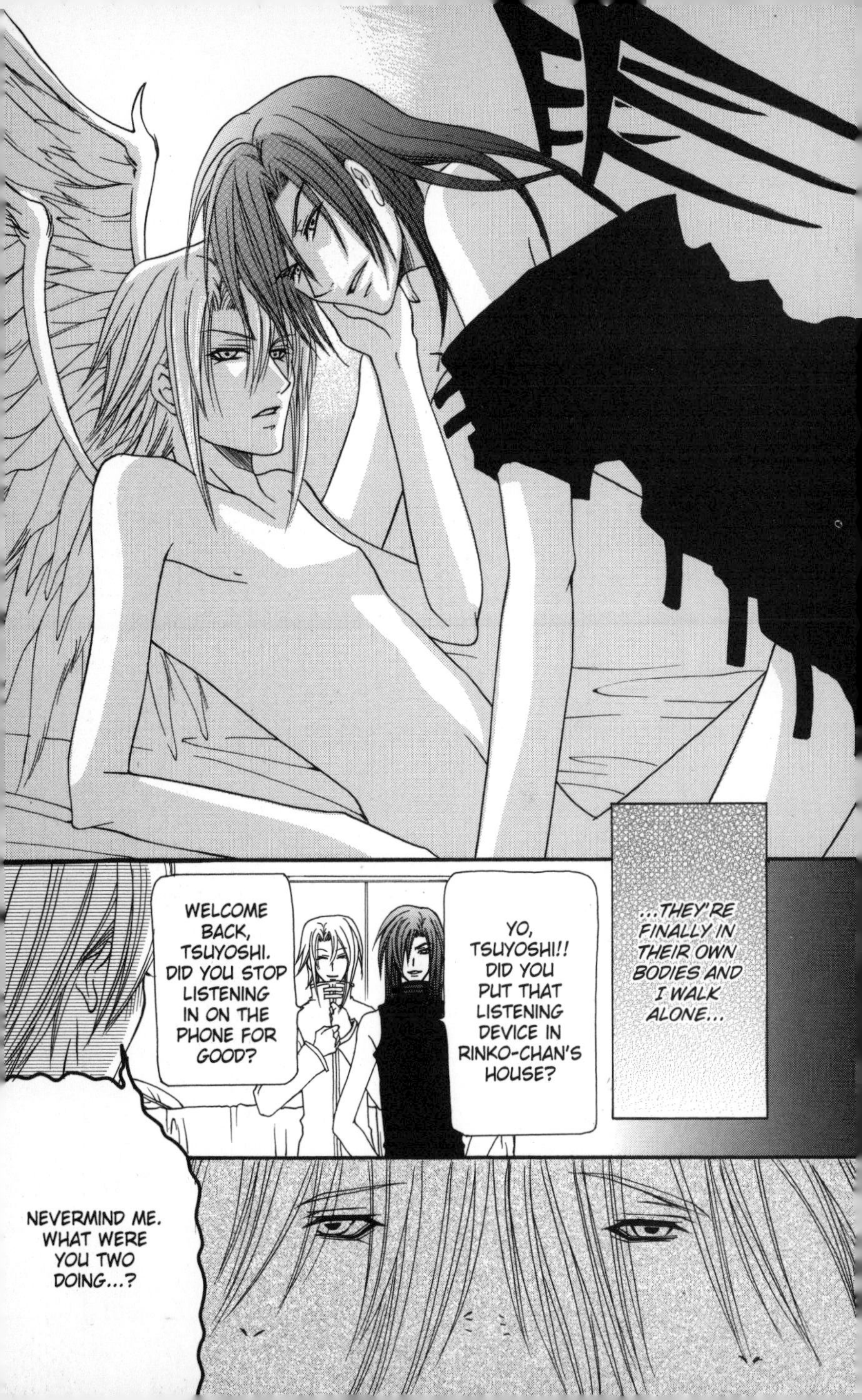
...THEY'RE FINALLY IN THEIR OWN BODIES AND I WALK ALONE...
YO, TSUYOSHI!! DID YOU PUT THAT LISTENING DEVICE IN RINKO-CHAN'S HOUSE?
WELCOME BACK, TSUYOSHI. DID YOU STOP LISTENING IN ON THE PHONE FOR GOOD?
NEVERMIND ME. WHAT WERE YOU TWO DOING...?

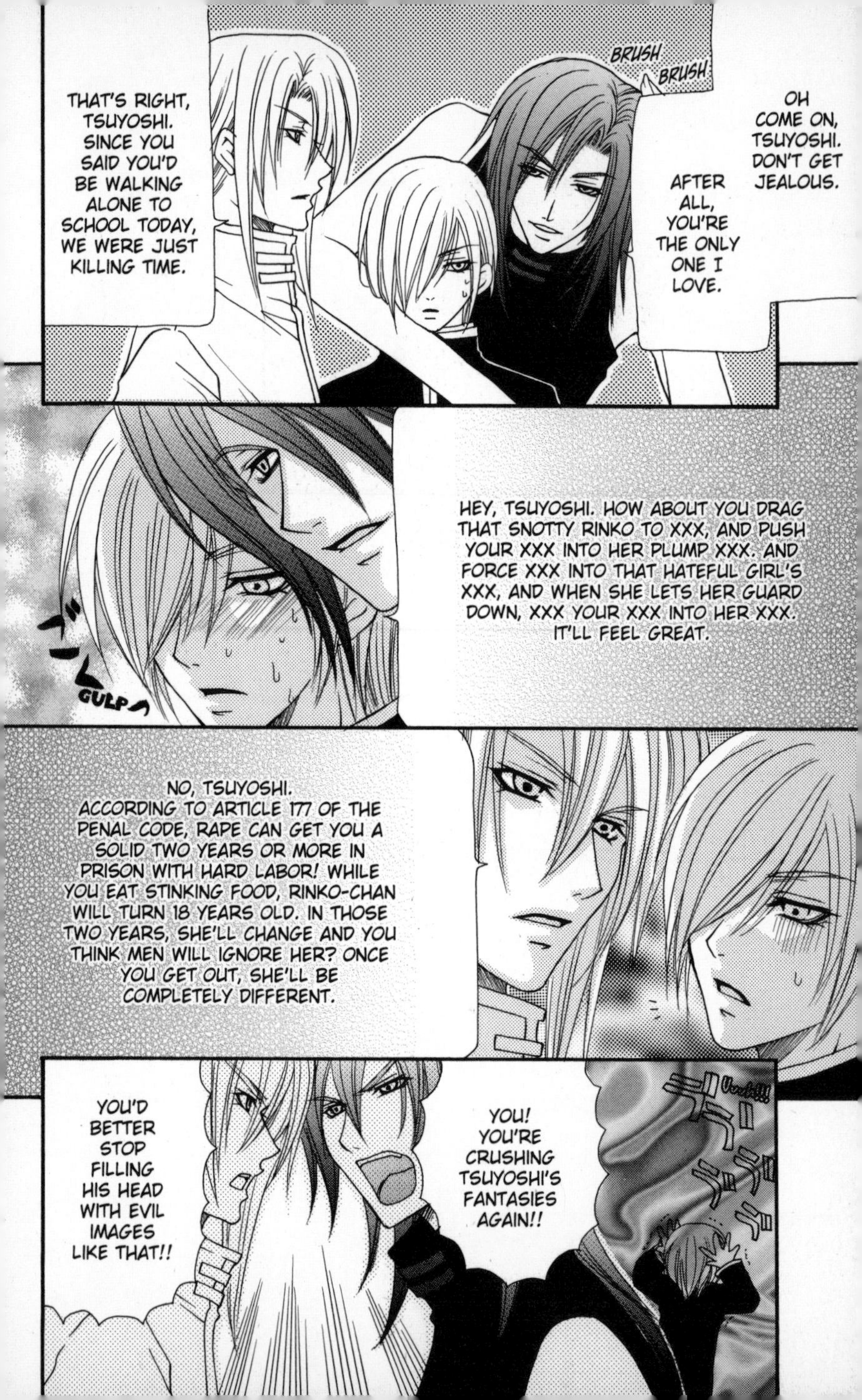
BRUSH
BRUSH
OH COME ON, TSUYOSHI. DON'T GET JEALOUS.
AFTER ALL, YOU'RE THE ONLY ONE I LOVE.
THAT'S RIGHT, TSUYOSHI. SINCE YOU SAID YOU'D BE WALKING ALONE TO SCHOOL TODAY, WE WERE JUST KILLING TIME.
HEY, TSUYOSHI. HOW ABOUT YOU DRAG THAT SNOTTY RINKO TO XXX, AND PUSH YOUR XXX INTO HER PLUMP XXX. AND FORCE XXX INTO THAT HATEFUL GIRL'S XXX, AND WHEN SHE LETS HER GUARD DOWN, XXX YOUR XXX INTO HER XXX. IT'LL FEEL GREAT.
GULP
NO, TSUYOSHI. ACCORDING TO ARTICLE 177 OF THE PENAL CODE, RAPE CAN GET YOU A SOLID TWO YEARS OR MORE IN PRISON WITH HARD LABOR! WHILE YOU EAT STINKING FOOD, RINKO-CHAN WILL TURN 18 YEARS OLD. IN THOSE TWO YEARS, SHE'LL CHANGE AND YOU THINK MEN WILL IGNORE HER? ONCE YOU GET OUT, SHE'LL BE COMPLETELY DIFFERENT.
YOU! YOU'RE CRUSHING TSUYOSHI'S FANTASIES AGAIN!!
YOU'D BETTER STOP FILLING HIS HEAD WITH EVIL IMAGES LIKE THAT!!

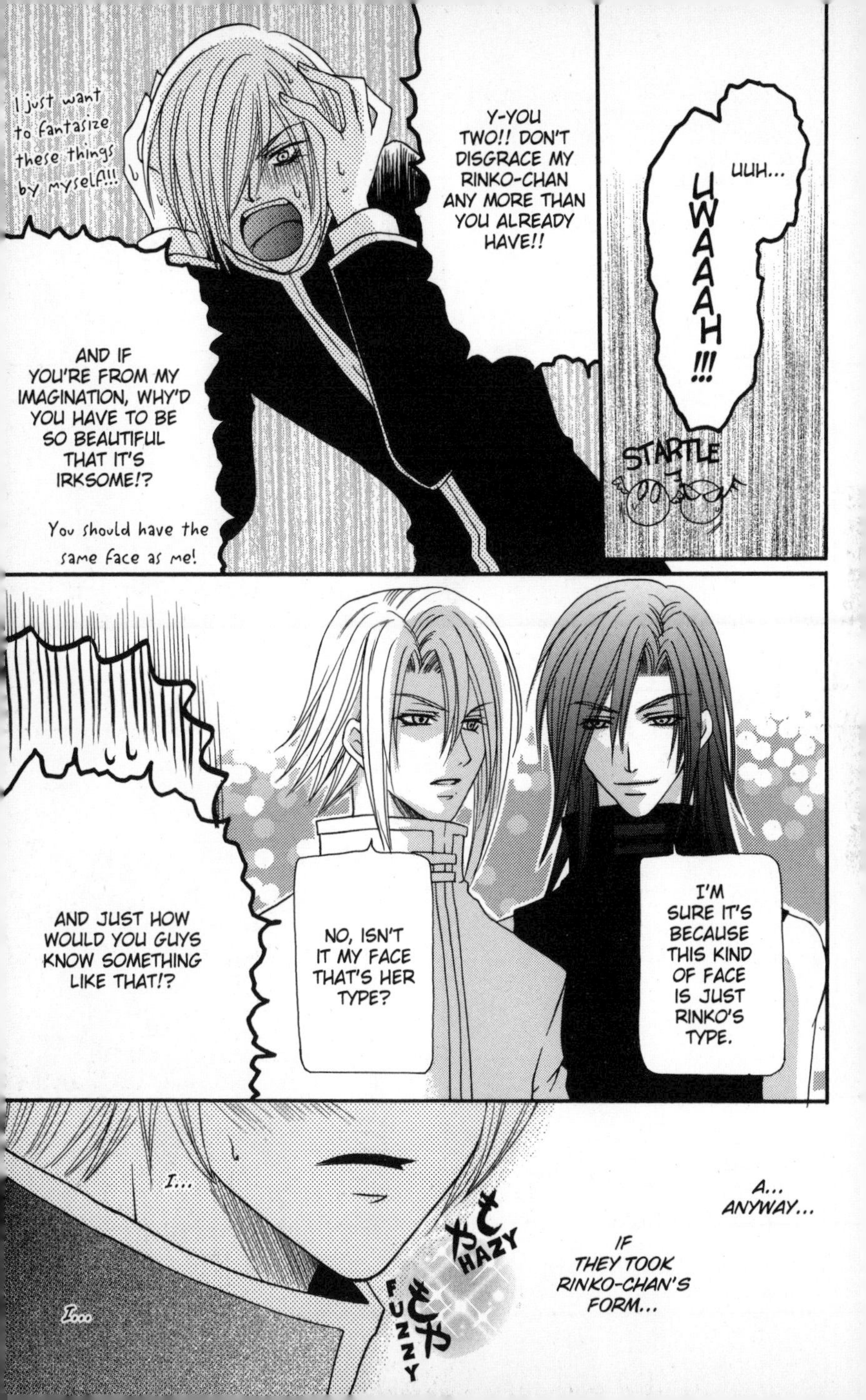
UUH... UWAAAAH!!!
STARTLE
Y-YOU TWO!! DON'T DISGRACE MY RINKO-CHAN ANY MORE THAN YOU ALREADY HAVE!!
I just want to fantasize these things by myself!!!
AND IF YOU'RE FROM MY IMAGINATION, WHY'D YOU HAVE TO BE SO BEAUTIFUL THAT IT'S IRKSOME!?
You should have the same face as me!
I'M SURE IT'S BECAUSE THIS KIND OF FACE IS JUST RINKO'S TYPE.
NO, ISN'T IT MY FACE THAT'S HER TYPE?
AND JUST HOW WOULD YOU GUYS KNOW SOMETHING LIKE THAT!?
A... ANYWAY...
IF THEY TOOK RINKO-CHAN'S FORM...
HAZY
FUZZY
I...

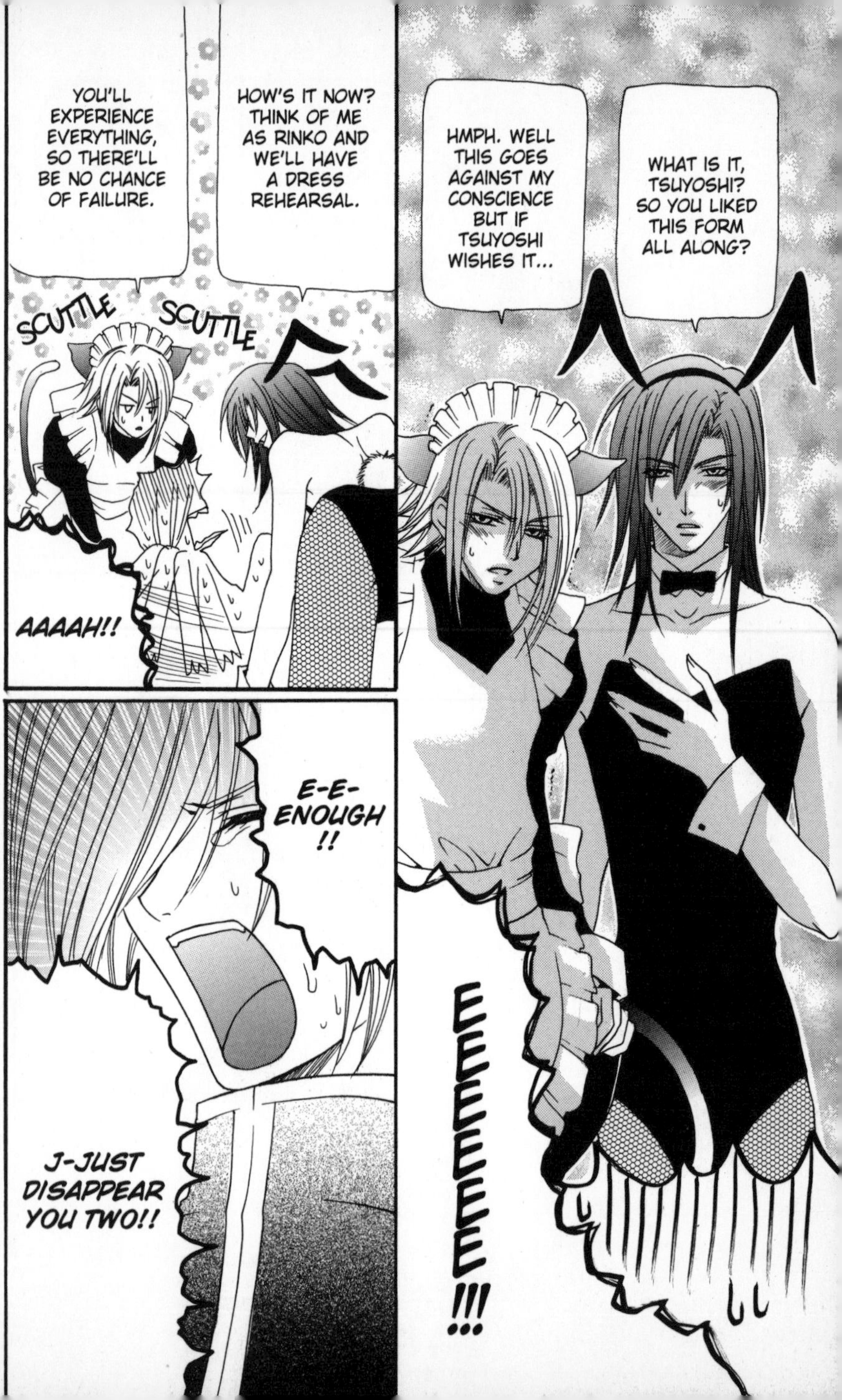
WHAT IS IT, TSUYOSHI? SO YOU LIKED THIS FORM ALL ALONG?
HMPH. WELL THIS GOES AGAINST MY CONSCIENCE BUT IF TSUYOSHI WISHES IT...
EEEEEEEEEE!!!
HOW'S IT NOW? THINK OF ME AS RINKO AND WE'LL HAVE A DRESS REHEARSAL.
YOU'LL EXPERIENCE EVERYTHING, SO THERE'LL BE NO CHANCE OF FAILURE.
SCUTTLE
SCUTTLE
AAAAH!!
E-E-ENOUGH!!
J-JUST DISAPPEAR YOU TWO!!

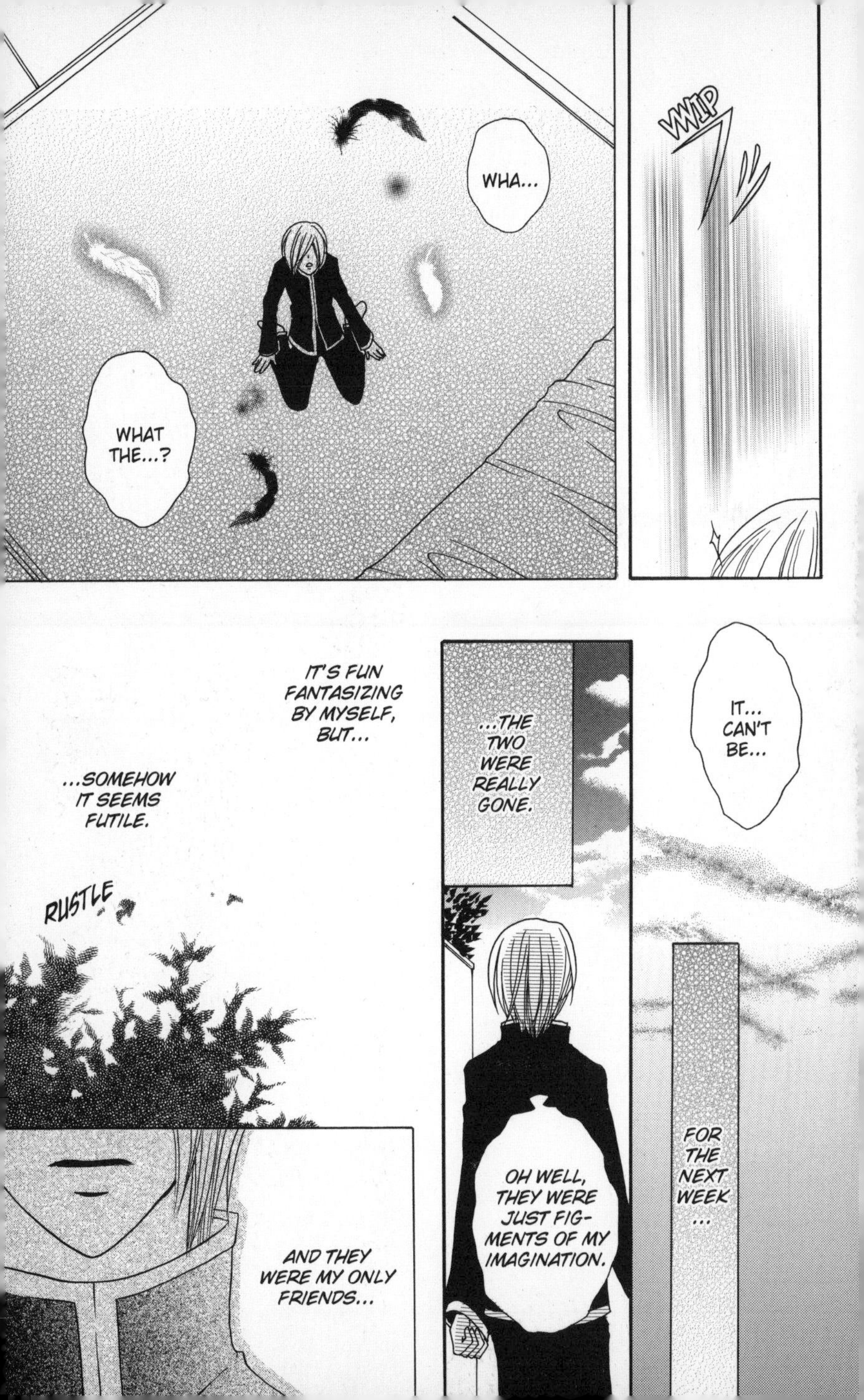
VWIP
WHA...
WHAT THE...?
IT... CAN'T BE...
...THE TWO WERE REALLY GONE.
FOR THE NEXT WEEK...
OH WELL, THEY WERE JUST FIG-MENTS OF MY IMAGINATION.
IT'S FUN FANTASIZING BY MYSELF, BUT...
...SOMEHOW IT SEEMS FUTILE.
RUSTLE
AND THEY WERE MY ONLY FRIENDS...

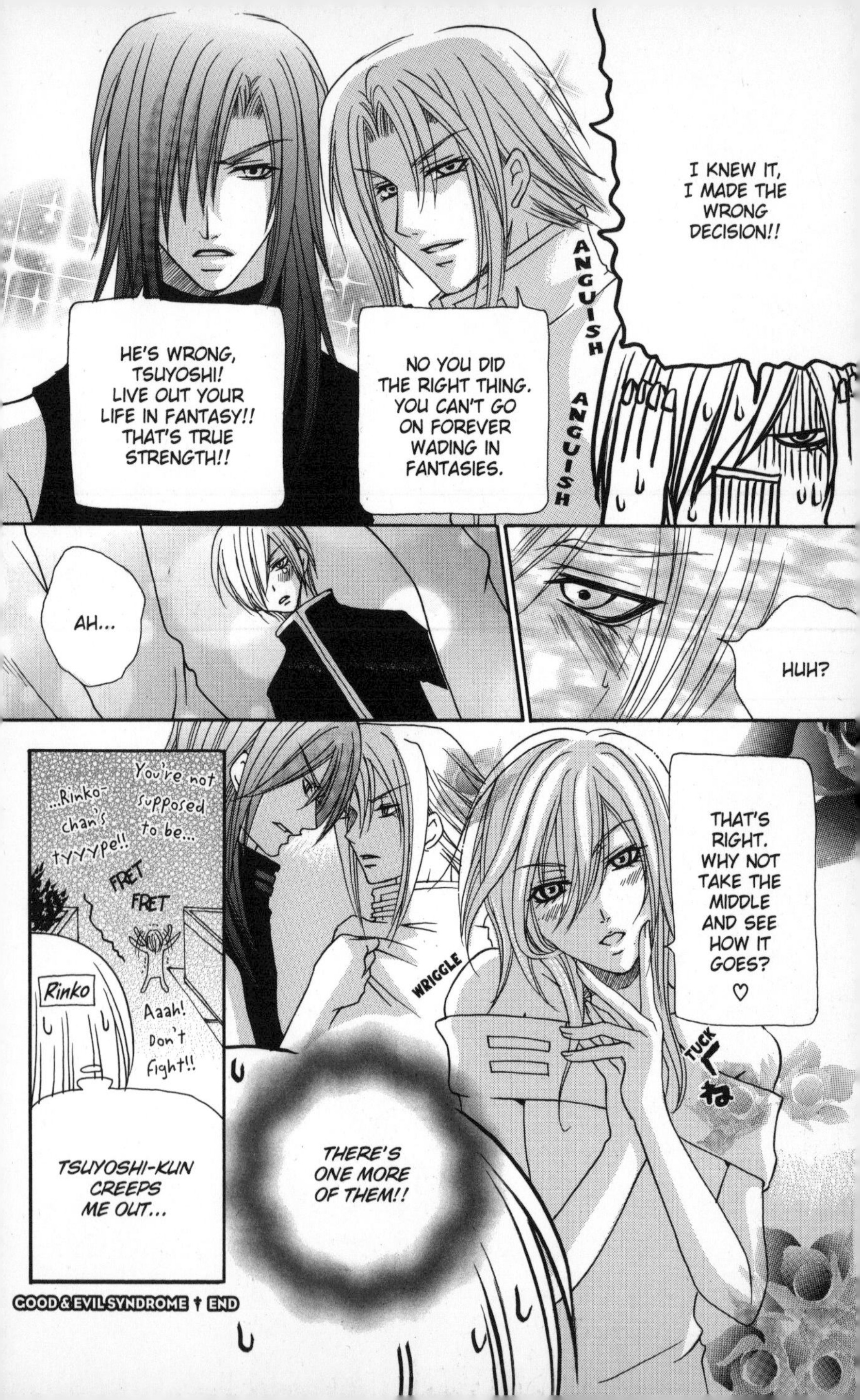

I KNEW IT, I MADE THE WRONG DECISION!!
ANGUISH ANGUISH
NO YOU DID THE RIGHT THING. YOU CAN'T GO ON FOREVER WADING IN FANTASIES.
HE'S WRONG, TSUYOSHI! LIVE OUT YOUR LIFE IN FANTASY!! THAT'S TRUE STRENGTH!!
HUH?
AH...
THAT'S RIGHT. WHY NOT TAKE THE MIDDLE AND SEE HOW IT GOES? ♡
TUCK
WRIGGLE
THERE'S ONE MORE OF THEM!!
You're not supposed to be...
...Rinko-chan's tyyype!!
FRET FRET
Rinko
Aaah! Don't fight!!
TSUYOSHI-KUN CREEPS ME OUT...
GOOD & EVIL SYNDROME † END

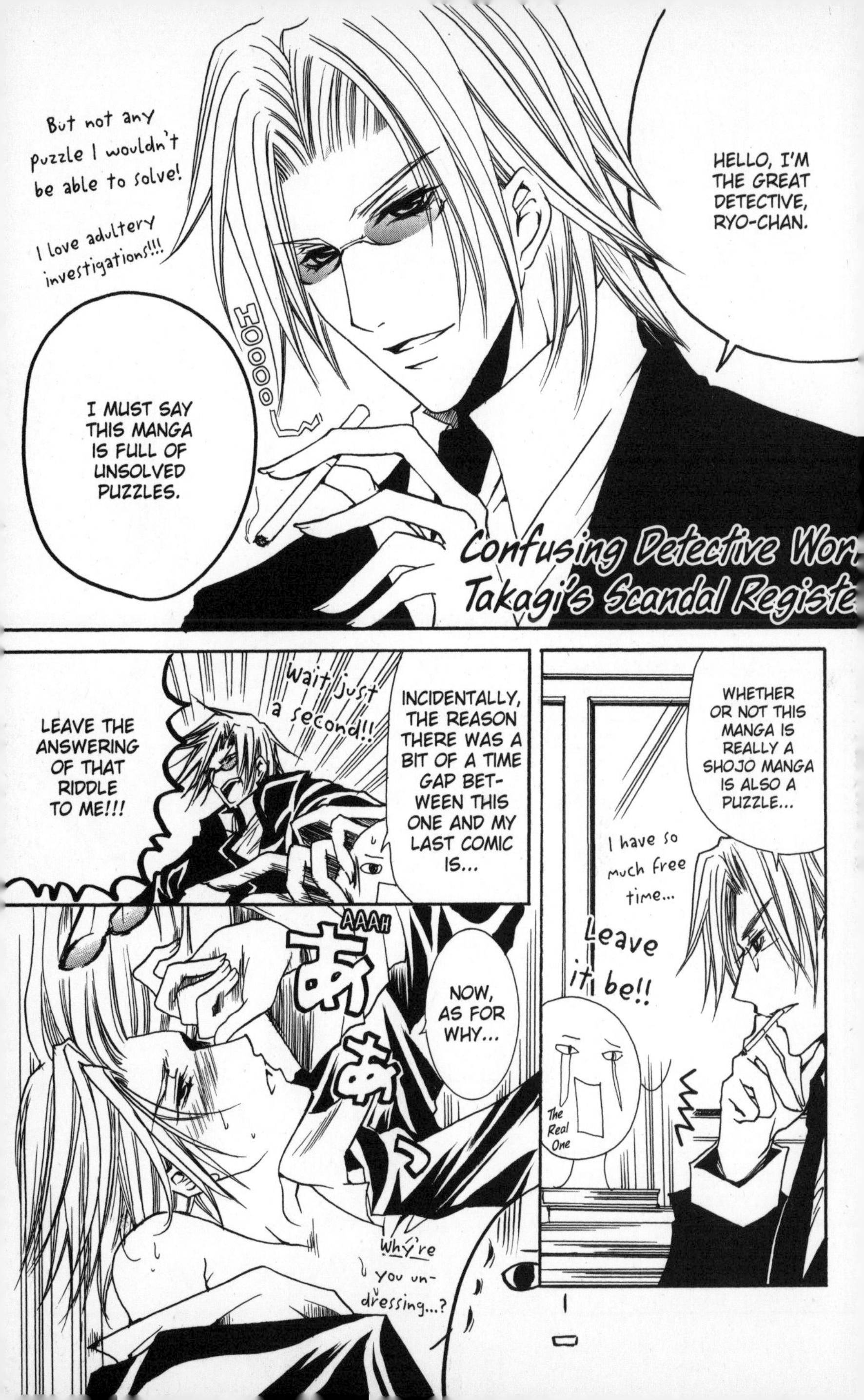
HELLO, I'M THE GREAT DETECTIVE, RYO-CHAN.
I MUST SAY THIS MANGA IS FULL OF UNSOLVED PUZZLES.
HOOOO
But not any puzzle I wouldn't be able to solve!
I love adultery investigations!!!
Confusing Detective Wor
Takagi's Scandal Registe
WHETHER OR NOT THIS MANGA IS REALLY A SHOJO MANGA IS ALSO A PUZZLE...
I have so much free time...
Leave it be!!
The Real One
INCIDENTALLY, THE REASON THERE WAS A BIT OF A TIME GAP BET-WEEN THIS ONE AND MY LAST COMIC IS...
Wait just a second!!
LEAVE THE ANSWERING OF THAT RIDDLE TO ME!!!
NOW, AS FOR WHY...
あああっ
AAAH
Why're you un-dressing...?

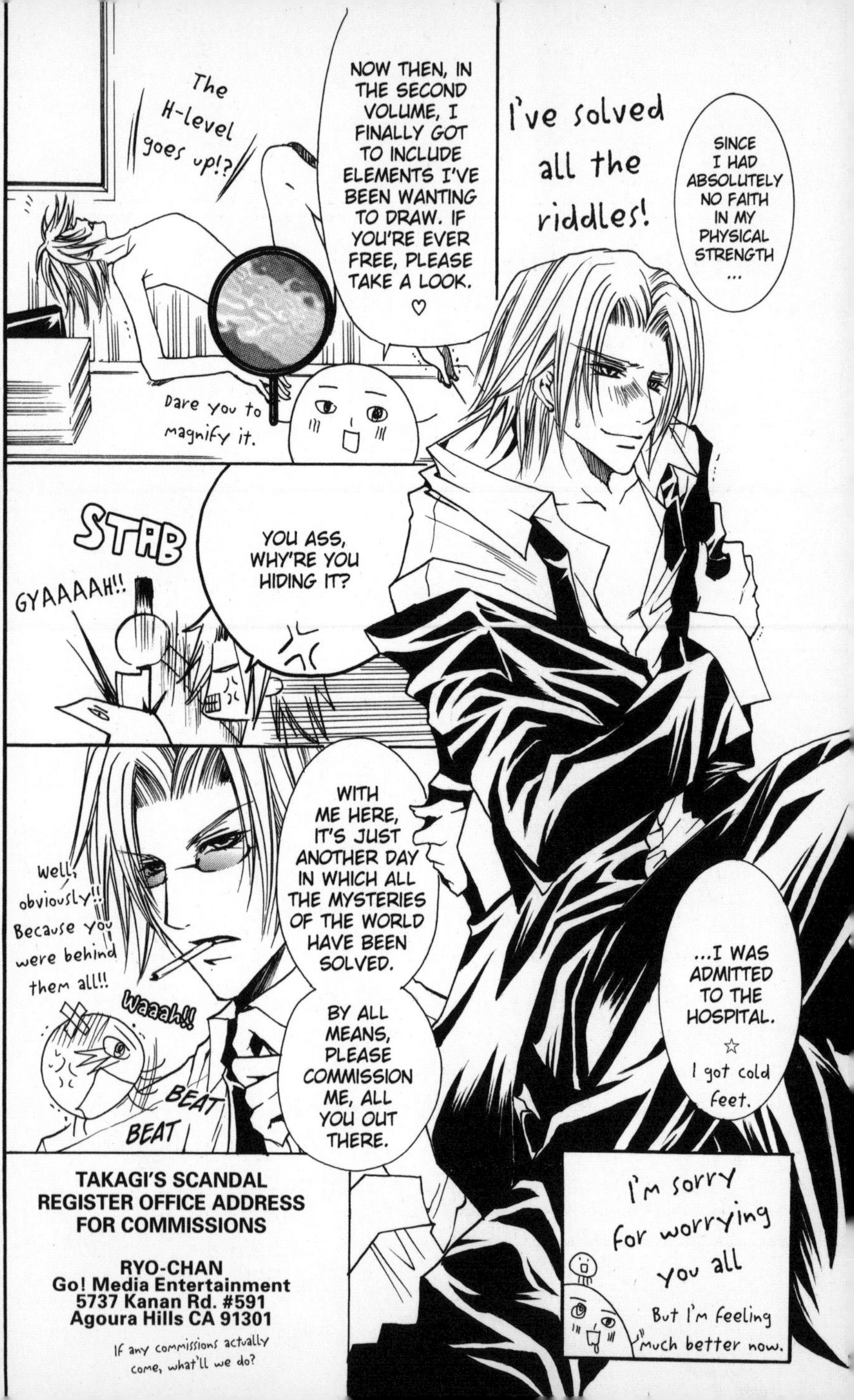
I've solved all the riddles!
SINCE I HAD ABSOLUTELY NO FAITH IN MY PHYSICAL STRENGTH ...
NOW THEN, IN THE SECOND VOLUME, I FINALLY GOT TO INCLUDE ELEMENTS I'VE BEEN WANTING TO DRAW. IF YOU'RE EVER FREE, PLEASE TAKE A LOOK. ♡
The H-level goes up!?
Dare you to magnify it.
YOU ASS, WHY'RE YOU HIDING IT?
STAB
GYAAAAH!!
...I WAS ADMITTED TO THE HOSPITAL. ☆ I got cold feet.
WITH ME HERE, IT'S JUST ANOTHER DAY IN WHICH ALL THE MYSTERIES OF THE WORLD HAVE BEEN SOLVED.
Well, obviously!! Because you were behind them all!!
BY ALL MEANS, PLEASE COMMISSION ME, ALL YOU OUT THERE.
Waaah!!
BEAT
BEAT
I'm sorry for worrying you all
But I'm feeling much better now.
TAKAGI'S SCANDAL REGISTER OFFICE ADDRESS FOR COMMISSIONS
RYO-CHAN
Go! Media Entertainment
5737 Kanan Rd. #591
Agoura Hills CA 91301
If any commissions actually come, what'll we do?

Translator's notes

Pg. 11 – big sister
They are not big sisters by blood or anything. It's just an intimate term girl friends can use amongst each other.

Pg. 11 – *shota-con*
"Shota-con" is short for "shota complex" meaning someone who has a sexual thing for young boys.

Pg. 19 – Patrasche
Patrasche is the name of the dog hero in the animated movie "A Dog of Flanders". Live action was filmed in 1999.

Pg. 34 – *onigiri*
Onigiri is that tuna-mayonnaise flavored rice snack she tossed him. The filling is surrounded by rice and then wrapped up in seaweed.

Pg. 40 – *bishonen*
"Bishonen" means "beautiful boys."

Pg. 53 – Elohim essaim
Chant is based on passages from Black Magic books and Hebrew texts. This phrase in particular was made popular in Japan through such manga titles as "Akuma-kun" (Ge ge ge) whose main character often used the phrase when raising spirits out of the ground. Elohim means "God" and Essaim means "Devil".

Pg. 85 – taking a dump
Apparently, some people believe it is a bad idea to poop so late at night.

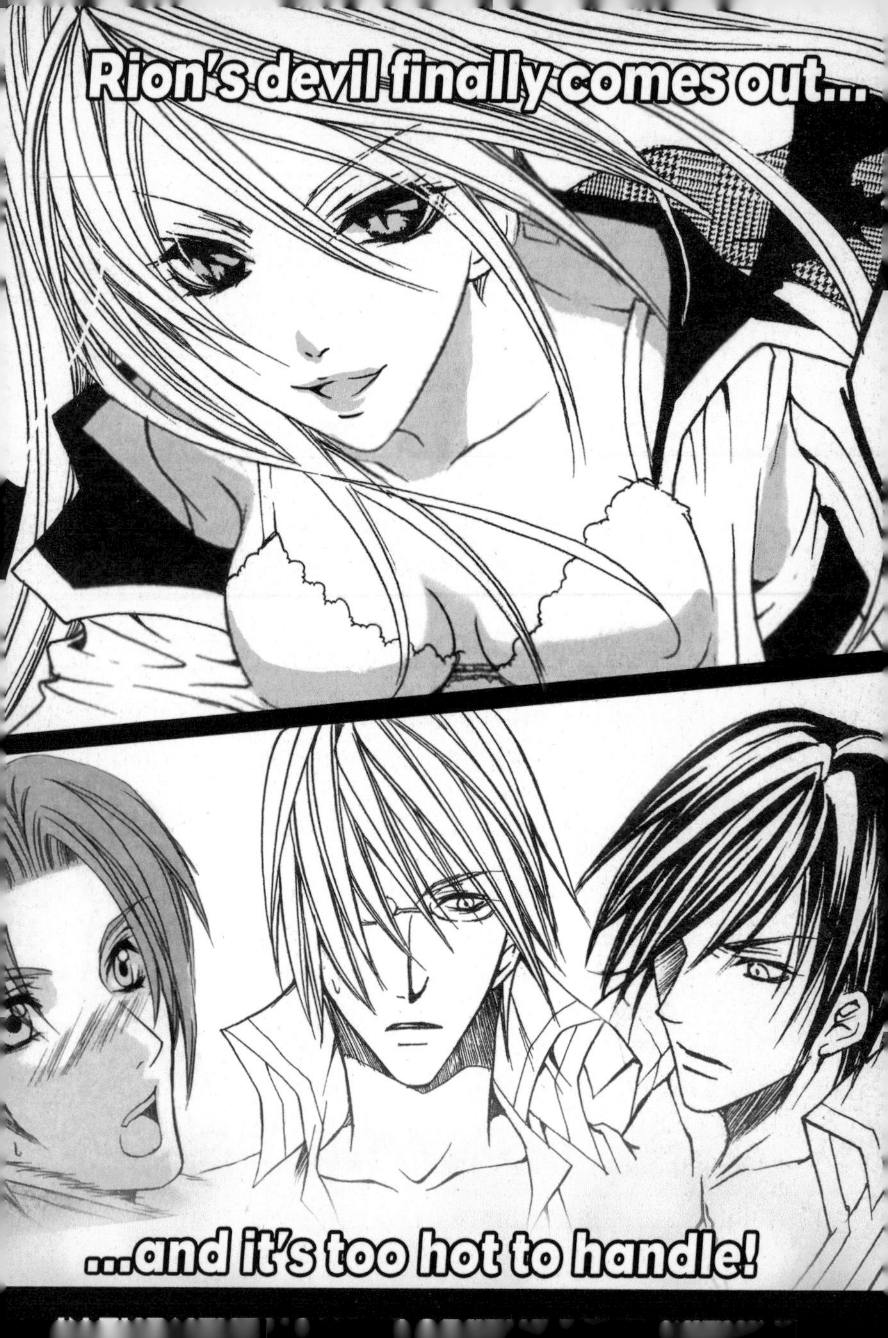
Rion's devil finally comes out...
...and it's too hot to handle!

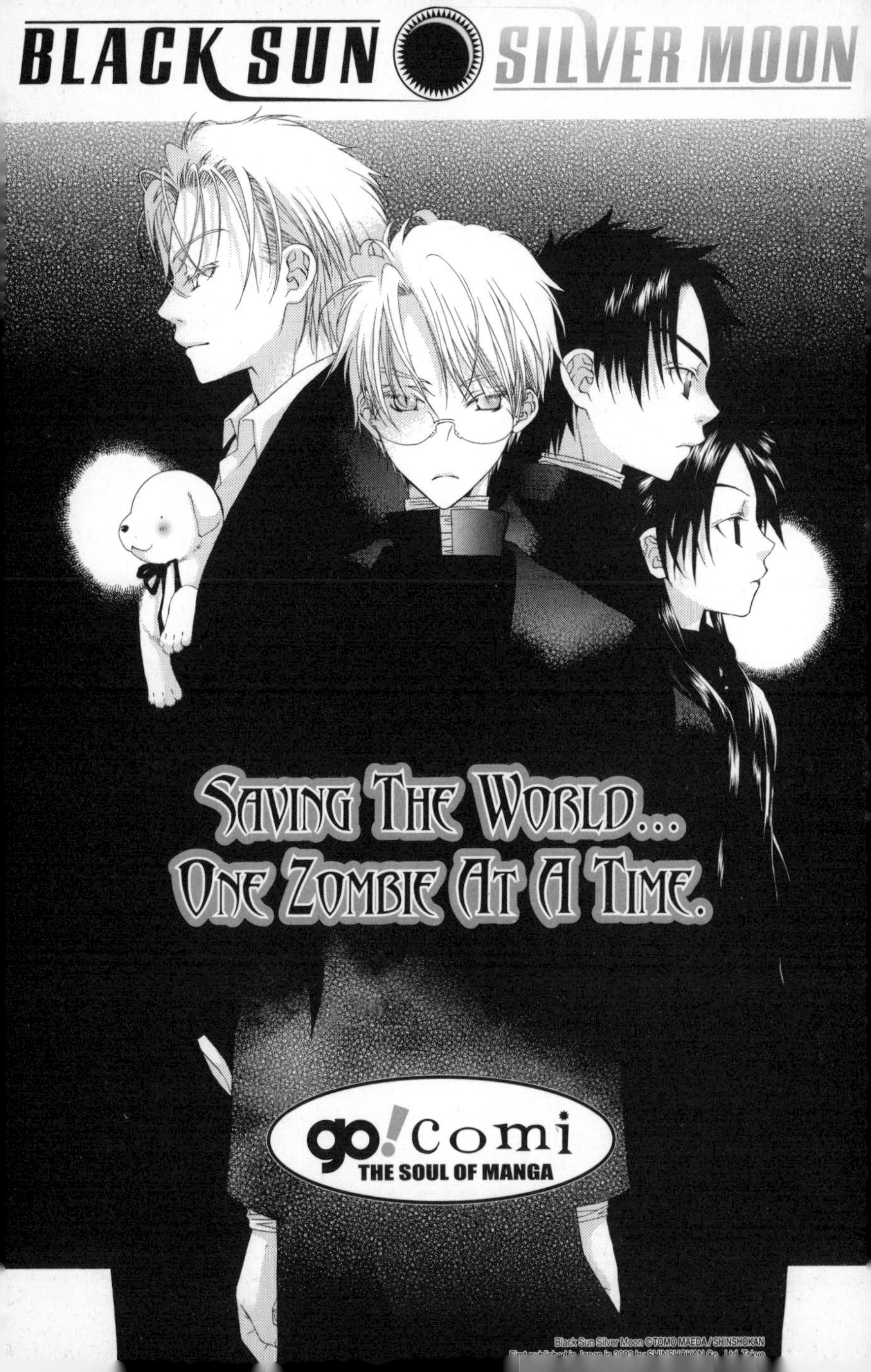
BLACK SUN SILVER MOON
SAVING THE WORLD...
ONE ZOMBIE AT A TIME.
go!comi
THE SOUL OF MANGA
Black Sun Silver Moon ©TOMO MAEDA / SHINSHOKAN

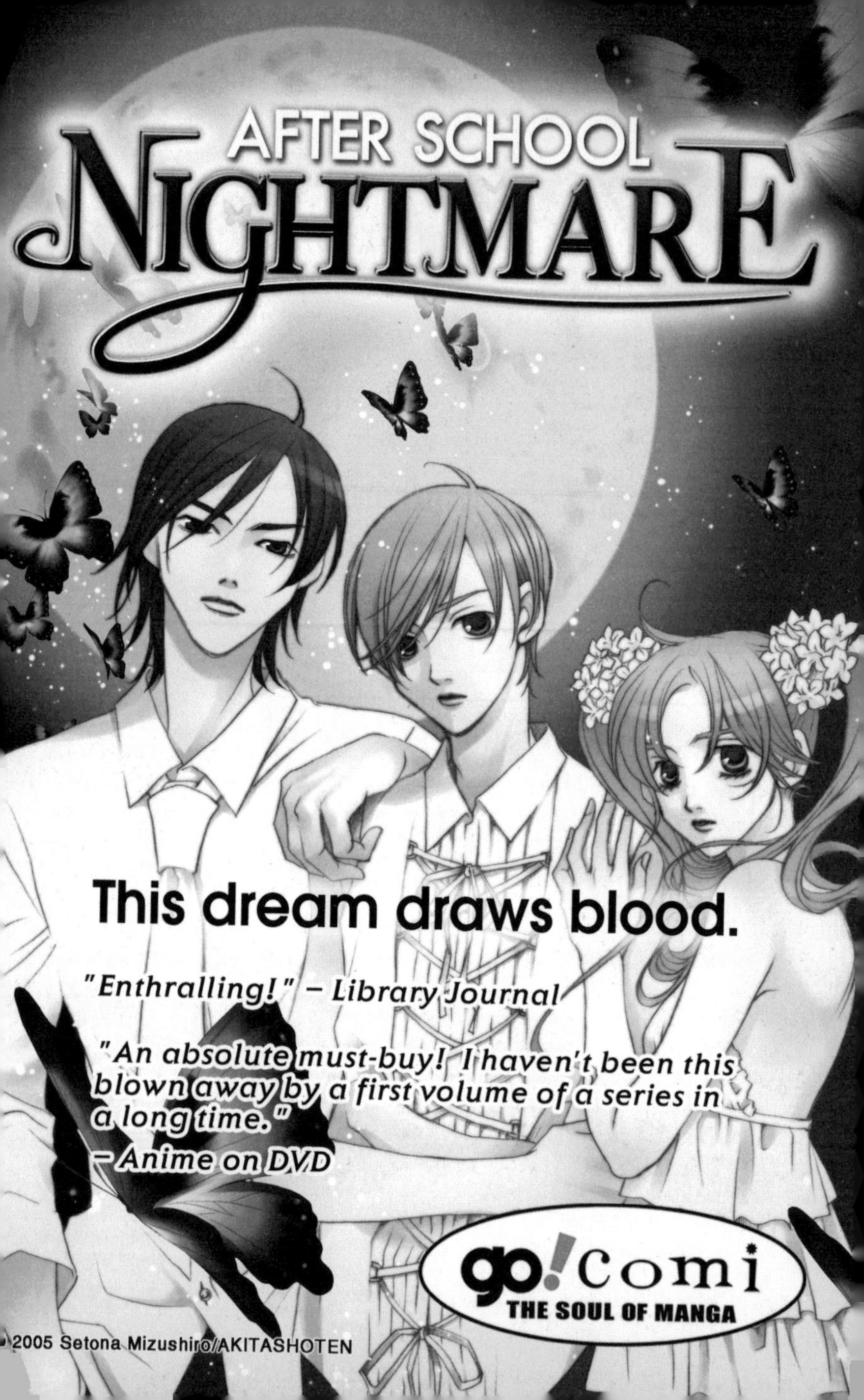
AFTER SCHOOL
NIGHTMARE
This dream draws blood.
"Enthralling!" – Library Journal
"An absolute must-buy! I haven't been this blown away by a first volume of a series in a long time."
– Anime on DVD
go!comi
THE SOUL OF MANGA

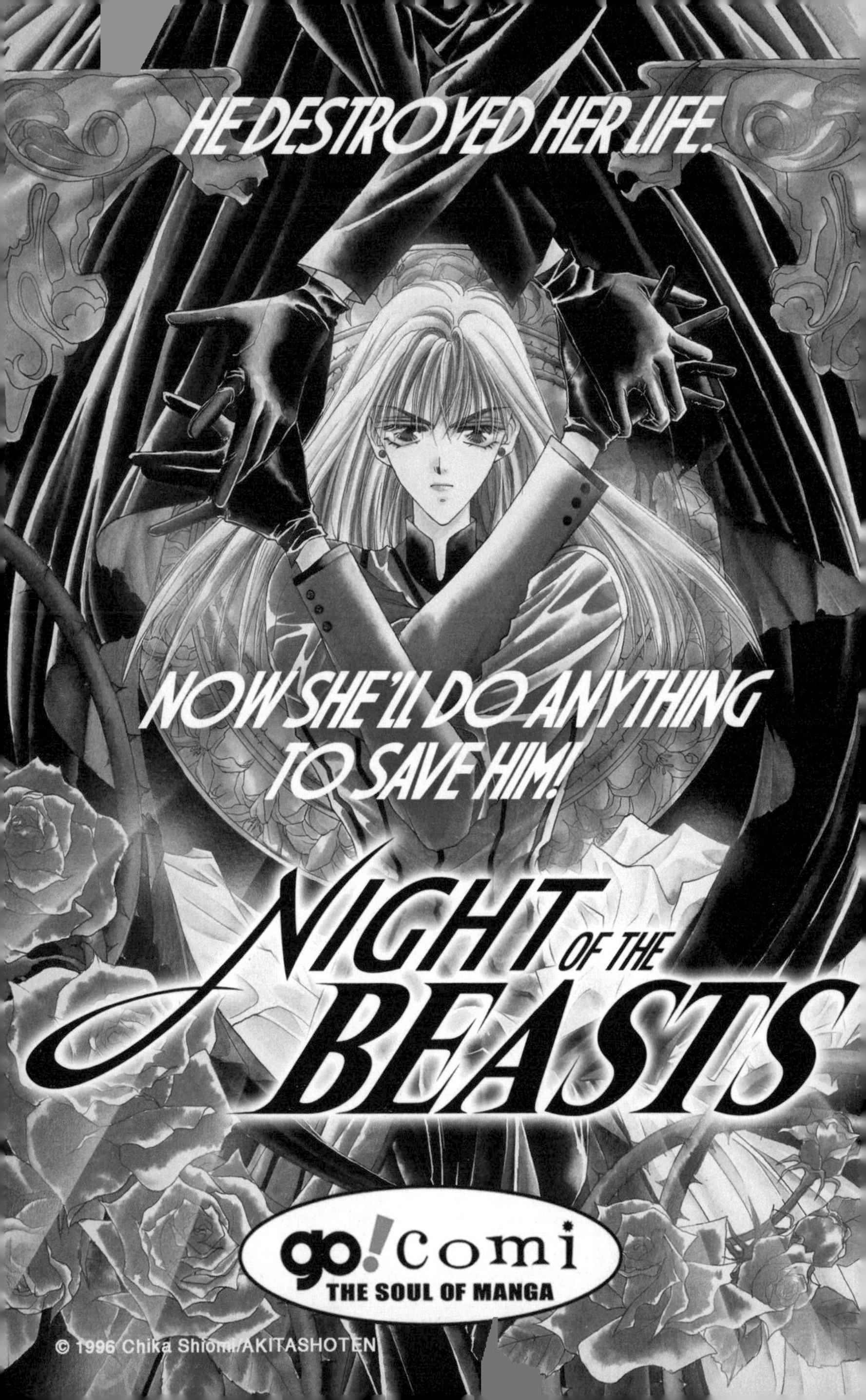
HE DESTROYED HER LIFE.
NOW SHE'LL DO ANYTHING TO SAVE HIM!
NIGHT OF THE BEASTS
go!comi
THE SOUL OF MANGA
© 1996 Chika Shiomi/AKITASHOTEN